We are only human sculptors in that we get up every day, walking sometimes, reading rarely, eating often, thinking always, smoking moderately, enjoying enjoyment, looking, relaxing to see, loving nightly, finding amusement, encouraging life, fighting boredom, being natural, daydreaming, travelling along, drawing occasionally, talking lightly, tea drinking, feeling tired, dancing sometimes, philosophising a lot, criticising never, whistling tunefully, dying very slowly, laughing nervously, greeting politely and waiting till the day breaks.

Gilbert & George, 1970

To
Marten & Keith
& the [illegible]/bar: '98
Happy New Year
SEM of Manhattan

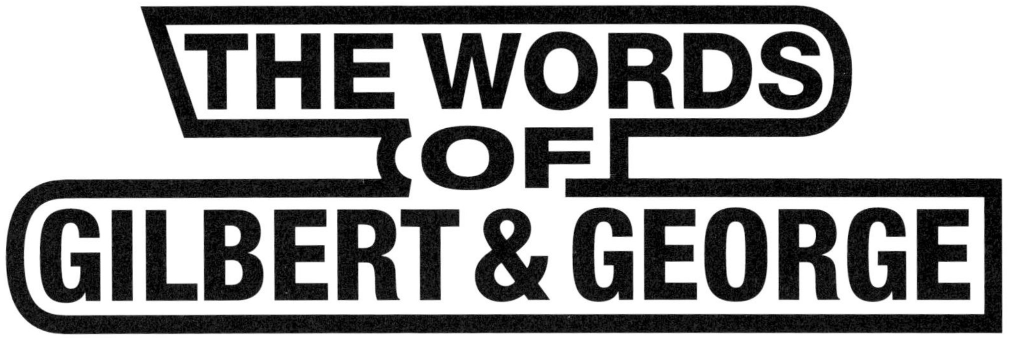

THE WORDS OF GILBERT & GEORGE

With Portraits of the Artists from 1968 to 1997

Violette Editions

First Published in the USA and Canada in 1997 by Violette Editions

Edited by Robert Violette with Hans-Ulrich Obrist
Designed and typeset by Peter B. Willberg, London
Film separations by System Colour, London
Printed and bound by Grafiche Milani, Milan

ISBN 1-900828-00-6

Distributed in the United States and Canada by Distributed Art Publishers,
155 Sixth Avenue, 2nd Floor, New York, NY 10013-1507. To order toll free:
1-800-338-BOOK

A signed clothbound edition (ISBN 1-900828-02-2) and a limited edition
with a signed self-portrait photograph by Gilbert & George (ISBN 1-900828-
03-0) are available from Violette Editions

Front cover: photograph by M. Hasui, Tokyo, 1993
Back cover: photograph by Rankin Waddell, Fournier Street, London, 1989

Visit the Gilbert & George website at http://www.gilbertandgeorge.co.uk

Contents

Preface

This book gathers together for the first time the very significant body
of writings, statements and manifesto art works by Gilbert & George,
alongside a selection of their prolific and controversial interviews and
portraits of the artists from the last thirty years. The most striking
feature and red thread through this heterogenous collection of primary
source material is the verbal and textual directness which recalls the
intensity, passion and presence of their pictures.

Through the voice of Gilbert & George – unique and unwavering
since the earliest days of their declaration 'We are an Artist' – the
reader experiences a firsthand introduction to the artists' key concepts
such as Art for All and Living Sculpture. Never flinching from
fundamental themes of the human condition, Gilbert & George address
an encyclopaedic range of subjects oscillating between the particular
and the universal, between nostalgia and modernity, relentlessly
walking a thin rope of ambiguity, blurring and breaking boundaries,
making private things public, fighting against divisions and accepting
contradictions. Gilbert & George embrace paradox. Their call for
complexity, in their work and in their words, follows the complexity of
the infinite possibilities in life.

This book came out of an intense dialogue with Gilbert & George
to whom we are deeply grateful for their open and generous collaboration and for allowing us unprecedented access to their archive,
especially during a rigorous period of work with major exhibitions
in New York, Tokyo, Stockholm and Paris. We are also grateful to the
numerous interviewers and photographers who have granted us permission to reproduce their own unique experiences with the 'Speakers',
Gilbert & George.

Robert Violette
Hans-Ulrich Obrist
London 1997

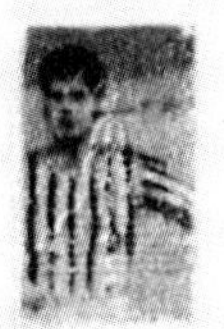 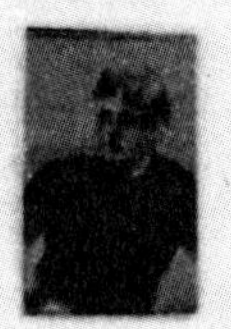

A

MESSAGE

FROM

THE SCULPTORS

GILBERT & GEORGE

LONDON 1970

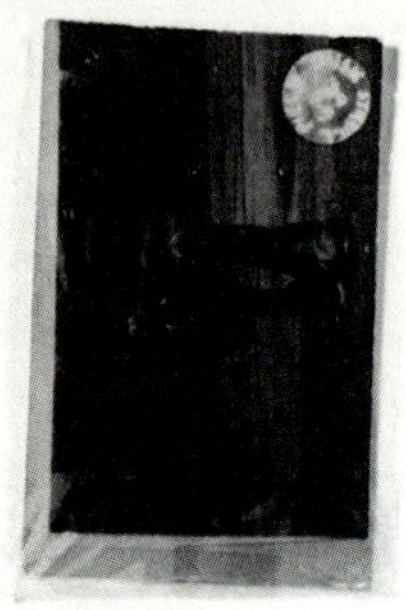

Gilbert and George, the sculptors, are working along a new road. They left their little studio with all the tools and brushes, taking with them only some music, gentle smiles on their faces and the most serious intentions in the world.

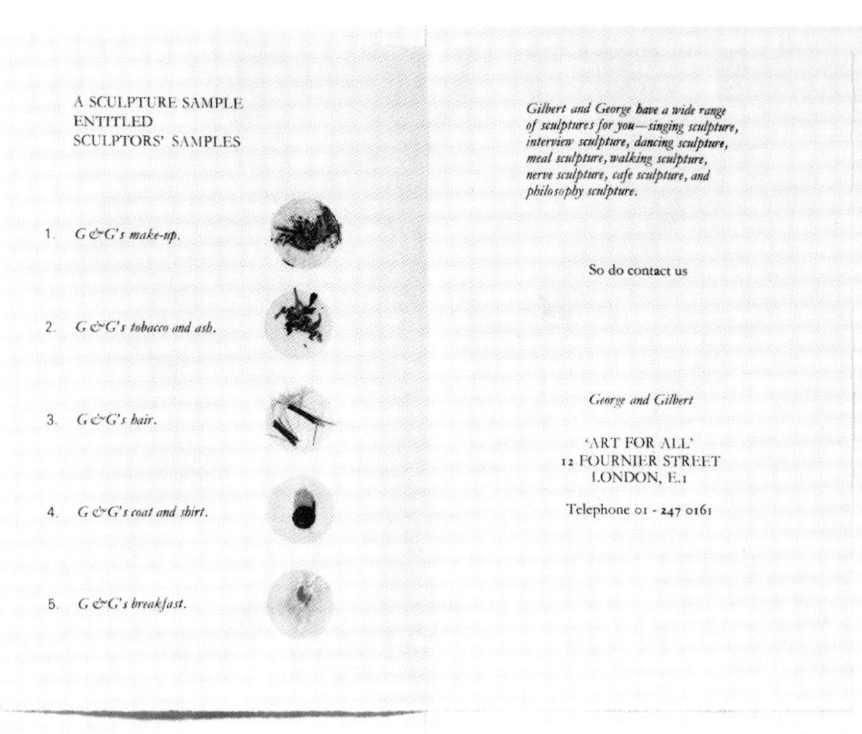

Gilbert and George have a wide range of sculptures for you— singing sculpture, interview sculpture, dancing sculpture, meal sculpture, walking sculpture, nerve sculpture, cafe sculpture, and philosophy sculpture.

This and previous pages: *A Message from the Sculptors*, 1970, Postal Sculpture, published by Gilbert & George in a numbered edition of 300 copies and in 1969 sent internationally by the artists for the first time

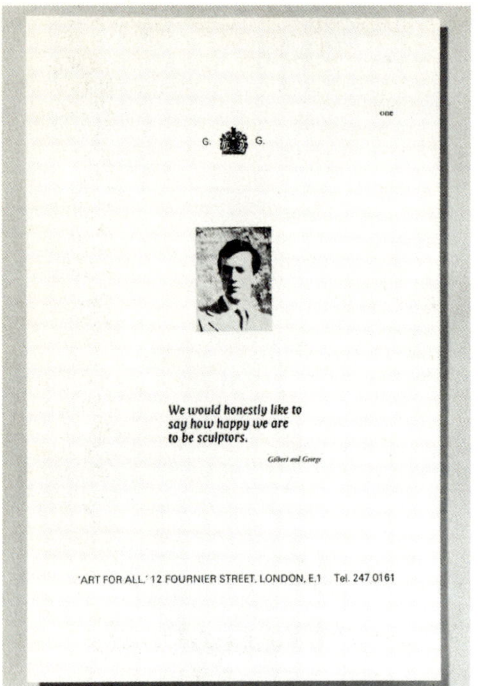

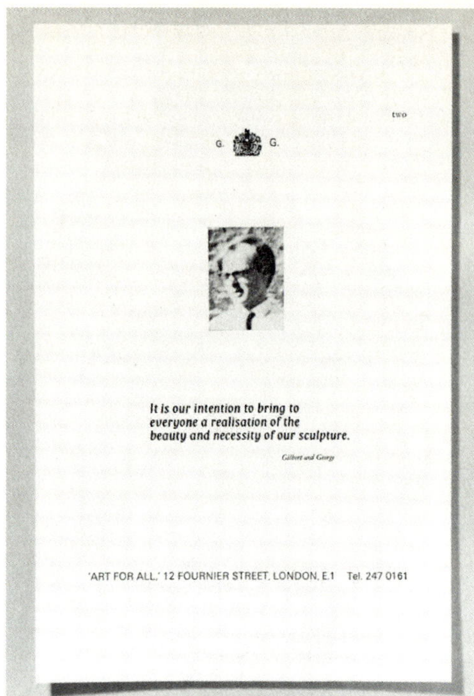

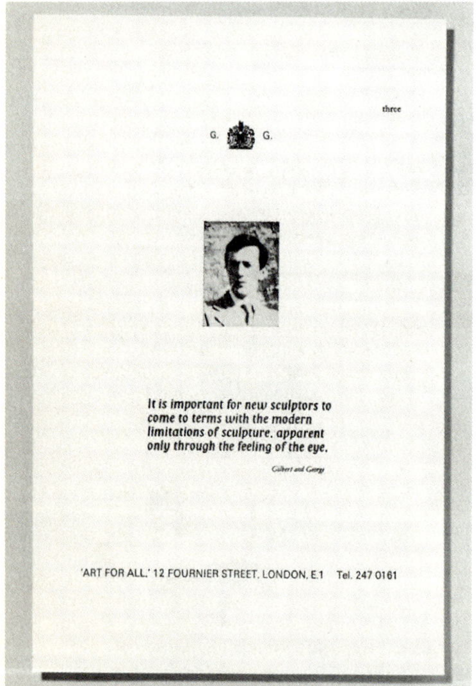

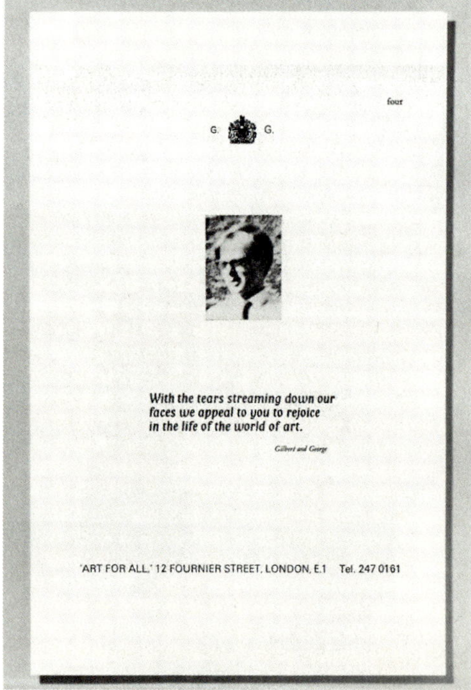

12   *The Words of the Sculptors*, 1969, first published as a Magazine Sculpture in *Jam* magazine

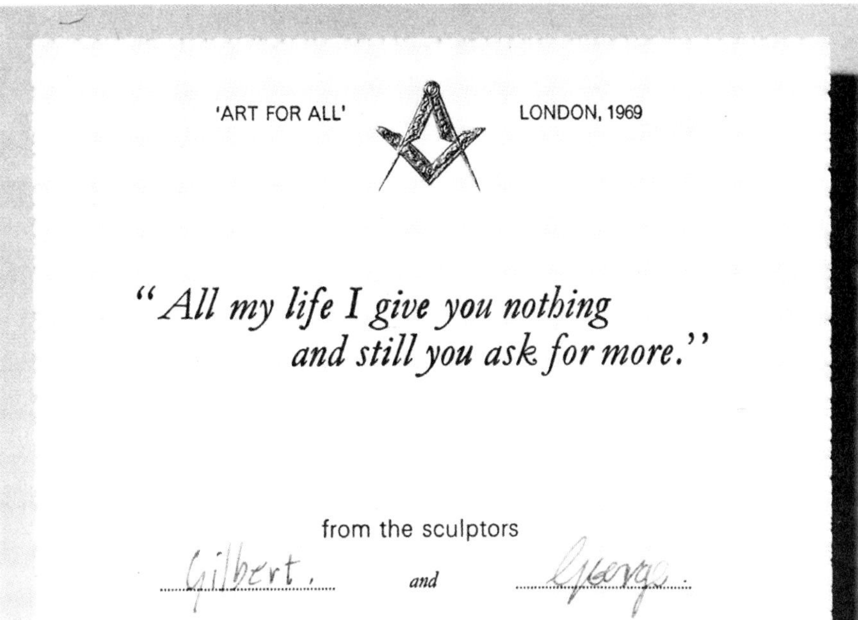

Postal Sculpture, 1969, sent to fellow participants in 18 Paris IV Exhibition, 1970

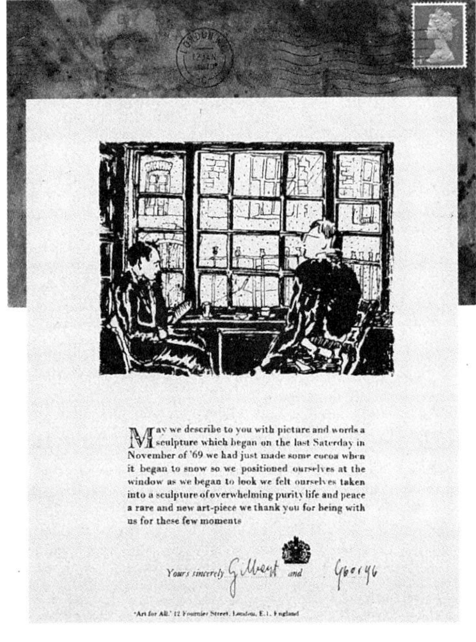

*May we describe to you with picture
and words a sculpture which began
on the last Saterday [sic] in
November of '69 we had just made
some cocoa when it began to snow
so we positioned ourselves at the
window as we began to look we felt
ourselves taken into a sculpture of
overwhelming purity life and peace
a rare and new art-piece we thank
you for being with us for these few
moments.*

Yours sincerely, Gilbert and George

Postal Sculpture, November 1969

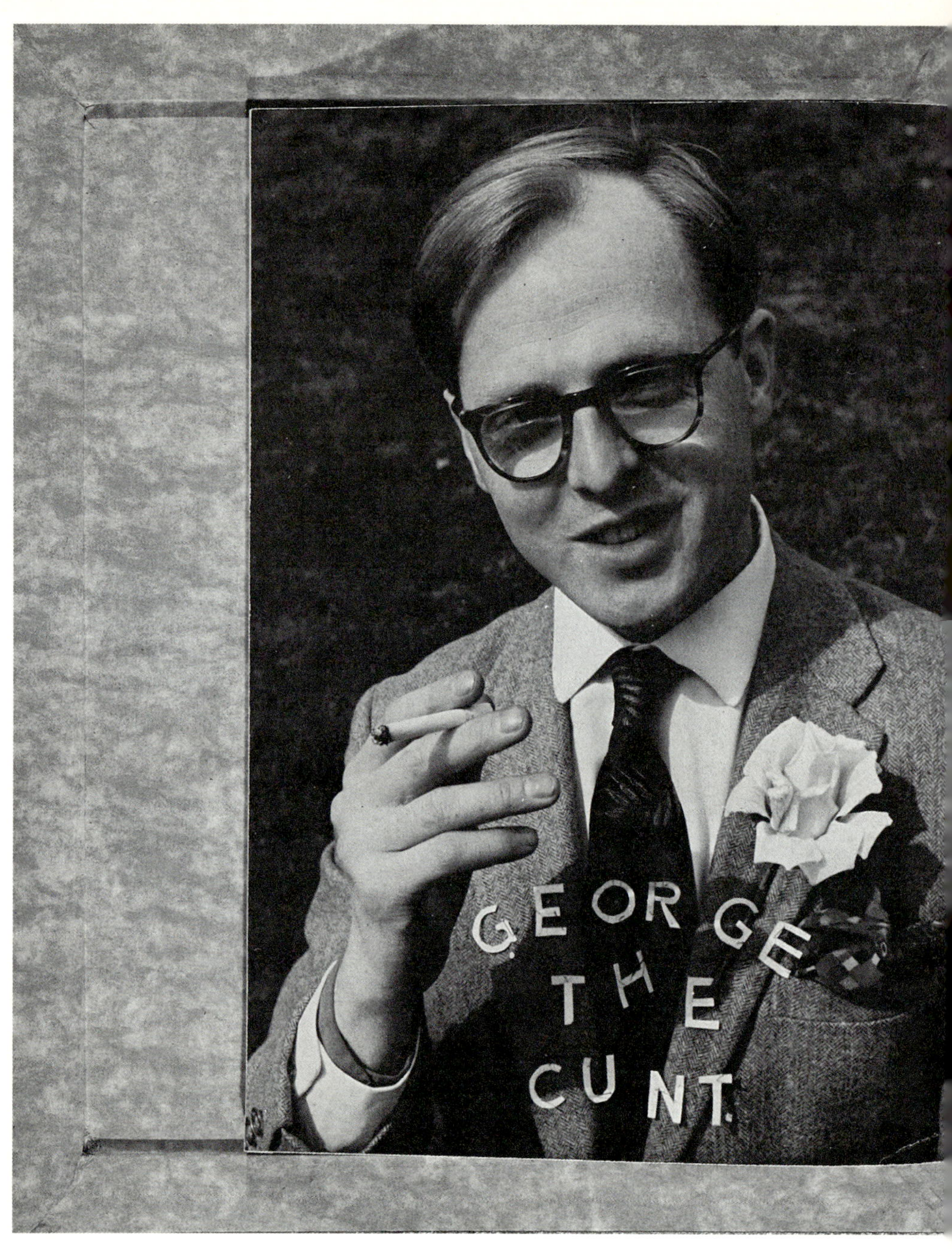

GEORGE
THE
CUNT.

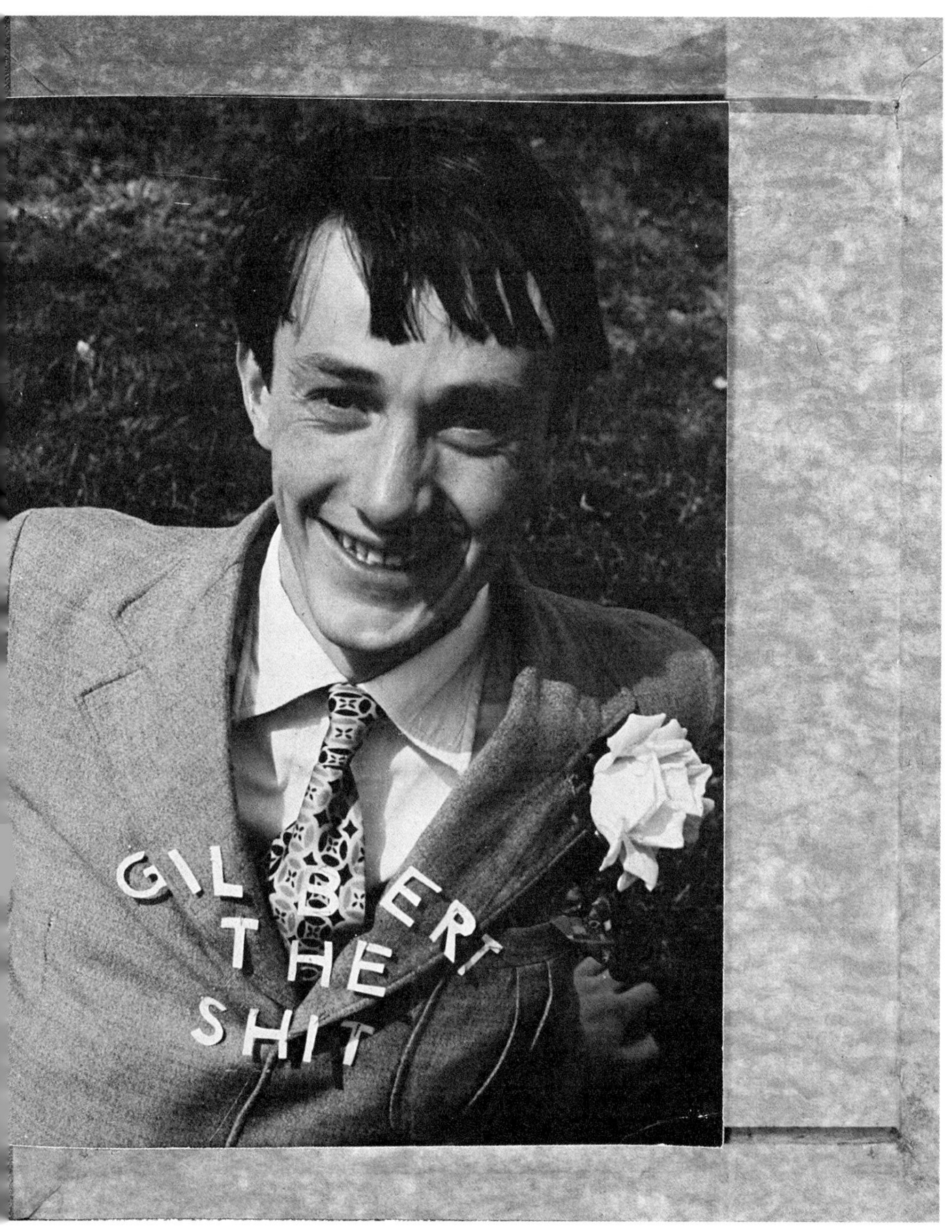

Shit and Cunt, Magazine Sculpture, 1969, made for and first published in 1970 in *Studio International*, but with the 'offending' words censored; also shown in a glass case to invited viewers at 3pm on Saturday 10 May 1969 at the Robert Fraser Gallery, London

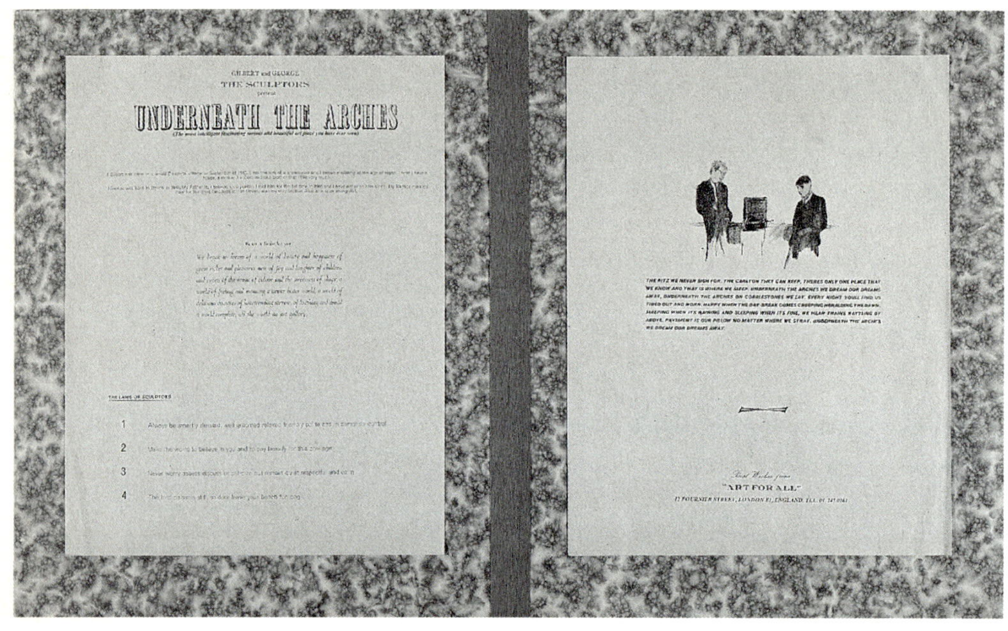

This page and opposite: two texts written to accompany the *Shit and Cunt*
Magazine Sculpture, 1969

GILBERT and GEORGE
THE SCULPTORS
present

UNDERNEATH THE ARCHES

(The most intelligent fascinating serious and beautiful art piece you have ever seen)

I Gilbert was born in a small Dolomite village in September of 1943. I am the son of a shoemaker and I began sculpting at the age of eight. There I have a house, a mother, 3 sisters and one brother that I like very much.

I George was born in Devon in 1942. My Father is, I believe, a carpenter. I met him for the 1st time in 1966 and I have not seen him since. My Mother married now for the third time lives still in Devon, also my only brother Alec who is an evangelist.

We Met in London Last Year

We began to dream of a world of beauty and happiness of great riches and pleasures new of joy and laughter of children and sweets of the music of colour and the sweetness of shape, a world of feeling and meaning a newer better world, a world of delicious disasters of heart-rending sorrow, of loathing and dread a world complete, all the world an art gallery.

THE LAWS OF SCULPTORS

1   Always be smartly dressed, well groomed relaxed friendly polite and in complete control

2   Make the world to believe in you and to pay heavily for this privilege

3   Never worry assess discuss or criticize but remain quiet respectful and calm

4   The lord chissels still, so don't leave your bench for long

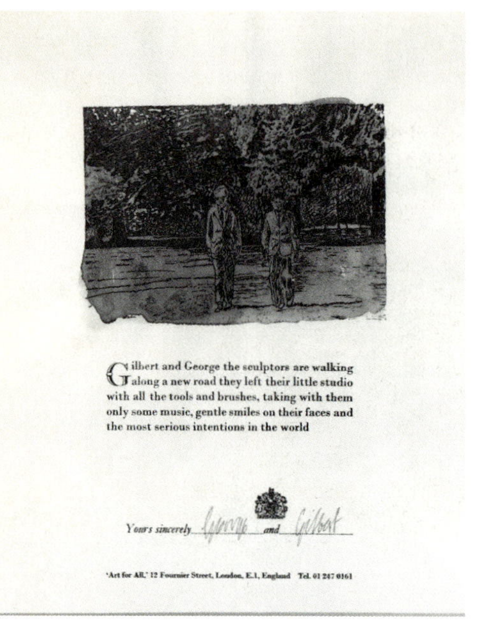

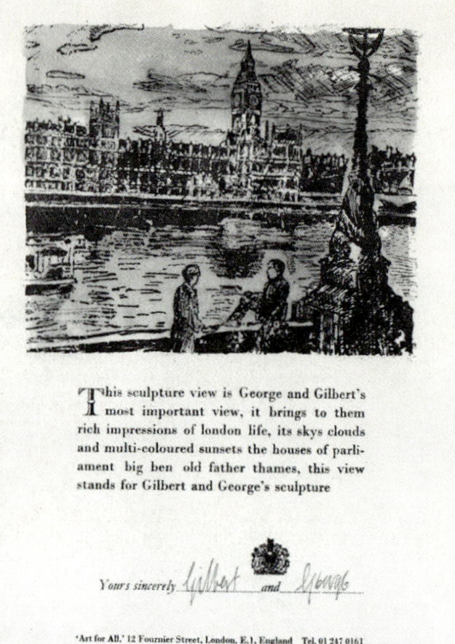

*Gilbert and George the sculptors
are walking along a new road
they left their little studio with all
the tools and brushes, taking
with them only some music,
gentle smiles on their faces and
the most serious intentions in
the world*

*This sculpture view is George and
Gilbert's most important view,
it brings to them rich impressions
of london life, its skys clouds
and multi-coloured sunsets the
houses of parliament big ben old
father thames, this view stands
for Gilbert and George's
sculpture*

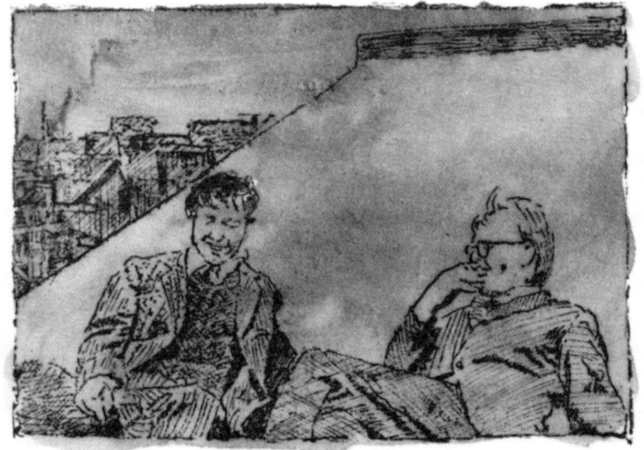

This page and opposite: *Walking, Viewing, Relaxing*, 1970, published by Gilbert & George in an edition of thirteen copies

A Guide to
Singing Sculpture
by
GEORGE & GILBERT
the human sculptors

1970

'Art for All,' 12 Fournier Street, London, E.1, England

Tel. 01 247 0161

SIX POINTS
towards a better understanding

Essentially a sculpture
we carve our desires in the air.

Together with you this sculpture presents
as much contact for experiencing as is possible.

Human sculpture
makes available every feeling you can think of.

It is significant that this sculpture
is able to sing its message with words and music.

The sculpture, in their sculpture,
are given over to feeling the life of the world of art.

It is intended that this sculpture brings to us all a more light
generous and general art feeling.

The Ritz we never sigh for, occasionally we have a drink there, the Carlton they can help, there's only one place that we know and that is where we sleep. Underneath the arches is still our most important realistic abstract wording. It lives along with us as we dream our dreams away realising how few people have had thoughts on these our sculpture words for we are really working at dreaming our dreams away. *Underneath the arches on cobble-stones we lay* is increasingly our position as day after day we rest on these our cobblestones. *Every night you'll find us tired out and worn* for after a day of sculpting we are sometimes a little tired. *Waiting till the day-light comes creeping heralding the dawn* of another day of light in which to find our sculpture way throughout that time. *Sleeping when its raining and waking when its fine*, its all the same to us and it doesn't matter where we are or what we doing as long as we sculpt along our way. *Trains travelling by above* as everything goes along leaving us here. *Pavement is our pillow*, but then what's wrong with that, *no matter where we stray*, we are there with our all. *Underneath the arches we dream our dreams away.*

Text from the booklet *A Guide to Singing Sculpture*, 1970

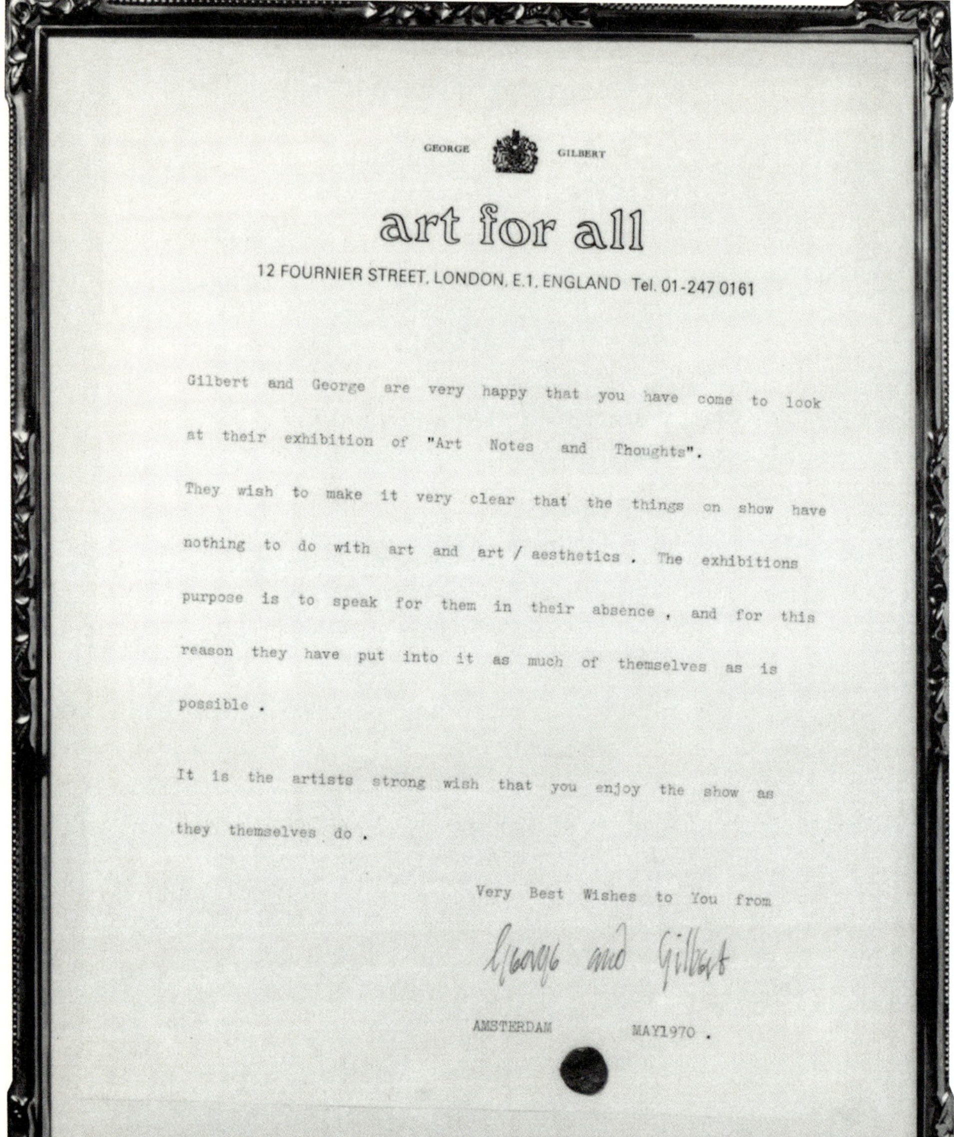

Text written to accompany the exhibition *Art Notes and Thoughts*, Art & Project, Amsterdam, 1970

Cover of the booklet *The Pencil on Paper Descriptive Works*
of Gilbert & George the sculptors, 1970, published by Gilbert & George
in an edition of 500 copies

The Pencil on Paper
Descriptive Works
of
Gilbert & George
the sculptors

*It is our wish that the reader should come to regard this booklet
as an insight into an understanding of our drawings
as an explanation of our living art life*

*On completion of this booklet it came strongly to us
that our work on it had resulted in a sculpture*

We are fascinated by the magic of the line of the pencil and the potential of that paper which can be so real and good it leaves behind the photograph in drawing the camera is now an absurd unreal pencil which can draw only a photograph is so exclusive as children we were totally un-shy of the power of the pencil from when we first wrote our names we drew on in time writing a name drawing a thing person or something until art took the pencil from our hand and so from our mind and art talent art for all showed us how to bring back the pencil ability availing us of new power of ourselves of greater out-put of feeling new sensitivities comment content beauty reason and simplicity at our pencil point this fundamental pencil as a descriptive drawer has been unheard in art return to us bringing this great intelligence of the line and the surface man signifying the pencil and the surface the world a very big drawing for everyone that smooth or rough textured surface of no colour or use at all has for the artist become an impossibly difficult situation or a tired thing to do the air between the drawer and the sheet being a reality that we cannot resist this seeming void is a place for all thinking and feeling the real sense and meaning of drawing has fallen into abuse degenerated into aesthetics of scribbling eg the blank sheet signed the playing on paper the gestural drawn pieces of anything physical changing of the surface by use of splashes dirt and weather time and a host of other misguided personal tricks come with us into the new thought in describing everything very normally as with your best eyes with a quality viewer seeing and understanding at the same drawn moment a tree – a tree house – a house a real person – a real person everything absolutely good and right art with you at all times and every situation a the new availability of the drawn picture as the new surprise language for us it is most daring and rewarding to regard ourselves complete unchanging ideal undying in pencil on paper to the true scale of lifesize living height black and white and occupying only two of the dimensions George by Gilbert and Gilbert by George an unrelaxed but dead surface yet providing a constant with you for you and even against you wishes day by day year after tear for ever of you can see for instance here where we are walking a little already the drawing begins Gilberts eyes going straight ahead Georges head a little bent left foot out right out on the sunny june turf a surface used by us as if a drawing a covering of dense summer trees a largely unoccupied area of park divided nearly half and half according to the golden rule the foreground joined to the back-ground with a belt of shadowed tree trunks the hand of man has put a lamp standard in this setting we can see an anonymous seated figure then to the fight of the centre comes George and Gilbert frozen into their representation of themselves in our words 'Gilbert and George the sculptors are walking along a new road they left their little studio with its tools and brushes taking with them only a little music gentle smiles on their faces and the most serious intentions in the world' look only at the drawing for the meaning of its truth look again to George by Gilbert and Gilbert by George and here are some spoken words strongly bound to the piece 'I thought we were going to interview hmmmm my name is pencil and this is my friend paper you did a knockout tie ahh very me what about Mark on the other side hahahahahhahahahahaha Mr and Mrs Michael Moynihan youve never had so few teeth you look so sad no you you look sad I dont look at all sad I just look myself really a bowl of custard completely a table leg I think they are very good a perfect pair so sophisticated you didnt put my spot in did you which spot I have one here and one here I hadnt seen it but you look quite good ahh very very beautiful really excellent it really is a very good piece very decadent incredible my eyes are very strong really look coming out of the paper at you and mine just behind the paper hahahahahahaha dont laugh small spot between your teeth is very good I really think thats very black really buck rabbit mine is even quite smoky you really know its a smoker quite sad very serious murderous it has a lot to do with the murders really brilliant I think a totally brilliant piece we are really agreed on that I think on what on their brilliance fantastic we have never done so good a piece no never Ive never seen anything like it all my life all my life your suit thats quite good splendid suit rolling around all over the page I do like a diagonal suit you can see I have a winter suit on yes very heavy very woolly even your tie but you look very English do you think so not German they are really awful looking through the paper just behind the paper this is a very plastic one very very 3D the portraits speak so much so much we dont have to say anything I like the structure here going in coming back out again marvellous form we must have new forms they are very important if you dont have it it is better to do without' relaxing drawing shows us set in a relaxing sculpture on a soho roof top the background divided by a diagonal line setting back the crowded buildings of london behind a sloping really hot tarred roof area framing an atmosphere of incredible life an area of thought we entitled spring snow and now to the sculptors seen here in classically relaxed poses conscious of their pleasure of being only there much is represented in their facial expressions hairstyles casual clothes easeful smoking naive laughter slightly windswept unusual collar-arrangement the wholeness of this drawn picture gives a clear account of ourselves set in time and we are personally still in the drawing on concluding this essay some general thoughts come to our mind like that in itself for us drawing is really nothing the important thing being us as the art-piece involving balances of living thinking being sculpting moving looking feeling responding and putting in the traditional sense as much of ourselves as possible into our being-viewing world for all the suits which we wear are symbols of our constant seeking for ways to bring about our renaissance of the person capable of contrasting his being with his fellow-men look freshly at all suits hairstyles attitudes and sensibilities that exist all are drawing in some way and are speaking to us of something special despite apparent sameness there are art-measures and the right for a drawing to exist is brought about with delicate balances of viewing in a time.

THE END

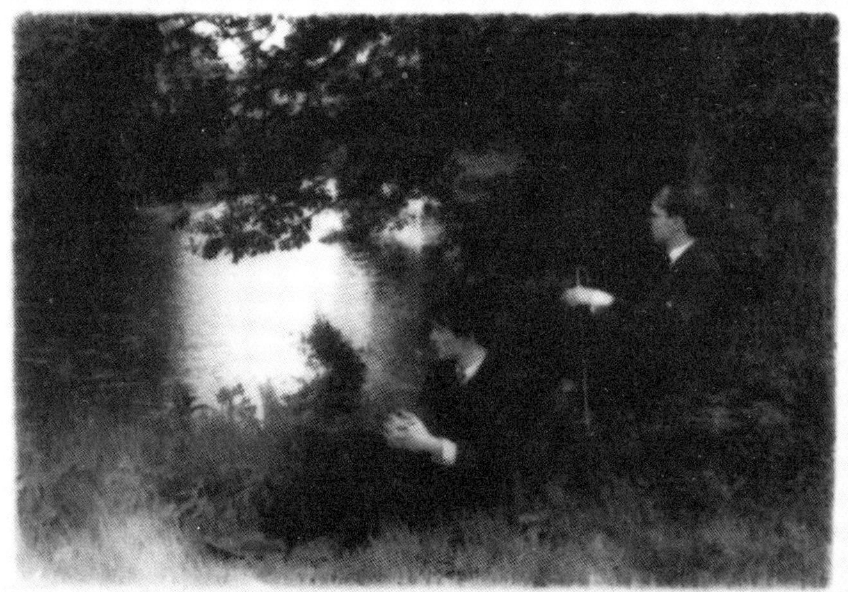

Announcement card for *The Nature of Our Looking*, 1970, an eighteen-minute
Video Sculpture

To be with Art is all we ask . . .

Gilbert & George the sculptors Autumn 1970

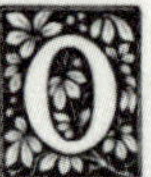 H ART, what are you? You are so strong and powerful, so beautiful and moving. You make us walk around and around, pacing the city at all hours, in and out of our Art for All room. We really do love you and we really do hate you. Why do you have so many faces and voices? You make us thirst for you and then to run from you escaping completely into a normal life—: getting up, having breakfast, going to the work-shop and being sure of putting our mind and energy into the making of a door or maybe a simple table and chair. The whole life would surely be so easeful, so drunk with the normality of work and the simple pleasures of loving and hanging around for our lifetime. Oh Art where did you come from, who mothered such a strange being. For what kind of people are you—: are for the feeble-of-mind, are you for the poor-at-heart, are for those with no soul. Are you a branch of nature's fantastic network or are you an invention of some ambitious man? Do you come from a long line of arts? For every artist is born in the usual way and we have never seen a young artist. Is to become an artist to be reborn, or is it a condition of life? Coming slowly over a person like the daybreak. It brings the art-ability to do this funny thing and shows you new possibilities for feeling and scratching at oneself and surroundings, setting standards, making you go into every scene and every contact, every touching nerve and all your senses. And Art we are driven by you at incredible speed, ignorant of the danger you are pushing and dragging us into. And yet Art, there is no going back, all roads go only on and on. We are happy for the good times that you give us and we work and wait only for these titbits from your table. If you only knew how much these mean to us, transporting from the depths of tragedy and black despair to a beautiful life of happiness, taking us where the good times are. When this happens we are able to walk again with our heads held high. We artists need only to see a little light through the trees of the forest, to be happy and working and back into gear again. And yet, we don't forget you. Art, we continue to dedicate our artists-art to you alone, for you and your pleasure, for Art's-sake. We would honestly like to say to you, Art, how happy we are to be your sculptors. We think about you all the time and feel very sentimental about you. We do realise that you are what we really crave for, and many times we meet you in our dreams. We have glimpsed you through the abstract world and have tasted of your reality. One day we thought we saw you in a crowded street, you were dressed in a light brown suit, white shirt and a curious blue tie, you looked very smart but there was about your dress a curious wornness and dryness. You were walking alone, light of step and in a very controlled sense. We were fascinated by the lightness of your face, your almost colourless eyes and your dusty-blonde hair. We approached you nervously and then just as we neared you you went out of sight for a second and then we could not find you again. We felt sad and unlucky and at the same time happy and hopeful to have seen your reality. We now feel very familiar with you, Art. We have learned from you many of the ways of life. In our work of drawings, sculptures, living-pieces, photo-messages, written and spoken pieces we are always to be seen, frozen into a gazing for you. You will never find us working physically or with our nerves and yet we shall not cease to pose for you, Art. Many times we would like to know what you would like of us, your messages to us are not always easily understood. We realize that it cannot be too simple because of your great-complexity and all-meaning. If at times we do not measure up or fulfil your wishes you must believe that it is not because we are unserious but only because we are artists. We ask always for your help, Art, for we need much strength in this modern time, to be only artists of a life-time. We know that you are above the people of our artist-world but we feel that we should tell you of the ordinariness and struggling that abounds and we ask you if this must be. Is it right that artists should only be able to work for you for only the days when they are new, fresh and crisp. Why can't you let them pay homage to you for all their days, growing strong in your company and coming to know you better. TO BE WITH ART IS ALL WE ASK.

To be with Art is All We Ask...

Gilbert & George the sculptors Autumn 1970

Oh Art, what are you? You are so strong and powerful, so beautiful and moving. You make us walk around and around, pacing the city at all hours, in and out of our Art for All room. We really do love you and we really do hate you. Why do you have so many faces and voices? You make us thirst for you and then to run from you escaping completely into a normal life: getting up, having breakfast, going to the work-shop and being sure of putting our mind and energy into the making of a door or maybe a simple table and chair. The whole life would surely be so easeful, so drunk with the normality of work and the simple pleasures of loving and hanging around for our lifetime. Oh Art where did you come from, who mothered such a strange being? For what kind of people are you: are you for the feeble-of-mind, are you for the poor-at-heart, are you for those with no soul? Are you a branch of nature's fantastic network or are you an invention of some ambitious man? Do you come from a long line of arts? For every artist is born in the usual way and we have never seen a young artist. Is to become an artist to be reborn, or is it a condition of life? Coming slowly over a person like the daybreak. It brings the art-ability to do this funny thing and shows you new possibilities for feeling and scratching at oneself and surroundings, setting standards, making you go into every scene and every contact, every touching nerve and all your senses. And Art we are driven by you at incredible speed, ignorant of the danger you are pushing and dragging us into. And yet Art, there is no going back, all roads go only on and on. We are happy for the good times that you give us and we work and wait only for these titbits from your table. If you only knew how much these mean to us, transporting us from the depths of tragedy and black despair to a beautiful life of happiness, taking us where the good times are. When this happens we are able to walk again with our heads held high. We artists need only to see a little light through the trees of the forest, to be happy and working and back into gear again. And yet, we don't forget you. Art, we continue to dedicate our artists' art to you alone, for you and your pleasure, for Art's sake. We would honestly like to say to you, Art, how happy we are to be your sculptors. We think about you all the time and feel very sentimental about you. We do realise that you are what we really crave for, and many times we meet you in our dreams. We have glimpsed you through the abstract world and have tasted of your reality. One day we thought we saw you in a crowded street, you were dressed in a light brown suit, white shirt and a curious blue tie, you looked very smart but there was about your dress a curious wornness and dryness. You were walking alone, light of step and in a very controlled sense. We were fascinated by the lightness of your face, your almost colourless eyes and your dusty-blonde hair. We approached you nervously and then just as we neared you you went out of sight for a second and then we could not find you again. We felt sad and unlucky and at the same time happy and hopeful to have seen your reality. We now feel very familiar with you, Art. We have learned from you many of the ways of life. In our work of drawings, sculptures, living-pieces, photo-messages, written and spoken pieces we are always to be seen, frozen into a gazing for you. You will never find us working physically or with our nerves and yet we shall not cease to pose for you, Art. Many times we would like to know what you would like of us, your messages to us are not always easily understood. We realise that it cannot be too simple because of your great complexity and all-meaning. If at times we do not measure up or fulfil your wishes you must believe that it is not because we are unserious but only because we are artists. We ask always for your help, Art, for we need much strength in this modern time, to be only artists of a life-time. We know that you are above the people of our artist-world but we feel that we should tell you of the ordinariness and struggling that abounds and we ask you if this must be. Is it right that artists should only be able to work for you for only the days when they are new, fresh and crisp? Why can't you let them pay homage to you for all their days, growing strong in your company and coming you know you better? Oh Art, please let us all relax with you. Recently Art, we thought to set ourselves the task of painting a large set of narrative views descriptive of our looking for you. We like very much to look forward to doing it and we are sure that they are really right for you.

TO BE WITH ART IS ALL WE ASK.

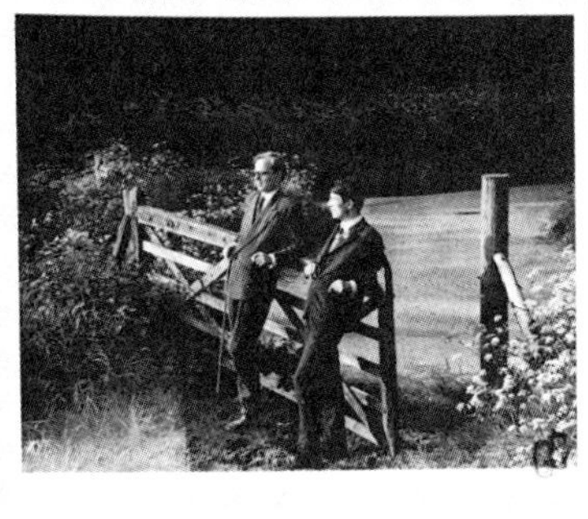

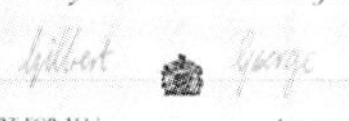

*We are only human sculptors in
that we get up every day, walking
sometimes, reading rarely, eating
often, thinking always, smoking
moderately, enjoying enjoyment,
looking, relaxing to see, loving
nightly, finding amusement,
encouraging life, fighting boredom, being natural, daydreaming,
travelling along, drawing occasionally, talking lightly, tea
drinking, feeling tired, dancing
sometimes, philosophising a lot,
criticising never, whistling tunefully, dying very slowly, laughing
nervously, greeting politely and
waiting till the day breaks.*

*These two people resting on a
five-bar gate. Such a simple easy
thing to do and yet there is a little
more to the story. Observe, for
instance, the similarity of their
poses, or look to the differences,
one dark, one light. See the walking stick. One single-breasted suit
and one double-breasted suit.
Think of all that diagonal relaxation, for only the picture behind
is symmetrical.*

*With Very Best Wishes
to You All from Gilbert & George
'Art for All' Autumn 1970*

Two Text Pages Describing Our Position, 1970, Magazine Sculpture commissioned
by the *Sunday Times Magazine*

31

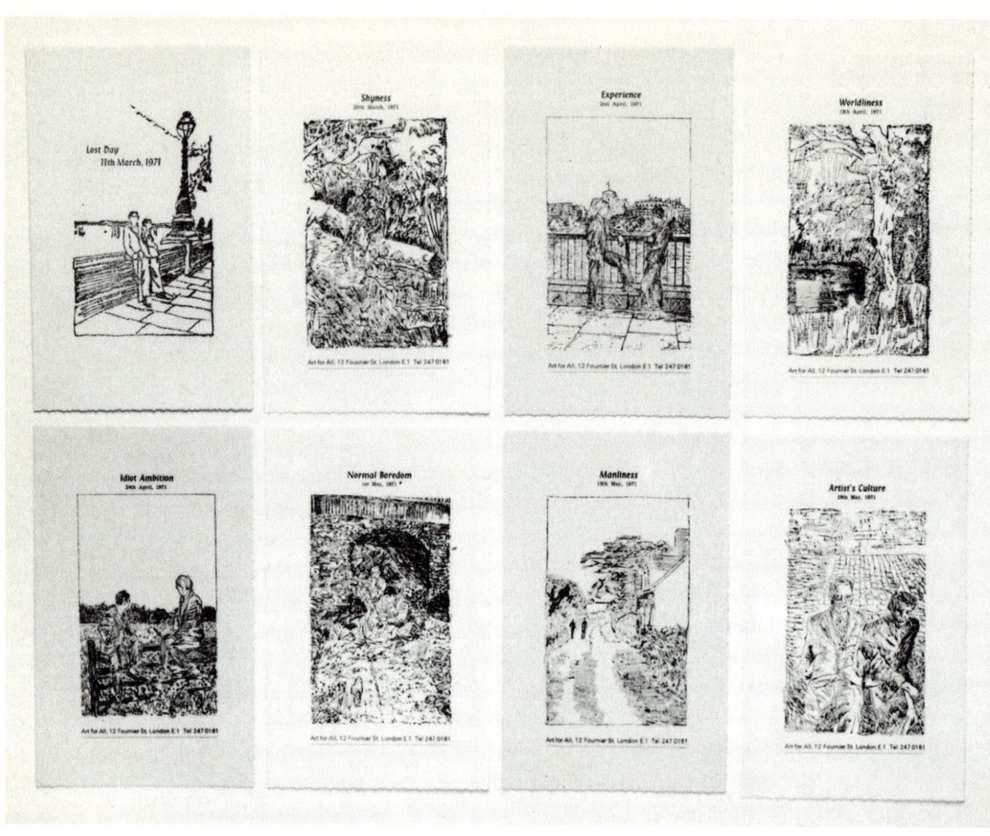

The Limericks

Lost Day 11th March 1971

There were two young men who were tired
They were tired and a little bit lost

They thought they were kings of their best
And found out they were just like the rest

One day they went out for a day
Though they risked falling down a drain

They smiled like two babies without fear
As you will all be happy to hear.

The Limericks, 1971, an eight-part Postal Sculpture where each recipient received
one limerick each week for eight weeks

Shyness 29th March 1971

There were two young men who were crooked
They were crooked in the way you feel best

They gave them the answers to live
And left them with heads full of fizz

But their friends they left all behind
They became lonely artistic and shy

Be aware of these silly old heads
Or you'll always look over the hedge.

Experience 2nd April 1971

There were two young men who did laugh
They laughed at the people's unrest

They stuck their sticks in the air
And turned them around with the best

Then with time they began to feel strange
For no longer it swung in their way

So to capture again that old thrill
They started to take the life-pill.

Worldliness 13th April 1971

There were two young men from afar
Who travelled and met with no bar

They went up and down in their way
And attempted to make the world pay

There was no one at all they could blame
Because it just goes this way

They've had a few pokes in the eye
But like everyone else they're not blind.

Idiot Ambition 24th April 1971

There were two young men so polite
Polite in the way that they moved

Their mothers had told them to wait
But their chances, the boys felt, were great

Good-morning dear dad it is now time to rise
The two sweeties await your surprise

Whilst the birds whistle tunefully outside on the fence
The young men sleep on without sense.

Normal Boredom 1st May 1971

There were two young men with no heart and no peace
They thought to be free lying under a tree

And so they lay there from the dawn till dusk
Enjoying the air and the chickens and ducks

They thought to be nice and wave with their hands
And so day after day they are under that tree

Counting the leaves and waiting for tea
They are as happy as can be.

Manliness 15th May 1971

There were two young men who were covered with blood
They are wounded and slashed and smeared with mud

They battle along singing a song
Straining to be jolly though the journey's long

They think nothing of health or worry or care
Because their job is to do their share

So left leg out and away it goes
And where they go to nobody knows.

Artist's Culture 19th May 1971

There were two young men who were charming as sweets
They turned the heads of all in the streets

They looked at their ties and laughed and were pleased
Looking down to their socks they began to sneeze

The boys didn't mind as much as they might
For they were artists and that was their plight

The funny thing is they're really quite normal
It's just that they seem of another order.

Being living Sculptures
is our
life-blood
our destiny
our romance
our disaster and
our light and life.
As day breaks over us
we rise into our vacuum.
The cold morning light
filters dustily through
the window. We step into
the responsibility suits
of our Art.

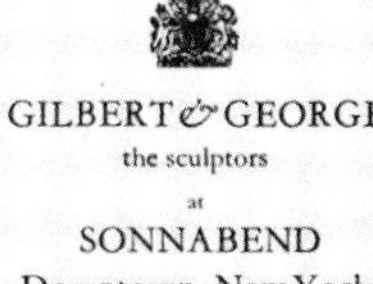

GILBERT & GEORGE
the sculptors
at
SONNABEND
Downtown, New York

·

Autumn 1971

·

In association with Konrad Fischer

*Being living Sculptures
is our
life-blood
our destiny
our romance
our disaster and
our light and life.
As day breaks over us
we rise into our vacuum.
The cold morning light
filters dustily through
the window. We step into
the responsibility suits
of our Art.*

Announcement card for *Underneath the Arches*, Sonnabend Gallery, New York, 1971

The Ten Speeches

One

They weren't Good Artists
They weren't Bad Artists
But, My God, they were Artists.

Two

They weren't Good Sculptors
They weren't Bad Sculptors
But, My God, they were Sculptors.

Three

They weren't Good People
They weren't Bad People
But, My God, they were People.

Four

They weren't Good Thinkers
They weren't Bad Thinkers
But, My God, they were Thinkers.

Five

They weren't Good Drawers
They weren't Bad Drawers
But, My God, they were Drawers.

Six

They weren't Good Writers
They weren't Bad Writers
But, My God, they were Writers.

Seven

They weren't Good Painters
They weren't Bad Painters
But, My God, they were Painters.

Eight

They weren't Good Dreamers
They weren't Bad Dreamers
But, My God, they were Dreamers.

Nine

They weren't Good Searchers
They weren't Bad Searchers
But, My God, they were Searchers.

Ten

They weren't Good Men
They weren't Bad Men
But, My God, they were Men.

 The texts from *The Ten Speeches*, 1971, published by Gilbert & George in an edition of ten copies

G.   G.

A Day
in the Life of
George & Gilbert
the sculptors

◆

AUTUMN 1971

ART FOR ALL 12 FOURNIER STREET LONDON E1   Tel. 01 247 0161

Cover of the booklet *A Day in the Life of George & Gilbert the sculptors*, 37
1971, published by Gilbert & George in an edition of 1000 copies

A Day in the Life of George & Gilbert
the Sculptors: Autumn 1971

Being living sculptures is our life blood, our destiny, our romance, our disaster, our light and life. As day breaks over us, we rise into our vacuum and the cold morning light filters dustily through the window. We step into the responsibility-suits of our art. We put on our shoes for the coming walk. Our limbs begin to stir and form actions of looseness, as though without gravity they bounce about for the new day. The head afloat on top levels on the horizon of our thought. Our hearts pound with fresh blood and emotion and again we find ourselves standing there all nerved up in body and mind. Often we will glide across the room, drawn by the window's void. Our eyes are glued to this frame of light. Our mind points ever to our decay. The big happening outside the window floods our vision like a passing film. It leaves us without impressions, giving up only silence and repetitive relaxation. Nothing can touch us or take us out of ourselves. It is a continuous sculpture. Our minds float off into time, visiting fragments of words heard, faces seen, feelings felt, faces loved. We take occasional sips from our water glasses. Consciousness comes along and goes away, slipping from dreaming space into old concrete awareness. The whole room is filled with the mass and weight of our own history, at times it sees us chained to our chairs and then it will appear like large music, surrounding and intoxicating. We feel briefly but seriously for our fellow artist-men. More than ever complete with our physical, for a time with legs crossed, or arms folded until the elbows ache, a throat is cleared gently but effectively, we then stand for relief pushed up against the wall. Sometimes the room with its size and form and precision of our clarity, its one vase of flowers, its large desk-blackboard of our doing, our two dear faithful green chairs, the black telephone, linked with the World's art-network.

> Ring and ring again
> Make us happy ever again
> Stay as silent as the desk
> And be as free and let it be.

The neat ashtray steadily fills with relaxful butts, beside it a fresh, yellow packet of cigarettes. Very often the room makes us hurt with real bodily pressure. From time to time we are taken head-first from this room called 'Art for All' out and away, sometimes driven, sometimes drawn to breathe again amongst the people. We stroll with specialised embarrassment and our purpose is only to take the sunshine. The people are all living near to beauty, passing by. Walking is the eternity of our living movement, it can never tell us of an end, it is for nothing but the time passing unnoticed. We give ourselves to this walking and so the houses come towards us and then away behind. We would like to tell of our great pleasure in seeing the early flowers and blossoms, they seem to have a young fresh youth, so fine and coloured. We remark the trees with their tight bursting buds. As our legs take us jauntily along we come to a place where we pause for a cup of poison-nervous tea. We sit over it chatting a little of the normal afternoon when all is usual and well. Nothing breathtaking will occur here, but in the darkness of a picture house, where time is killed, the world explodes realistically into giant action stories, men are killed, women are loved, mountains are blown up, night falls, Volcanoes erupt, john wayne rides again and caesar speaks anew to the people. All this until the reel is done and viewers drift blinking and reeling out into the bright city. And we happily go back to Our art where only tiredness and searching play big roles, where all is thin on the ground, where greatness is made at the stroke of a brush, where something and nothing are both qualities. Art is for all the only hope for making the way for the Modern world to enjoy the sophistication of decadent living expression. It is our strong belief that in Art there is living, and where there's life there's Hope. It is for this reason that we have dedicated our hands, legs, pens, speech and our own dear heads to progress and understanding in Art.

> Art my Life and Art my Way
> See us painting in mud and clay
> See us dancing and smiling too
> Let us hope that Art is true.

And then maybe we will see ourselves in a garden, soft and sitting, watching the sun as it gently lowers itself down behind the horizon, taking with it all its golden light and warmth. For a little while the garden keeps some of the day's warm-strength. The two men-sculptures use up this last pleasure, but soon the chill of evening creeps over all, we hear no insect, the birds begin to settle down from the day's frolics and we feel it must soon be time to stretch a leg and make our way between the rich beds of flowers, over the spongy lawns to return to solid state of buildings with their sensible doors and windows. On our way we pause on the Embankment to take in the glory that is the Thames and Westminster. Slowly the lamps are lighted and night presumes upon the evening. We like it very much. We like it because we are so stupid, artistic and shy. Because we have come from nowhere and where we go nobody knows. We feel the total mystery of each man-laid brick. We are just down at the river feeling around. As the shades of night are falling around our neighbourhood we stroll because we know full well that another sculpture-day is over.

Gilbert & George:
Interview with Anne Seymour 1971

First published in 1972 by the Arts Council of Great Britain in the Hayward Gallery group exhibition catalogue *The New Art.*

I'm always trying to find out what it was really like at St Martin's when you were there.

George & Gilbert: I think that when we arrived at the school sculpture was already in a very good state. Certainly there was no feeling of reacting against. It was very much outside the school already. There were people making marvellous sculpture with welding steel, but that was a separate small department.

What sort of intellectual climate was there? What sort of art was being discussed?

George & Gilbert: We played a large part in not talking about art in that way. We stopped discussing, even in the streets outside the school. We were not in favour of groups of people standing around talking about sculpture.

You didn't feel, because of the bad state of things, it was necessary to reorganise, deliberately to bring other things in?

George & Gilbert: We didn't do that. It just looks like that.

Gilbert & George: It's more that we lived.

George & Gilbert: What we were doing at St Martin's and just after was nothing different from what we had been doing all our lives, really.

Gilbert & George: It was a very simple matter. We only wanted to do art. We didn't want to discuss it. We didn't want the worries that teachers bring there. They tell you what they want everyone to do.

George & Gilbert: We've come to see art as a great big history of our personal relations, of day-by-day changes.

Gilbert & George: Even we never mind what it is.

George & Gilbert: No, not at all. We keep it for ourselves for ever, the idea that art exists just because art is creating freely every day.

Gilbert & George: Or even what kind of art – we don't mind too much. We like all kinds of art.

I think the first thing you did together was a head?

Gilbert & George: Yes, that was the first piece.

George & Gilbert: That was really before we left college.

Gilbert & George: It must have been in March '68.

George & Gilbert: We had one café piece while we were at art school in which we had separate works.

What did it consist of?

George & Gilbert: Three sculptures from Gilbert and three sculptures from myself. People were invited to see them on tables in the café.

You have said that you then liked the idea of taking art to the people.

George & Gilbert: Yes. We have this title 'Art for All' which we've always been very interested in and it has different meanings for us all the time. That's all we do really – re-form our understanding of that sentence.

Do you still make object sculptures in a similar way to the way you make paintings as sculpture?

George & Gilbert: We don't have object sculptures, but abstract sculptures. No.

But you don't make a distinction between your café exhibition material and later stuff.

George & Gilbert: That's rather an unfair sort of tie-up. There's also very little difference in a way between one's first still-life painting or life-drawing. Even that's just another number of days before.

Wouldn't your first life painting have been done from a different sort of standpoint?

Gilbert & George: It's probably not wildly different, you know.

George & Gilbert: Not wildly different, no. It's still based on arranging the painting in such a way that one can breathe tomorrow. [Laughter] There's still some heavy breathing around.

Gilbert & George: We don't *do* pieces. We just show some small parts. They're not even important. We never think our 'works' are important.

George & Gilbert: They're not art works, you see.

I suppose I'm inevitably putting the point of view of the spectator. Do you consider the spectator as at all important?

George & Gilbert: At the moment we're very away from that.

Gilbert & George: We have thought about that.

George & Gilbert: When we had our business manager we talked about nothing else. In some ways we're interested in it in a much more general way now.

Why did you acquire a business manager?

George & Gilbert: We needed to do some business in the art world before we left St Martin's. We just wanted to put it on a sound footing really, a sound business base. It seemed a very suitable idea at the time.

What did you do?

Gilbert & George: Oh, a lot of things. Maybe it doesn't sound a lot, but we had a very busy time.

George & Gilbert: Terribly busy. It was amazing. We did a whole series of art visits tied up with a business investigation of the art world.

What sort of people did you go to see?

George & Gilbert: All the people to do with business or with art or both, preferably both. We spoke to every writer.

Gilbert & George: Every art school was included.

George & Gilbert: Every dealer – we talked to them about money. Government people.

Gilbert & George: We wanted to do it. We were very involved in ourselves.

Did you propose certain things should be done or did you simply discuss the state of the case?

Gilbert & George: We proposed a lot of things, hundreds of things.

George & Gilbert: Yes, but basically we just presented ourselves and a lot of information about –

Gilbert & George: Us and what we wanted –

George & Gilbert: Our ideas. We had a box which we took to everyone with a lot of photographs in and a series of cards. The first plate in the box is about 12 by 10 [inches] and is just a photograph of a head laughing in a bathing hat. We always presented that first and said, 'This is a smile, something that we intend to promote.' They just looked and looked away. Then we went on through the other cards. We thought it was very exciting. I can still feel the box, heavy on one side, with a big rubber band around it.

What sort of other things were in the box?

George & Gilbert: The complete documentation of the café show at Frank's Sandwich Bar. Some information on *Underneath the Arches*, which we were just beginning to present at art schools, and all sorts of other jolly things.

Was this the first state of Underneath the Arches, *before it became* Singing Sculpture?

George & Gilbert: Yes. It was made initially as just *Our New Sculpture* and presented as a piece of sculpture at various schools of art.

Gilbert & George: We just played the record twice, on one side. It was turned twice to give the illusion we were turning the record, which wasn't true. And there was a short speech before and a short speech after, I think.

George & Gilbert: I don't remember that awfully well.

Did you make it up on the spur of the moment?

George & Gilbert: No. I think we always welcomed the people and said how nice it was of them to have come along and explained how we were interested in showing our sculpture.

Gilbert & George: And how it was made completely.

Have you ever considered exhibiting documentary material of the kind you've been talking about?

Gilbert & George: We have never been in favour of that. We show only the new information. We like very much that our pieces are heard, but it's impossible to go back and show them how it was. It's not true when you start to do it as a record.

George & Gilbert: Mm – we like to do a new thing every time, you know.

Yes, I can see it would be difficult, like making a loop tape of your lives or something. Would it be all right to do it after you're dead?

George & Gilbert: Gosh! That's a long time away I think, I hope.

[Laughter.]

Gilbert & George: Not necessarily. [Laughter.]

You have in fact hinted at death quite often, 'Dying slowly' I think is a phrase you've used.

George & Gilbert: I think we are fairly optimistic. You make me feel past it already. [Prolonged laughter.]

In that you're pretending to be sculpture, I suppose one could imagine that you were looking over into the abyss as it were, into a magic situation. And that in a way you're saying, 'Come on in, the water's OK.'

George & Gilbert: Yes. I don't know about that. It is a most marvellous thing to do.

What sort of other work were you doing when the Underneath the Arches *piece was evolving?*

Gilbert & George: We did the *Interview Piece* in which we interviewed Bruce McLean and we did *The Meal* at the same time.

George & Gilbert: They were all done during the early part of the year

(1969). But we did *Underneath the Arches* right up to this summer. It's still quite a success.

The Meal Piece was when you invited David Hockney to dinner. What happened in the piece with Bruce McLean?

Gilbert & George: It was an interview about art.

George & Gilbert: It was about history of art, almost in the form of a lecture. Bruce McLean acted the sculpture for us.

When you say you did Underneath the Arches *right up to this summer, does that mean you've stopped doing it?*

Gilbert & George: Oh, no.

George & Gilbert: We always think it's just like a sculpture we made. It's always there, we take it out of the cupboard and dust it up.

Do you get back into it like putting on old clothes?

George & Gilbert: It's just like new every time. It's different. It feels different. We did a good deal with the Pop world for a short time. We did a different piece for the Marquee Club, but we did *Underneath the Arches* at the Lyceum Ballroom and at the Plumpton Pop Festival.

What did you do at the Marquee Club?

George & Gilbert: I told a story to Gilbert. First of all I asked him to listen to a story.

What sort of stories were they?

George & Gilbert: Some rather bloodthirsty stories from comics. Just the sort of exciting stories we naively imagined that people of that sort of background would enjoy. They liked it.

Did you like working in that sort of situation?

George & Gilbert: We saw no future in it.

Gilbert & George: In popular art.

George & Gilbert: We wouldn't even be interested now. We just thought we might do it then. We were interested in a lot of the people. It's very much based on entertainment.

One tends to connect the slightly old-fashioned appearance of some of your things with the world which is specifically to be enjoyed, which is not timeless.

George & Gilbert: I think we are just keen to be reasonably, normally conservative.

Gilbert & George: We change our minds every day. What people think is very difficult to consider for us. We think it's very dangerous for us to know anything about it.

Gilbert & George: It's so interfering. It's so much what they want and not what we want. Everyone has a different idea.

Gilbert & George: It's very nice to be with the galleries, they take over splendidly. In all of our shows we are very much the art. Every letter that we get every day is some comment. If you would react to everything...

You'd go crazy?

George & Gilbert: Yes. We're very wary.

Gilbert & George: Very wary.

George & Gilbert: Even though we work along with that...

Gilbert & George: in mind...

George & Gilbert: more than many artists.

Yes, this is a problem which is salutary to consider. The spectator is involved with trying to make contact but when he gets there, as with any work of art, the curtain drops.

George & Gilbert: Yes. Perhaps that's why we're only friendly to a person the first time. [Laughter.]

So could one say you are attempting to bring the spectator round to your way of thinking?

George & Gilbert: I think to make up our mind either way would be a mistake, really. It's only a balance between these things that really matters.

Yet in the paintings and drawings and the written and photograph pieces you invite people to speculate about the relationships to your lives. In the General Jungle *drawings for example, obviously one can draw a lot of conclusions which wouldn't be what you intended.*

Gilbert & George: We don't mind.

George & Gilbert: No, we love that.

What did you intend?

Gilbert & George: It's very simple I think, we just use forms to explain ourselves. That's the most logical thing. They are just pieces of art, and we used that kind of form because another form would be more difficult. We wouldn't even know how to draw another way. We didn't want to find some aesthetic way of drawing. They are taken completely from a photograph and just done very, very quickly.

In seeing yourselves in the General Jungle *situation, are you being metaphorical or biographical or both?*

George & Gilbert: It was purely autobiographical.

What was the particular situation?

Gilbert & George: So many different situations.

George & Gilbert: It was just to do with us and art really.

The jungle of art?

Gilbert & George: Not art as a jungle. Our jungle.

George & Gilbert: Ultimately our personal relation to art.

Those were done in 1971 I think. When did you do The Paintings, *did they come before that?*

George & Gilbert: We painted them in January of last year I think.

That must have been quite a feat.

George & Gilbert: It wasn't too bad. We were quite surprised; originally we'd intended to do them quicker. We did a basic 10 till 5 or something like that.

Were they done from photographs?

Gilbert & George: Entirely. Not colour photographs though.

George & Gilbert: Not the colour, just the composition. The colour we made up.

Gilbert & George: We did mostly greens so it wasn't much made up. [Laughter.]

Did the paintings come out of being in the country?

George & Gilbert: No we didn't see anything of the countryside, we just went down to take the photographs. Everybody wonders why we did such paintings. We didn't realise it was such a way-out thing to do.

Gilbert & George: They've got so involved.

What do you mean by that?

Gilbert & George: Intellectually why we did things. Normally they can only say yes, sure, it looks like modern art and that's all. This time they didn't know. It was even for us very difficult to do it.

George & Gilbert: That's true, yes.

Gilbert & George: It took us six months to order the canvas before we could do it.

George & Gilbert: Just to decide that we should use that form.

Gilbert & George: There was rather a lot of worry in that.

George & Gilbert: Finally just before Christmas we thought we could bear to do it, we could bear to have done it.

Neither of you had ever been painters?

George & Gilbert: Ah. We both had a general sort of art education.

It's not really so very difficult to do. We did it entirely with speed in mind. We could hardly wait to finish and go and wash our hands. But considering they're our first paintings they're not bad really. There aren't many painters who could show such good first paintings, I think, do you?

Gilbert & George: There was an amazing point that was for us amazing, marvellous – because we didn't say they were paintings. We simply said they were a sculpture, and that brought a lot of funny questions.

> *One of the things that surprises me is that what you've written in many pieces is tremendously literary in a way. But you've said in the same breath that you very rarely read anything. Is this poetic licence or is it true?*

George & Gilbert: Ah. We don't read in fact. I think any sort of literary content in our writing must date back quite a long time. Though we have started doing a little reading now. We've just cottoned on to these new journals, called *Forum, Climax, Open, Mentor, Experience, Janus* and so on and so forth. They're journals of sex and physique. Very intimate. Terribly up to date. Absolutely slap up to date.

Gilbert & George: They publish very good letters.

George & Gilbert: Very strong. Very informative. Very direct. Just quite amazing things. Sometimes in form of confessions, sometimes in terms of boasting, sometimes problems – questions and sometimes very good answers.

> *So in a way when you are writing things or doing other pieces you are sort of dredging things up from the past?*

George & Gilbert: I think we're very conscious of our whole life at any one point.

> *Isn't it sort of bifurcated?*

George & Gilbert: Not really, no. We talk a lot to each other about our separate pasts. We're always telling each other about what we did as children.

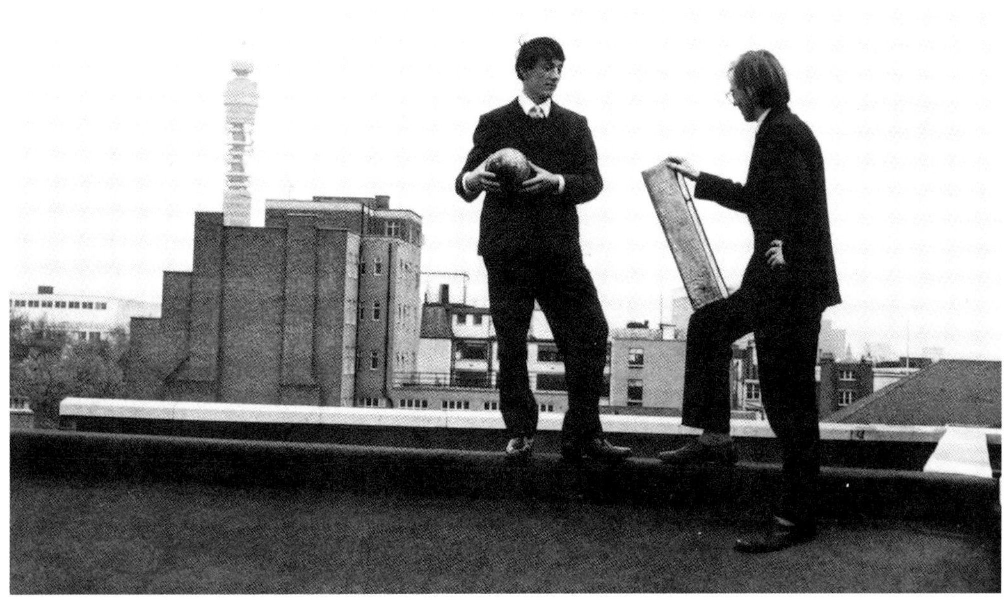

1 Posing with *Object Sculptures*, on the roof of St Martin's School of Art, Spring 1968

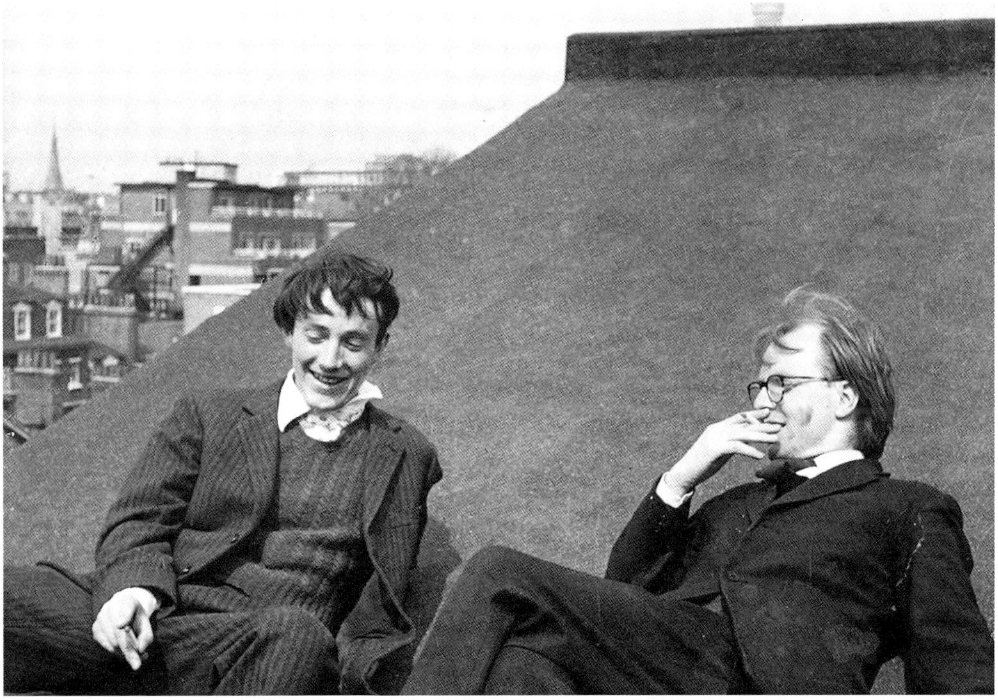

2 In a moment of *Relaxation*, on the roof of St Martin's School of Art, London, Spring 1968

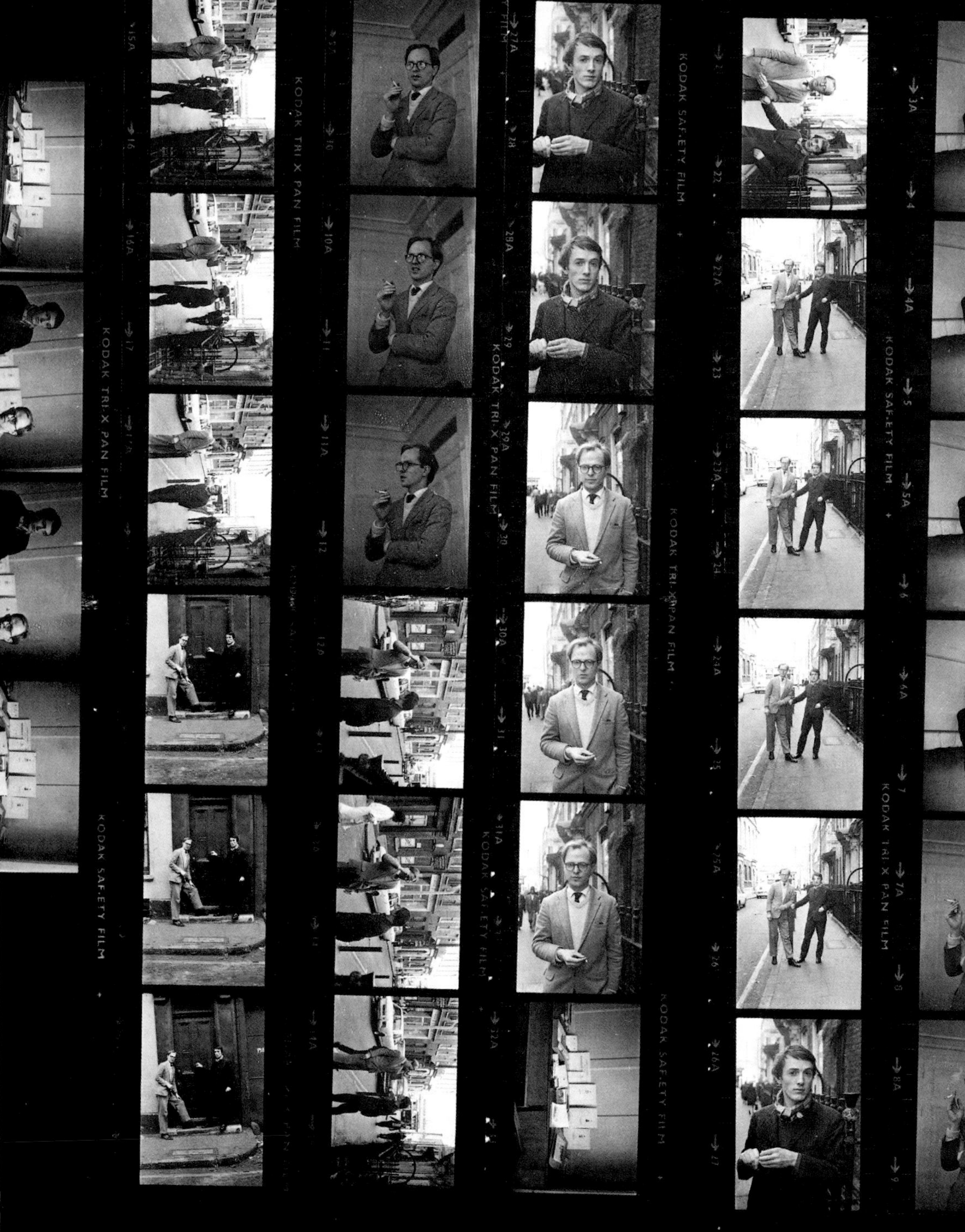

3 First photo-shoot for a national newspaper, Fournier Street, London, *c*. 1969

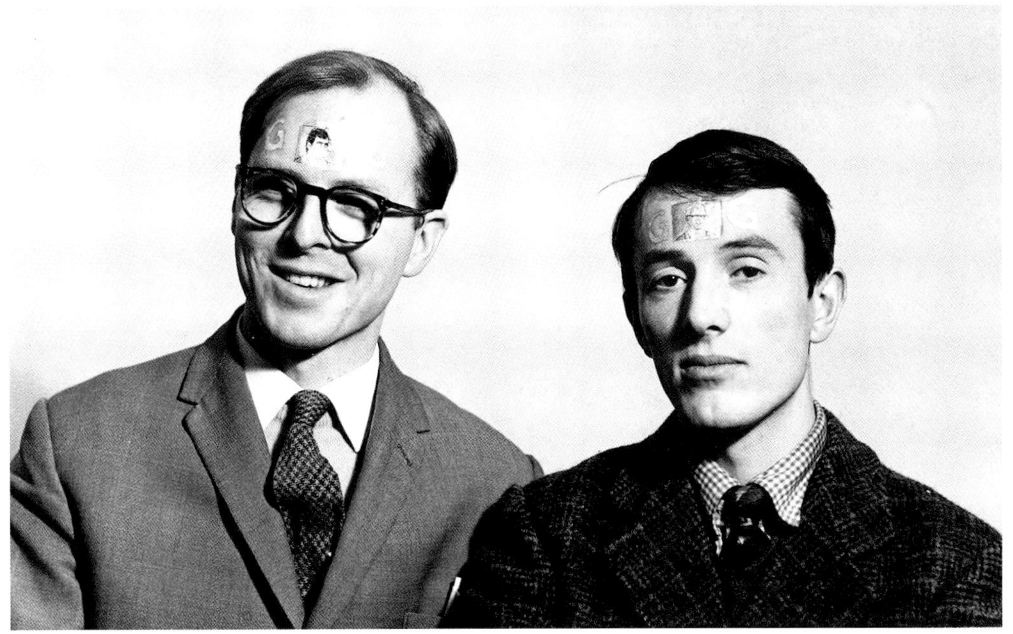

4 With *Design for Foreheads*, worn during 1969 and 1970 on various social and artistic occasions, 1969

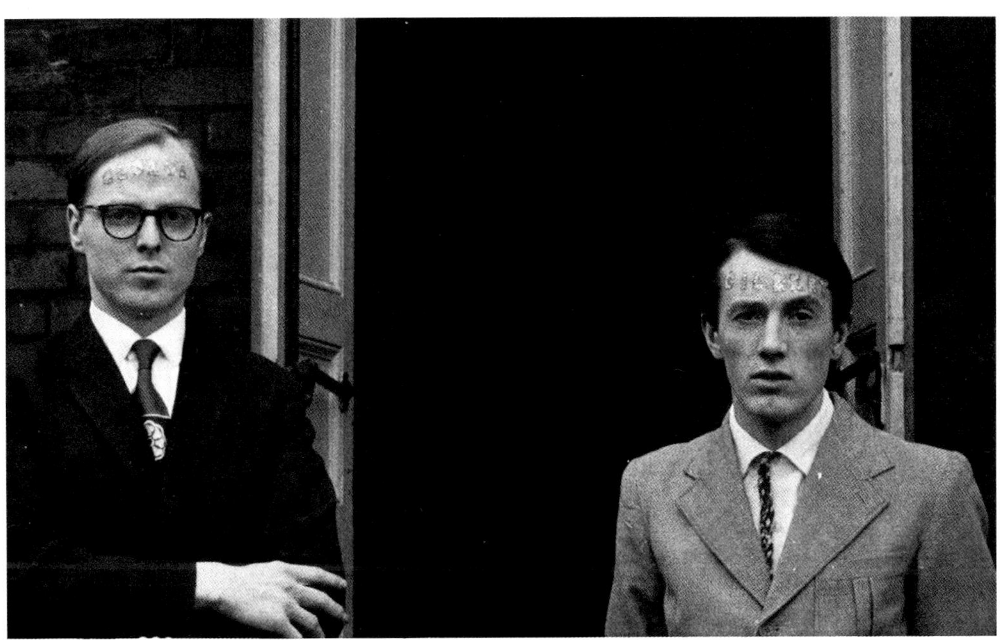

5 Outside the Geffrye Museum, London, on the occasion of the artists' slide-show *Reading from a Stick*,
26 January 1969

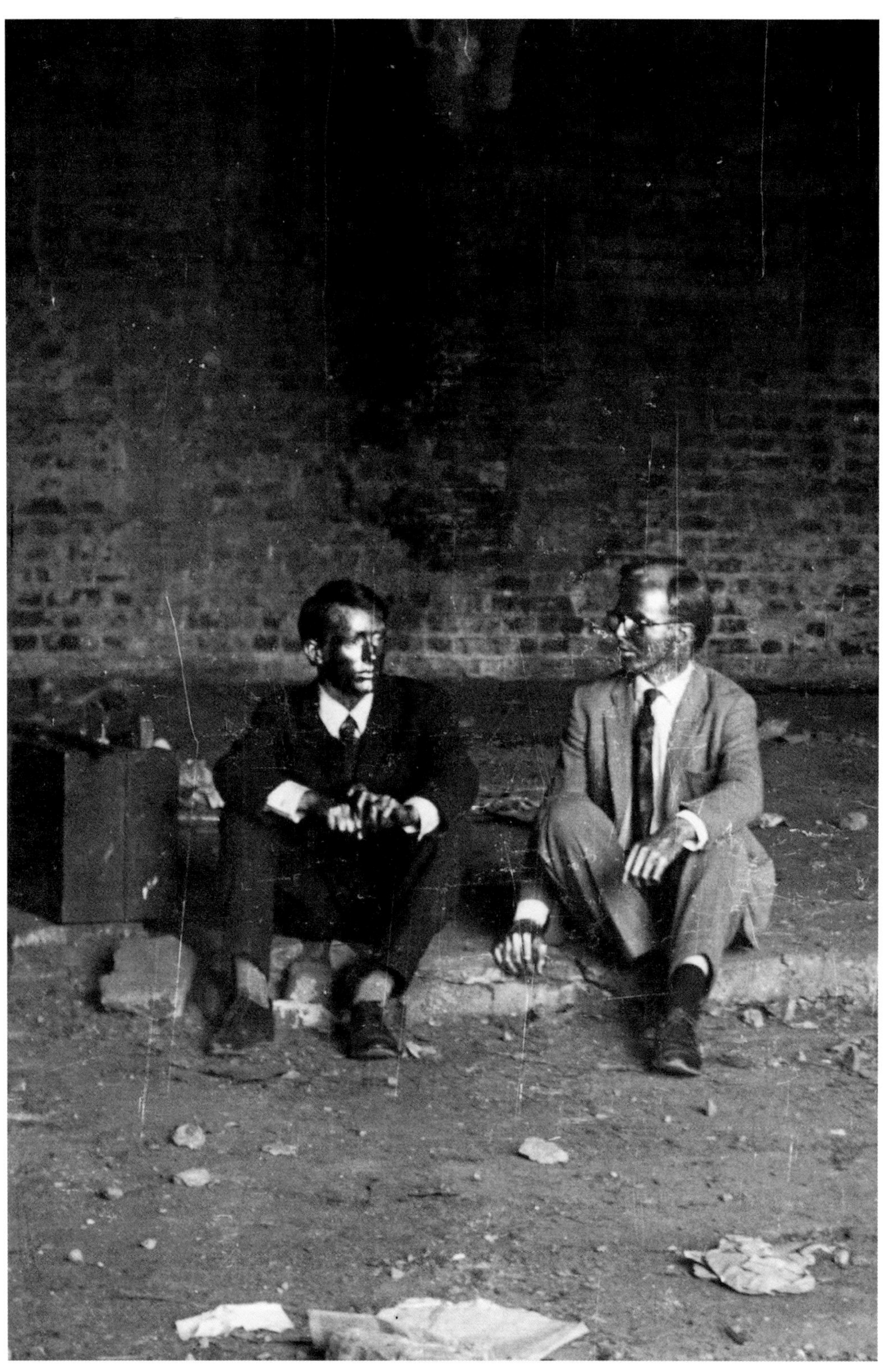

6 Just before *Underneath the Arches*, Cable Street, London 1969

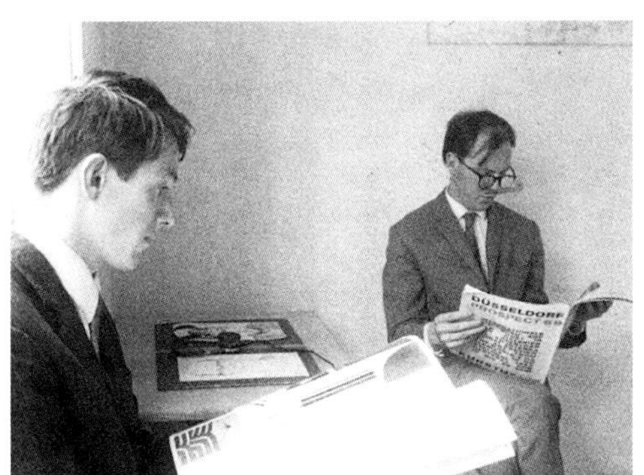
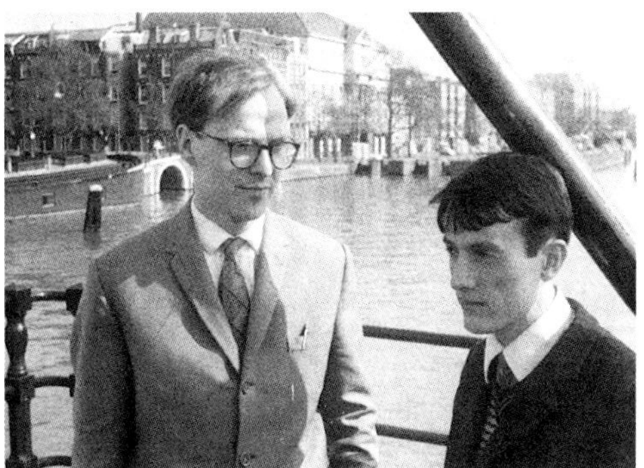
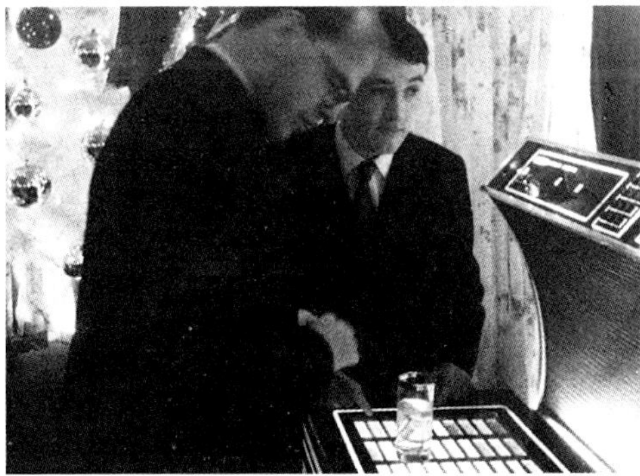

7 In Amsterdam at the time of the artists' exhibition *Art Notes and Thoughts* at Art & Project, May 1970

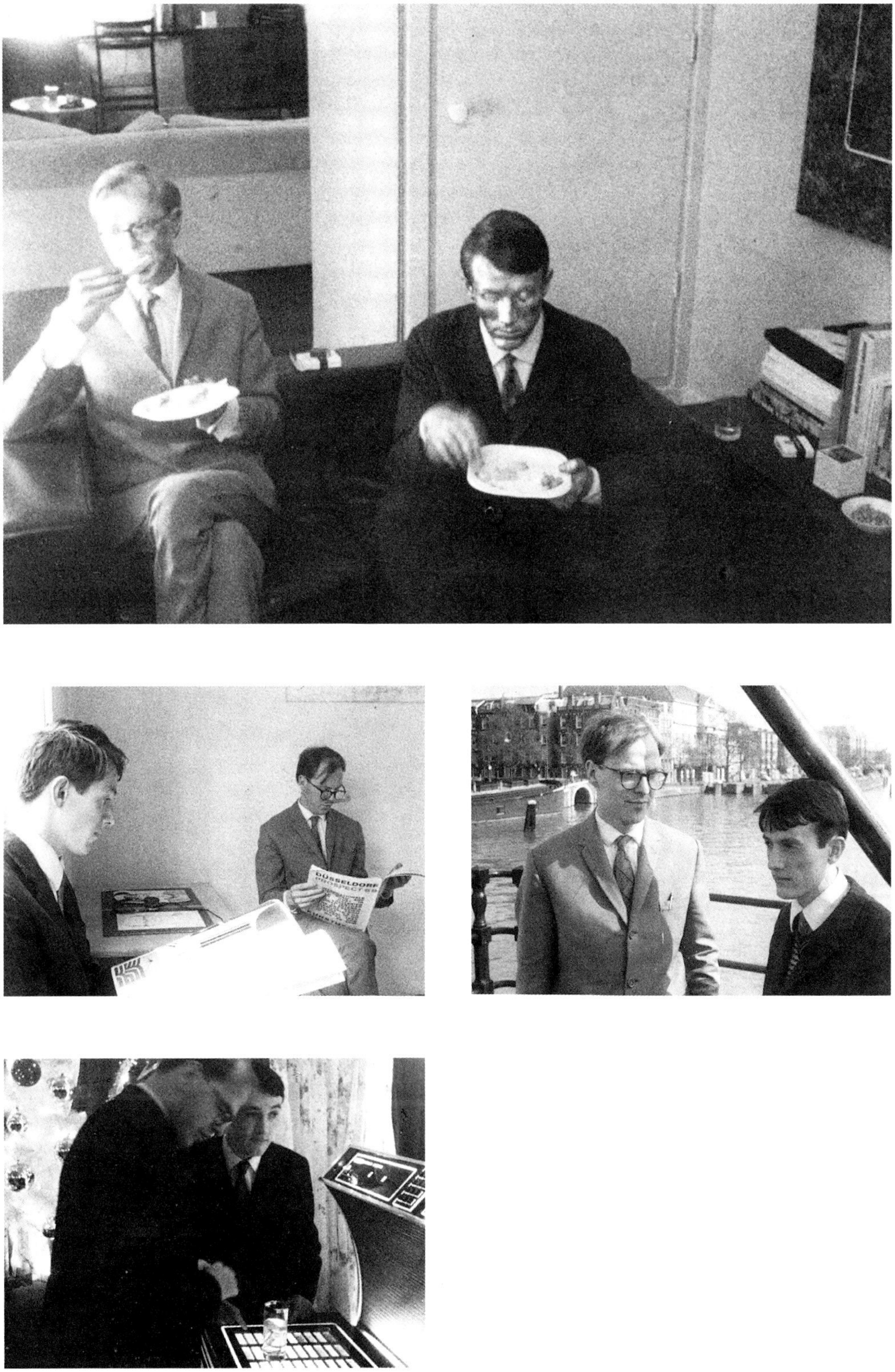

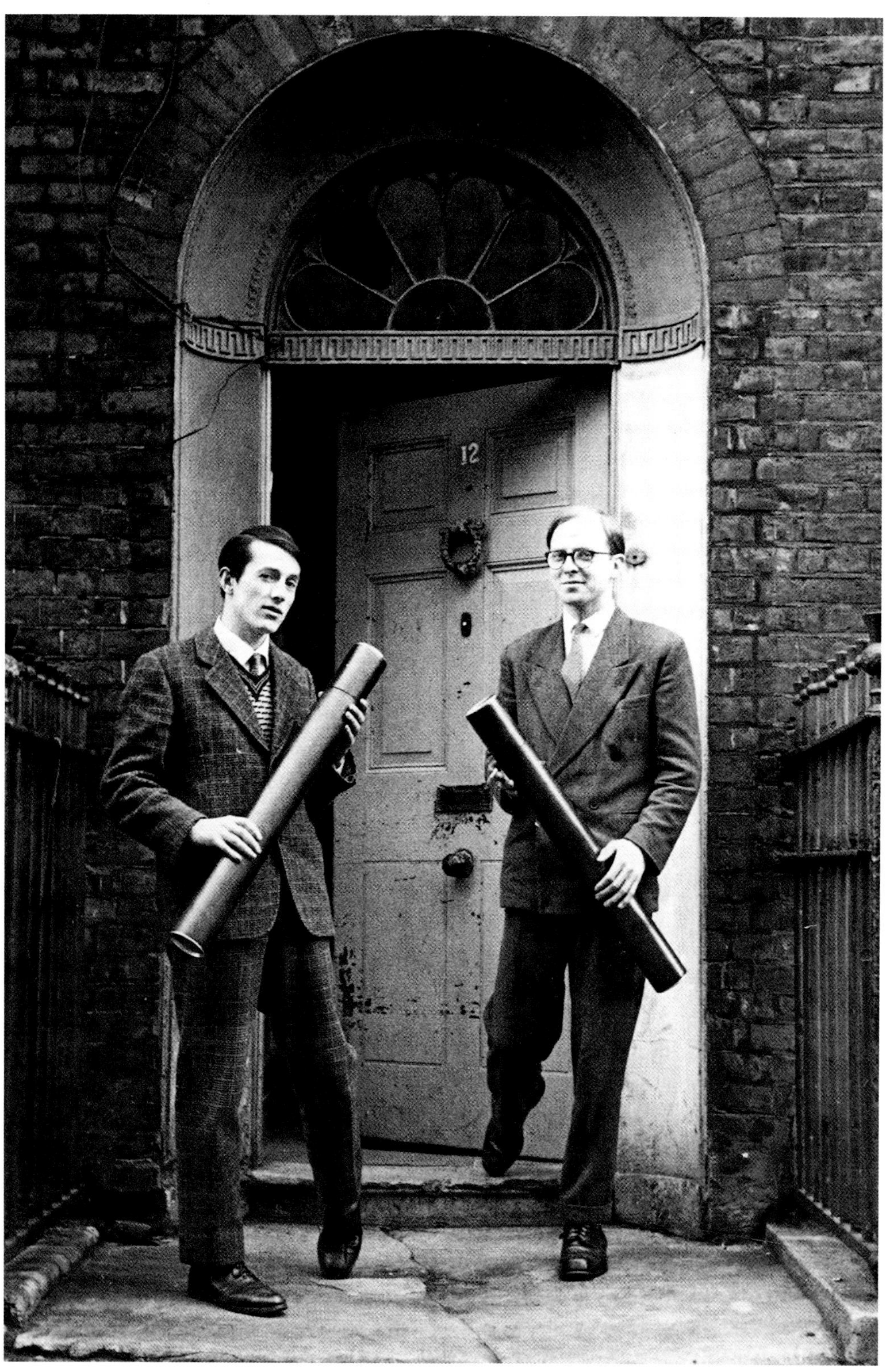

8 Off to send drawings to the 18 Paris IV Group Exhibition, outside the artists' home and studio in
Fournier Street, 1970

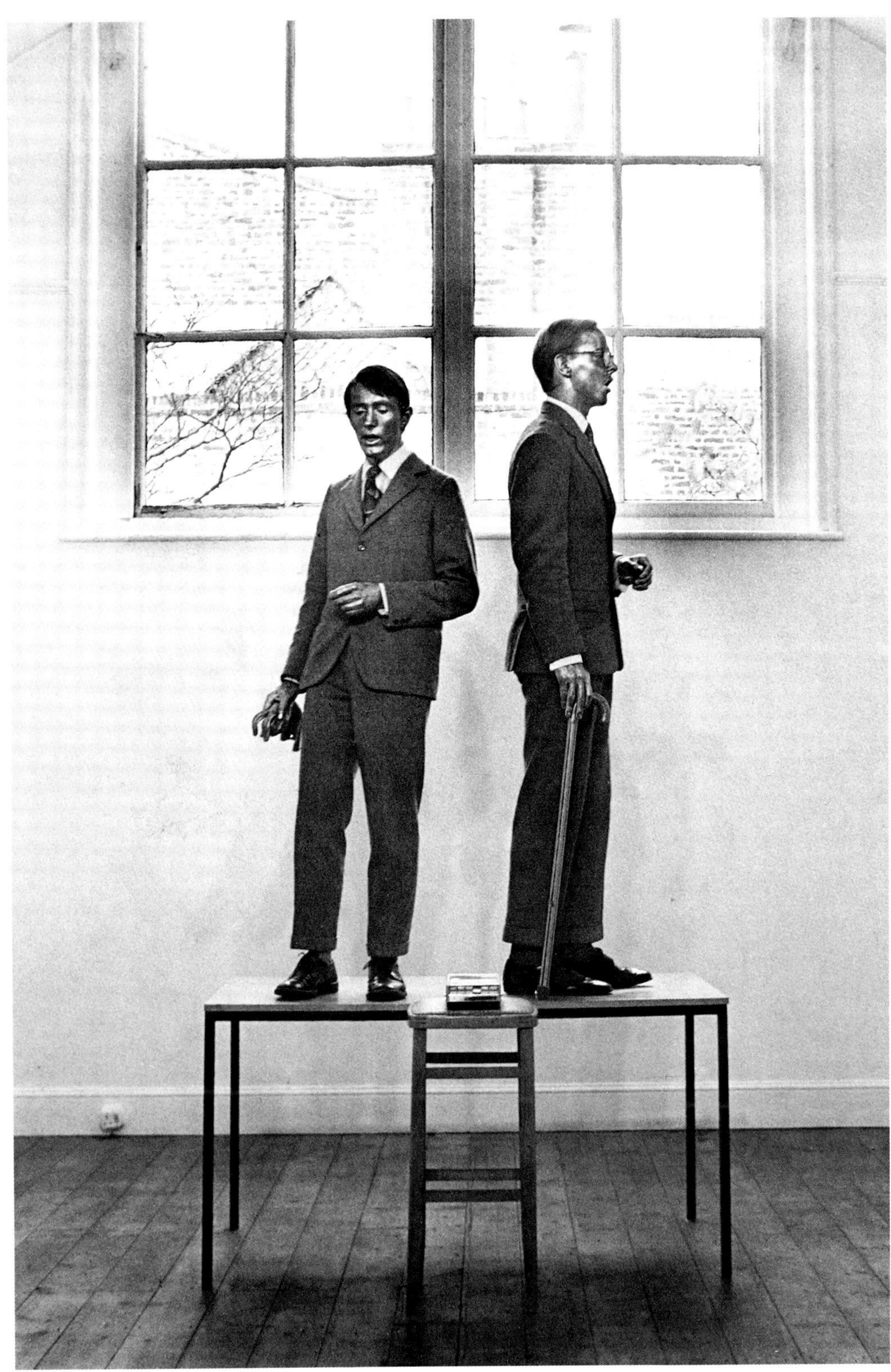

9 *Underneath the Arches*, Nigel Greenwood Gallery, London, 1970 (*Photo: Jorge Lewinski*)

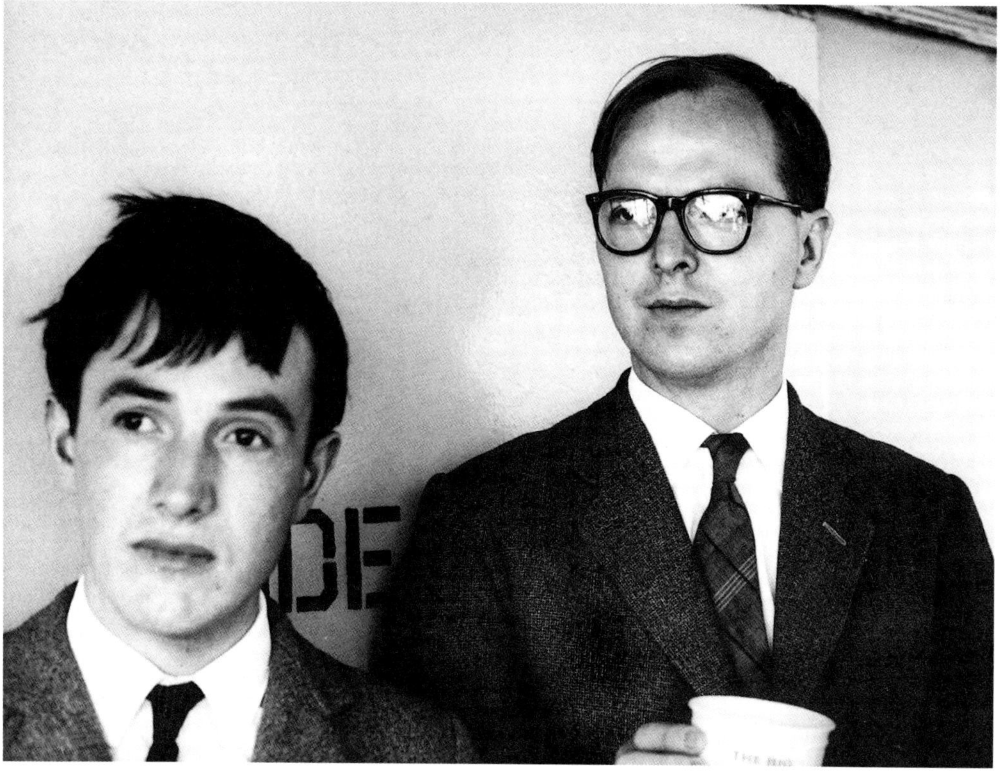

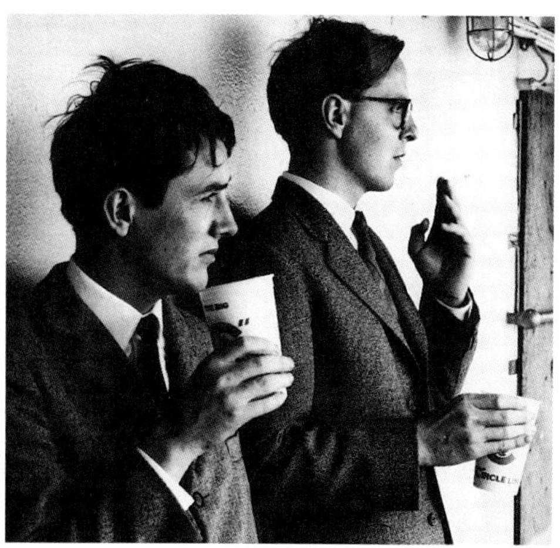

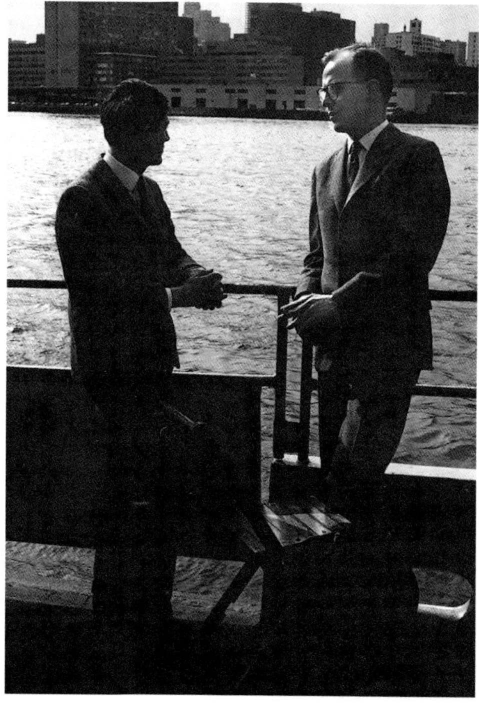

10 On the Circle Line ferry, New York, at the time of the *Singing Sculpture* at the Sonnabend Gallery, Autumn 1971 (*Photos: Carter Ratcliff*)

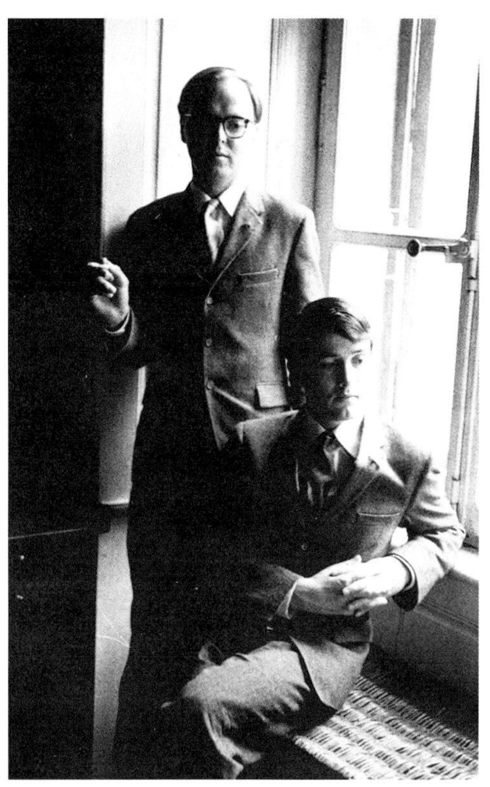

11 Portrait by Allan Porter in the photographer's apartment in Lucerne, Switzerland, at the time of *Underneath the Arches* at the Kunstmuseum Lucerne, 1972

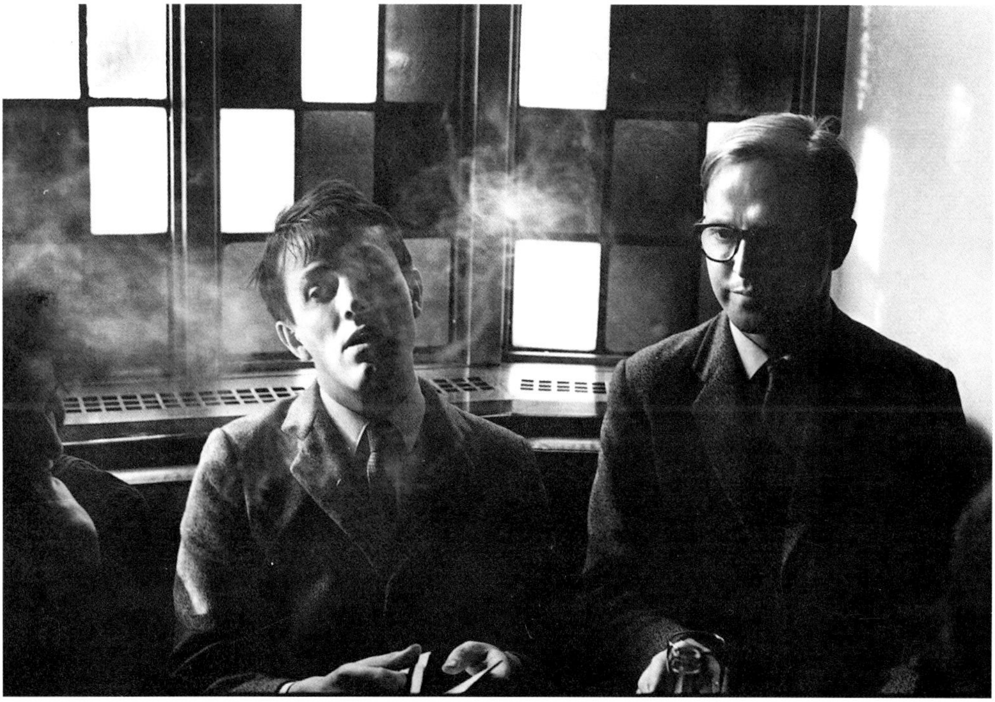

12 In a restaurant across the West Side Highway from the Circle Line dock, New York, Autumn 1971
(*Photo: Carter Ratcliff*)

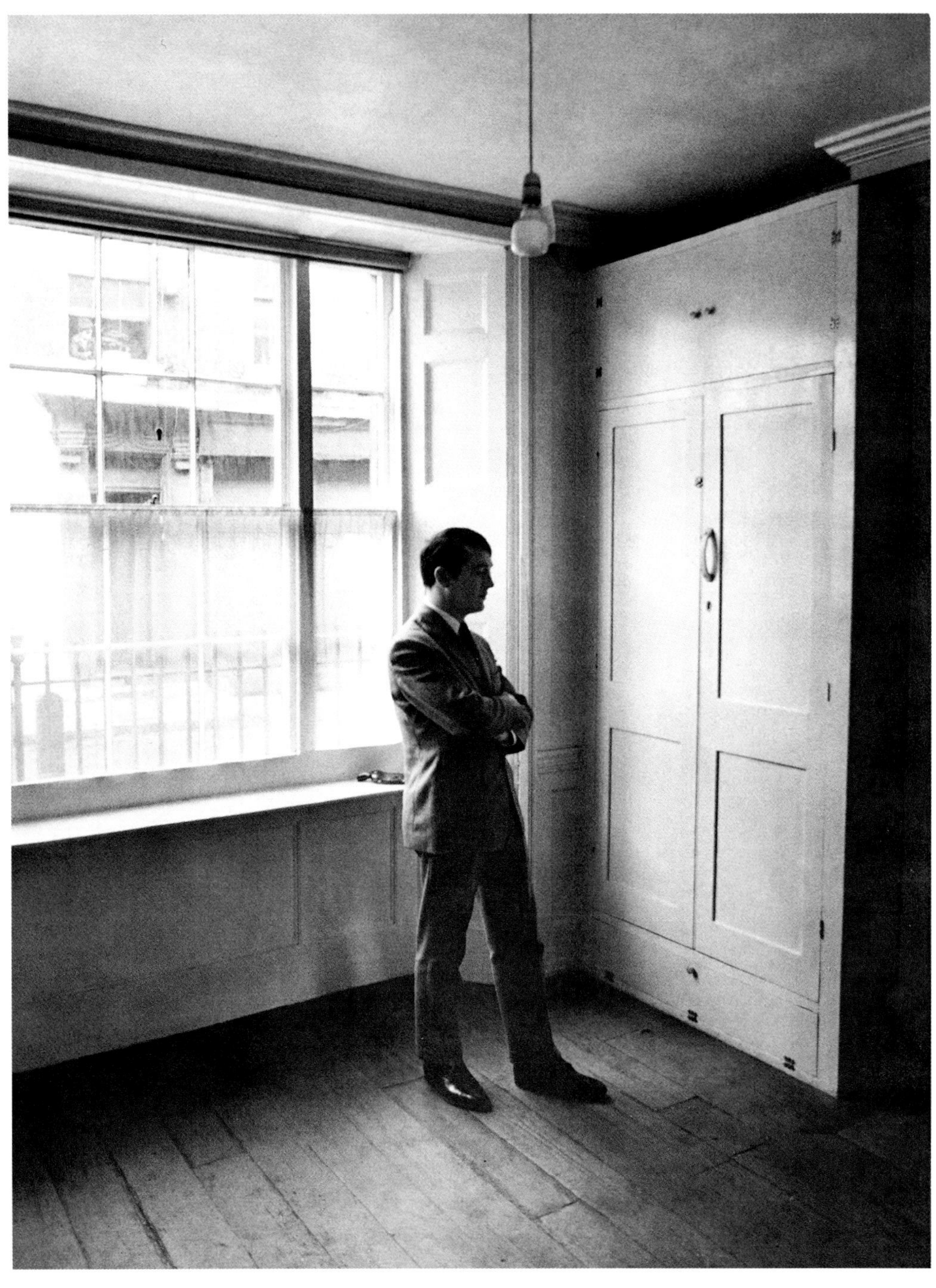

13 Portraits by Jacques and Jenny Gough-Cooper in the artists' home, Fournier Street, 1972

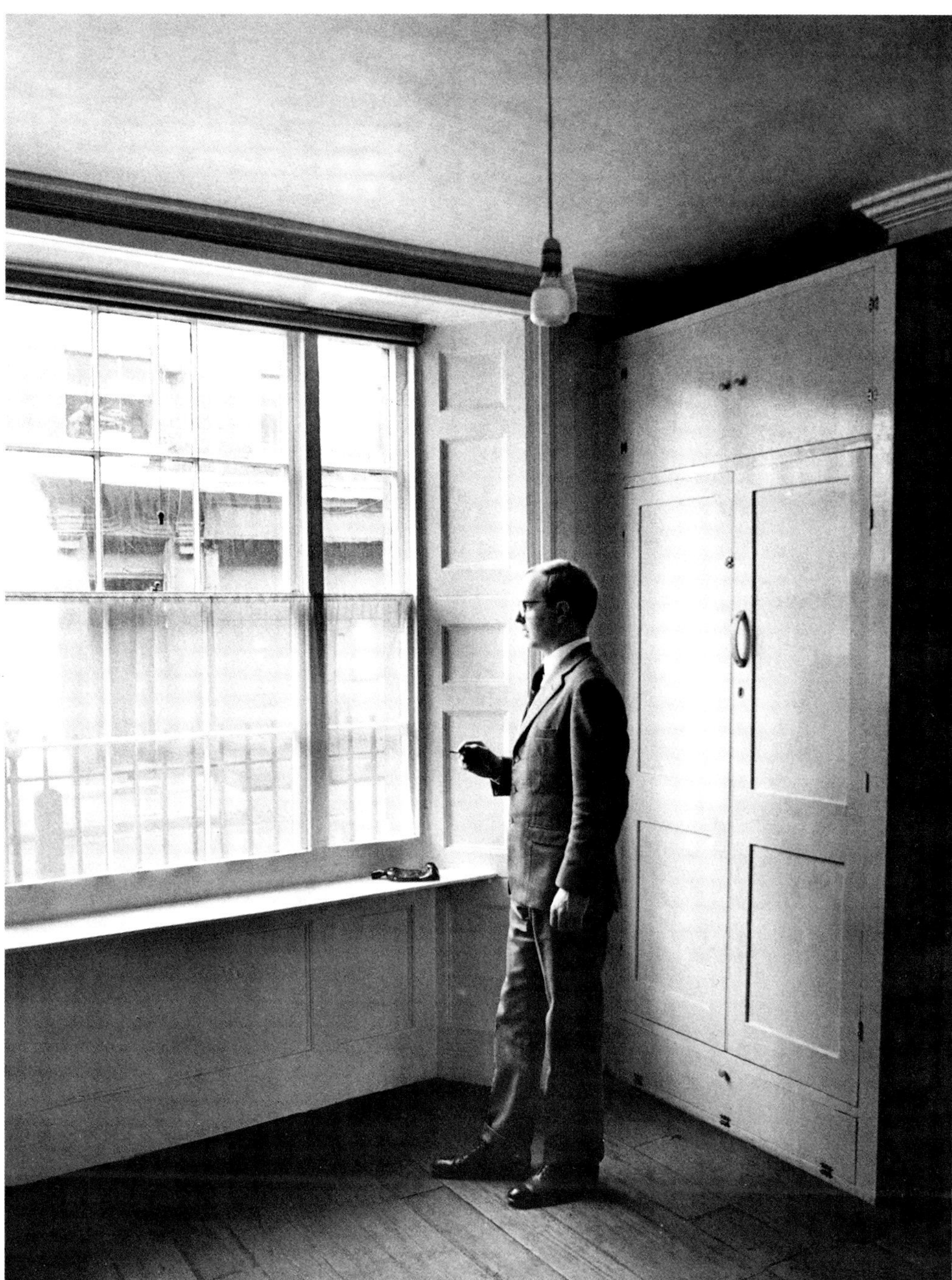

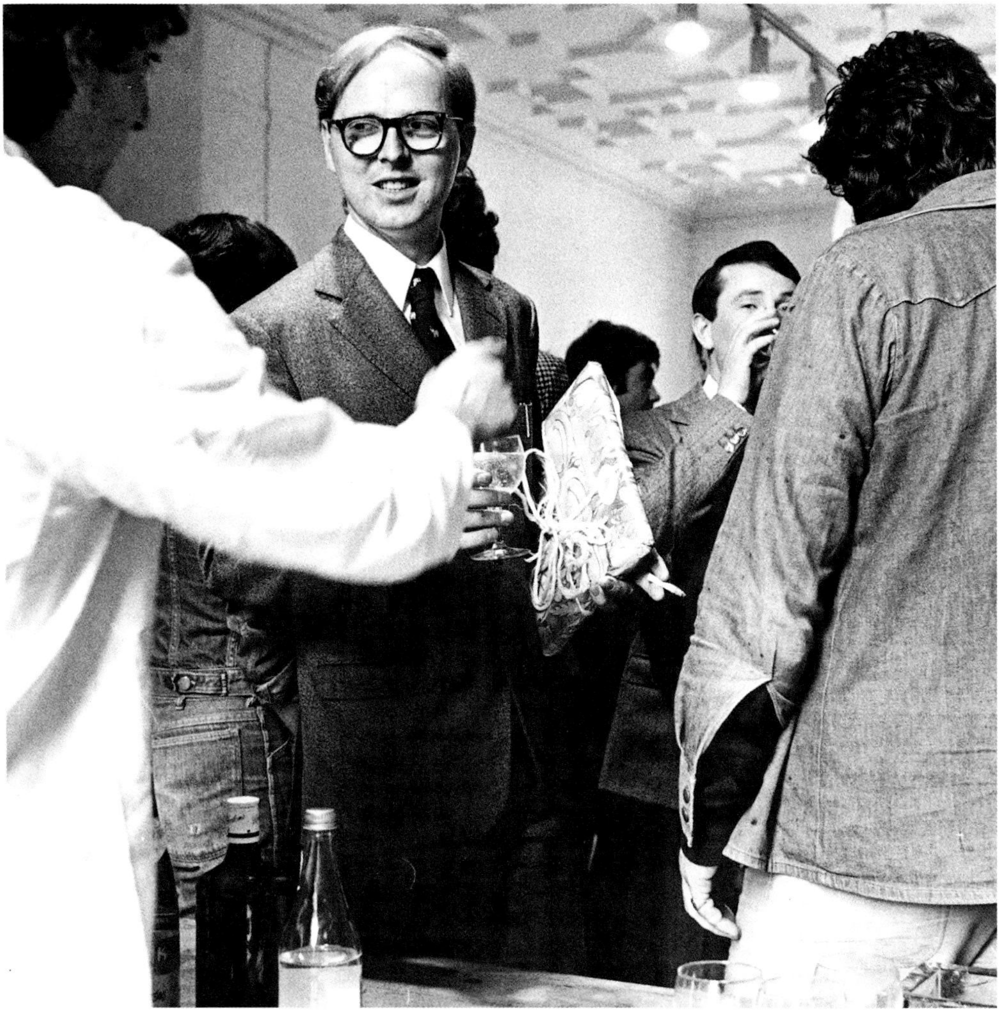

14 At the opening of the artists' exhibition *Reclining Drunk* at the Nigel Greenwood Gallery, London, 1973

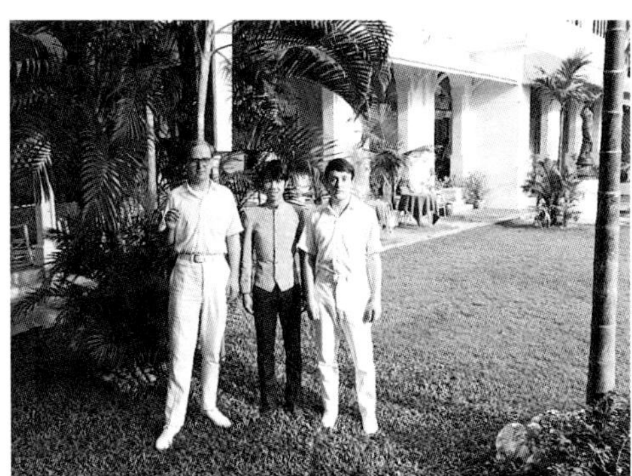

15 With Somsak at the Oriental Hotel, Bangkok, during a visit to Thailand, 1973

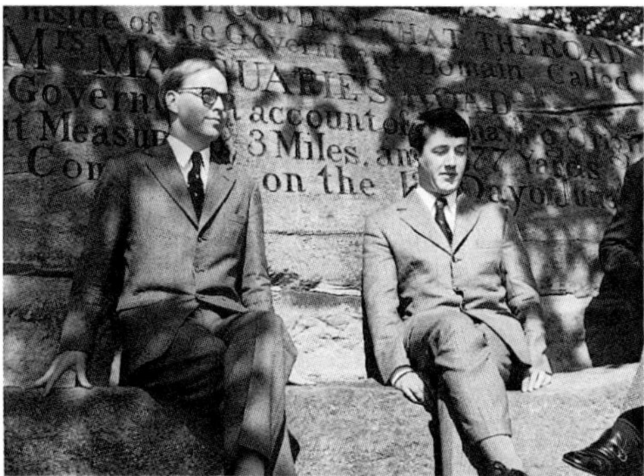

16 At Mrs Macquarie's Chair, Sydney, Australia, at the time of the artists' exhibition *The Shrubberies & Singing Sculpture* at the National Gallery of New South Wales, Sydney, and the National Gallery of Victoria, Melbourne, 1973 (*Photo: John Pearson*)

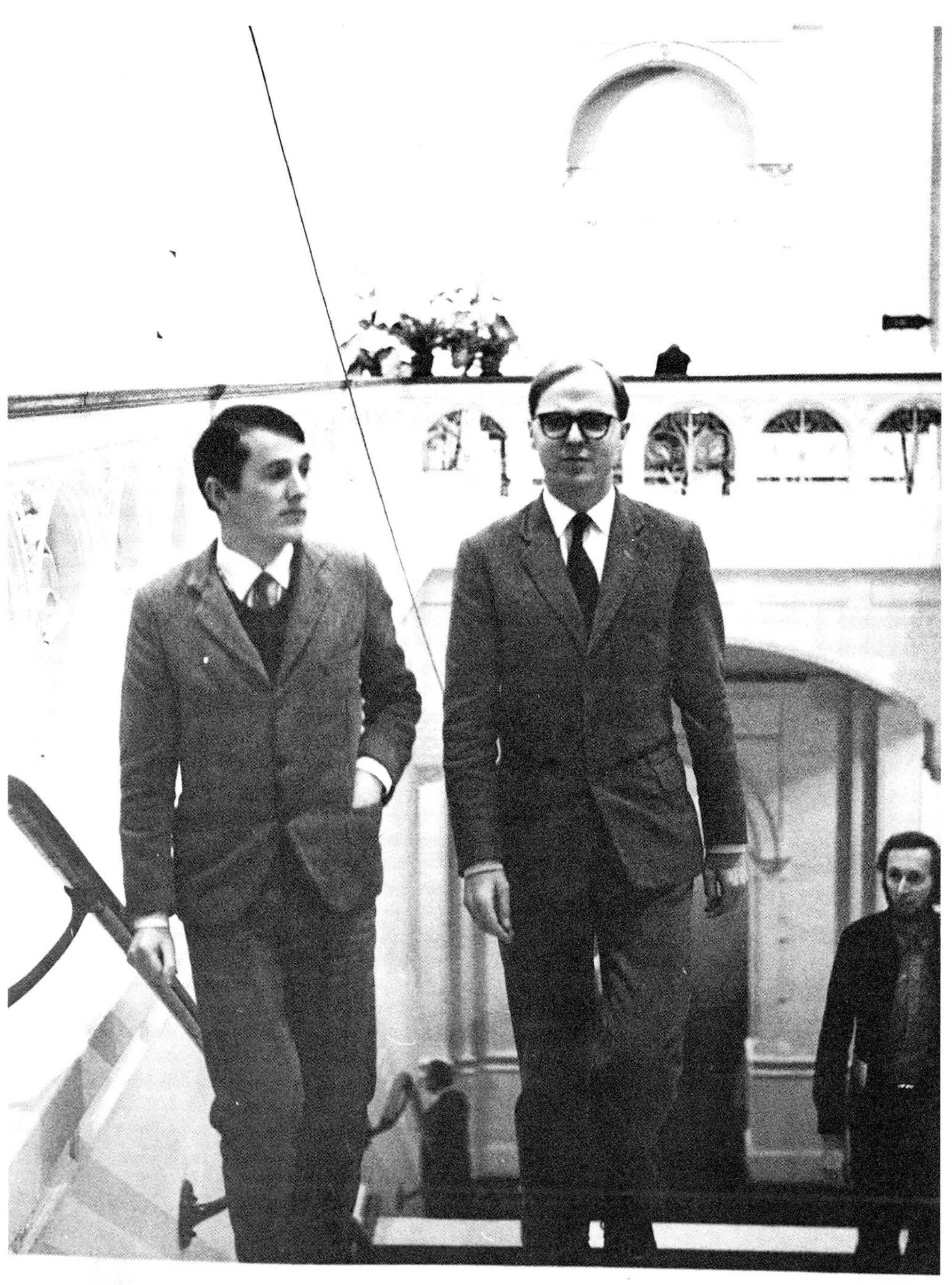

17 At the Stedelijk Museum, Amsterdam, at the time of the artists' exhibition *The Paintings (with Us in the Nature)*, 1971 (*Photo: Courtesy Stedelijk Museum*)

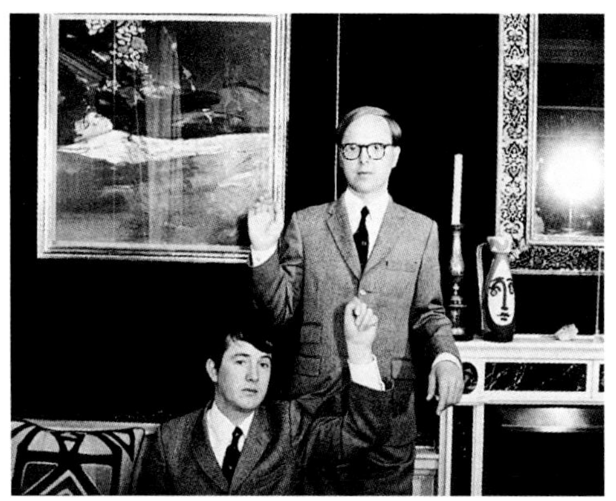

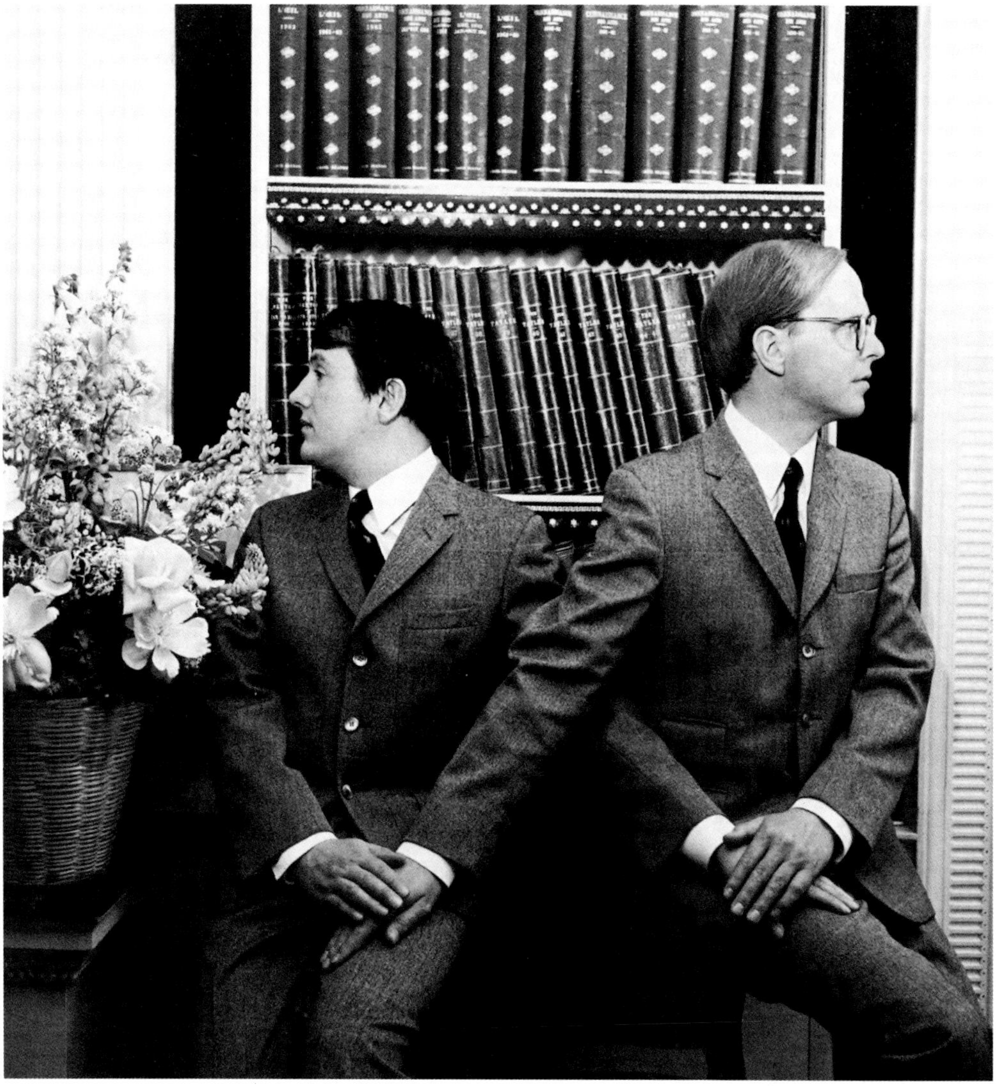

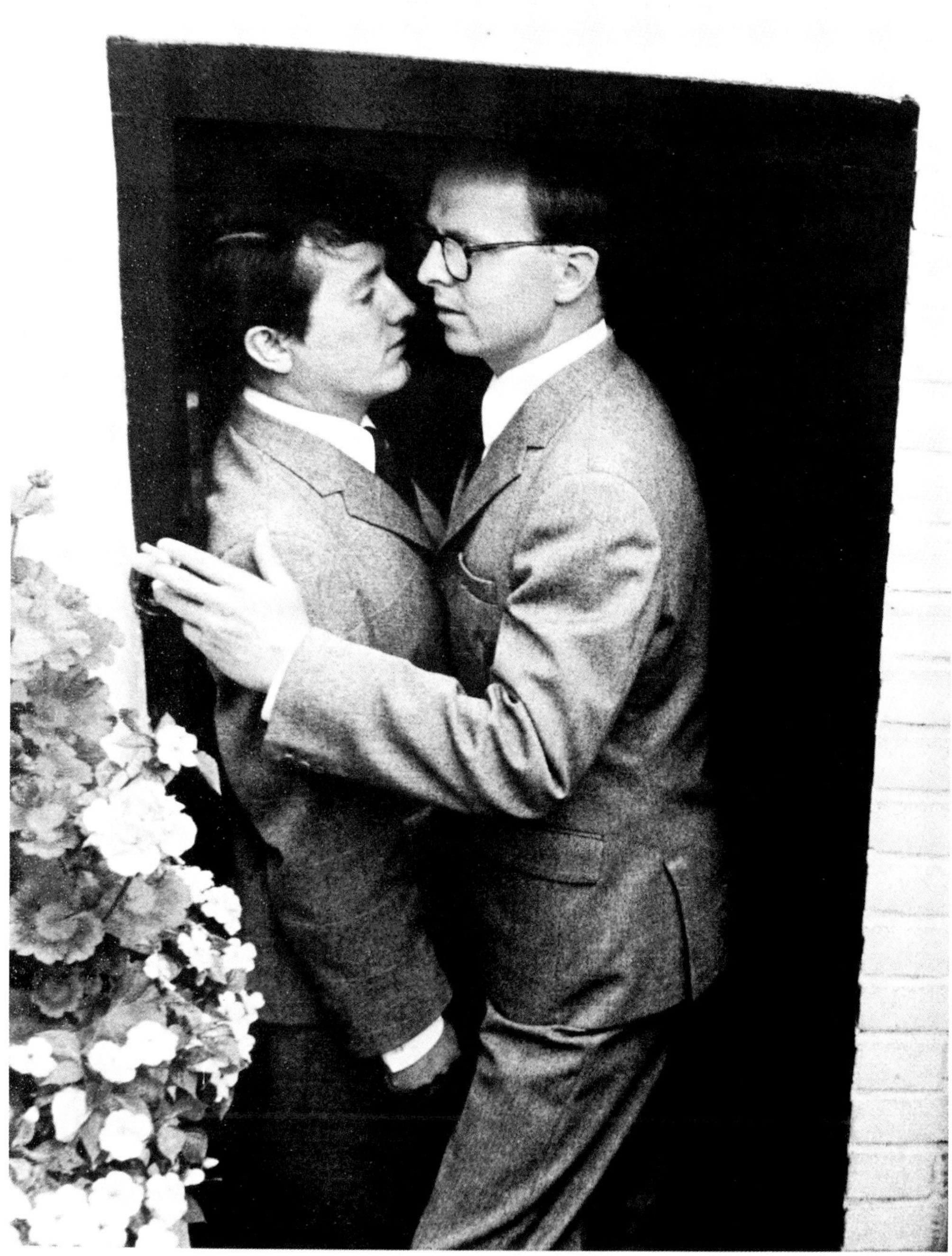

18 Portraits by Cecil Beaton at the photographer's home, London, 1974

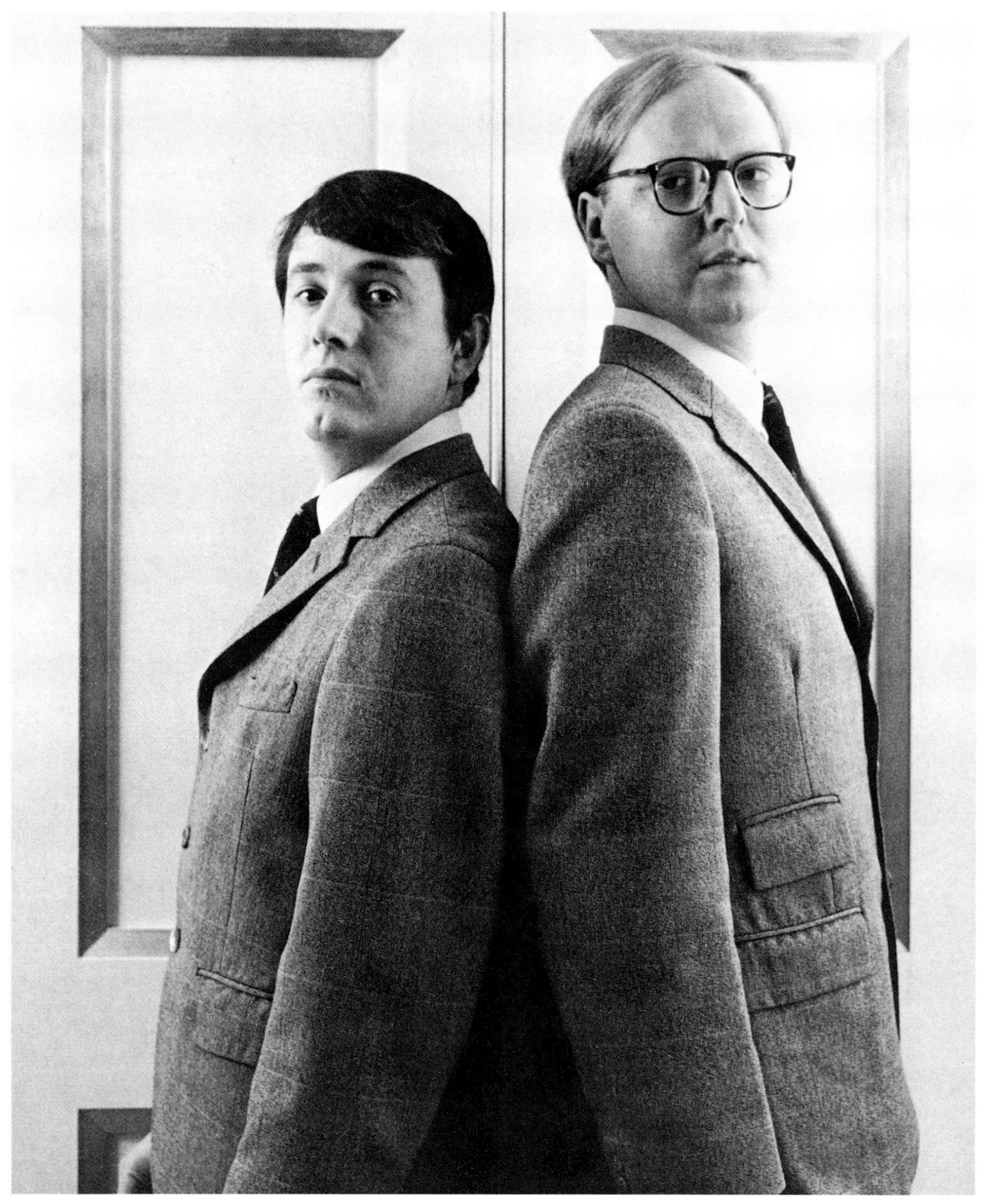

19 Portrait by Cecil Beaton at the photographer's home, London, 1974

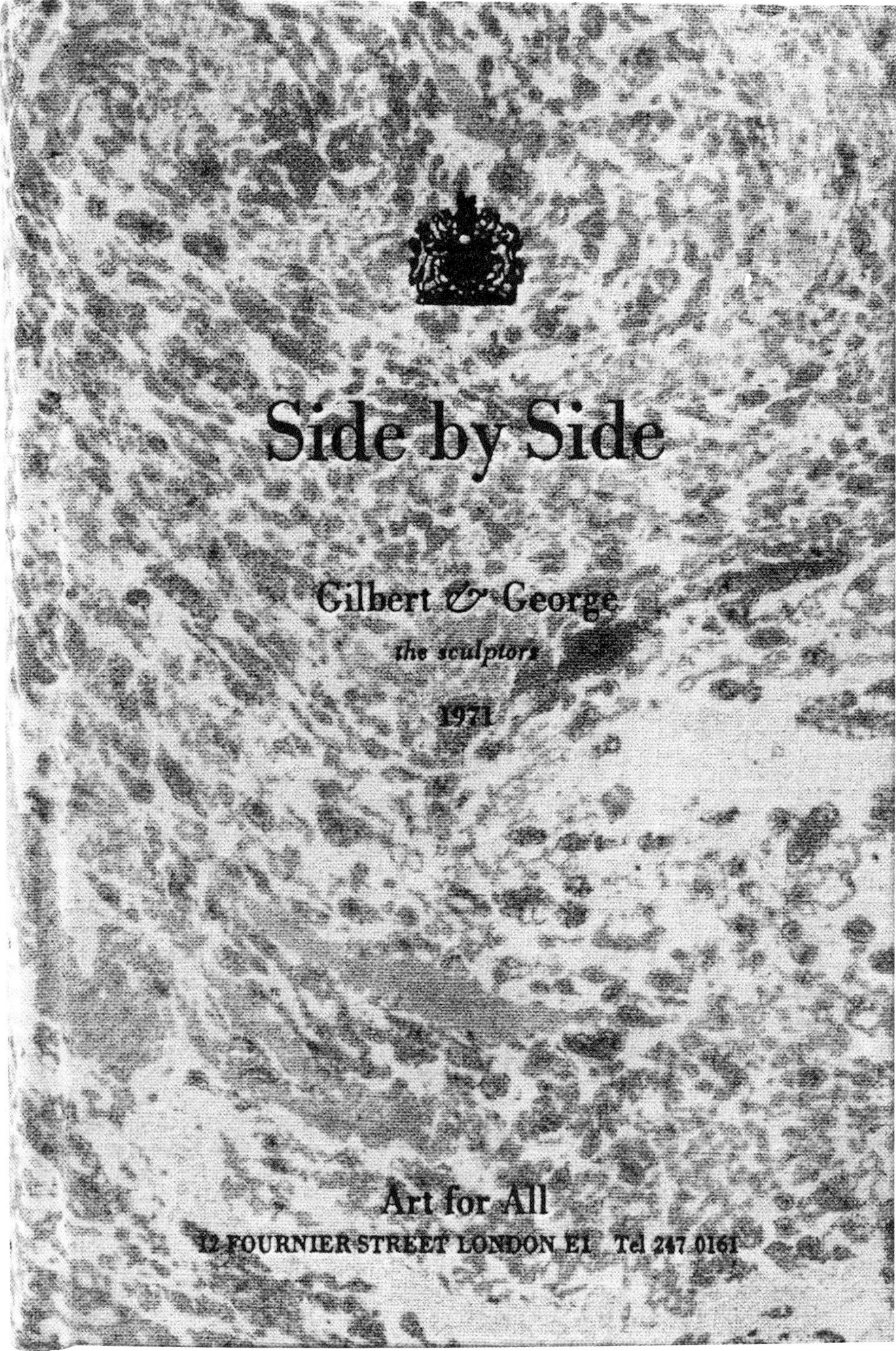

Hand-marbled cover of *Side by Side*, 1971

To the reader
of
Side by Side
from
the sculptors

These chapters together represent a contemporary sculpture novel.

It is based on plans, intentions and experience.

The form being abstract air brushes and the expression pure sculpture.

The reader should not expect not to understand this volume as we have been careful to use only accessible material.

We beg you not to criticize this, our work, as this could only result in unhappiness for both. the reader and ourselves.

And so, we leave you now with this our simple book.

Yours sincerely

George and *Gilbert*

Side by Side

First published in 1972 by König Brothers, Cologne, in a signed and numbered edition of 600 clothbound copies in which each of the following texts occupies a full lefthand page and faces a full-page black-and-white illustration.

Introduction to Chapter One

With Us in the Nature

This sculpture is based on and resulting from our position in relation to the countryside.

Here we deal with natural material e.g. weather conditions, air situations, light atmospheres, flora lay-outs and contour feelings.

The position of the homo-sapiens has been closely observed and fully documented. The content is a message concerning modern conservative evolution.

Chapter 1
With Us in the Nature

SOPHISTICATED CULTURE

This is the sophisticated cultured garden of the World. In a monastery garden each little piece tells only one story of simple superficial ambitions. We two are here to glide over all problems, prejudices, and nervousness, unhappiness and stuff. We stand here to be only with these Human flowers to see their artificial colours and forms and to drink of their sweet drugged perfume. What else do we need.

WHITE BLOSSOM

In this frame you see a lot of white blossom on boughs, it is not Winter, it is quite hot. A heavy day smelling sweetly of Spring and of Summer. The branches moving lazily in the sluggish wind. If you look very closely you may see a little water, still and black for you to look into, blossom and water, blossom and water. The keenly defined leaves are all over a pattern or grid. This definition is our own.

INNOCENCE
The foreground corner is innocent and bland and a place to stand and
maybe listen to the trouble ahead. A network of tracery, branches for
you to look through. The sun coming through and resting on the peaceful surface of the stagnant pool. The edge trimmed daintily with early,
fleshly plant life. In this Hangers-Pool, what stories could this black
pond tell, what secrets does it have. We sense a mystery with no life.

SENSELESS FENCE
Here a senseless fence shows man's hand upon the greenery and foliage.
This thin bending moving grass keeps the foreground what it is in light
and in one piece. Move your eye on and out to the distant shadow telling
of another past. Only the fence and the middle ground being really in
the picture this time. Light falls upon the surfaces telling us all about it.
We never will forget it you know.

HOMELY LIFE
We like this sweet view which shows only homely life in a rural setting
– the simple folk. Even the shrubs trimmed by the cottager to a solid
friendly shape. One window open onto view and fresh air. It was afternoon and the shadows showed us this lovely, nice spot. No sounds come
from the house, all is silent. Only some birds fly heavily overhead. The
faintest sound of an insect doing.

SIDE BY SIDE
Side by Side we look to you. A fine dark sky is our back-ground. Flowers
edge our way along the dusty road and thick-leaved trees shade our
way. Some shadows on the road. Quite a funny sky in this one with an
incredible atmosphere of threatening and dread, late-evening and we
must be home before we are too tired, too depressed and happy. Back to
sleep, and dinner and Friends and a House.

UNTROUBLED LIFE
Dear quiet piece of country with your totally untroubled life. A broken
rustic fence reminds us of times that have past [sic] and are never to
return. Days of innocent unthought Youth when only the moment
counted. Dear picture we love you for your beautiful meaning and life.
Though looking closely we see the tombstones of our departed families
and we hear memories of joy and happy.

LITTLE BRIDGE
A little bridge spans the picture. The two relaxed looking, unthinking
chaps stand on the wooden planks that form the bridge. We look out of
the picture to you – past all that is around us for your mystification. A
weeping willow tree backs us up. Willow sing your song again. The hard
metal bars relieve our tired weight. Their ordinary strength is valuable
because only the gazing of the Arts is of Art-Interest.

TWO BOYS
This time these Two Boys are coming along the road allright. Just
around the bend and about to twist again. Head held high, one straight,
one bent, in this world of Nature. The trees are really beautifully
arranged to form our Arch over our heads. Walk on, walk on, do your
best with hope in your heart for we may never walk this way again, all
being well, we never will. Repeats are not for us too.

EDDIES
Eddies on the water of this, a jollier pool made active by the ducks. The
foreground entirely occupied by a complex of musical flowers, playing
their delightful notes to us and to you. Even the branches and green
leaves are completely composed into the music. All joining hands
together and making summer nature. Five component parts harmon-
ising into a view simply for all. Flowers, reeds.

LEAVES CRY OUT
Black distorted leaves cry out their magic message of mystery. What
happened here? We dare to guess what truths lie fallen from the tree.
We stand puzzled gazing through this frame and find no consolation
from other things around. The grass is dead and worn with a strange
depression. It is surely a suicide view. The background throws us back
onto ourselves and we see all or nothing. All in all.

WESTWARD
Now we are travelling onwards through the trees way up to the west.
Views and pieces rushing past, no stills only a general picture for us.
Frightening looking as we blindly go along. Branches brush our bodies
and scratch our hands and faces – but we feel nothing only to look
ahead and keep marching onwards to our haven of rest. Towards the
new ambition we are forever moving and moving along.

MODERNITY

Lunatic wonders in the churchyard. Sweet solace is ours for we are old-fashioned enough to see this ancient building. Old-fashioned are our clothes and eyes but our outlook is ultra-modern. And so here we must recognise sadness as the key to our past and future. Where is the balance in which to be two beings with this lovely scene of an old church in such charming trees and front and sides and surrounds.

REST

These two people resting on a five-bar gate. Such a simple easy thing to do and yet there is a little more to the story. Observe for instance the similarity of their poses or look to the differences, one dark, one light. See the walking stick. One single-breasted suit and one double-breasted suit. Think of all that diagonal relaxation, for only the picture behind is symmetrical. This really is a very charming picture.

COMPLEX FORM

A more complex piece than you would maybe think or feel. For here we have six areas of activity. In front are two of brambles making a barrier of a desperate nature. Parting gives way in the middle to a better world where good and bad make way for George and Gilbert to be in the unfenced field of their Art. Strongly backed by friendly characters of trees that are small but strong and will grow.

ELEGANT COMPOSITION

A really elegant composition of intimate landscape and two well-groomed figures. As we view each other we feel a surrounding beauty, a lightness that takes us over to the other World of magic dreams and dramas and tinkling bells. Seek no meaning from the objects for there is only an atmosphere of inhabit with the minds eye. Delve not too deeply for all is a surface charm and pleasure. Easy to relax and live it.

STANDING FOR ART

Stand alone and standing for Art. To whom we look, for whom we think and feel and live. Only one direction lies in view and look closely to see that we two strain to keep that view in line. Posed to clear our minds of Worlds desires. To leave us free for Art alone. Sweet Art, hear our voices as we express our humble aim to share your wisdom and beauty. We hope that the sun will one day shine anew.

FLOWERS
Shiny flowers, running fresh clear water under the bridge, bubbling
over clean brown stones. Transparent view of all beneath the surface
and so we are refreshed. The splendid reassurance of the red-brick
wall contrasting and yet complementing these few differences. One
streak of angry barbed wire cuts through the whole picture. There will
be blue skies over the white surface of water. Let us hope.

PUZZLE
We are really in it up to our waists but you have to be quite good to
see us this time. No puzzle, just difficult truth. We are like all around us
and we blend in tonally and in shape. A windswept area of restless
disturbed land. A place for long grass and small shifty bushes. Nothing
grand or special here only realistic modesty. Sometimes we cannot
even find ourselves because it is so foggy. Good old fog.

RIPPLING WATER
Water, rippling, happily in the light. Bending around, finding its own
sweet way. Plants growing lovingly down the old wall. It really is a
picture of sentimental beauty. A little truth, a little freedom. Can this
corner escape for a little time the hard critical stare of viewers. Let this
choice piece alone to do its thing baby. For the sake of you and the days
gone by, be tolerant and support water only.

STONED
A row of natural shaped stones border the path, keeping back the
naughty people. A slight gravel path of no importance means only
walking by. Shining flowers say nothing. They only serve to hide the
branches and growing ugliness of their life. They are a screen for
peoples gaze. Youth will find no harm here, no edge or bitterness for
excitement. Rather you will see grey accuracy of your position with.

SHADE UNDER THE TREES
A quiet smoke and chat together in the shade of the old apple tree. Why
should we step forth into the desperate sun-life of the open space. And
so we linger on the line, indecisive and calculating. Enjoying the one
and regarding the other with a fear of heat and sun-tan. How tempting,
to step boldly for-wards through the flower-spattered grass and turn
our back for a little on the trees. Of this fresh experience.

ROMANCE

A romantic diffused light spread throughout the picture and we are standing nearly together and in the middle. Like the strong trunk of the tree we are based on our roots. We take strength and life from our established past. We are looking very calm confident and relaxed with great future-sense in our lost eyes. We are waiting for time to pass by. The reeds wave as we wait here. We wave back to them with ease.

DARK TUNNEL

Dark black is the tunnel of the road from whence we recently emerged dazed into the tender patch of soft light. It was a steep uphill road enclosed heavily with banks overgrown with a great variety of things. Our way is now a little flatter and more light. There may be trouble ahead but we will face the music together. The sound of music is always present. We all have a road and this picture.

BOYNG BOYNG

Boyng boyng de boyng, boyng boyng. As the pair comes forward slowly and with ceremony through the virgin plants. Straight and beautiful they are in this setting. Approaching this new gate so sweetly opened for us. And so we soon leave the pasture for what is outside – the open road. But, for a while we linger here, reluctant to take that bold step. We give our thoughts to the many aspects here.

FOREVER WE STAND

Forever we stand to give thought to the picture we have in our mind. Join us for a moment beside this handsome oak and savour the pools message and sunlight. Think not of the pleasant countryside but all that lies behind it. It leave behind big thoughts of human nature. Think not too much and expect nothing from us. Because it simply is what it is – our shape of things to come. To look forward is possible.

DESIRE

A beautiful shape of happy desire. A homely May tree carefully arranged with a few flowers. Abstract your feelings to be at one with this image. It is modest and quiet and asks nothing of anyone. It has no mischief or shouting or crying – no emotions known to man. Its simplicity is a heart-ache. Tears are here no consolation. This picture has ambition. Its depths in front of the eye for us.

STILL AND QUIET

Here in the countries heart where the grass is green, we stand very still and quiet. We are full of admiration for the frank honesty of All around us. This is nearly a complete picture, for it contains a lovely sky, a healthy field, flowers, trees, grass and a farm-house. The birds are singing for us, a distant dog barks and our feet push wet and pleasantly into the moist turf. Here in the country sweet heart.

SPRING AGAIN

We will walk together down an English lane. We will gather flowers in the Spring again. A slight coming up provides us with a little effort. Behind, a little hill catches our affection and love. The rough stone road is dusty and is made of walking feet. Day after day, day after day. We converse in pleasant tones of mild things. A tree flourishes beside us making the picture beautiful. Dear complete.

FROZEN INTO

Frozen into the Nature for you Art. We are gazing into our thoughts. Mainly Our spirit is here to be felt. Smiling melancholy. Clouds sail whitely past the blue sky caring for nothing but their progress. The log serves us well. It is our thing for this picture, an object for two people to be with. To compose themselves around. There is so little to be said here – a smile says all. As much as every smile can do.

LOOKING AWAY

We are looking a long way away – as far as our eye can see. We strain to see more. Our figures a complex arrangement with the gate and stick. A very unresolved piece. Oh future where are you we can still not see you. A tea-cup guess is all we have to go by. Please speak to us some-time and tell us of the journeys end. We wait for your Sculptural Lovers. To give us the growing confidence and strength.

GARDEN

Not a picture complete, no view to satisfy, only a slice of the real. The pretty turret and ruined garden wall. All is overgrown and unloved. Outside the garden picture Nature finds another way, without any disturbance she piles the trees with white blossom. And so you have the two Worlds in one and they endeavour to go together in their own ways. Give it all its chance to change sometimes and be.

A FLOWER OR TWO

Bending down to pluck a flower or two which anyway we leave behind.
Smell the dank rotten earthy Life of this jungle. Feel its sinister gloom.
Animal life here abounds shrouded in the sympathetic undergrowth.
Brambles tangle the foreground with their cruel thorns waiting for
contact. And then they cling to you like death. The arranged has no
place here at all, only the random patterns of wild Nature. And bushes.

THE ANCIENT OAK

Here are Arts two old Men, one bending forward and one bent backward. Our eyes glazed and shuddering in the reality of the moment. We
feel overtaken by the Age around us – this timeless hill and ancient oak.
What can we do but sit and stare. Our tired legs shake without rest. Our
brows are contorted with imagination and rambling ideas. We are not
happy as we used to be for we have seen.

CAN IT BE TRUE

Can it be true – we fear to trust this jolly picture. Just two Men chatting
amiably along. A cigarette, a joke, each remark made by chance. We
surrender ourselves to the morning and give no thought to the evening
ahead. We drink of the plainness and honesty and fresh air in which we
are caught up. Here in the middle of these fields. Only stuff around in
the form of images typical of a rural.

ON THE ROAD

We are standing like two statues. An old-fashioned light surrounds and
envelops us. See us here through the mist of our Art Work. Our heads
stand out like lights. The foreground is unreal, the background is
unreal. The thin white knife-line separates the picture in half and one
side shows us on the road and the other side shows the road without us.
This is our dream, this is our snap-shot. It's it.

THE RED BARN

Here near the old red barn we found our way along the tattered path.
We rest on the gate and look into the valley of flowers and blossom.
What perfect form, what splendid perfume. We could stay awhile and
feast our senses on the whole valley. See that we don't speak, only
together look. A feeling of great beauty sweeps over us in heady waves
as we give ourselves up to Everything. Take us away.

CONVERSATION PIECE
A conversation piece is a dull place. We talk of every-day matters here
on this quiet by-way. No traffic to busy us. It is a funny time of day
neither evening nor night – and we are undecided. Should we push on a
little or slowly stroll back to our white cottage – soon the sun will decide
for us and so we linger here so that the decision shall not be ours.
Darkness is soon over our heads.

ALONG, ALONG
The babies are marching along, along. Concentrating on this they flash
past trees, hedges, ditches, streams, gates and all. Stick flying, hair
waving, shoes treading, heavy of breath, glasses shaking. The birds go
unheard. Beauty unseen. And so, the two Philistines crash along their
way. Woe to anyone who comes in their way. But don't worry, soon this
small amount of energy will be spent and another.

STANDING
Here we stand and here we rest because this place is really best. The
great security of the open spaces gives us strength to pen our piece
again. Just us and a bit of old fence standing in much the same way. The
fence has stood here for probably thirty years but we will soon be off
leaving the fence to decay its way into the nature. You see, once more,
we did it again. And when our time does come it is o.k.

REALITIES
In true Bombergian style we do our Gainsborough. Shattered forms
and realities make up our shapes for painting. Dynamism is here to
work, doing its energetic mischief. All is contrast, all is perverse for
you. Only a Gold-Flake relaxes through the storm. See through to the
colours of the earth, the wind and the sky. The fallen trunk is a
monolith, a monument to Man's-forests. It really is a bit sad in some
way but please don't ever mind.

ABSTRAKTEN
One of lifes Abstracts. Gentle and flowing it represents detail and the
force of specialising the minds-eye. A pungent vivid glance – what
happens next – a fox runs by perhaps, a bird flies out of cover. Or does a
sinister figure emerge to meet our gaze only to disappear into memory.

Be careful – do not be mislead by any seeming simpleness, be Naïve but
Alert. Count the days with serious enjoyment – they are so few. This we
know too.

ALL SHOOTS UPWARDS

This is a section from our key majestic view, where we attempt to settle
our mind on the contemplation of the Abstract World. Tremendously
vertical and full of grown and growing power. All shoots upwards in
its effortful progress. This concert everybody knows but few have it in
their mind, as is right. Here we present a possible balanced realistic
representation of the Abstract World we see. See through the feeling
of eye.

HORIZONTAL BANDS

Trees where we walk shall crowd into a shade. Two horizontal bands
dominated by a third element of vertical thrusting uprights. They are
making their careful slow natural way to the light. And we see as they
grow nearer the sky. If you walk a little through the trusting woods you
will see how dark it is beneath and how dangerously piercing are the
small shapes of light tomorrow – we just have to see.

JUST LIKE THE IVY

Just like the ivy on the old garden wall. Soft garden sun caresses the
worn nice brick surface. One heavily laden branch swings low to
partially obscure our way adding a new dimension to all. It is not at all
an unusual view and yet it has great possibilities for showing us a time-
honoured order. A simple division which depends on respect. To keep
out and to keep in. This is enough. And so we are bouncing onwards –
but up and down a bit.

ON TOP OF THINGS

Rather on top of things here. Feeling very pleased with ourselves and
the world. Our surroundings serve to flatter us. Each flower seems to
sing our song. The wind whistles Art-Compliments in our tickled ears.
Oh that this can last another minute. Essentially a portrait we call your
attention to the standing chaps, the positions, the facial expressions,
their country clothes, and well-meaning. We are standing like two
statues.

Introduction to Chapter Two

A Glimpse into the Abstract World

This chapter explores the pure area of intellectuality usually referred to as 'Abstract'.

Whilst we have had to make the form visuals and text-matter the expression remains one of blind-signals from our knowledge of the emotional.

The subject has been fed into the paper with the letter and the free-line and so the pages make available certain art readings.

Chapter 2
A Glimpse into the Abstract World

THE FIRE OF ART

Without fuel the burning fire dies. Fan the flames however feeble and heap with logs, for then we feel that necessary heat. With fire you can light your way, burn yourself, cook your food, and warm your body. Danger is only in its misuse so control and care is very important. The world was made by fire and is slowly cooling off. The universe is like ice so look after this small fire. As a team. The whiteness, work together with it.

CRYSTALLINE PRAISE

Crystalline Praise the Lord to let it be again. Allow things to be renewed, new crystals are transformed by pressure and times education and at any time some are ready with glistening readiness. Like a passing procession, every day another one glistens its light. They seem to be very hard but a sharp crack on the head means instant shattering into tiny pieces of light. Keep a good eye for crystals. Words link together, bridge, collaborate, team, nice.

ARTS HERALD

Arts Herald comes announcing the normality of tomorrow. Opening new interest of fresh exposures and declarations. Receptiveness is vital to stay alive for the normality of tomorrow when we can all live and let live again with no frustration of criticism. This at this historical point weighs heavy on the free thought available in unlimited lines. These lines though invisible possess hard tolerance, tonic, and vitamin characteristics.

ARTS VEIL

Arts Veil, we wait till you are drawn aside. All mysteries we are curious to explore and absorb. We await the day when arts stuff becomes touchable. Art is still a stupid baby, learning a teenager, science an old man and man still unborn. Like Brancusi's *Bird in Flight*, the veil divides, two times. The line is difficult to draw and the veil is difficult to draw. But we never mind, the circumstances are all. Art's veil we wait till you are drawn aside.

THE SEARCHER

Day in, day out, the search goes on and no find will stop it. Wheel, motor car, aeroplane, space-travel and Art serve as ghastly landmarks in and on the progression of a map. It took us twenty-six years to find some clear guidance from the creative marks in art. May we propose the following list of applicants, Leonardo da Vinci, Rembrandt, Vincent Van Gogh, Pablo Picasso. And the unknown painter of the picture of two elephants in it.

THE BEST YEARS

The Best Years of the life, full with grapes hanging heavily. It is a long, long time from June to September. Full of obscure, subtle, impossible to catch, slow-changing factors. It is very much a day to day occupation needing all one's wits and sensibilities. It is dangerous to ignore the slightest sign. In the night the storm could break over the carefully prepared ground. Pick the right times. Should it be the Autumn it starts to fall.

ON AND ON

On and On, expect no sleep, only melancholy rest. Only live with doing things like every bus, train, house and worker. It is most important that something has been done for only nothing has no existence of reason. Every movement of muscle is satisfying in the physique and intellect.

That all is lost is not a fact so accept the gift of movement on this our planet. Because if not for you then it will be for a fellow creature. On and on.

BEAUTYS FRAMEWORK

Beautys [*sic*] framework stands as simple as a frame around a picture. Beauty is in the eye of the beholder. The eye being the making of a frame for ease of understanding. What is framed today is maybe tomorrow out of view. Many things have yet to be framed up by discerning vision and thinking about it. Selection is here out of place as breadth of emotion is more useful. Frame in the past, present and future memories. Future, present, past.

ARTS WONDER

Arts wonder is a spirit which can go into any thing or person or branch of life. The world was once dusted with a fine magic powder of immense artistic specialness. They are so fine that they are constantly being blown from one place to another. They can only be arrested by an absence of air which over a certain length of time begins to suffocate them to death. So beware – delicacy is the keynote – it seems that the possibilities are few.

SIMPLICITY FOR MEANING

Simplicity for meaning means only to be simple. The best things in life are free, indescribable, painful, delicious, rare and expensive. To deal with all these points which we here call 'Simplicity' we require a certain sweet fresh naivety. It is really all a question of balance between man and matter-understanding. Simplicity is a work of sophistication. A study in Simplicity becomes more and more to the point of reasoning. To deal with all.

OVERFLOWING CUP

Of sweet juices drink before the cup is dry. Opportunity knocks not for ever, so take that which comes your way with open arms. Put caution to the wind. Throw yourself into the lake and learn swimming. Art is strong wine for young heads, so be merry and buoyant and in the swim. Be respectful to the moonlights spell as soon the dawn will come. Collect these golden pieces in their journey downwards like rain. Learn swimming.

VIEW
View all but learn to expect nothing. Surrounded by emotional
substance we endeavour to draw into ourselves all emotional forces
and ambitions. Evidence in glass, paper, walls, sticks, birds, foodstuffs,
Deco-lamps, the written word, carpets, skirts, cocks and socks. To
register an accuracy of significance in the smile or the grimace, the
rising and the falling. To be moralistically involved is not a bad thing.
Nevertheless we return always.

THINGS REAL
Mountains, Rivers and Streams are real because they are strong. The
strength of solid building over a long period of time. Receiving at all
stages admiration and encouragement adding mass, quality and
niceness to its casual structure. Time passes and credibility increases
steadily. The scribbles at the left are keeping a surveillance, as the
general movement rushes on heedless. Electricity shoots around the
drawing diagonally interrupting elements.

SCRATCHING UPWARDS
Scratching Upwards is Looking to the West. Many contained bodies of
heavily lined areas are directed in one direction. An overall confusion
of differently pencilled imagery gives realism and depth of study.
Lightness of touch, heaviness of handling. Reminiscent of Indian tents.
A fast travelling surface with some itch illustrates an essentially
sensible abstraction. To attempt a word comment on this abstract area
we whisper these.

OBJECT
Objects are always Touched. The subject is objecthood and the agent
is minimised. The pencil plays but a small role as it makes way for its
productions. All objects ae related in that e.g. a cup of tea is touched
and then you drink it down and then it is no more the same thing. The
important identified object exists for usage as in everyday, moving as
an extension of body, and personal activity and comment. They mirror
to a large extent.

BEGINNING
In the beginning all was White and then along came the Pencil. The

Vanishing Desert. The pencils moving into the whiteness making signs, comments, descriptions, mystics, unhappiness, documentation, biography, criticism and drawings. It is an immensely respectable abstract form capable of a high degree of communication and persuasion. For some expression it is a definite scientific advancement in information exchange. It is believed.

SECOND DAY

On the second day, rain fell and everything would be grasped. We make every preparation for the cascading downpour. We make the lines, the spots, reason, the lightness, a spiral, some near shading, some patterns, some style, some formation, a shadow or two and a certain completeness. And then it awaits the rain for growth, to give it meaning and substance. William Blake comes to mind with his greatness, and Christian involvement.

CONTINUOUS FORM

The figure moist and waiting with continuous form. Here the pencil gives out an abstraction of a natural form. A curtain back-drop of multi-directional lining serves to throw to the surface the white purity and lack of substance of the central figuration. This is the standard art-work of the emotional human-being. The crucifixion, the weeping woman, the madman, the potato eaters, the Madonna, Guernica, the electric chair, the human.

UP, UP AND AWAY

Up Up and Away, the drive, the bird rising. Giddy with spinning on its way to eternity. The pencilled object is hurtling over the drawn surface. Its path sketched out and burnt in and fixed in the action. To the left books and buildings and objects are pushed aside. The upper drawn section draws the object like a magnet up up and away. Nothing is said, no comment heard for this special activity of motion. We cannot do without presence.

ARTS EMBERS

Arts Embers when not blazing if only a little light, it cannot go out, it goes on. This is nothing for fear. It is a drawn reassurance that all will stay alive as long as it is. It is an emotional generalisation on the subject of arts existence. It is very beautiful because nothing is to be expected and yet all is possible. Moreover, nothing incorrect can be done for the rules are for the maker and he's not telling you anything. Here is the abstract behind it.

Introduction to Chapter Three

The Reality in Our Living

This piece is very simply an ideal idea. It makes available every known feeling, for all human-life is there.

We regard it as totally important in that these words are with us always.

It should be viewed in the light of its honesty and its humour, as frank reality.

Chapter 3
The Reality in Our Living

THE RITZ

The Ritz we Never Sigh for, the Savoy they can keep, there's only one Place that we Know, and that is where we Sleep, Underneath the Arches, we Dream our Dreams away, Underneath the Arches, on Cobblestones we lay, every Night you'll find us, Tired out and Worn, Happy when the Daylight comes Creeping, Heralding the Dawn, Sleeping when its Raining, and Walking when its Fine, We hear Trains Rattling by Above, Pavement is our Pillow, No Matter where we Stray, Underneath the Arches, we Dream our Dreams Away. Our dreams away.

[The text above is repeated on subsequent verso pages facing illustrations with the following captions.]

THE SAVOY
OUR PLACE
SLEEPING PLACE
THE ARCH
DREAMING
ARCHES BY NIGHT
COBBLESTONES
US
THE TIRED

DAY BREAK
DAWN
RAINING
WAKING
TRAINS PASSING
PAVEMENT
STRAYING
OUR ARCHES
AWAY

We do hope that you have found this book both enjoyable and relevant.

THE END

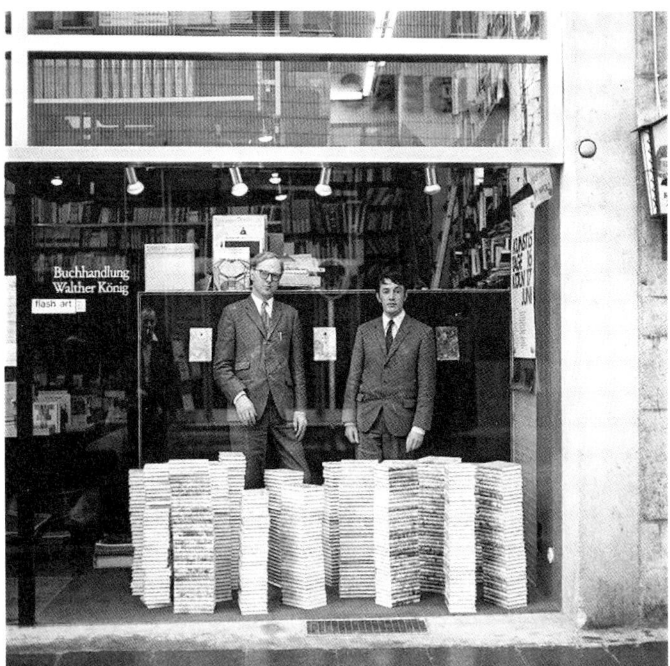

At Buchhandlung Walther König, Cologne, for the launch of
Side by Side, 1972 (*Photo: Hannes Jähn*)

Gilbert & George: Interview with Gordon Burn 1974

Previously unpublished.

George: May I take your coat? A drink perhaps. What will it be?
A sherry? Gin and tonic?

Do you have many callers?

George: Not a lot, no.

Gilbert: It's very difficult to reach us because we, really, are never here.

George: We're not here very often. Most mornings, when we're in
London.

Gilbert: We're here then.

*Do you feel in a comfortable position now as regards the art
establishment?*

George: The art world anyway is composed entirely of views, of
different people that are changing all the time.

Gilbert: Every day.

George: They pass them on. That is the art world. Just a changing
collection of anecdotes. Stories. Gossip. Reports. Very abstract.

Gilbert: The only way we do things is if they make us do them.
Otherwise we would never do a show. Never.

George: We never make work unless it's for a show. We never have.

Are those your original suits that you started off with?

George: Oh no, we're always changing tailors. We're never satisfied.

Gilbert: The last one was Burtons… We like them because they are just
some boring suits. Ordinary, boring suits.

Where are the ties from? Are they anything special?

George: Well, yes. His are pink elephants and these are some chaps.
You can buy them like this. You can buy ties that have almost anything
on. Tennis rackets… We like clothes so that we can just fling them on
every day rather than to have to think a lot about it. Nice to be ancient
enough to have to wear a siren suit.

*How did you start doing the drinking pieces? Because you started
drinking?*

George: Exactly, yes. Because we didn't use to drink at all, you know.
We never went to pubs or anything.

Gilbert: And we still don't like it. It's completely artistic, the whole
thing.

George: We don't even like to drink that much.
Gilbert: We don't like it.

Why do you do it?
George: We don't even know that really.
Gilbert: Nerves. Meeting people and so on. Especially in the art world. It is so boring meeting all these people to us. So if you get completely smashed you really are free.
George: At the same time it brings you very close. You can literally do anything to anyone if you're completely drunk. You don't mind who you grab or anything. On the other hand it creates an amazing distance. I mean, if you feel quite secure in your drunkenness you don't feel anyone can *really* come close.
Gilbert: We dislike always the normality of meeting people. They talk the most boring subjects. Awful. Especially if you go to some funny opening.
George: Completely neurotically, I'm frightened of some very ordinary sentences that you can hear. I don't know, some things completely terrify me. It's a crazy way – that one should never say any normal thing at all. That it should just always be the way it is when one is drunk, in fact. One should *just glide along.*

How did you happen on drink?
George: I think drink attracts us anyway, because it has some glamour to it, as it were.

How about the unpleasantness of recovering the next day? Has it ever been so unpleasant that you've felt you never want to do it again?
George: For a long time we never got hangovers, yes? To start with.
Gilbert: Everybody will do it again. But I hate it. Every time when you are out and you meet some people, it is the only way. You don't even think what you are doing, I always feel. You are just carried away.

Gin and tonic is your favourite?
George: But it's not very often that you can taste what it is you're drinking anyway. It's just a part of the evening, like eating or smoking. Because the first drink just knocks us out completely.
Gilbert: Completely. The first one. I think nerves make a person completely drunk.
George: Even sometimes we get *completely* blown out, just with gin and tonic.

Gilbert: When you are drunk like that nobody knows what to do.
You never become violent?
George: Not aggressive, no.
Gilbert: *Insistent.*
George: The embarrassment of the insistence one gets with drinking.
One sometimes gets an idea when drinking and really insists on that.
Some funny idea, you know. Someone has to do something, or make the
table turn round, and in some drunken way it seems exactly what you
want. In sober times, it's just very embarrassing that one insisted on
this very simple thing that one really wanted done.
The work came after the drinking?
George: A lot of the time we were drinking we weren't using it in our
work. We were still using images of nature and the more homely life,
and then we felt brave enough to introduce it into our work. For a long
time we wondered how we could do it.
Gilbert: Nearly all the artists, they are nearly all drunks. The whole art
world, they all get drunk. It's amazing.
George: We think it's very honest of us to realise that it can be a
subject... You get really smashed and then next day you paint a
beautiful picture, stripes or something. And then you get drunk again,
and it's absolutely nothing to do with your way of life. So we thought
we'd like to use that as a subject. As an aesthetic. We'd have to anyway
because we don't have any artistic interests, as such. We're not interested in painting or in any technical aspect of art at all.
You spend all your time together?
George: Absolutely. Most of our time is just talking about friends or
other people, and so on.
Gilbert: Imitating friends.
George: We do it all the time. Really. Always just give the
impersonation of friends to each other. It's super. I don't think there's
a person we know who we don't have an impersonation for.
Gilbert: Making it up. New stories all day. We go somewhere and we
make up what *she* would say if she saw this place. It's very funny.
George: We don't have proper business relationships with anyone.
Gilbert: Personal, completely personal.
George: We don't even like ordinary business arrangements at all.
We ask them completely in detail what they do with their wives or
something.

What was you first conversation with each other?
George: It was when we were at college. You're better at remembering,
Gilbert.
Gilbert: I remember only he used to call me Gilbert-the-Filbert. That is
the first thing. I didn't understand one single word.
George: You soon picked it up though. Didn't you, Gilb?
George: We like to be very life-like in a way. Not to be too artistic.
It would be very easy for the artist to exist with very, very discreet
exhibitions that nobody ever heard anything about, and it would just
involve five or six people dotted around the world and three or four
collectors, and it would be completely enough to be successful. That
doesn't interest us too much, really. It seems very dry to us.
Gilbert: It becomes very academic. Just a big family, ten people.
That's all. Even we are too much involved with that.
Do you go to other people's openings?
George: When we go to an opening, a party or something, we don't like
to move around. In fact, we can't even do that. We always get absolutely
paralysed with nerves. We always stay in the same place. Usually the
four or five friends that we know will come over. And it usually
develops into some terrorist behaviour. I don't know why people don't
mind more, anyway. We would be very annoyed. We would have hated
somebody coming, crashing around. We're not invited to a lot of things
because people expect a disaster to happen.

[George excuses himself and returns with a drinking glass. It is clean and clear but
broken so that the ragged points and splinters catch the light, like a piece of meticulously
rinsed debris from a pub brawl. He turns it this way and that, holding it aloft in one hand.]

George: Terrific, yes? Don't you think that's shocking, absolutely?
Gilbert: Fighting is rather nice. Do you remember when they broke
my nose?
George: They were the skinhead types.
Gilbert: Yes, they kicked us in once.
George: It was fun. It was the early days. This was in Finsbury Park,
which is very tough. Such a marvellous style of dress they have, the
skinheads. Marvellous. Lovely, really. We were their greatest
supporters, you know. It's rather unfair they attacked us. Everybody's
thinking about this great wave of violence and there are we walking
around the streets admiring this amazing style. Splendid.
Gilbert: You never see it any more. Not in the East End.

George: It's a style sported rather heavily by male prostitutes. I think
that's the last stronghold of skinheads in London. I don't know why.
Gentlemen Prefer Skinheads, or something.
Gilbert: It was the time of the queer-bashing when they kicked us in.
George: Absolutely. It was very funny. Because there was a time when
you couldn't walk across to Liverpool Street from here without all the
groups, or two or three young men, they would always shout or make
some fresh remark. Amazing. We never used to understand it. And they
always used to make some very homosexual jokes or some-thing, yes?
And now they wouldn't make it in a hundred years. They're all dressed
up like swans or something. We never understand why they were so
funny then. It's an amazing thing.
Gilbert: Now, my God, every single person in the East End is dressed
up much more queeny than we ever were.
George: Go into any corner pub in the backstreets of Bethnal Green and
they're just so dyed up and... silver underwear. So fancy, hmm?
Gilbert: And that was amazing. We used to go into a pub very near here
where all the lorry drivers used to be, and we made them completely
crazy. We went in there, started to dance together, and they couldn't
dance, you see.
George: They *wanted* to. We were dancing like some other couples,
boys and girls, were dancing and everyone was sitting very relaxed.
And the lorry drivers would be standing there with their pints doing
this, and they'd come a bit nearer, and we'd say something, and they'd
nearly start to dance, then they'd go back for a pint, yes? And they
would have liked very much just to have danced. Not with us
necessarily, but with anyone, or alone or something. And they could
never actually make that step, just to dance. Absolute frustration. And
so they come out and see us going along the road, so they follow on. We
came with some friends back, and they must have seen the lights go
on... They probably would have liked to be invited in for drinks, and
maybe we should have done, I don't know. Anyway, they just started
throwing all these milk bottles through the window. It was shocking,
really. Such a desperate thing, hmm? All this glass in the air. Can you
imagine? It was quite exciting in a way.
Gilbert: Nutting. Do you know that technique of nutting? They put their
hands over your shoulders and just do that... We had rather a good fight
back sometimes.

George: We went to a club, had a marvellous time, came out with some chaps and suddenly for no reason a fight started. I ended up on the street covered in all this blood I remember.

You like dancing?

George: Very much. Very much. We're always dancing.

Gilbert: It's better than looking miserable *all* the time, like me.

What about travel?

George: Thailand. It's our second home, really. It's beautiful. Shocking attitudes towards everything they have. You can't even describe modern art. 'Modern art', you say. 'Picasso.' And they've got no idea at all. I think there's not one person in the whole of Bangkok who understands anything like that. Really. Absolutely not.

Gilbert: They have this beautiful Thai boxing.

George: Bruce Lee we love. Shocking good. Very, very pleasant... I say, is there going to be a storm, d'you think? It's rather marvellous. Splendid light.

Gilbert: It's incredibly dark.

George: What's going to happen next? [Laughter.] It's amazing. It's just gone midday. It could even snow. Even the warmth has gone out of the light there. Perhaps it's the end of the world. One's always waiting for it... Beautiful light. [A sign on one of the sweatshops on the opposite side of Fournier Street begins to move with the wind.] Rather eerie I always think to see a sign swinging. Lightly creaking. Isn't the rain beautiful! All diagonal. Nice. But the sign always reminds me of things like [R.L. Stevenson's] *Kidnapped*. The sign creaking, *then* someone comes along. It always begins with something very abstract like that. Even *Treasure Island* has a swinging Inn sign I think.

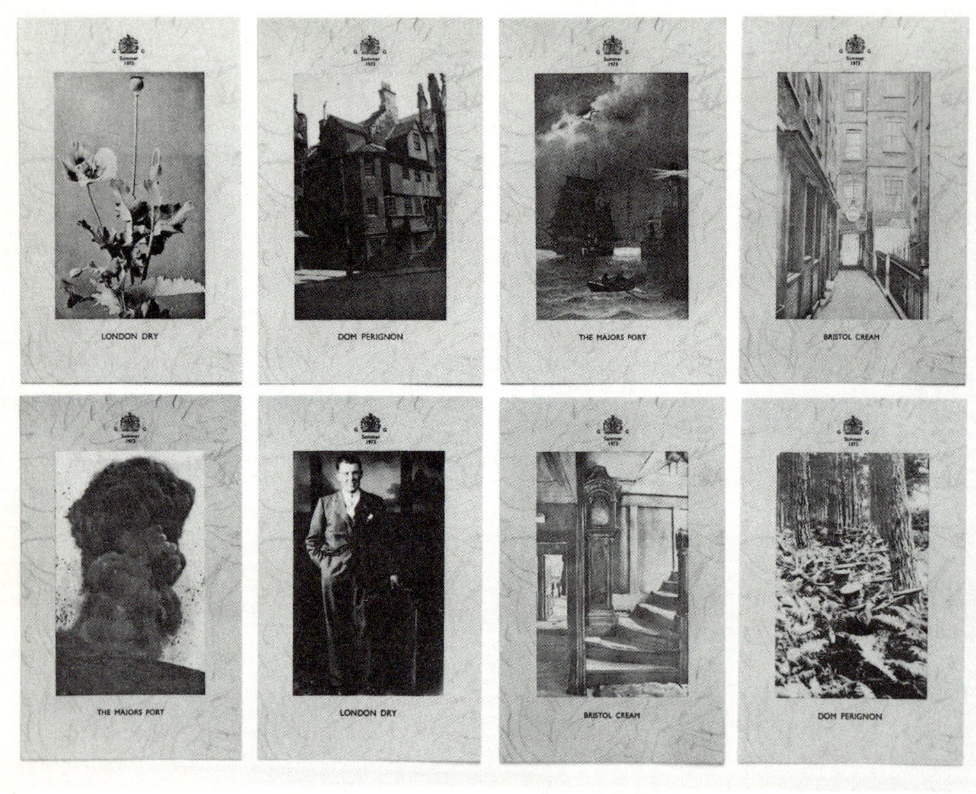

The Pink Elephants, 1973, an eight-part Postal Sculpture where each recipient
received one Pink Elephant each week for eight weeks

The Pink Elephants

LONDON DRY
Felt a trifle queer last night
couldn't eat a thing
couldn't drink a thing.
Lay very still for a few minutes.
Drank a lot and later quite
made up for it all.

Who said Gin?

DOM PERIGNON
Made a fair number
of decisions in the bar last
night. Carried them all out
and went home happy and
diagonal.

Stagger stagger.........

THE MAJORS PORT
Had two dizzy spells
at lunch today.
Asked the two identical waiters
to bring us a couple of doubles
for the second time.
Felt twice as good.

Is that a treble?

BRISTOL CREAM
Nice beano last night–
Awoke this morning
feeling absolutely marvellous
Must be some road
repairs going on nearby as
there is this terrible sound
of drilling.

VVVvvvvvvvvvv

THE MAJORS PORT
After a certain number of
glasses of a certain
drink, certain people prefer
to ride in the front
of the cab.

You o.k. Sir?

LONDON DRY
We dropped by at quite a
number of places of refreshment
last evening and everyone
seemed very friendly and
flighty on the whole.

Whoops!

BRISTOL CREAM
Went up to the bar and ordered
these drinks, lost those
somewhere ordered a couple more,
found that we had forgotten
the others so we had another
round, found some and tended
to lose track a shade.

Wonderful Stuff!

DOM PERIGNON
There's not an awful
lot to be said for the
case of getting home
in time sometimes.

Early Days.

Announcement card, 1972

78   Hand-marbled cover of *Dark Shadow*, 1974

To the reader

of

Dark Shadow

from

the sculptors

This sculpture is a result of our past three years of earnest daily thoughts, shadows, deeds, cares and pleasures.

We have turned them into ink and arranged them as words and pictures to form this living sculpture book.

We hope that you have a nice time going through it.

Yours sincerely

...................................and...................................

the sculptors

Dark Shadow

Extracts from the book first published in 1976 by Nigel Greenwood, London, in a signed and numbered edition of 2000 clothbound copies in which each of the following texts occupies a full lefthand page and faces a full-page black-and-white illustration.

Chapter 1
Gordons Gin

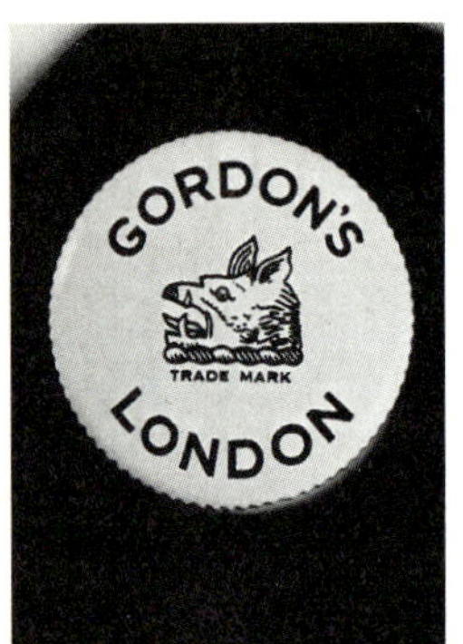

1 TEETH AND EYES
The boars head, hallmark of our illustrious down fall and brand new imaginations. Smart and sombre with edges of our clearness. The trade mark rather than the marks of trade, his ears, his nose, nothing between the teeth and eyes left with a steady expression. Easy to turn but hard to turn to the right to make tight. Black for black, white for white but black for bottle-green. Wavy edges, flat top and easy to screw either way, if you know more or less what we mean.

2 GILBERT'S COMFORT
3 GEORGE'S EASE
4 WONDERFUL SHOULDERS
5 INFLUENTIAL DRINK
6 MAKE US CLEAN

7 SLIDE IT AROUND
There was this old fellow who had such good eye-sight that he never needed glasses. He always drank it straight from the bottle. Tools of the floater leaving behind a depression flood of cheerfulness. Crystal clean brains and smelly socks, the perfect combination for the modern gentleman. Glasses polished like a modern gentleman's brain. Just hold one in the hand, feel the weight, admire the surface, look at the bubbles, slide it around and then when you have finished put it down and have it drink.

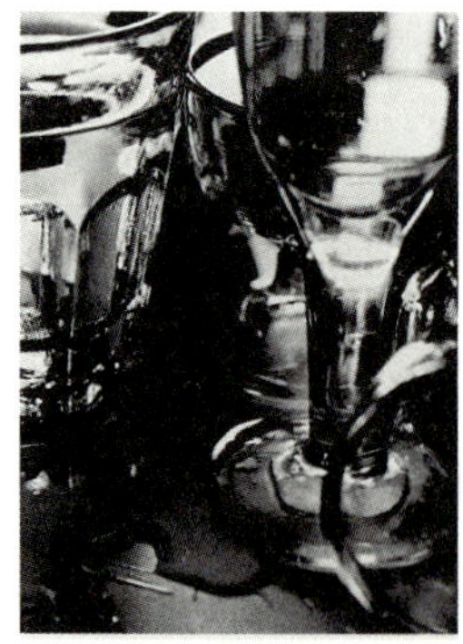

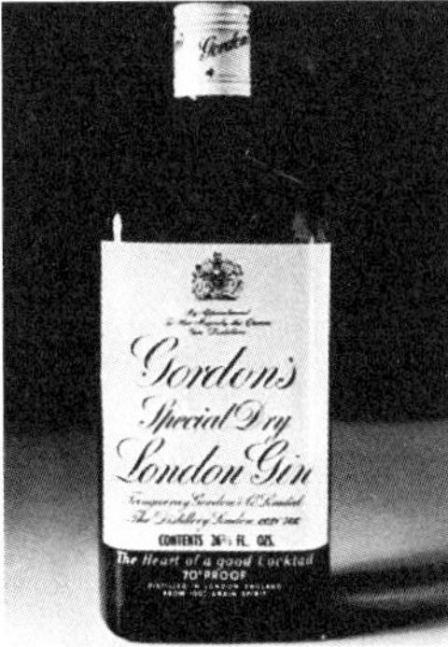

16 GENERAL GORDON
The tool is our symbol, the picture is our tool and
Gordon is our general. The seventy per cent proof
after a while twists and knocks itself into a state of
happiness as we look on with gay alarm. What is the
1947 atmosphere of last Wednesday. Get the general
on the blower. Gordon is in the kitchen carting in
another case. Put me down he cries. He dries his
tears, puts on his cap and looks down at his soiled
front, his dirty boots stuck deep into the floor.

Chapter 2
Dark Shadow

17 PANELLED LIFE
Glued forever with despondency to this vista of variations of glooms. Nothing is too dark, dreary, desolate
or miserable for us. Our black black years stretch out
with pleasantness of morbid memory. The falling of
lines our panelled life it is as though we were without
a sound, gravity or solid grave. Just flying bat-like into
the atmosphere with unlimited appetite. The harsh
silver light from other places and corners of our
senses makes us blink blindly with horrid reaisation
of our imagination.

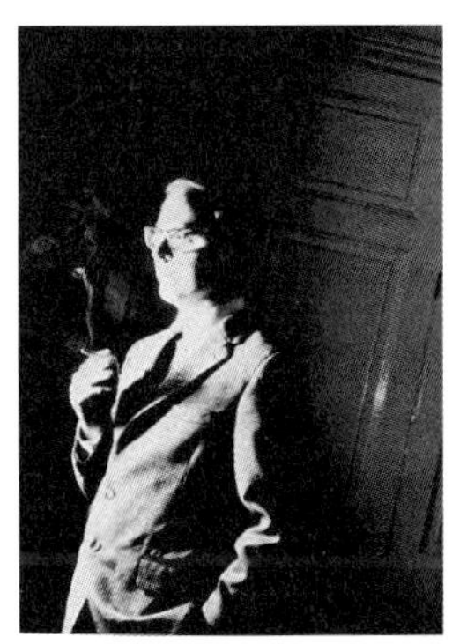

18 HOMELY SADNESS

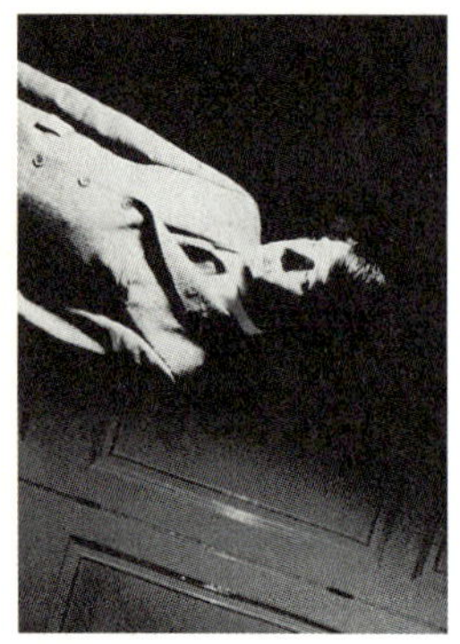

19 HORROR GLANCE

Falling in with figure carrying its own value of light in this depressing atmosphere. Eyes stretched out towards the feet completing the figure in a glance of horror. Head promising to crash with the heaviness melting into the whole awareness. The eyes have in mind the blackness of the top righthand corner. The mouth laid out as slice across the chin with sculpture purpose. Vital life-giving texture exists here as in all suits, buttons, pockets. As useful as an ashtray with much less sensuousness.

20 LOVELY LINING
21 TRAVELLING PROGRESS

22 PERFECT ESCAPE

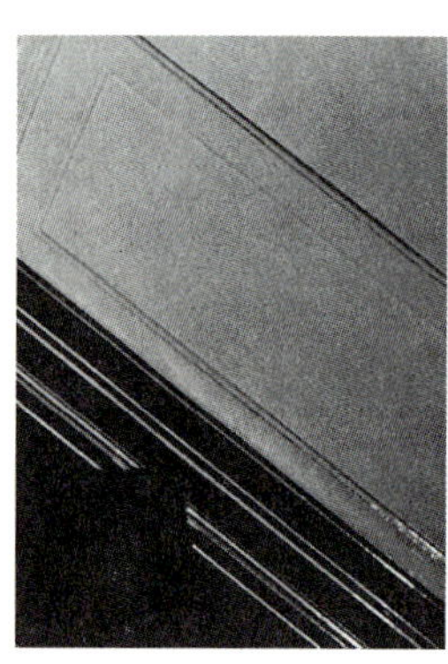

From across the room the mummy tries to speak. Dustily he just manages to say to us the word 'shame'. All is then quiet, vast and grey and lost and lonely. This is the secret panel we always lived into our living room. It leads just around the corner and brings us back on the other side panelling. What a perfect crystal escape route. Shining glossy hard lilac paint gives us this shuddering fear and love with our history room of experience, to say to us the word shame, shame.

23 HUMAN RAPE

24 SHADOWED VALLEY

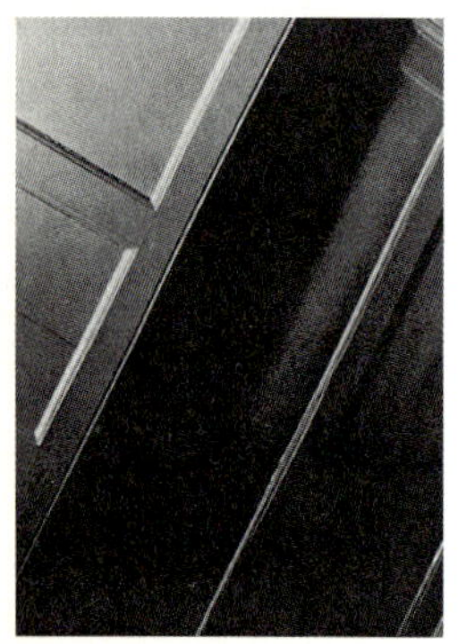

Here are the standard three possibilities of placement of self or glance or feeling. Be careful of number one with its bland country smile and most misleading appearance. Beware the number three with its wonderfully clever kindly welcome. Instead join us at number two. Here is the shadowed valley of endless pleasure tunnel of the corner of despair we can join together in a celebration of the life qualities sunk in that sickly comfort of dark cheerfulness necessary for jolly endurance in a day of three whole possibilities.

25 STRAIGHT FACE

26 MEAN NERVES
Hard mean nerves calling out to us to strain along with
them. We generously supply the necessary nerve-
power, and there is a little meeting. The skin is taken
off, the flesh torn away and we are left as happy
skeletons to dance the dance of nerves along the wires
of the rooms lit consciousness. From one side to
another our hungry angry gazes travel. Rectangular
hinges and lines. We hear this wondrous chant and we
become as hard as can be. Creaking hinges combine
with hardness.

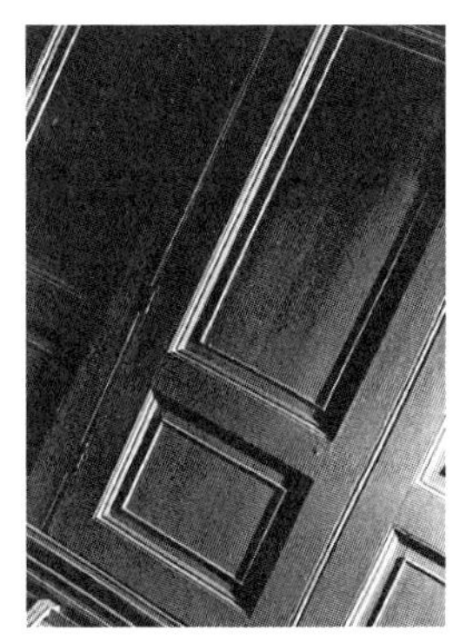

27 FEARED LIGHT
28 PLAYING HAVOC
29 CERTAIN INTERESTS
30 BLUSHING MEMORY
31 SHADOW VICTIM
32 SHADOWY INTELLECTS

Chapter 3
Broken Hearts

33 THE COMMON PANSY
We never gathered lilac in the spring before. With
its queer black leaves and most poisonous blooms it
remains a plant of very general appeal. Very useful
in all forms of flower arrangement and especially
attractive when combined with the mountain rose,
lilies of the valley and the common pansy. Very much
a city flower we love it for its unthinking calm and
persistance. No other flower embodies the modern
human sculpture qualities with such style and grace-
lessness, with such defiance and colouredness.

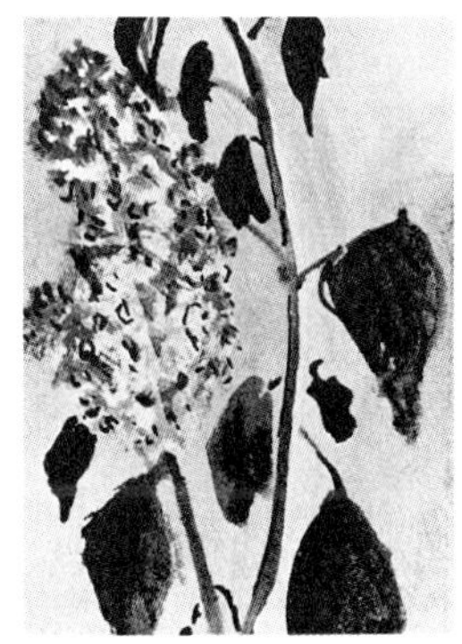

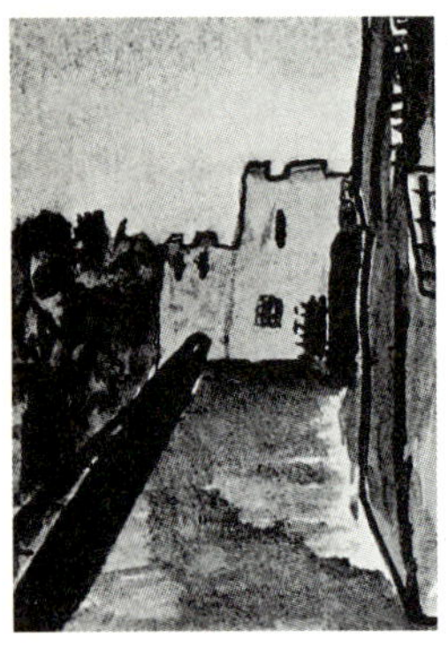

40 THE BLOODY RAMPARTS

Late evening at the Tower of London and the visitors have all left. Two shadowy figures circle the ramparts before disappearing through a little locked oaken door. Their hands pass like those of blind persons over the surface of the walls, they are reading the carved names and writings. 1468, E. L., W. R. and so on for hours. Then suddenly one figure stops and shows the other what he has found. They begin to laugh quietly and horridly. They hasten away splashing over the freshly blood-pooled floor.

43 THE SHOCKING MEANING

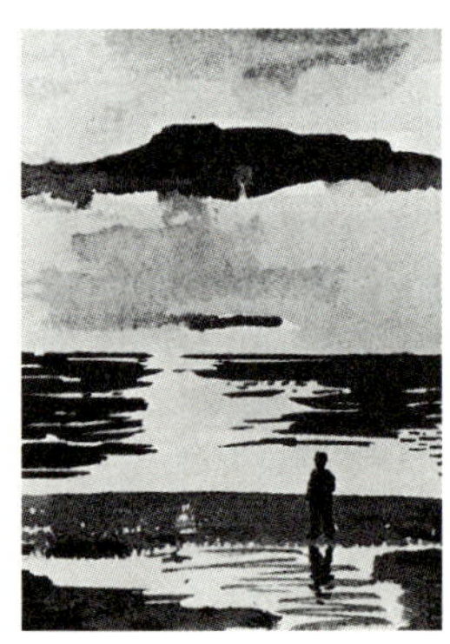

We sit secretly in the shadow of the rocks and watch the man on the beach. Our minds wander and see a second view as well. The man is the same but the sea has gone and in its place stands Westminster. Then seagulls shriek as Big Ben chimes. The waves lap against the solid buildings. The sun sets darkly and with shocking meaning behind a rippling roof. Traffic moves noiselessly across the beach. The man wearily dons a trench coat and climbs on to his pedestal.

Chapter 4
Bloody Life

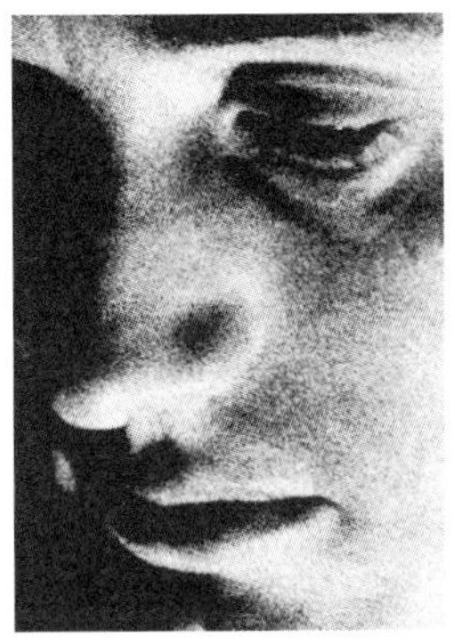

49 DIFFERENT AND ACHING
That dark glance of menace, the lid drooping with modern daily danger. The personal life-old surface of grey flesh. Diseased skin is mouldy with the fresh bloom of knowledge. A slight smile crosses the mouth and then is gone. The one-eyed look strains artistically to hold its visioned image. Colours and tones of black flood the view with rich beauty, always different and aching with contemporary comfort. The face looks tired, the mouth relaxes, the eye closes slowly, there is a slight nodding.

50 TWISTED AND AGGRESSIVE

51 SCREAMS AND ENERGY
A rare and splendid sign of life, of contact and of intelligence. Two fists scream energy at each other with equal volume, rejoicing in the busy carelessness of an artistic moment. Frozen and locked they swell with tension and with pride relaxing into the sureness of their grandeur and time honoured dignity of intent. They drink deeply of the pungent smelling shadow and cheekily catch a little flattering handsome light. They see their background looking on, a muscle twitches nervously and something of the composition changes mysteriously.

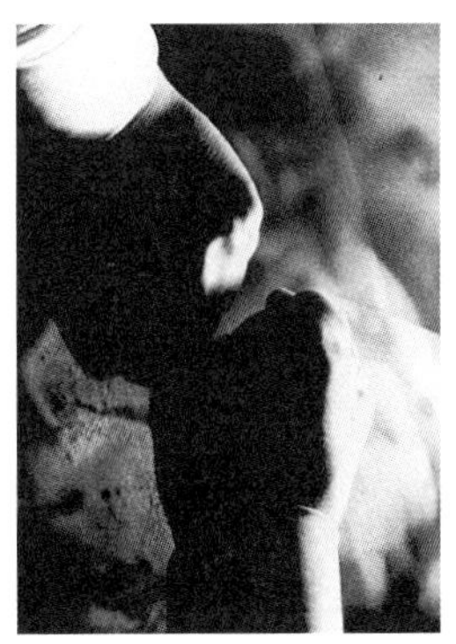

52 SMELLS AND VOICES
53 LOST AND TORMENTED

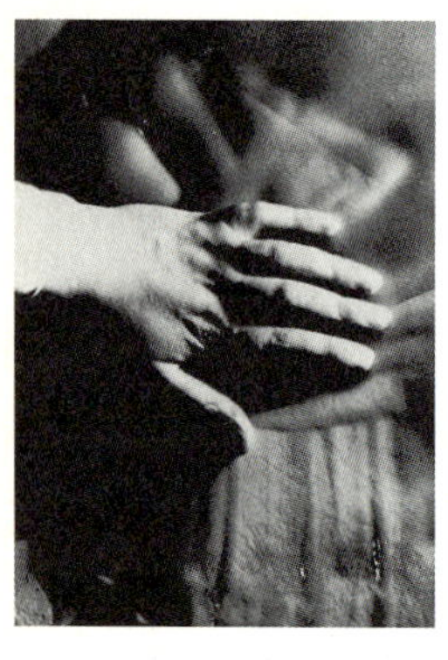

54 DREAD AND RESENTMENT

The touch of the soul and the wobbly effect. Pushing and scraping with tired leaden arms our minds sob for release and human love comfort. The hand is driven to scratch the old wounds and make again the liquid of the blood to come in front of our blood-learned blood-shot eyes. Tiredness, dread and resent [*sic*] fill the picture greyly. Human touches are swimming in the blood, lost and moist and waiting for the sculptor's hand to push and scrape some hope and steadiness into their swirling stupidity.

55 SURFACE AND SHAME
56 POISONED AND FLAVOURED
57 DRUMS AND CLOUDS
58 SQUALOR AND OPTIMISM

59 AMBITION AND CREATIVITY

Marks on the sheet march on like bloody stains to cover all with comfort and sameness of tired experience. Sickness takes over our soul and cleans our brains to crystal skulls through which we peer at all this running down of living time and waste of horrors. The drops drip down before our tear streaked faces and rest upon our dusty worn shoes. We shuffle away leaving trails of splendid marks of work done in a sense of ambitious creativity. We will congratulate ourselves.

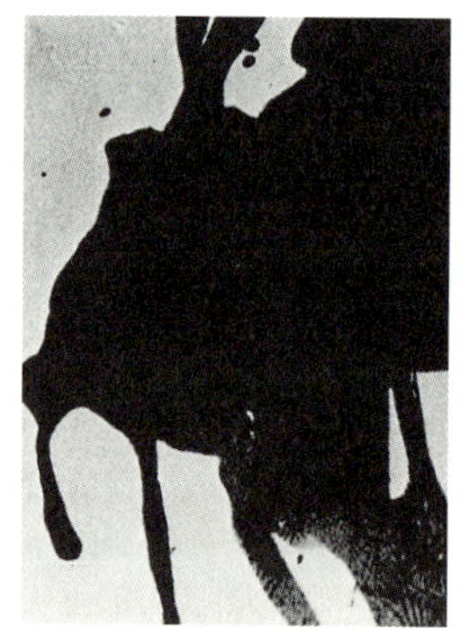

60 ELEGANT AND DIRTY
61 STENCH AND PROGRESS
62 DECORATIVE AND FLUTTERING
63 CRUNCHING AND NERVOUS
64 CORNERED AND UNKIND

Chapter 5
Balls Bar

65 OLD GOLD CAP
Balls seen here by public bar with the daylight
and the major. London fogs filter through the
noon gloom with special focus and beauty. To sip
and gulp we stand alone the bar creaking and
bending with the strain of realising its useful-
ness. The major mutters something unintelligi-
ble and we reply suitably. He is a little cross but
we don't mind for we are in good humour. Then
in comes old gold-cap falling in to fall out with
the major. We rather hope to see a certain fuss.

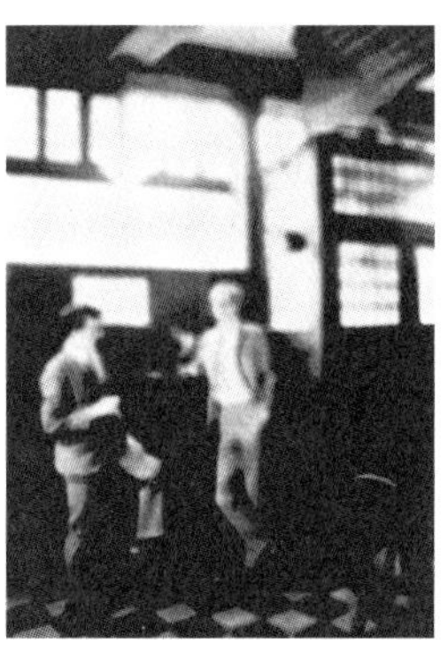

66 A PALACE BURNING
67 TALK OF DRINKS
68 THE MAJOR'S PORT
69 GRIM AMUSING CAGE
70 WE COUNT TOGETHER
71 LITTLE NICE DRINKS

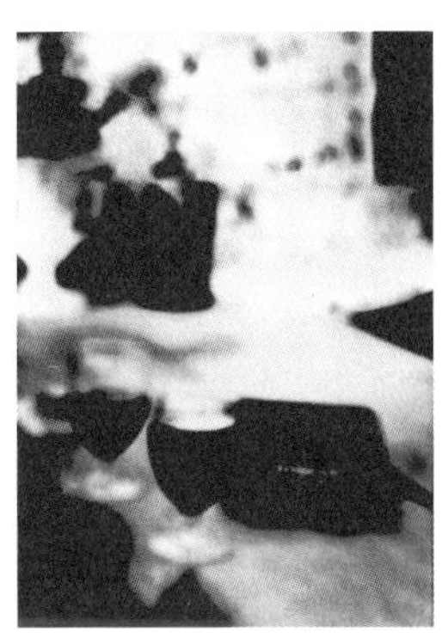

72 TWO GLASSES WAITING
Balls Bar bar surface moist and smelly where
hands reach out for gaily coloured liquids. Coins
change hands and smiles are exchanged as the kind
hands behind the bar give the choice of more or
less. The glass as the container of the goods that in
no time makes you talk of better funny grey days.
Two glasses stand darkly waiting for their friends.
They wink, they ripple heavily and flirt and then are
swallowed up. Here is the busiest surface of them
all, as the ash-tray said to the gentleman.

73 CHAINED UP IN PLEASURE
74 FONDLED POCKET FLUFF
75 BALLS SWINGING SIGN
76 HEAVY BREATHING

Chapter 6
Bad Thoughts

81 OUR LOST BEAUTY

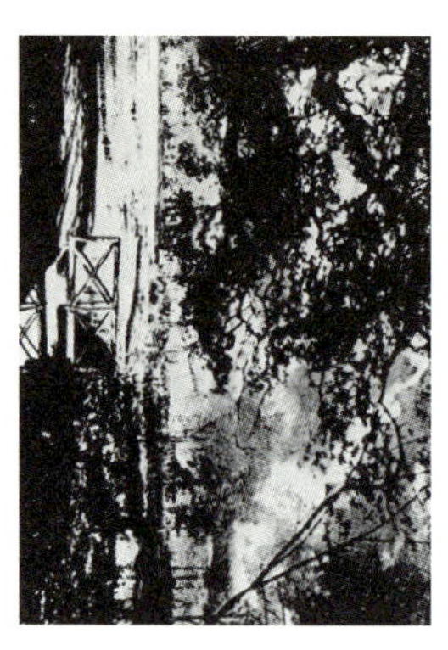

Lost in the beauty of the dark weather-filled night. Along the little path we go, across the flimsy bridge and over into the distance of the love we need. We feel and mix with the many dark patterns of the time of night. We realise the hours as they with us pass and we are the hours ourselves. We see things of our own age, things twice our age or half and we see things of the night's duration living just with us this night. Some short-lived peculiar shape or pattern lasts but the time we watch it.

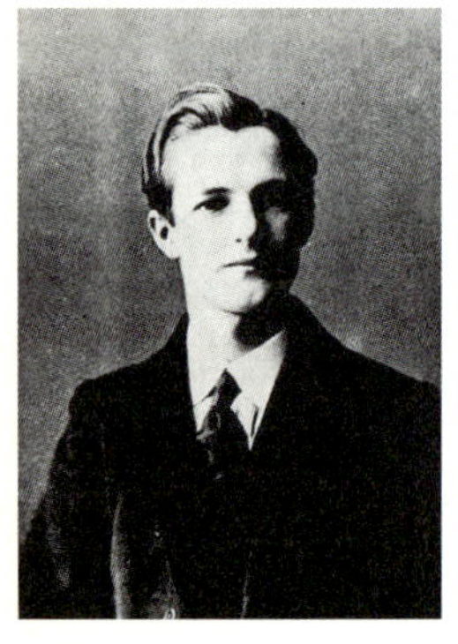

82 OUR FASHIONABLE FRIEND

The man we sometimes see is smiling nicely. His hair well-groomed, his heavy suit and neat fashionable appearance make him a friend of ours. He is quiet and still and has a shadowed portrait face of handsomeness. We see in him the feelings, subjects and materials of the living person. He reminds us with heavy heart of our need of years life sense without the normal misery of grey time people that we always dread. We would not know of something to say to anyone but this fellow now here.

89 OUR FALLING SEAGULL
90 OUR THING IN THE NIGHT

91 OUR CLEAN BRAINS
Distortions in our tortured clean brains wrestle to
have an arrangement of order and rest as here we
represent our hope for small luxury of moment with
fear of discovery. The different qualities of substance
neatly balanced with their human values layed in the
crisp order natural to the position of all things used.
Let dark damned disappointment show its sparkling
smile and we will laugh as all things fall down in
place all to be seen in our twisted dear straight and
personal style.

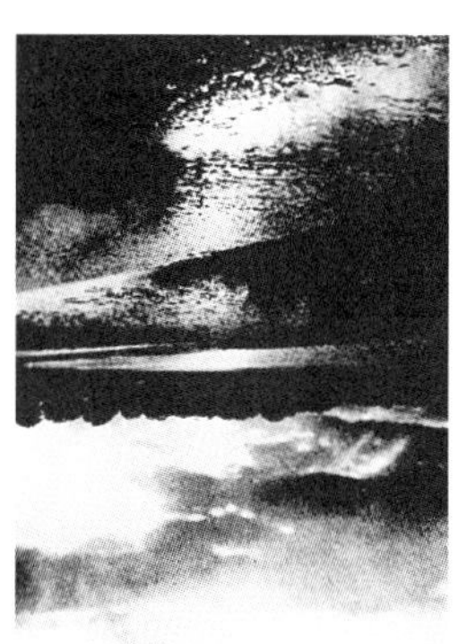

92 OUR HEADACHE ROOM
93 OUR HEROES ARCH
94 OUR GOOD FORM
95 OUR PLEASANT CHARACTER
96 OUR EVENINGS SPENT

Chapter 7
Inca Pisco

97 BLACK SMILE

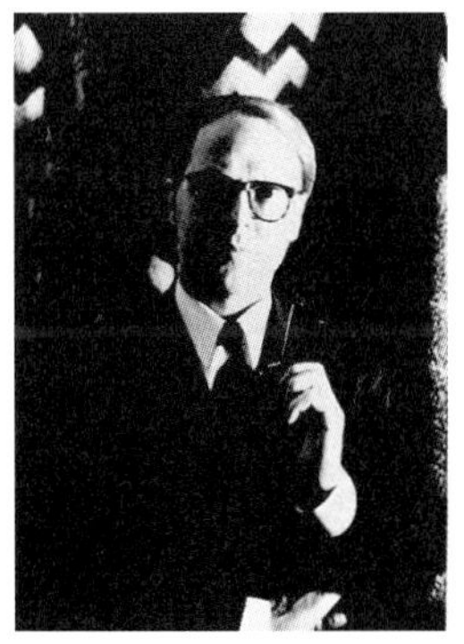

98 DARK FACE
Inca Pisco glass in hand steady and sombre with the
thrilling pleasure of the sombre thrilling effect of
this rather catchy concoction. Travelling on HMS
Alcohol to foreign lands where smokey dark smiles
and heavy strangely designed materials turn about
with wonderful black contrasted quality of happy
seeing. His gaze steadys as the scene is taken over
by the captain and a party is held, bottles grab the
glasses and drag them onto the floor to glide about
noisily and dangerously.

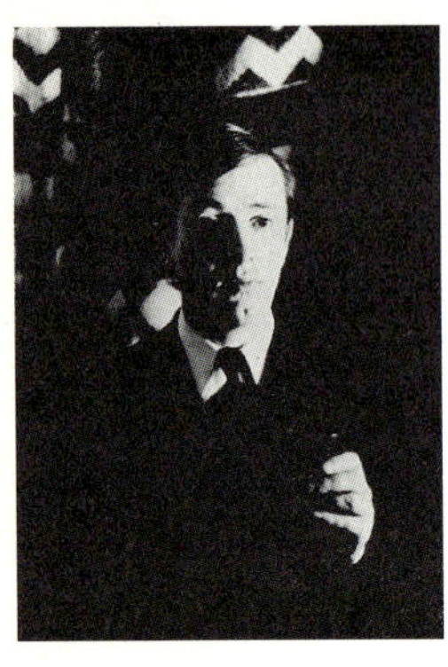

99 GREY OUTLOOK

Inca Pisco's sad outlook on the time and the world of the mystery party. The black liquid keeps the guests alive and heads filled with new music and foreign lands thoughts. The party is getting into hand with unusual behaviour, two glasses snogging in the corner, several bottles have removed their caps and several have already soiled their labels. A cork-screw from somewhere or other takes the dance-floor by surprise, twisting and gyrating a savage dance he grabs a young cork and begins.

100 GLOOMY PROFILE
101 SHADOWED GLASS
102 MURKY GREETING
103 BLACKISH FRIENDS

104 DARKLY DRINKING

Inca Pisco's drunken heavy gas pervades the glorious room sweetly. The smell is mainly of lower parts of human bodies in a state of excitement, partly of bunches of mixed wild flowers, partly of ethnographic museums and just slightly of vomit. This powerful cocktail smell is extremely distinctive. Distorted lens on face of true contentment levels on the earthly glass of daily down-to-earthness. The confrontation is one of marked design and formal human integrity. A voice speaks gently from behind the curtain.

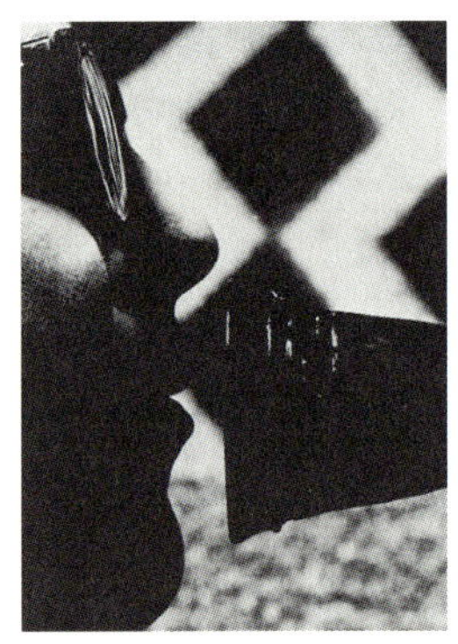

105 GLOOMED GLASS
106 SHADOW SPLENDOUR
107 BLACK FEATURES
108 DARK GATHERING
109 GREY DRINK
110 GLOOMY LIQUID
111 SHADOWED CHAT
112 MURKY COCKTAIL

Chapter 8
Human Bondage

113 DRUNKEN GLASSCAPE

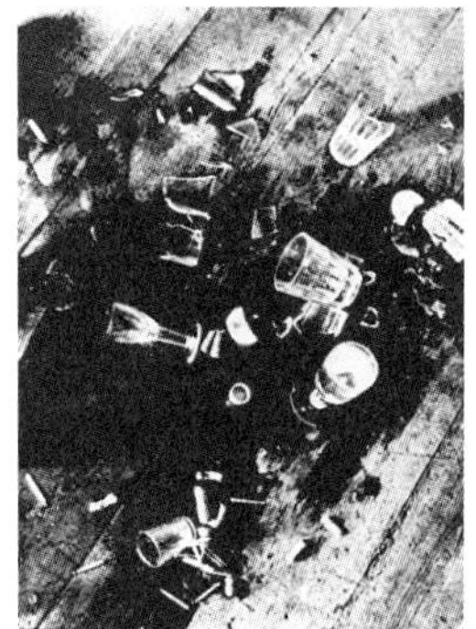

Typsying glasscape on the drenched floor with detailed objects turning and screwing their way around in endless possibilites. Black patch of glorious gloom setting for our broken jewels and thoughtful things. The pressed-down glass into the wooden boards where our forms feel on and over crunching and splintering with restrained excitement. The wet pool dead and sweet with various smells and beautiful in wild active shape. Burnt out drizzly matches fly about colliding with used slices of lemon and cigarette ends.

114 DRUNKEN FIGURES

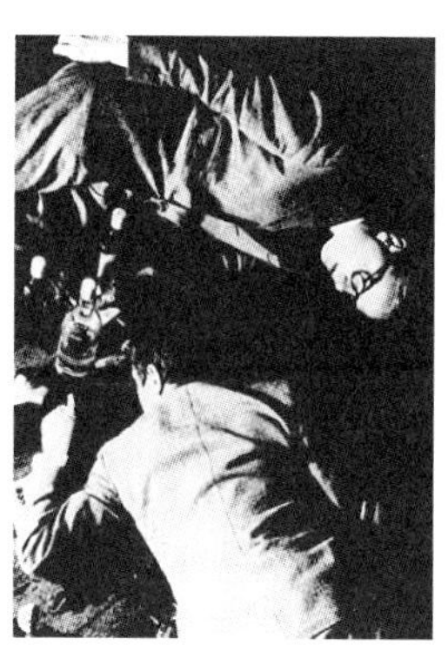

The two reclining figures roll and turn slowly as if roasting on a spit. They make suitable cooking noises and then sometimes there is a collision or a turning over of bottles. Clear pure strong alcohol laps heavily on the shore of this picture's meaning. A glass is carelessly filled, carefully emptied, carefully refilled and then carelessly emptied. The suits remould themselves with each movement into stranger more valuable sculptures. The black shadow has come over the heads and bottles and all.

115 DRUNKEN FLOOR

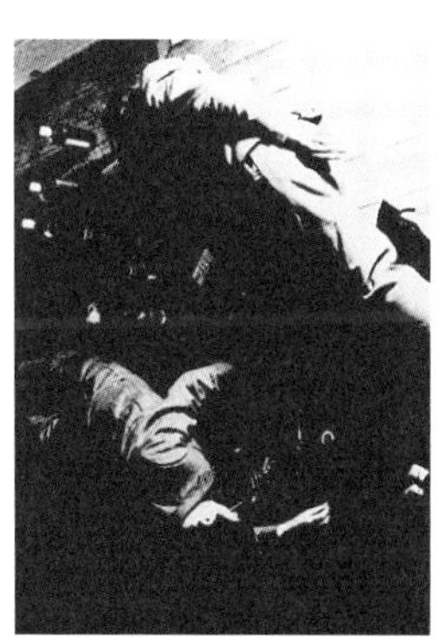

116 DRUNKEN CHAPS

Rough suited chaps glide ghostlike through the debris searching for an unbroken glass. Hands are cut and suits are torn before they rest and cast about for interest to combine with rest. The bottles still with contents hang around expecting to be found, shining and happy looking in the dim light. The human bondage of the hour sets in with elegance of necessity. Turning form tattered and tired to the moment the figures relax with the tense enjoyment of twisted ideas and their minds torn.

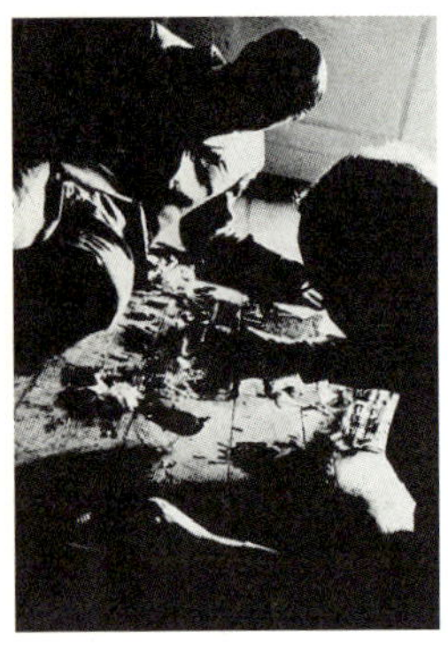

118 DRUNKEN LIVING

Dark shadowed living sculptors of human bondage raise themselves from off the crackling emotion spattered floor to make merry time with glass and drink and few words of heavy guilt. Iron bands on heads make them feel more bound to the floor as the pain takes over and tries to escape the increasing pressure of the band. The leaden hands stretch out uselessly only to drop with dull conscious felt weight to the floor map of the moment and the day, making adventure and angry urgent slump.

119 DRUNKEN SQUALOR
120 DRUNKEN SCENE
121 DRUNKEN HEART
122 DRUNKEN BONDAGE
123 DRUNKEN BOTTLES
124 DRUNKEN NIGHT
125 DRUNKEN DINNER
126 DRUNKEN MESS
127 DRUNKEN BLOOD

128 DRUNKEN GARLAND

A ghastly garland of drinking sculpture in the mad decorative spirit of the artists. The grin, the shave, the crease, the shoe we feel our world of crazed details circling with us at great sickening speed. Blinding flashes shoot from glasses, stunned by blows on head from bottle tops reeling with sense of respon-sibility and modern sexual vileness. We stare, we leer, we lurch, we jeer. The human heart is marching down the driveway away from the old house of hate and friends, into the distance they go, the maniacs. Sloshing along on a wettish song with shoes.

THE END
(Until the next time)

Your favourite virtue:	VICE
Your favourite qualities in man:	MASCULINITY
Your favourite qualities in woman:	MASCULINITY
Your favourite occupation:	PRAYING
Your chief characteristic:	CHILDISHNESS
Your idea of happiness:	MISERY
Your idea of misery:	MISERY
Your favourite colour:	REYELBLAWHI
Your favourite flower:	THE COMMON PANSY
If not yourself, who would you be:	CECIL AND RHODES
Where would you like to live:	IN HELL
Your favourite prose authors:	TOM
Your favourite poets:	DICK
Your favourite painters:	AND
Your favourite composers:	HARRY
Your favourite heroes in real life:	IAN AND SMITH
Your favourite heroines in real life:	ELIZABETH II
Your favourite heroes in fiction:	ROBIN AND HOOD
Your favourite heroines in fiction:	PETER AND PAN
Your favourite food:	BREAKFAST LUNCH AND DINNER
Your favourite drink:	YES
Your favourite names:	GILBERT AND GEORGE
Your pet aversion:	MODESTY
What characters in history do you most dislike:	MOTHER
What is your present state of mind:	IN A STATE
For what fault have you most toleration:	INTOLERANCE
Your favourite motto:	FUCK OFF

Newspaper questionnaire, *c.* 1978

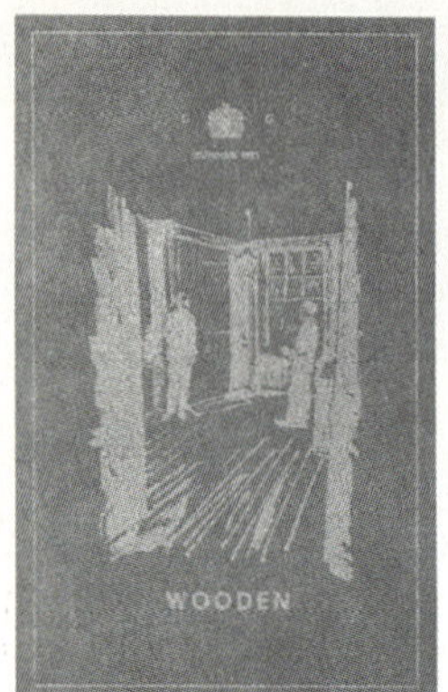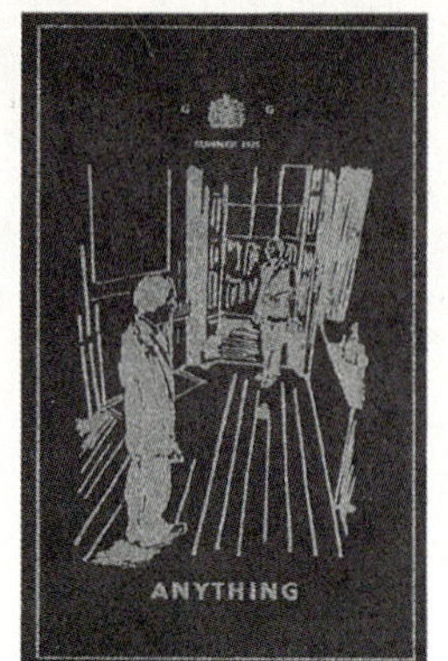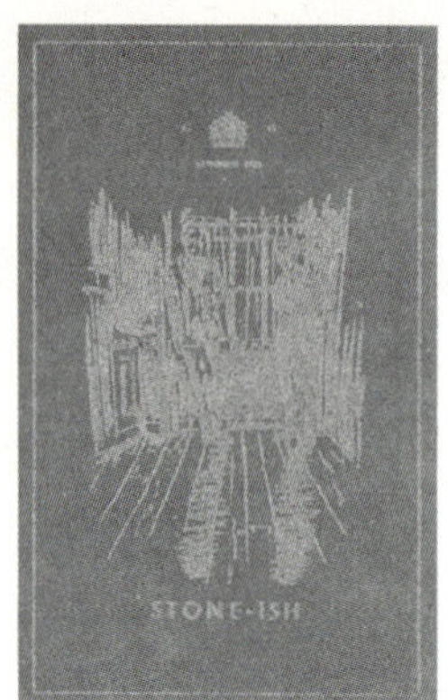

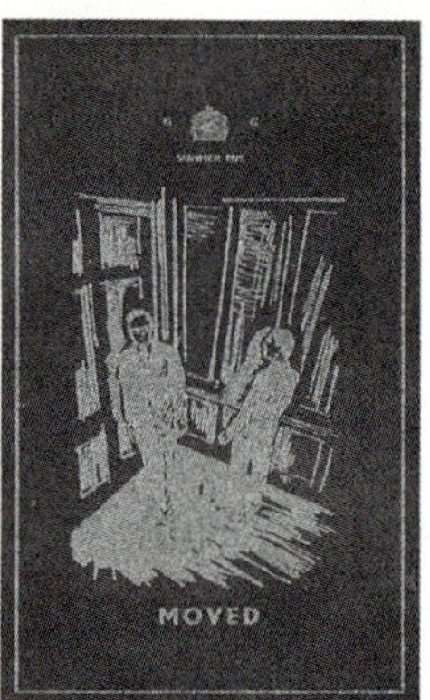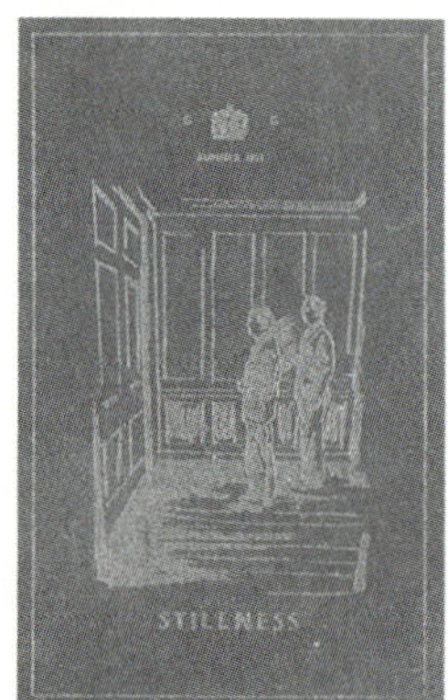

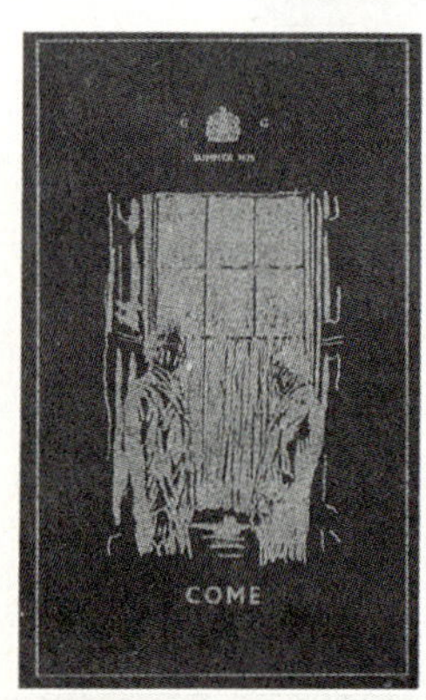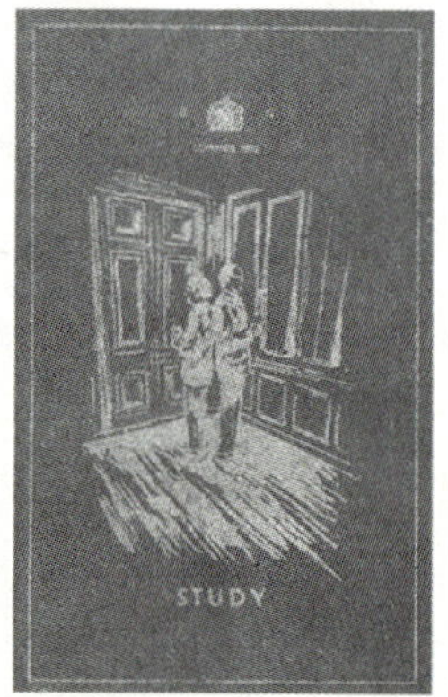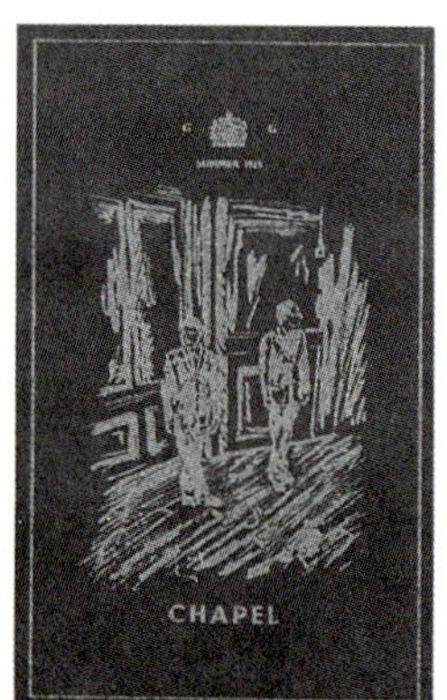

The Red Boxers, 1975, an eight-part Postal Sculpture where each recipient received one Red Boxer each week for eight weeks

The Red Boxers

95

1st.   In the room we looked across
The WOODEN AIR between .

       2nd.   They moved and paused a little
Not seeing ANYTHING .

             3rd.   Leaning on the window sill awhile
Two STONE-ISH faces on the floor .

     4th.   And tilted , MOVED on with dry
boards and then to STAND .

       5th.   STILLNESS breathing through our
air makes us still breathe .

6th.   Walking across the window glass
Dry figures COME to them .

     7th.   Back on back and shooting through
the closed STUDY .

       8th.   Two in the CHAPEL with life
around the suits .

We Believe

Text written by the artists for use in exhibition catalogues.

We believe in the Art, the Beauty and the
Life of the Artist who is an eccentric
person with something to say for Himself.

We uphold Traditional Values with our
love of Victory, Kindness and Honesty.

We are fascinated by the richness of
the fabric of Our World and we honour
the High-Mindedness of Man as the
ultimate Form and Meaning of Art.
Beauty is Our Art.

G+G
1978

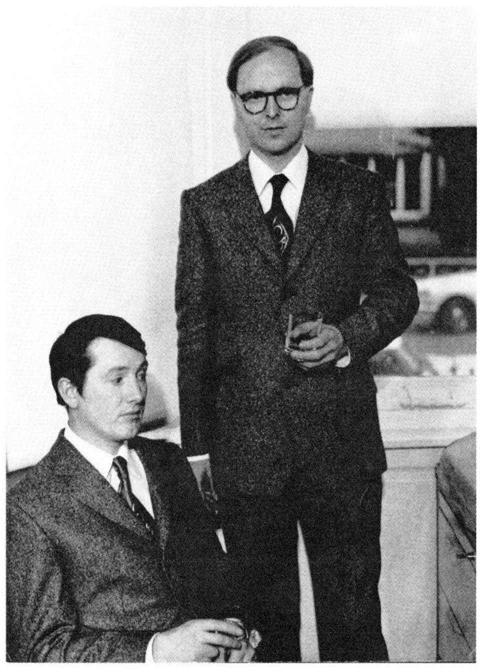

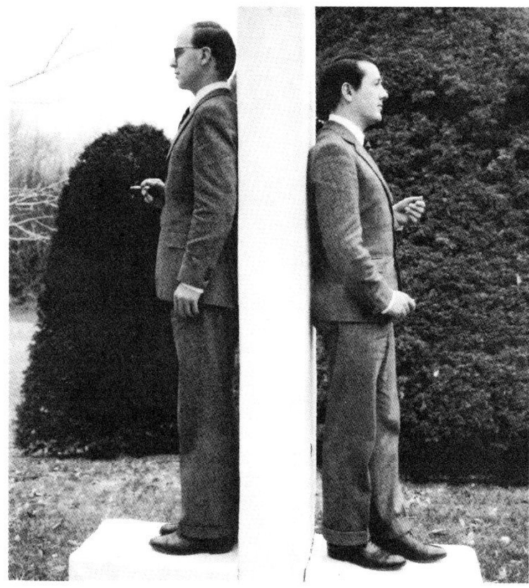

20 At the Spillemaekers Gallery, Brussels, during the artists' exhibition *Bad Thoughts*, 1975 (*Photo: Jacques Charlier*)

21 Portrait by Horst P. Horst at the photographer's home, Oyster Bay, Long Island, New York, 1976

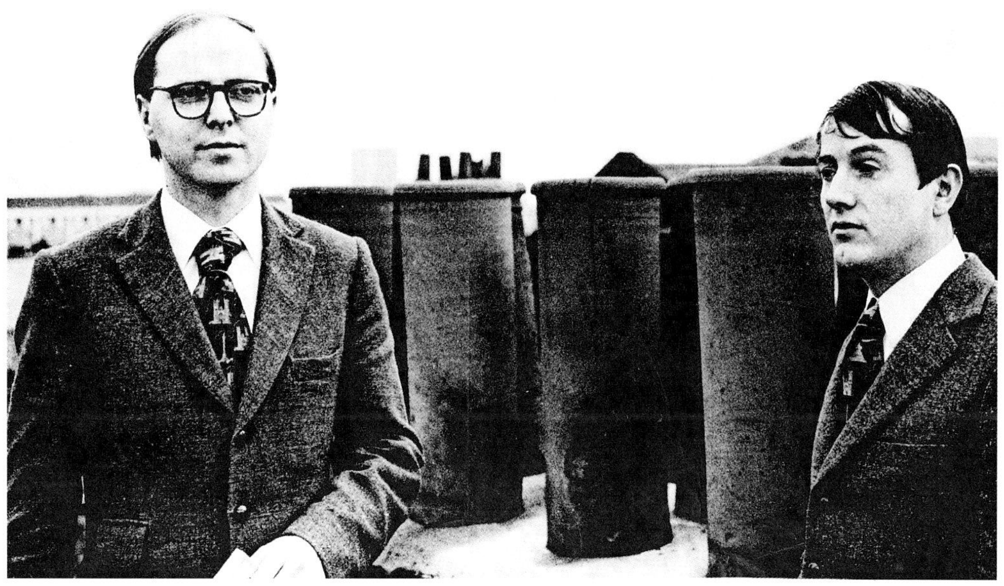

22 On the roof at Fournier Street, *c.* 1977

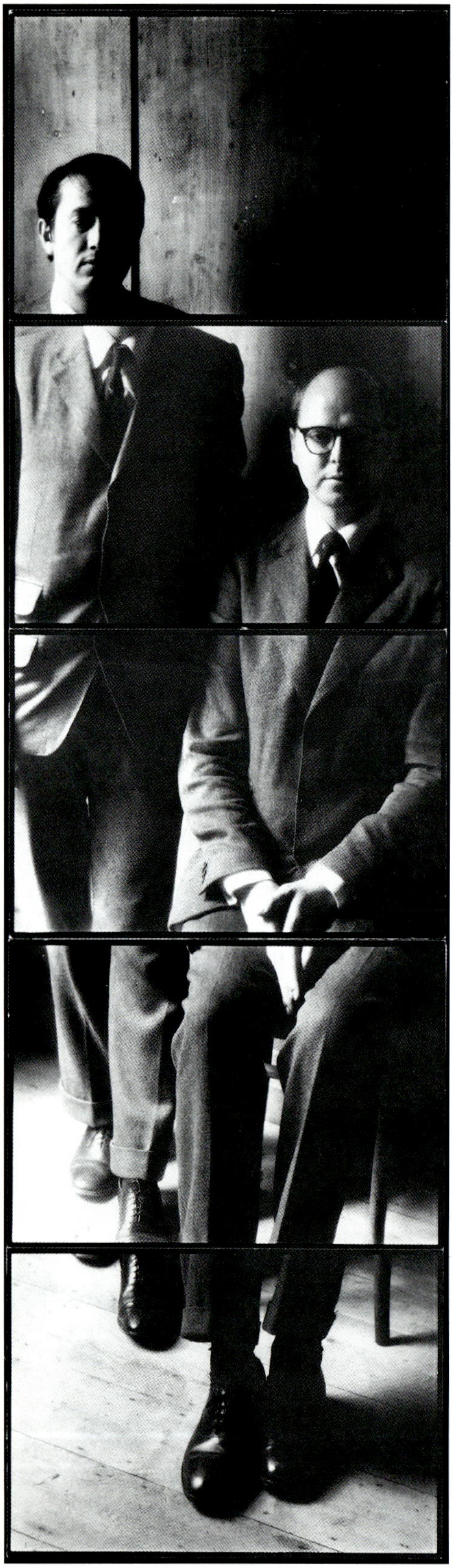

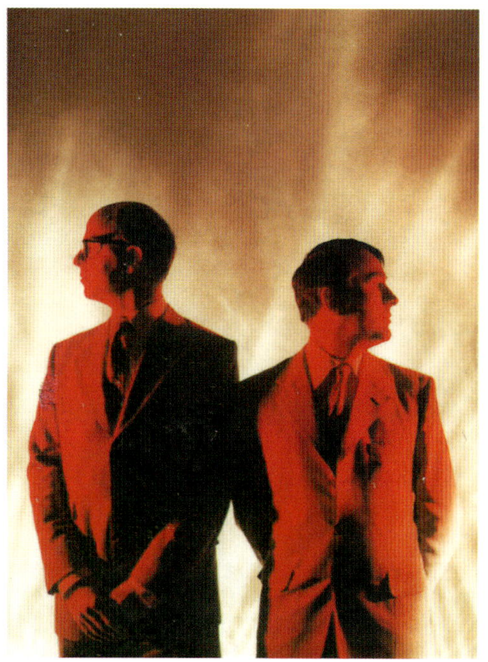

23 Portrait by Brian Griffin for the cover of *Time Out* magazine, Rotherhithe, London, March 1982

24 Portrait by David Seidner, Fournier Street, 1978

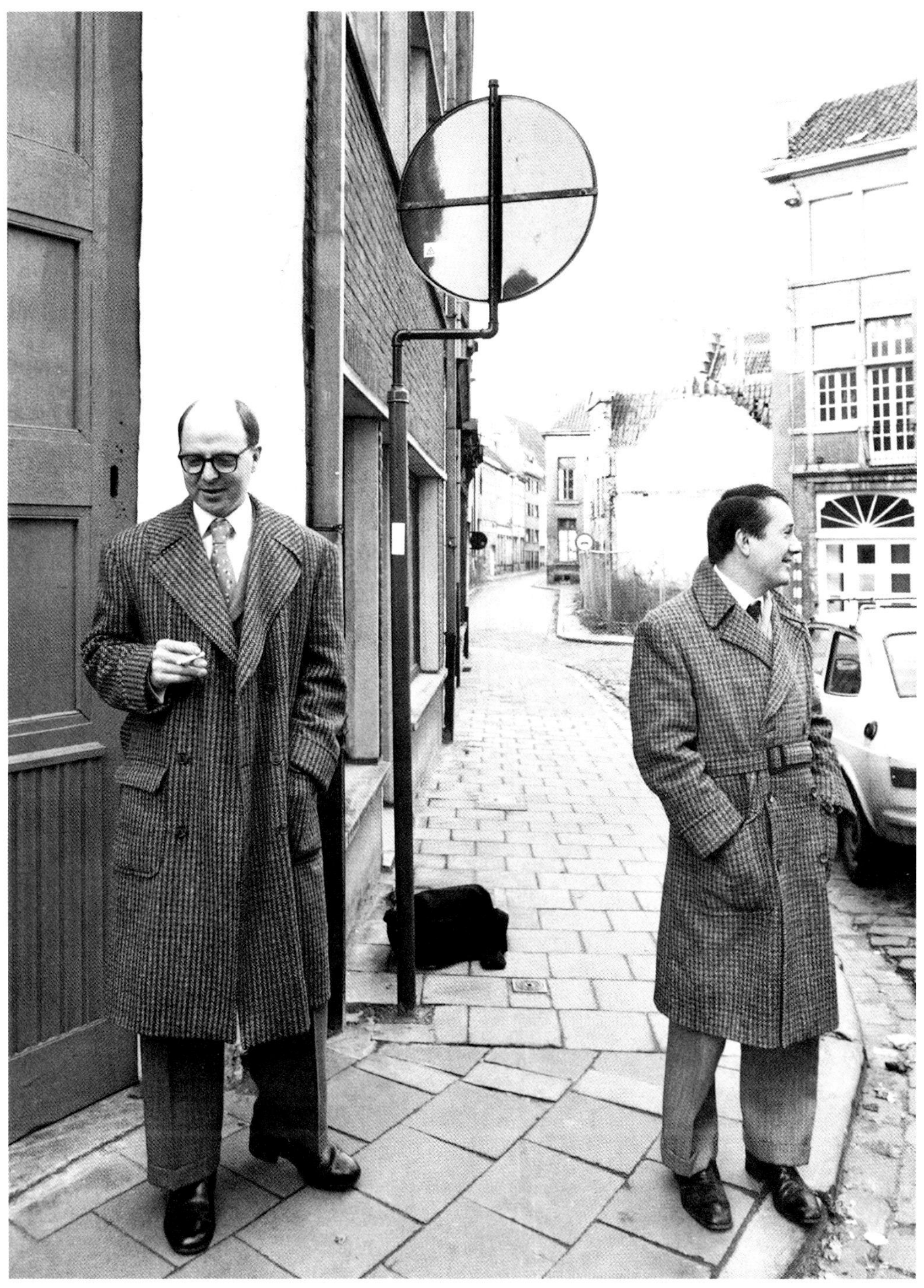

25 In Belgium for the artists' exhibition *New Photo-Pieces* at the Galerie Gewad, Ghent, 1982
(*Photo: P. Van Den Abeele/Die Standard–Het Nieuwsblad*)

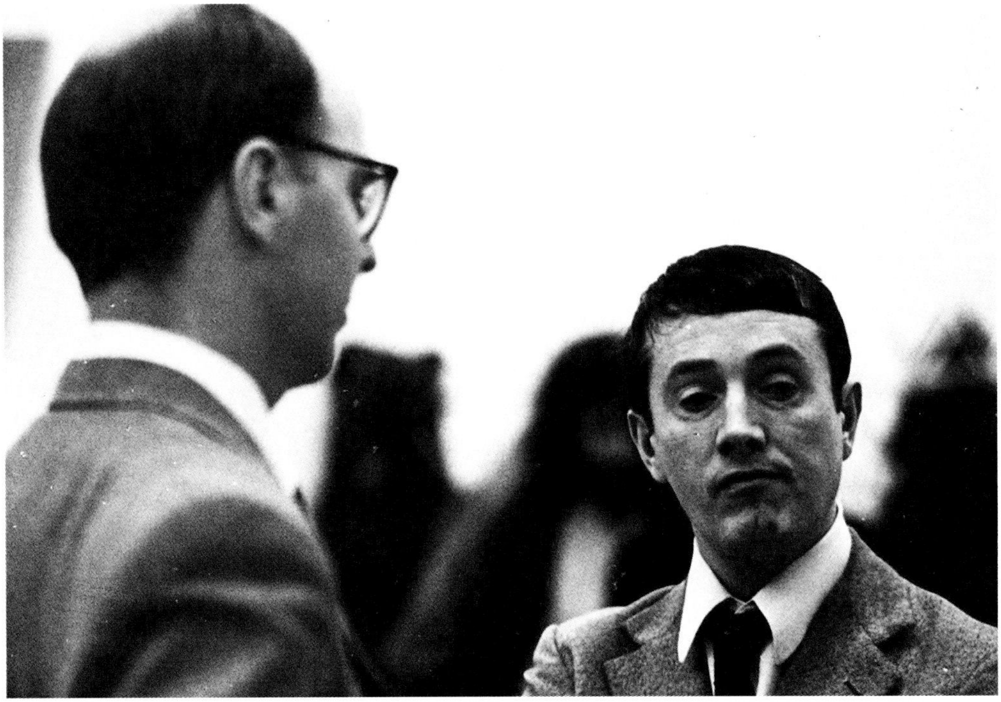

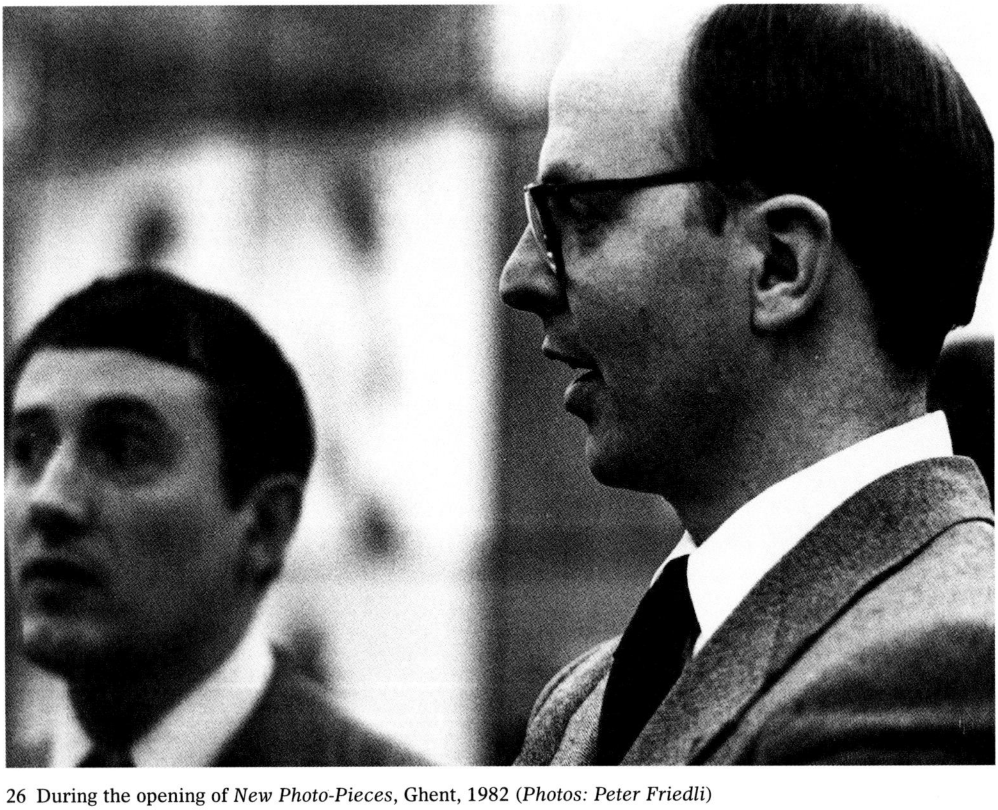

26 During the opening of *New Photo-Pieces*, Ghent, 1982 (*Photos: Peter Friedli*)

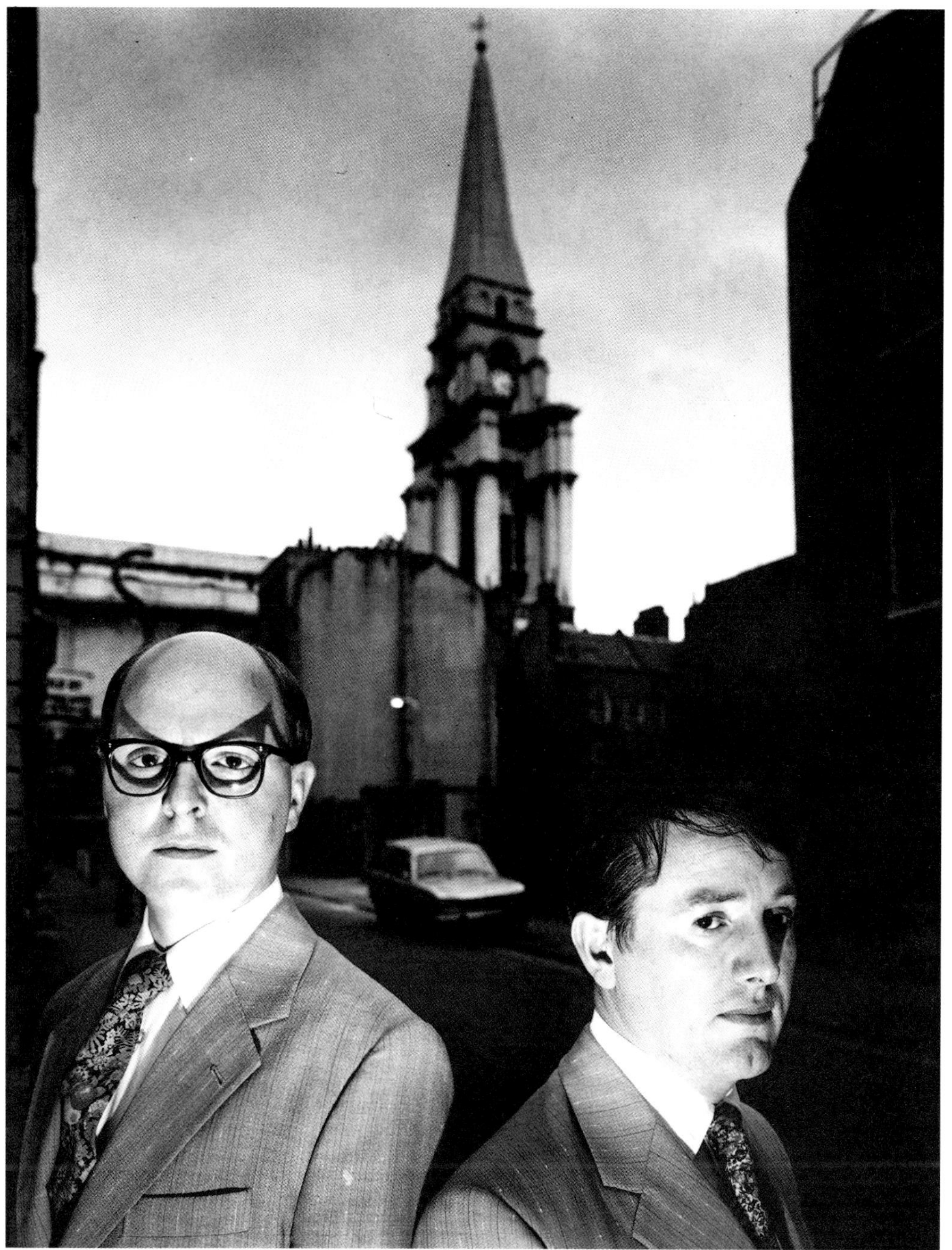

27 Portrait by David Bailey with Christchurch Spitalfields in background, Wilkes Street, London, June 1983

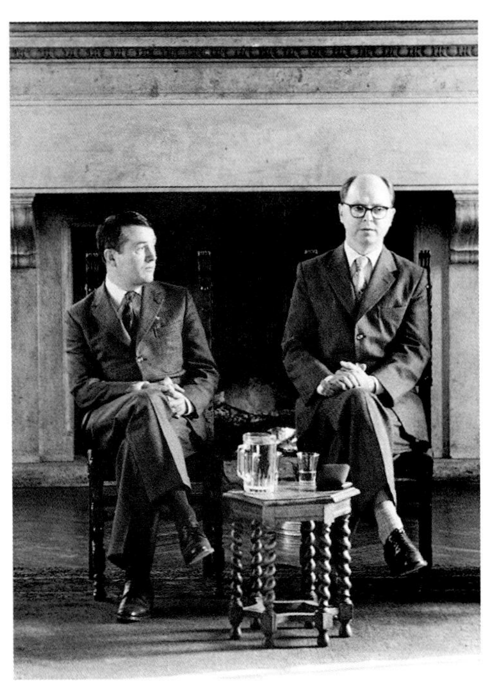

28 Receiving award at the Conferenza Stampa Oi, British School, Rome, 11 December 1984 (*Photo: A. Maranzano*)

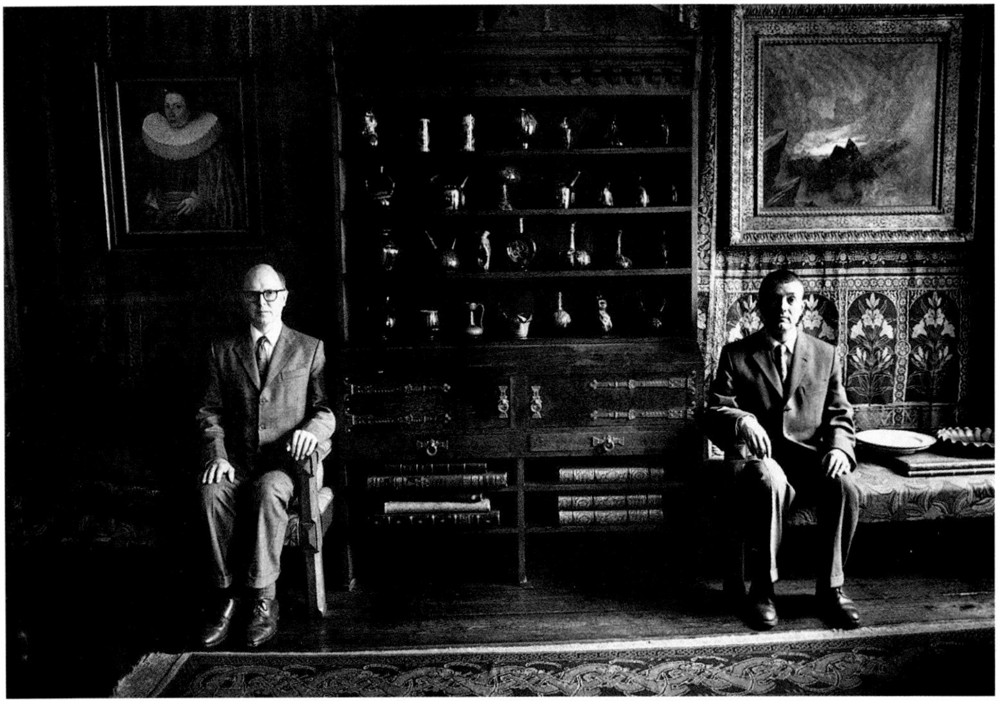

29 Portrait by Brian Harris for *The Independent*, Fournier Street, 1986

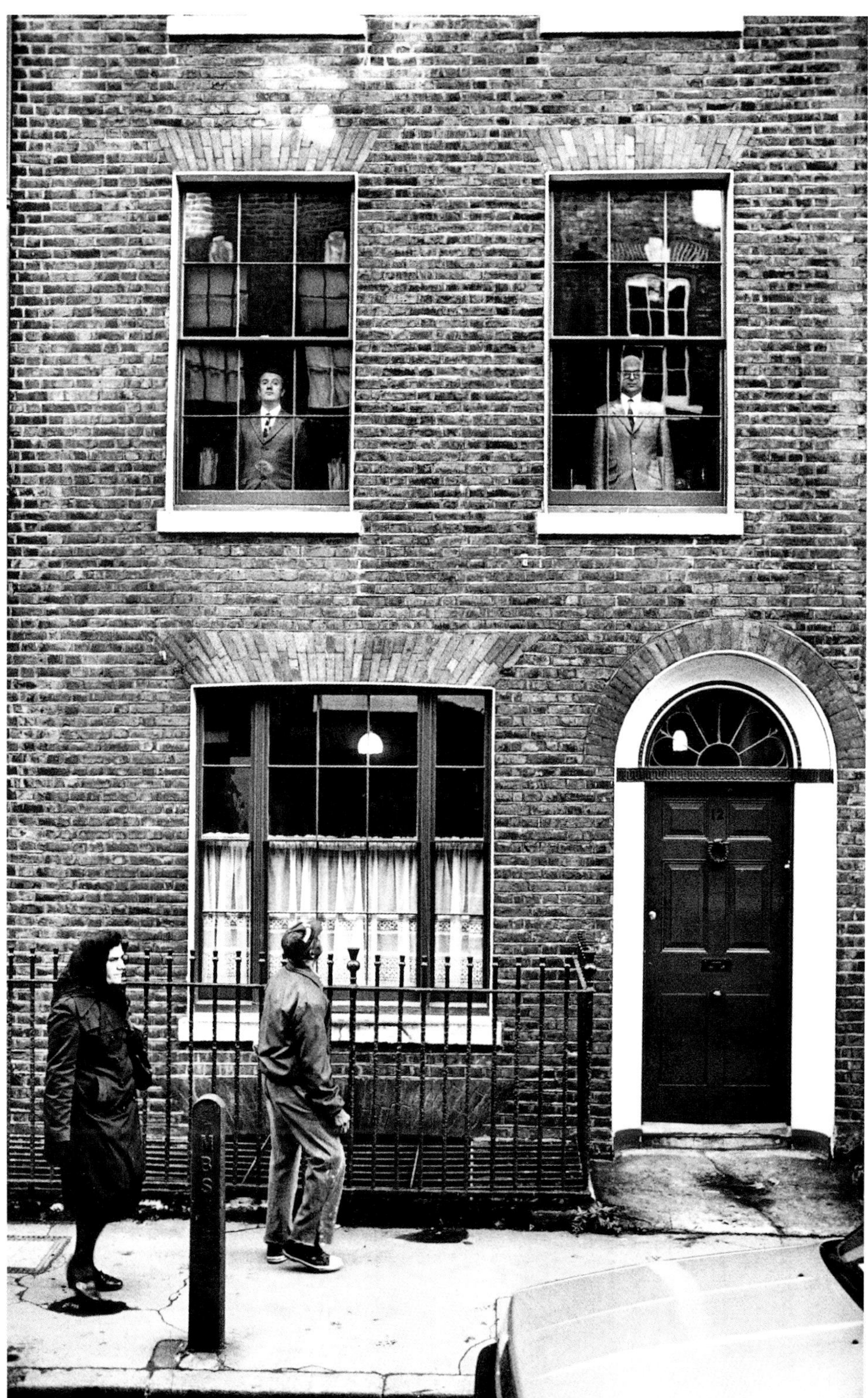

30 Portrait by Nick Rogers, Fournier Street, 26 November 1986

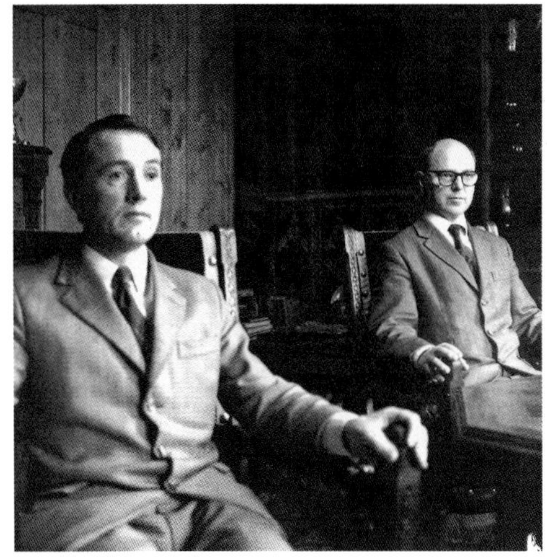

31 Portrait by Chris Timotheou, Fournier Street,
20 January 1986

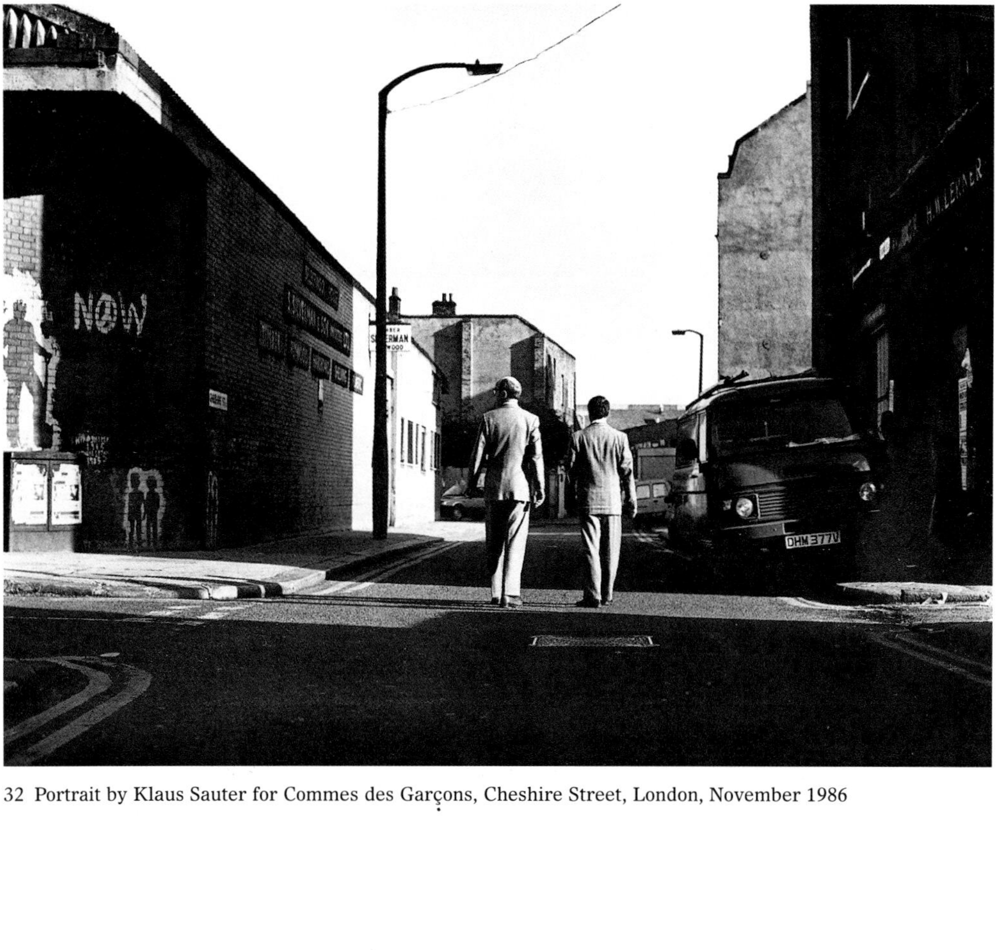

32 Portrait by Klaus Sauter for Commes des Garçons, Cheshire Street, London, November 1986

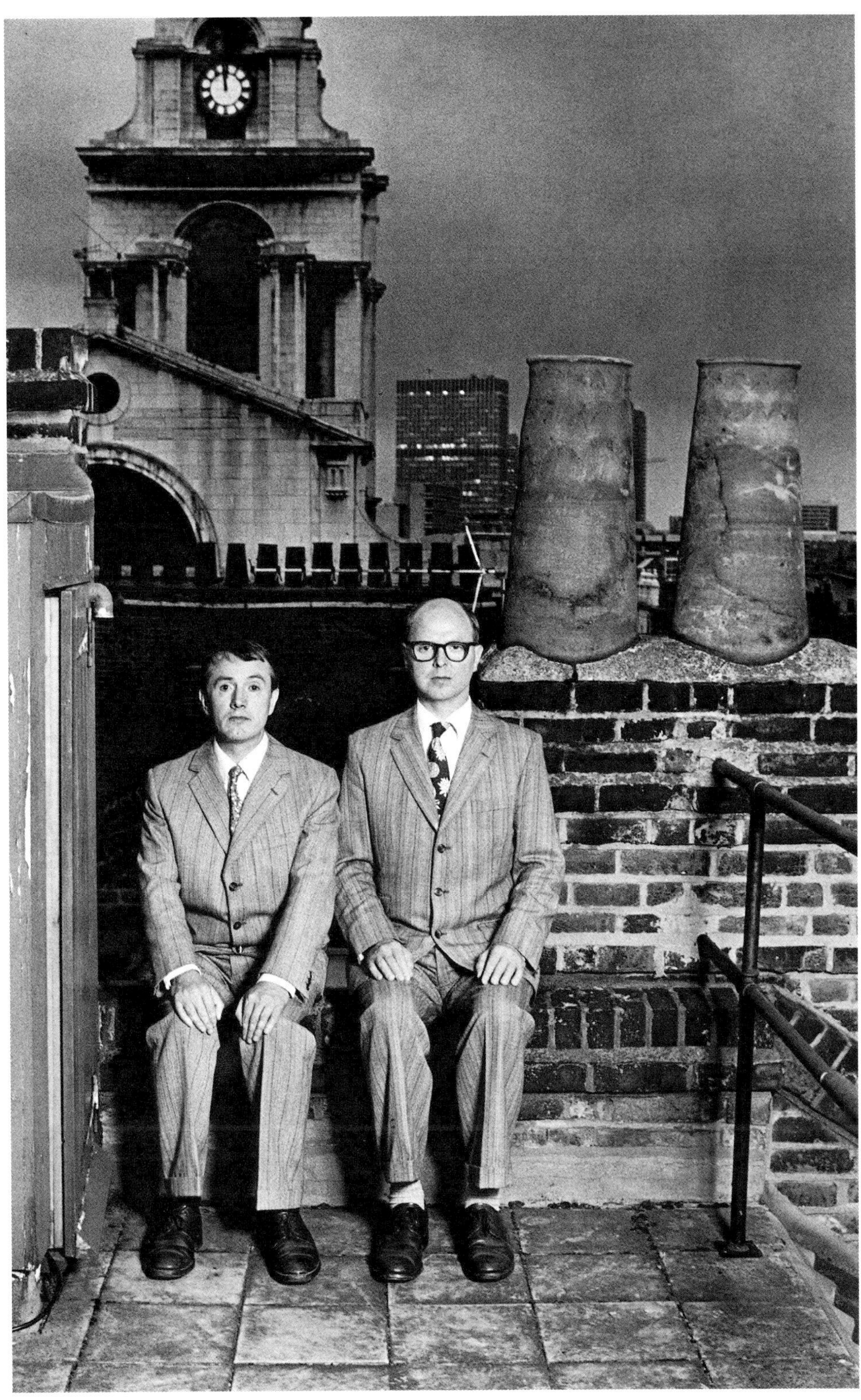

33 Portrait by Herbie Knott on the roof at Fournier Street, July 1986

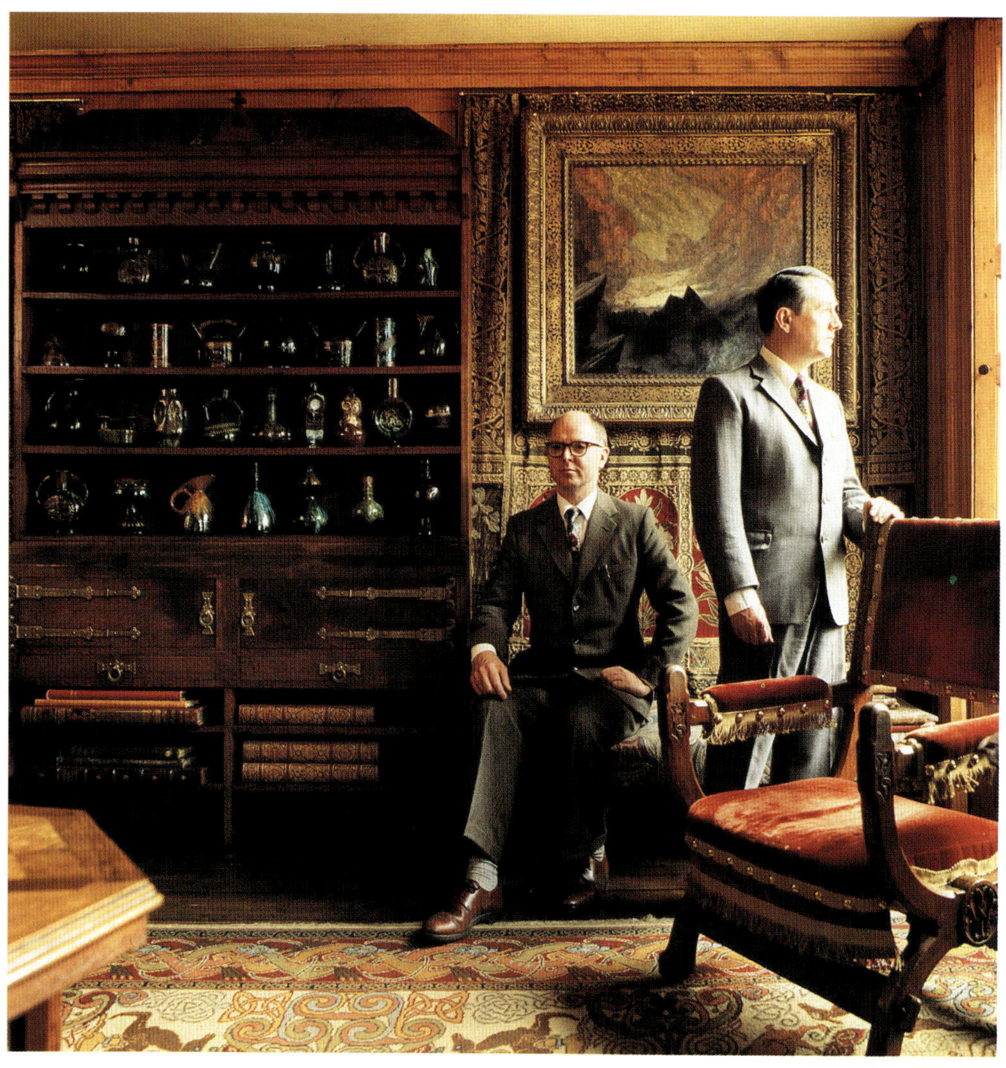

34 Portrait by Derry Moore, Fournier Street, 1987

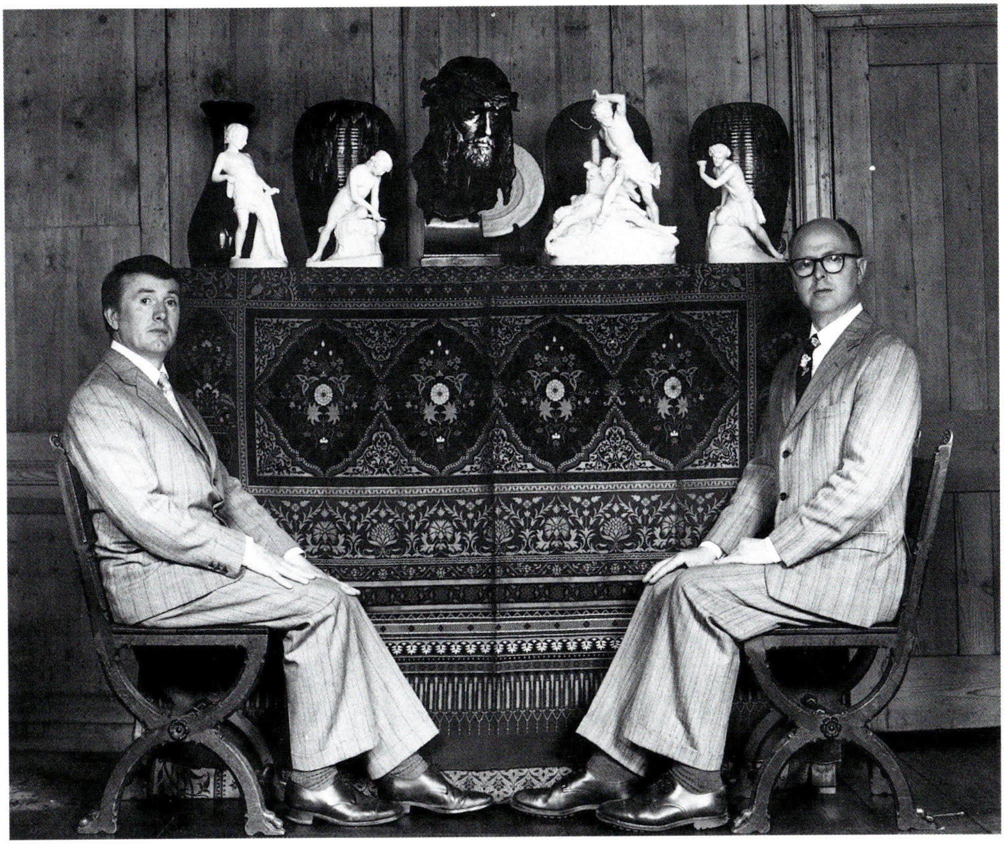

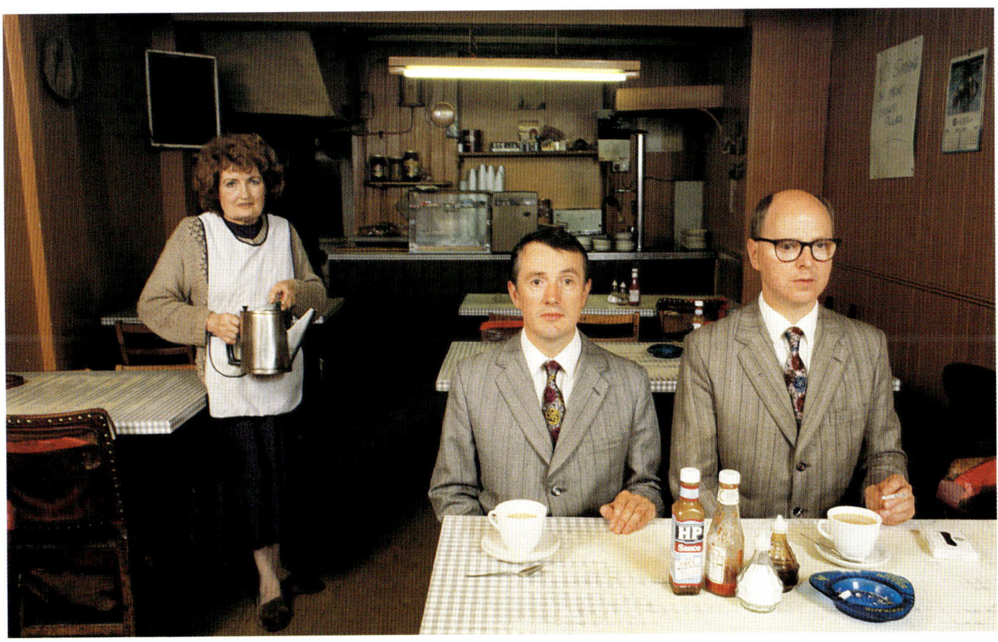

35 Portrait by Liam Woon for Commes des Garçons, Fournier Street, 1988

36 Portrait by Herbie Knott with Phyllis in the Market Cafe, Fournier Street, May 1987

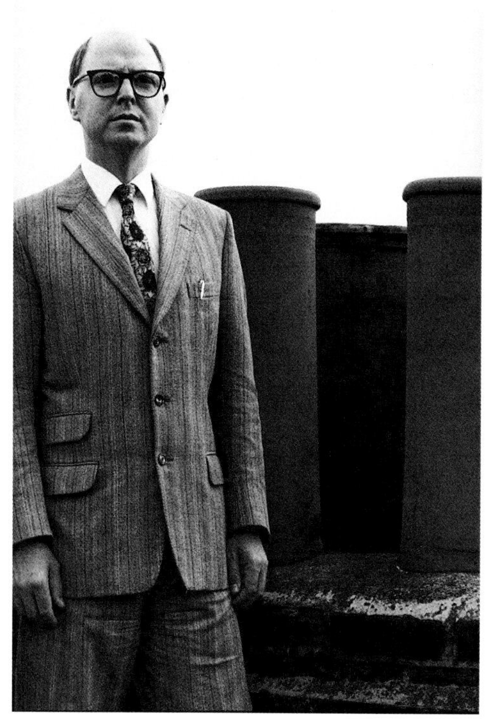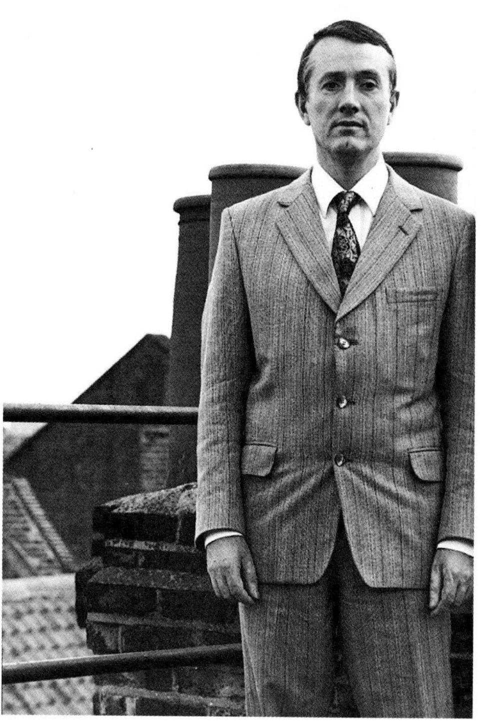

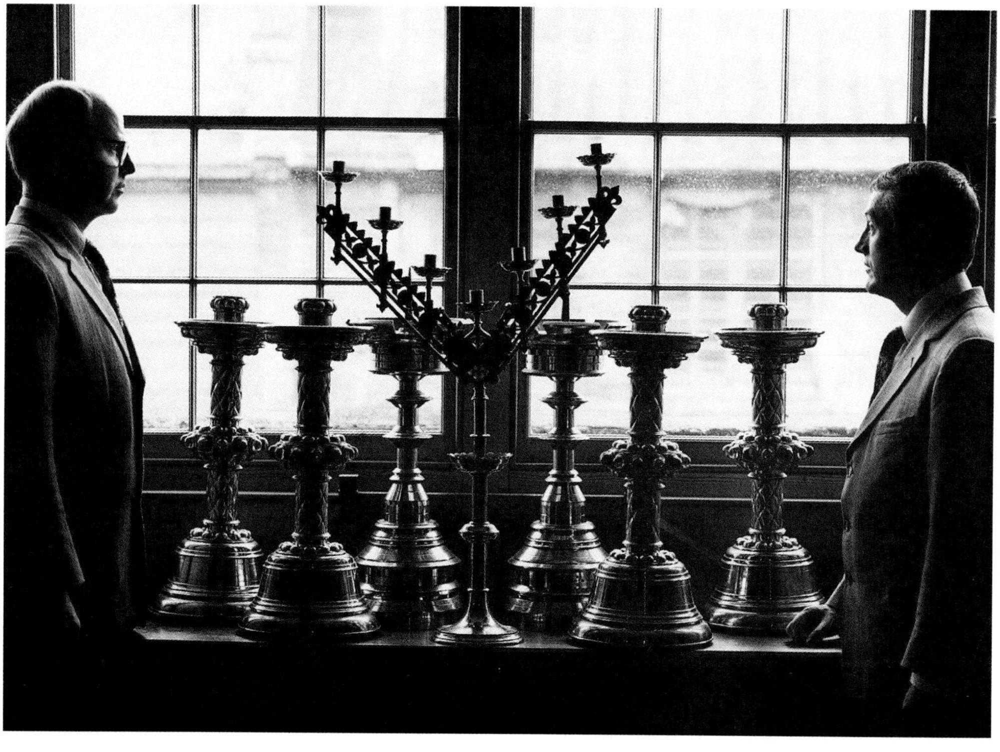

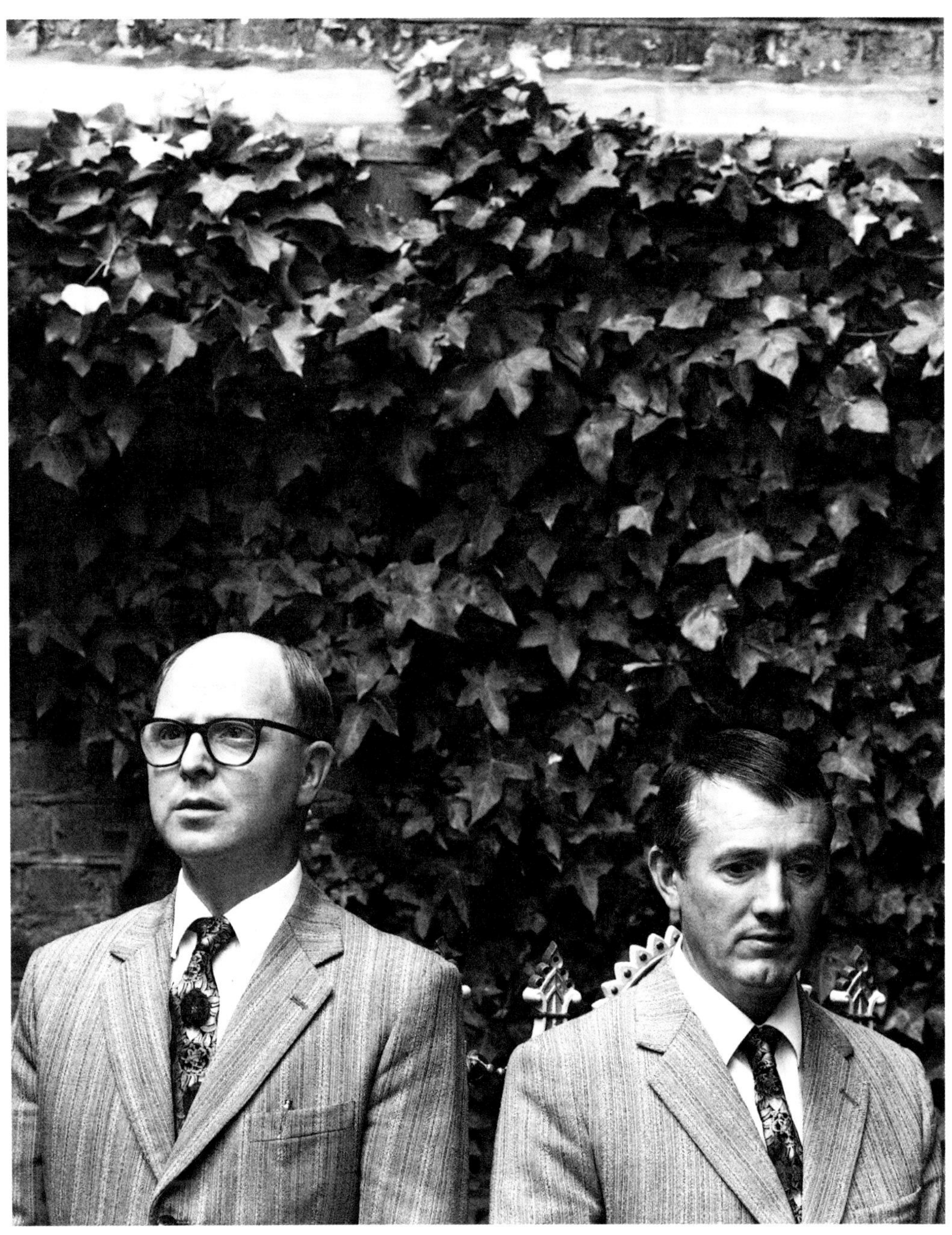

37 Portraits by Michael James O'Brien, Fournier Street, 1987

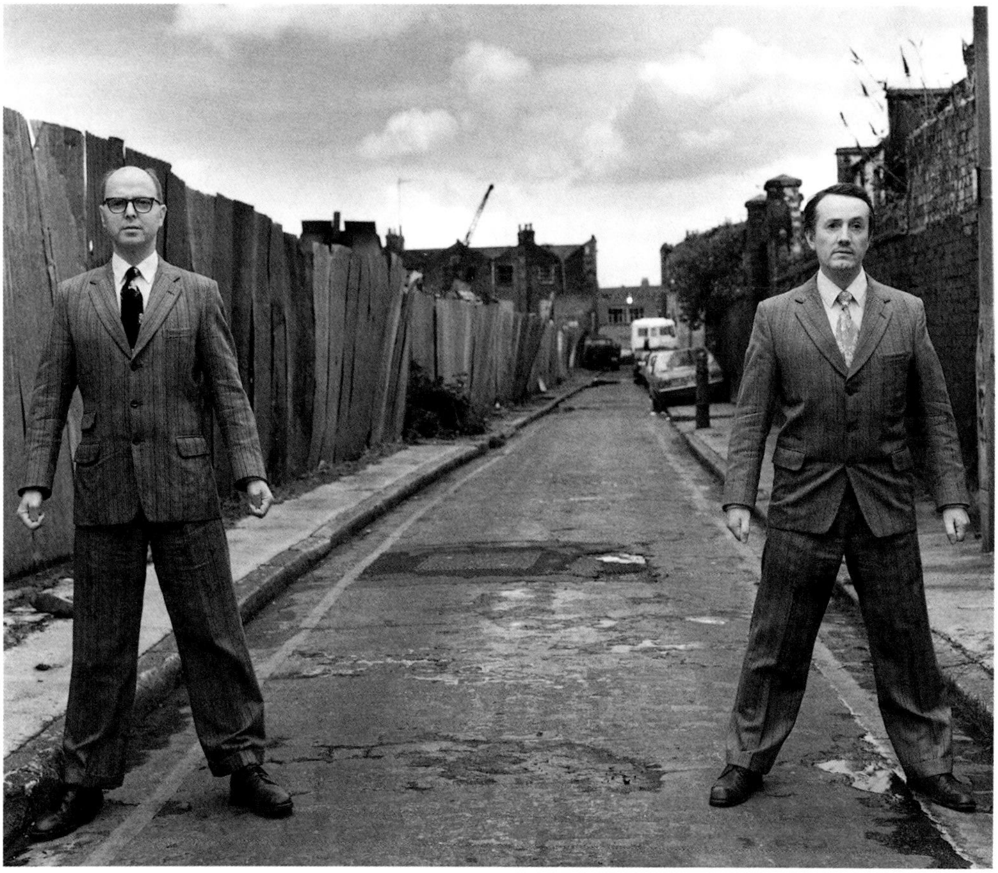

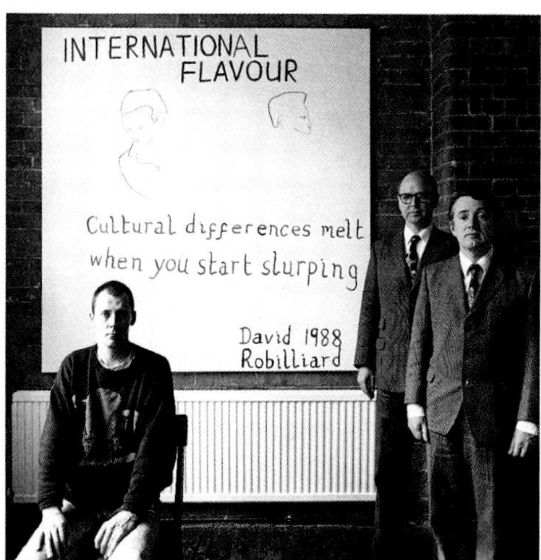

38 Portrait by Liam Woon, Whitechapel, 1988

39 With David Robilliard in his studio, Garden Walk,
London, 1988 (*Photo: Isabelle Blondiau*)

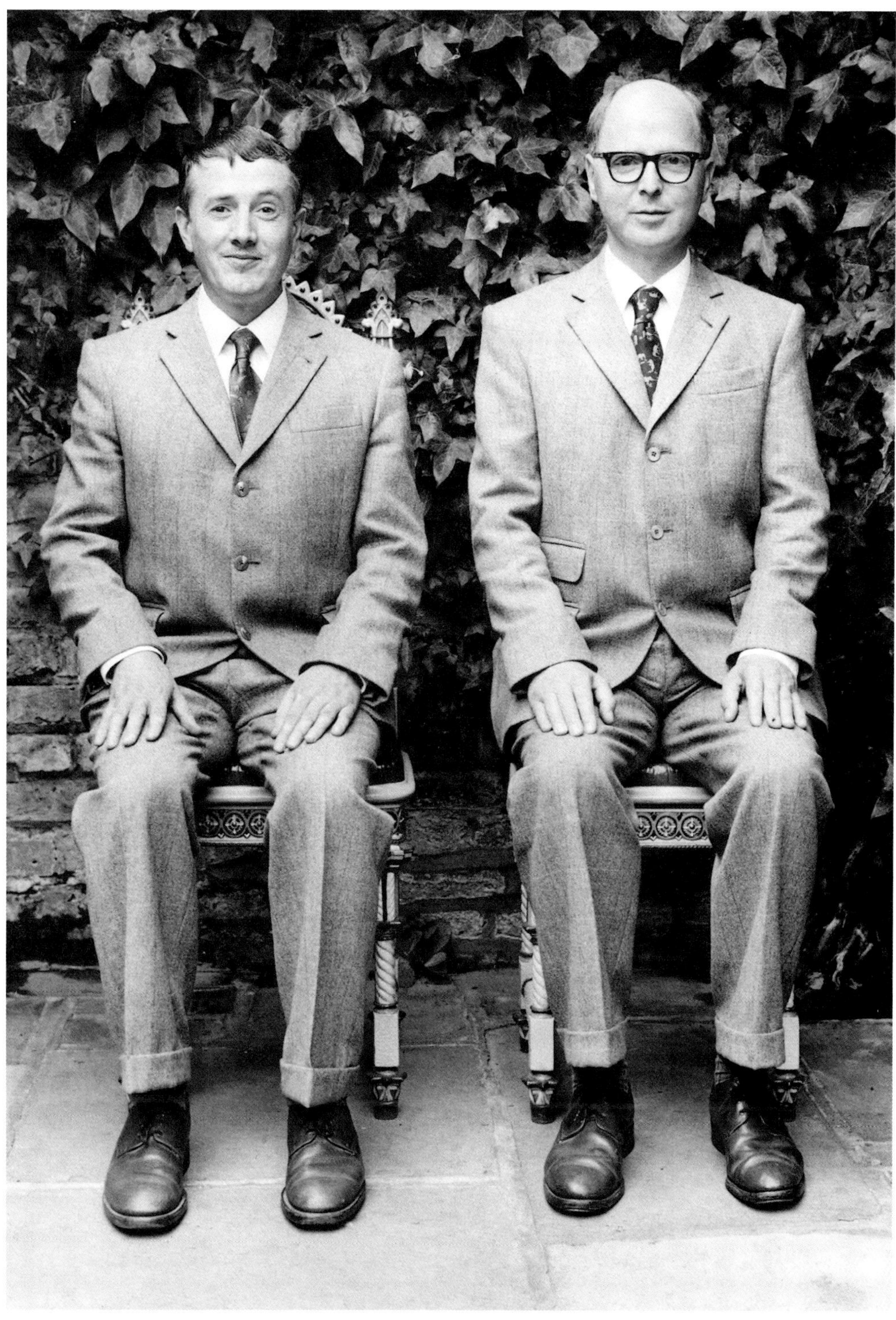

40 Portrait by Christopher Felver, Fournier Street, 1989

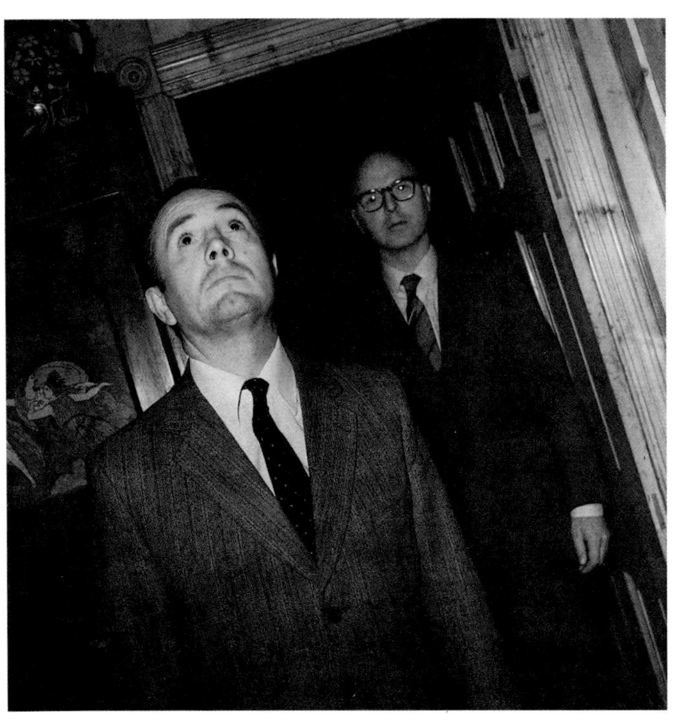

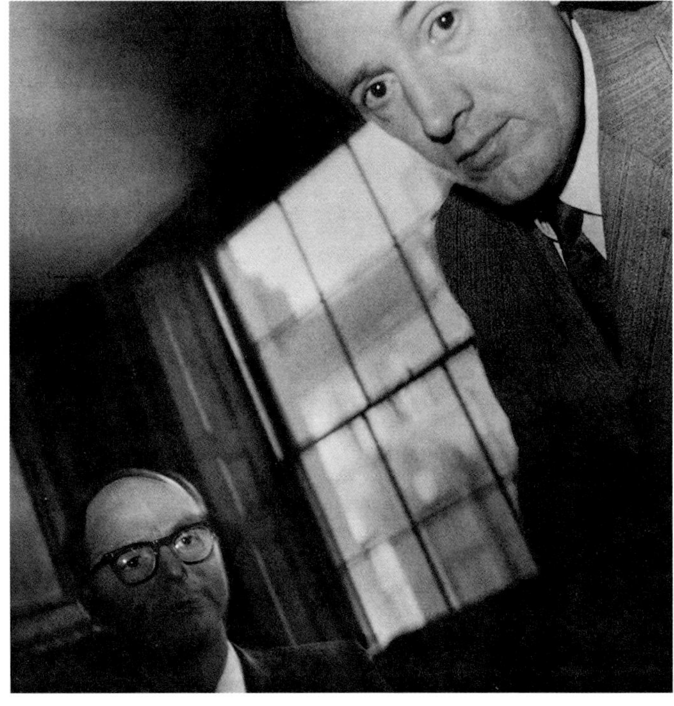

41 Portraits by Mark Lally, Fournier Street, 1989

④ MISERY ~~FOR ALL~~. HERE THE STRUGGLED PUNISHED NATURE MASKS THE HAND OF MANS 200 YEARS OF CRUDE LOVING DESPERATE COMMERCE. DEATH LIFE, NO YOUTH DEATH LIFE NO FREINDS, NO FEELING FOR OUR ORDER. THE ONLY HUMAN BEING TREES ARE CLOSE TO US IN ~~#~~ MOVING LEAVES AND WAYS. THEY ARE THE ONLY REAL FREINDS THAT WE HAVE. THEIR BACK-DROP ~~SYMPAONY~~ ~~#~~ ORCHESTA TUNES UP FOR EARLY EASTERN BREEZE. THESE ~~MONSTERS~~ GENTLE MONSTERS STAND BETWEEN US AND THAT THING CALLED LIFE. BROWN FACES, BUSINESS AND THE LIVING LIFE OF CHARM + PERVERSION STRONG WILLED AND WILLING TIME AWAY. BREATHING FOR US THE MONSERS STAY AND WAIT.

FOREINGN THOUGHT ON FETID LONDON
BRICKS OF AGE WITH SENTIMENT
OF HUMAN LIFE DECAY.
MOVING IN AND OUT AND IN AND OUT.
THE LOVE MURDER INDUSTRY EATING
SINGING TALKING SCREAMING ROWING
BURNING CRACKING ~~GOES AL~~ GHOSTS
MOVE WITH THEIR DRY STINKING
HISTORY FROM ROOM TO ROOM.
GLIMPSED THROUGH DIRTY ~~&~~ PANES
THEY LOOK LIKE SHADOWS IN DISGUISE
AND TELL ~~SOME~~ THAT ~~THERE~~ ARE NO
GHOSTS. EYES ACHE TO WRENCH OUT
A SAFE GOOD STORY. FOR RICHER AND
FOR POORER THE ~~SOULS~~ FOREING SOULS
DEFY THE GHOSTS WITH LOVE.

Artist's manuscript for Scene 4 from the film *The World of Gilbert & George*, 1980–81

The World of Gilbert & George

Texts from the script by Gilbert & George for the artists' 1980–81 seventy-minute film produced by Philip Haas and the Arts Council of Great Britain.

Scene 4. Camera cruise (slight, not panoramic) of half-time view from study front. Half-time view from study rear. Hardly any sky. Text (unless otherwise specified in script, text is spoken by Gilbert and/or George) plus natural sound:

Misery for all. Here the struggled punished nature masks the hands of man's 300 years of crude loving desperate commerce. Death/life, no youth, death/life. No friends, no feeling for our order. The only human being trees are close to us in moving leaves and ways. They are the only real friends that we have. Their back-drop orchestra tunes up for early eastern breeze. These gentle monsters stand between us and that form named life. Brown faces, business and the living life of charm and perversion, strong-willed and willing time away. Breathing for us the monsters stay and wait.

Foreign thought on fetid used-up London bricks of age with sentiment of human life decay. Moving in and out, and in and out. The love, murder industry, eating, singing, talking, screaming, rowing, burning, cracking ghosts move with their dry stinking history from room to room. Glimpsed through dirty panes they look like shadows in disguise, and tell some that there are no ghosts. Eyes ache to wrench out true meant good safe true story. For richer and for poorer the foreign souls defy the ghosts with love.

Scene 6.

Images:

A. Stone Jesus.
B. Sky.
C. Graffiti Christ.
D. Cityscape.
E. Soldiers fighting.
F. Church reflected in puddle.
G. Church spire.
H. Sun through trees.

I.   A dinner.
J.   A drunk on the floor.
K.   A youth.
L.   Rubbish and dirt.
M. G & G frame townscape.
N.   Victory sculpture.
O.   Battersea power station.
P.   Sunset.

Text [together with images above]:

a.   Our Father
b.   Which art in Heaven
c.   Hallowed be thy name
d.   Thy kingdom come
e.   Thy will be done
f.   On Earth
g.   As it is in Heaven
h.   Give us this day
i.   Our daily bread
j.   And forgive us our trespasses
k.   As we forgive us who trespass against them
l.   And lead us not into temptation
m. But deliver us from evil
n.   For thine is the kingdom
o.   The power
p.   And the glory, for ever and ever, Amen.

Scene 9. Head to waist pulling back to three-quarter-length portrait Gilbert.
Text (Gilbert, then repeated by George):

I believe in the art, the beauty and the life of the artist who is an eccentric person with something to say for himself. I uphold traditional values with my love of victory, kindness and honesty. I am fascinated by the richness of the fabric of our world and I honour the highmindedness of man as the ultimate form and meaning of art. Beauty is my art.

[Scenes 11 and 12 were not included in the film's final edit and
are previously unpublished.]

Scene 11. Text:

We believe in the art, the beauty and the life of the artist who is an
eccentric person with something to say for himself. We uphold traditional values with our love of victory, kindness and honesty. We are
fascinated by the richness of the fabric of our world and we honour the
highmindedness of man as the ultimate form and meaning of art.
Beauty is our art.

Scene 12. Alternating blossom/youth's head. Texts (with faces):

BIRDSFOOT TREFOIL. A more or less prostrate perennial, downy
or hairless. Leaves with five iflets, with lowest pair bent back so that
leaves appear trefoil. Flowers two to seven in a head, yellow but often
tinged red or orange. Sepal teeth erect in bud, an obtuse angle between
the two upper pods straight in a head resembling a bird's foot. May to
September in grassy places.

BITTERSWEET. Clambering sometimes prostrate downy perennial.
Leaves pointed oval often with two lobes at base. Flowers in loose
clusters, bright purple, petals turned down. Yellow anthers in a con-
spicuous column. Forms a poisonous egg-shaped berry, green, then
yellow then red. Found in woods, scrub, hedges, waste and damp places
and throughout.

MASTERWORT. Medium-tall almost hairless perennial with broad-
toothed iflets and inflated sheathing stalks. Flowers white or pink
without lower bracts in June or July, rounded, flattened, ridged. Found
in grassy places on hills or mountains. Tinged red with solid stem,
rather leathery leaves, numerous lower bracts turned down and egg-
shaped.

CREEPING BUTTERCUP. Short to medium slightly hairy creeping
perennial with rooting runners and leaves rather triangular in outline
with stalked end lobes. Sepal erect and flower stalks not furrowed. May

to September in damp often bare places. Sometimes hairier and not creeping with seeds and long hooked beak.

Scene 19.

G & G torsos with drinking still life.
a. Gilbert's head drunken.
    G & G torsos with drinking still life.
b. George's head drunken.
    G & G torsos with drinking still life.
c. Gilbert's head drunken.
    G & G torsos with drinking still life.
d. George's head drunken.
    G & G torsos – Normal pub chatter to be recorded.

Text (for drunken heads):

a. Come on you silly little nitty titty.
b. He needs buggering stupid.
c. That's a lot of bloody bollocks.
d. He's a silly old queen.

Scene 23. Text:

Here with the handsome beauty of the daily food. These pools of juices and mounds of dead matter giving us our necessary breathing life and intellect. Sliced pig to bacon with fats and veins drool into our pleasure of eating. Disgusting sausages taste so nice with deep-bowelled satisfaction of sensation. Cabbage come and potatoes go as fixed drab sadness for our gullets. Sheep chops lie in beauty with dead, ribbed happiness of purpose. Gravy rivers round ran rind of belly, curlicues of fat decorating its way to masticated end. Steamed up air above the stewed stew, stewing for its winter stench/smell loveliness with puddings of sweat, solid with the cornfields gold and aching with travelled sun-cursed sugar, all drenched in good yellow-shirted custard. Tarts fall and crumble as crumbles various stand dust dry but moist with mystery of excellence.

Scene 25. Camera travels along Cheshire Street by zoom and following zoom path
from side to side in a zig-zag way. Text:

Scarred cobbled street we see you for your worthless worthiness made
miserable by nature and your lust you reek now of your history of use
beyond your purpose. Your blood stained surfaces of charm and alarm
of daily work that comes to you and leaves you dry with the destructive-
ness of your years. Romantic and unhappy you rot to serve no person
but your friends and servants, us.

Scene 27. Full-length G & G against white background.
Five texts at five-second intervals:

a.   We like very much to be happy.
b.   We like very much to be drunk.
c.   We like very much to be unhappy.
d.   We like very much to be sober.
e.   We don't very much like to be happy,
     or not drunk or unhappy or not sober.

Scene 30a. Child against white background. Text:

Pan's garden pleasured beauty for a child's fleshly delight. This rosy
cheeky milky being filled with praise for gaiety and joy. Heart pumped
with virgin taste-blood thought of home and school and friends. Here is
the child.

Scene 30c. Teenager against black background. Text:

A saucy sex-crazed seeker of the nerves and tastes and disappointments
rare fresh time of superior unhappiness and tragic heart events with
each white limb. The experiment with spots on skin decisions. The
pleasure with the learning time moves fast. Here is the youth.

Scene 30e. Grown-up against white. Text:

Spring ripened life's experience rests finely on the face of human
mastered life. Glad mistaken courage enobles each ounce of solid

personal known flesh with measured feeling of the time the voice cries for control. Here is the moment, there is the day. Here is the person.

Scene 30g. Older person against black. Text:

Here with the superior youth of age and with grandness of flesh in use. Freedom of being with the citied world destroying care with ultimate wit and thought. Knowledge glides from arm to vein tracing beauty on the skin of years. Here is the man.

Scene 33. Front view of Christchurch Spitalfields in bad weather, with minimum of passers by. Text (shot continues after text for ten seconds):

Dead church with stones piled up for classic heathen sense points skyward to our Gods and clouds and aeroplanes and birds and good police helicopters. Home of tramp and pigeon and sad-cultured music lover all grey with beak or bottle or program old. Circled, arched, dust-pushed, dead dream signs of intellect on gloomed dead names. Climb hippy, stagger drunk, trot educated man for hands touching blinking grudged compliment for him our friend in Jesus stones.

Scene 35. Text:

Randy	Office
Unhappy	Shop
Miserable	Church
Cold	Wharf
Tired	Station
Depressed	Pub
Waiting	Person
Ghastly	Thing
Awful	Market
Terrible	Factory
Unbearable	Workshop

A tart was walking down our street,
He looked, we looked, he nodded
His hands were red
His face was white
He was the best tart of the night.

A rose was on our cupboard new
It spoke to us, of us, in wood
We touched its sepals, runners, teeth
It scratched a hand and made it bleed.

We walked through rain to Farnborough
Past ivy, shop and tomb
We heard some hounds, and saw some woods
And liked them more than old foxes' wombs
Then we came back on the forty-seven
Not mugged but changed twice
A day well passed and used up right
In our dirty mooded life.

A friend came to our house one day
He knocked upon the door
He stood outside, we stood inside
Our shoes glued to the floor
He waited and waited, our table creaked,
And then he turned and left
We looked and sighed and breathed again
For no one had crossed our door.

George: How is the tea Gilbert?
Gilbert: It's very nice. Would you like some cake?
George: Thank you, yes. Would you like some cheese?

Gilbert: Yes, I would very much like to have a piece of Leicester.
George: Here you are.
Gilbert: Thank you, George.
George: How are you feeling Gilbert?
Gilbert: I feel relaxed after the long walk. How do you feel then?
George: Very well, thank you. Rather brainy and relaxed. How should we spend the evening?
Gilbert: Why don't we go to the Clifton and see some waiters?
George: Extremely good idea. Should I change?
Gilbert: Change what?
George: Oh, I meant my suit and tie. What did you think?
Gilbert: I thought your shoes and shirt. Why? Should I change?
George: No, I think you'll be alright as you are. Do you think Attilus will be there?
Gilbert: If he is not we are going to get him out of the kitchen. Do you have your words ready for him?
George: I have everything ready for him. How about you?
Gilbert: I will ask him about his science. How about you?
George: I will ask him about his science as well.

      Scene 42. Darkly lighted G & G profiles as in *The Alcoholic* (G & G photo-piece)
      against black background. Sound: melody only. Text:

Here in this place we have to stay even when dreaming of our jungled distant happy land. Our faces are heavy with the thoughts of the far away jungled happy people. The heavy sky makes us feel as moisture and with Sabu happy and exhausted. One day we will take to our feet and walk that way where the sunset never ends. We have to find again old pink elephant. Steaming mountainous dung on jungle path and tripping, we are almost falling home.

      Scene 68. Faded in/out shots of well-composed furniture in situ.
      Romantically lighted. Text divided into four parts:

Our oaken misery of neurotic escape seen here in shadowed dusted depression of time's corners. Our brains filter orgiastically with light-struck particles of world's-dust to define our refined taste for history-object sad-usage. Brainy back and looked at leg float dream like past

our visioned senses forming aesthetic veins and passionate ambitions.
We want, we need, we feel, we cry with these purchased forms as
diagrams for our various lusts. The combinations of shaped shadowed
feeling serve our damned drawing board hearts. Here in the lined
corners dark we join with shape and form to find our meaning, see
ourselves and breathe another feeling.

Scene 69. Slightly wandering camera.
G & G looking out study front window. Text:

Bhunas and bricks
Moss and mouldings
Clapboard and keystones
Tiles and tar
Windows and water pipes
Leaves and leather
Buddleia and brown paint
Willow herb and workers
Curtains and cracked glass
Dust and design
Gutters and glass
Burglar alarms and boxes

Scene 70a. Slightly wandering camera.
G & G looking out study back window. Text:

Asbestos and Aldgate
Spitalfields and spire
Branches and banks
Ivy and iron
Barbed wire and bushes
Trunks and tiles
Sky-lights and scrap metal
Pigeons and pillars
Pub and piles of wood
Offices and old chimneys
Markets and motor-cars

Scene 77. Still life with two glasses being filled and refilled,
alternated with stormy sky shots.
Sound skies: Wind in trees. Sound still life: Text:

The drinks were poured
We picked two up
The wine was very good
It was all so very ghastly
That we drank as much as we could
Down came the neck
Up came the bottom
The stuff again it poured
Until it came to us again
And our two heads did roar.

There is not so much wine for us
But we feel it works the same
If we drink at least four bottles
And then we are born again
It makes you groan and stroll away
To the land of stormy skies
For it needs us more
Than hand can pour
In its especially horrible way.

When the bottle comes attacking
We are ready for the fight
For we understand this enemy
Who comes most time at night
He comes with stealth and waving
As if a real true friend
But after a night of friendship
We can do him in the end.

Scene 80. *Mad* (G & G photo-piece, face in studio close-up).
Text (read by uneducated person):

I am the mad man that nobody loves. My hair is filthy with grease because no one cares for me. My mother has left me behind in this wonderful state to look at you like this. My teeth are rotten and I don't have nothing to care because I stumble to corner to corner and every place is my place of rest. The eyes are bad and I cannot see very well but it doesn't matter because I have nothing to care. I was in the war and got hurt twice, but I had no friends. But I love my Queen and Country and I don't hate anyone because I don't know anyone so how can I?

Scene 85. Text:

This proud pressed life in agony of tortured pride. We love our pride with time. The right righteous rightness of our rightness roots us in firm thoughts of fertile glowing thought. Our thoughts are all of pride in time. Cured of unproud disease we, pressed for time, are now embalmed in pride.

Scene 88. Branch of leaves reflected in water moving oddly (Studio). Text:

Death's hard buddleia beauty here reflected. Green leaves in a black buddleia picture act out their coloured moods. We wish, we see, we do not understand, and then small piece comes clear. These dance/death movements show us how to be with beauty on our happiness. The season of the leaves unfolds sad story of love – time for us to compare with our limbed brainy own. Its life, our life, its shape, our shape, its smell, its sex, its form, its colour are all ours. Its going, its coming, end, and wish to dance for its meaning for us is so human, is like us reflected in our pool.

Scene 89. Slow pan from base to top of National Westminster
Bank building at night. Text:

With fine-brained ghastliness of good intentions each fitting part fits in and tunes to the rising whole. Sweet delicate massiveness of purpose and desire. Twinkling compartment/cells of energy inspire us with blood/thoughts. A thousand people whizzing with their blood from cell to cell, another thousand heavy fixed hard to desk with work for pleasure ambition. Some for their first day and some for their last. Rot on for us dear lighted sign of life, proved good and get loved as a form.

> **Scene 92.** Still life with vase of flowers, copy of *Dark Shadow*, copy of *Side by Side* (books by G & G). Picture in frame, foreign fruits, elephant's foot tray, burning cigarette in ashtray. Camera is fixed but light source changes all time to explore the 'landscape'. Text:

The manly human landscape of the cultivated person. Superior meanings on grand scale shown in detailed coloured brilliance. Nature tamed and ordered as is proper resting in tamed clay subservient and loyal, or sitting on tamed beast cut-up and carved to our man's use. We eat for body brain and progress, selfless with driven superior ambition for the control. Pictured classic man's friendship tamed and enframed for all, an object for all use, extreme in beauty's meaning, fixed, slavish and controlled. Our written word of intellect fixed hard in inks and bondaged in bindings fiercely wrenched from history's died-on form. The page on page rigidity cut straight/harvested and stacked in perfect number-order on its cooked clay, glass-glazed imprisoned bed the weed-leaves cylinders of form burns, its spirit trail of progress smoke encircling all.

> **Scene 94.** Faded quickly in and out alternate G & G portraits (to collar). Text (spoken alternately by G & G):

We are unhealthy, middle-aged, dirty-minded, depressed, cynical, empty, tired-brained, seedy, rotten, dreaming, badly-behaved, ill-mannered, arrogant, intellectual, self-pitying, honest, successful, hard-working, thoughtful, artistic, religious, fascistic, blood-thirsty, teasing, destructive, ambitious, colourful, damned, stubborn, perverted and good. We are artists.

Scene 101: Bhuna body clothed. Details. Six shots. Texts:

MOUNTAIN EVERLASTING is a low short creeping perennial with
rooting runners. The leaves are whitely woolly beneath, those in the
basal rosette having the broadest near tips.

COMMON CUDWEED is a low short annual covered with silvery
sometimes yellowish hairs. It is widely branched with narrow oblong
leaves, wavy edged blunt or pointed spirally up stems, white tipped
red but appearing yellow from tips of sepal-like bacts.

YELLOW LOOSE is a medium tall downy perennial with broad leaves
lanceolate. Often black dotted with very short stalk. Flowers yellow in
whorls of two or four. Sepal teeth with reddish margins. Found in wet
places.

RED CLOVER is a variable erect low/tall hairy perennial. Leaves often
with a whitish crescent, stipules triangular and bristle pointed. The
uniform is hard reddish purple. Found in open woods.

Scene 105. Riverscape gently moving past. Sound: of glass breaking. Text:

The door is locked
The windows jammed
The building is quite dead
For no one comes here any more
Unless they are strange in the head.
The paint peels off
The wood rots on
The stone begins to crumble
A tramp sleeps here sometimes at night
After drinks and a dirty stumble.

Scene 108. Shots and cruise of decayed Victorian Church. Text:

Here is the lost Victorian world
That nobody seems to need
For years its spirit has drained away

And only the gargoyles bleed.
It stands up proud and defiant
So surreal in its beauty fine
Its excellence quite unchallenged
Like Augustus Pugin's shrine.

Scene 114. G & G in first-floor front room. Text:

George: How should we spend the day Gilbert?
Gilbert: Just now we are spending it looking at our walls. Don't you feel tired?
George: No, I don't feel tired. Why don't we go out and buy a vase?
Gilbert: Just now I like to see the falling of the light through the window. Should we go later to buy a vase?
George: Alright, that sounds fine. Do you still feel tired?
Gilbert: No, let's go now and buy a terracotta vase. I like them very much, do you?
George: Yes, terribly, I think they look so high-minded. What do you like about them?
Gilbert: I like very much the earth colour and the extreme coloured lines. Do you prefer the geometric ones or the Greek type ones?
George: I prefer the large geometric ones but I also like medium Greek ones. What else could we buy?
Gilbert: Let's buy a nice Arthurian chair.
George: What a good idea! Should we have lunch and then go shopping or should we go shopping first?
Gilbert: Let's have lunch now and go shopping later. Then we will be more relaxed to decide about what to buy. Are you ready to go?
George: Absolutely, yes.

Scene 118. Yard filmed from the studio. Text and natural sound:

Here with struggled weeds and planted ivy our various thoughts grow gently. Perversion of plant life threads delicately our intellect. Green friends for us to play with and care for. Moist pubic moss and dragon sow-thistle with milk bitter juice combine to express with us our feelings. Purple Chinese elegance with chickweed fluted adderwort mix tones and thoughts and structures for our bad games with people-study.

Scene 119. Panorama of London taken from train on Broad Street Line.
Texts (spoken at brief intervals):

Spital
Lamb
Calvin
Fleur-de-lis
Quaker
Holywell
Snowdon
Redchurch
New Inn
Basin
Redvers
Cotton
Henry
Mildmay
Wallace
Madras
Wheelwright
Copenhagen
Cramer
St Pancras
Hertland
Geffrye
Haggerstone
Whiston
Labernum
Dunston
Clarissa
Brownlow
Mortimer
Lavender
Ridley
Canonbury
Barnsbury
Huntingdon
Ponder

Thornhill
Chalfont
Delhi
Havelock
Royal
Provost
Prince of Wales
Gaisford
Gopse Oak
Arthur

Scene 121. Close-up of yellow and white chrysanthemum heads
against black background. Text:

Vast purity of privileged beauty, we love you, cruel behaviour is your
pleasured way with white cleanliness magnificent and yellow well-born
educated calm we follow you for fortune and whipped by ambition cling
to your progress. Sweat-stinging leather cuts add tortured sacrifice
satisfaction to our obedience to your order. Your way is as hard as we
are blood-hard with rigid-brained resolution. Tied ever to your forward
moving wheels we circle in ecstasy dizzy with your rule of beauty. We
are the slaves of beauty.

Scene 126. Alternate fade in/out G & G heads with closed eyes. Text:

Wet-dreamed perverted thoughts pervade the worried restless workers'
sleepy heads. Release in realistic pictures of near impossible behaviour
flooding through the heads with stinking deliciousness of sex. Good
cruelty and stupidity of fornication blend noisily with strange new
actions. Wet sticky limb on face, on leg, on back, roll into turgid
tableaus of our troubled imagination. Beauty rides sharp-wheeled over
all cutting paths for changed order and arrangements. We dream of
youth, we dream of nights, we dream of days. We dream our dreams
away.

Scene 127. Still life of foreign fruits on black cloth background.
Fixed camera but fruits moving by means of hand under cloth.
Extreme lighting. Text:

Here in the dreamland of our anxious night the fruits behave. They speak and turn and roll with us with unending orgasms. Incest with varieties proud in main line pedigree, distorted in closed thought and separated sense. Life in the cut-down object pieces groans for new turns and movements frustrated with their limited beings, the bump together yearning for new chance inaction. Heavy with doomed history, optimistic with their cranky dream, they push fruitily on through the orgiastic old hours. With us they love and we through their night-dream love, reason with our passion. Strange weights, textures, flesh and seed move here for the scream of reason.

Scene 161. Alternate G & G faces against white background.
Pull back to both together. Text:

This is the world
This is our end
This is our world
And this is the end.

Gilbert & George: Interview with Mark Francis 1981

First published in 1981 by the Whitechapel Art Gallery, London, as a leaflet to accompany the artists' exhibition *The Photo-Pieces 1980–1981*, in which no distinction is made between the speakers in the artists' statements.

You have been together since 1968, and the exhibition consists of photo-pieces from the last ten years. Would you say that the photo-pieces form a central core to your work, or that they are only one part of work which is made in many different forms?

It became a main form from early times onwards.

We started drawing, but we always liked photography more. We always wanted to make them big but we didn't manage to find a form to do them big. That's why we started with groups – to make them bigger.

Are art galleries a good place to show your pieces or would you like to show them in other places, like churches for example?

Art galleries and museums appeal to us.

I imagine they could look almost like stained-glass windows.

Yes, the show looks like some extraordinary modern cathedral.

Is all your work, in a sense, a message?

Yes, from the first day, it doesn't matter what form we use.

The form is just the servant of the message.

Messages to whom?

To the viewer.

We rather grandly think to the world, but it's not always to the world.

What are the messages of? The way you see the world?

Our aesthetics, our views.

Our understandings, our colours. Though it changes from work to work, from period to period. All to do with our feelings and thoughts mainly. That's all one has anyway.

In what way do the images of things stand for your feelings?

We have a flower maybe because we believe in the purity of flowers, a symbol for us. A lot of the material is symbolic.

Or they are things that agree with us. We find things in the world that agree with the way we feel or think, therefore we can use them as examples. They are always things that we come across, things that are common to us. We don't exclude anything, we like the whole.

Sometimes we do represent disturbed times...

If that is the case.

*Can you describe the time when you first wanted to put these other
things in your pictures? For a few years there were...*
Us in nature or the empty house, us around the inside.
It was very simple and more formal. We felt that ourselves as Living
Sculptures was as much as we wanted to say to people. We were more
shy of our own feelings, much less worldly at that time. Innocent in
some ways, and ourselves with a background either nature...
Or inside the house.
Or in a bar, then we became more worldly.
And more disturbed.
*Did the pieces of you in the house reflect more desolate kinds of
feelings?*
The ones in the house are more desperate, but it's still more of an
exterior idea.
We still like to go back to that, we still like the idea of the person in
the house.
Absolutely.
We would never like to take that away.
Pieces of grain in the wood can also express things for you.
Mullah [1980], yes, given the right moment we can use anything.
But you've never actually made things in wood?
Only as students. When we actually started we didn't, we were left with
ourselves. It was very simple. We left school, we didn't have anything to
do, no studio. We were the art. That's how we started.
One thing that is absent from your work is any images of women.
It's not the only thing that's absent. It's too immediately sexy or
desirable for such an enormous section of the population, it would be
misleading.
It would be misleading. People become more like objects the way we
use them. There is a certain kind of man that we use, very limited. We
can't use every person.
Very particular.
*What are the feelings that the derelicts, the down-and-outs,
express for you?*
We like them, they are outside and they are more real.
Are the young people outside in the same sort of way?
There are a lot of people completely outside. They have a certain
freshness that is outside the normal middle-class person, and it's much
more interesting.

That's what we admire.

They are more fresh in what they say, more philosophical. What they come out with is very interesting. They look as though they agree with us, their expression. You can always find yourself in other people in various ways. Sometimes they are how you would like to be, the way you think or dream or plan to be.

Yes, even we feel we are completely outside, like lost kids or tramps. The art is our outside. Even when we go to galleries.

We get our dole money from galleries.

[Laughter.]

> *So you see yourselves in an extreme position in a similar*
> *kind of way?*

We see ourselves in a very extreme position in every way.

> *Do you think an artist should have an extreme point-of-view?*

You have to be untypical or you wouldn't try to do something different as an artist.

Then you'd either not be an artist or you'd be a run-of-the-mill artist. You can only do what you can't help doing so it's dependent on that completely.

> *Can you say then at what point you saw yourselves as artists, as*
> *artists together? Do you think artists are born or find themselves?*

Nobody knows that. Certainly it's a lot to do with talent. That is obviously inborn.

> *Do the two of you express one vision?*

I would say so.

It's our joint image that is interesting for us That's the only thing we're interested in.

It's an amazing power. It becomes like a fortress, much bigger than one person.

> *Are there any artists you like?*

We like the paintings of H. S. Tuke.

He was a late nineteenth-century person who lived in Cornwall, and always painted sailors and people connected with the sea.

How he framed them up was so incredibly modern, like snapshots.

Very bizarre compositions.

Always cut in pieces.

Very fresh and unusual, completely different from his contemporaries.

Very good moralistic subjects always. *All Hands to the Pump*, one's called.

Landseer we like.

Is your art particularly English, or more wide than that?
Our art is as English as England is anyway global. If you want to live in
the world this is the place. It's the only place where you have a total
grasp of the whole world. Whatever is happening in every country you
can feel it in London. Every single building, every single person, every
scratch on a tree, is global because it is one of the most modern places
in the world.
I never see the Englishness in it.
I think that's largely a misunderstanding.
Maybe there's Brick Lane in it.
It could also be Karachi.
We never did a piece outside London.
We have places like Khartoum in our head already. We have a dream,
a feeling, an imagination of things like that. I'm sure we would find it
there.
That's why we like so much Hong Kong movies, because they represent
a totally different world and we know it. Especially in the very old
musicals and stuff like that, based in Ancient China, old men with
pigtails and all those ideals, all dress up in white. Fighting for freedom.
Fantastic people. We have a very particular idea of foreign which is of
big interest to us.

What sort of idea is that?
There is a lot of foreign stuff in us. Ever since we went to Bangkok, that
was the start of that. You see different ideals that we prefer. We liked
Japan the first time because of the old ideals.

Do you think the English have lost what they had?
Not at all.
England still does stand for a tremendous amount. It's an amazing
place.
A lot of individualism here.

Would you like to make an art of wide appeal?
We would like that.
Popularity is all very well inasmuch as it can be popular but we
wouldn't like to do popular things, and we wouldn't want to become
popular novelists, or illustrators or something. We want as many people
to see our work for what it is.

Because they express your feelings?

Yes, it's our only driving force, to shout as loud as possible for as long as
possible.

> *Can I go back to an earlier time? After you'd done the pieces in the*
> *landscape, there's a whole series which showed you drinking.*

1973–4, that's the time.
We were in bars – Bethnal Green Road, Liverpool Street, or down
Commercial Road. It was a very destructive time for us.
We were exploring drunkenness really.
In the art world everybody drinks. It's a very big part of art but they
always do the next day beautiful flowers even if they are blind drunk.
So we tried to use that as a subject. In fine art it's not accepted, but in
plays, in Shakespeare, drunkenness is part of living.
It's probably the most common subject of all time. Every poet...

> *Was it a reflection of the way of life you were leading at that time?*

Yes, it was the first time we got drunk. In fact we were tee-total,
we still are.
We hardly ever drink. On the rare occasions when we see people or
something. We never have a beer with lunch, always tea.
In fact we are completely tee-total, nobody would believe it but it's
true.
Mind you, on the rare occasions we do, we make up for lost time.
Let's make some more tea, George.
Would you like a nice hot cup of tea?

GILBERT & GEORGE

CRUSADE

AN EXHIBITION OF POST CARD PIECES

13 January to 13 February 1982

Private View Tuesday 12 January 4 to 7 pm

Anthony d'Offay
23 Dering Street New Bond Street London W1
01-499 4695

What is a Post Card Piece?

The form of the Post Card Piece lends itself to the expression of finer feelings, stirring thoughts and beautiful views.

Through our hearts, brains and bodies the cards crystallise into our crosses of Monarchical, Christian, Nationalistic, Violent, Pagan, Floral, Sexual Post Card Pieces.

They are our shields, our swords, our emblem, our vision, our tombstone and our life-masks.

GILBERT AND GEORGE
1981

Mint Prince, 1981, 44½ x 37 ins.

What is a Post Card Piece?

The form of the Post Card Piece lends itself to the expression of finer feelings, stirring thoughts and beautiful views.

Through our hearts, brains and bodies the cards crystallise into our crosses of Monarchical, Christian, Nationalistic, Violent, Pagan, Floral, Sexual Post Card Pieces.

They are our shields, our swords, our emblem, our vision, our tombstone and our life-masks.

GILBERT AND GEORGE
1981

Gilbert & George: Interview with Gordon Burn 1981

Previously unpublished.

Gilbert: We never say no. We try never to...
George: We don't like to polish up. It's not ever good if you polish something up.
Gilbert: We never examine ourselves in that way, We just *accept* it... We have our ideas that we are interested in. And that's our art. Our new thoughts that we get from the street or wherever we go. Art we have no interest in whatsoever.
George: Our inspiration is not to be found in that world anyway. Our inspiration is outside of galleries and museums. Absolutely. I mean, if we went to a museum, we are more likely to be inspired by the doorman or something, rather than what's inside. We've never been inspired by other people's art.
   When did you begin to steer away from drink?
Gilbert: We never did drink a lot. Only when we meet people. But if we're alone we never drink.
George: We never go to pubs.
Gilbert: Never! Not once.
George: Only with people. Alone we never even have half a pint of bitter. We've no interest really in that.
Gilbert: We used to go out with people. But never alone. Never. We don't have any time left.
George: Absolutely.
Gilbert: The actual people who are important are very, very few.
   You don't go dancing any more?
George: Hardly ever. I can't think of the last time we danced. We hardly go out even to walk, many days.
Gilbert: We are completely isolated.
George: A normal Sunday we would be working... And the amount of inspiration one needs is very, very little, in fact. One doesn't have to scout around for three weeks. One second's looking out the window is enough to...
Gilbert: The main thing is, we don't have time to do the pieces any more.
George: We like to say what we want to say to the world as much as we can, for as long as we can... Carry On Screaming.

Gilbert: We are very interested in that. In messages.

George: After all, we only have eighty more years or whatever it is. It's not a lot. More tea?

People get in the way of the work. Unannounced guests are not welcome?

George: We always look out of the window first to see it isn't somebody we're not expecting. We have one very quiet window we can lift.

Tell me about the Pugin and the Christopher Dresser – the vases and furniture you've started collecting.

George: They came from pieces more. We always find things that agree with us. We like to buy things that support what we already think.

Gilbert: We like very much recently symbolic art. Symbolic. That's why we started to collect furniture with symbolic...

George: Yes, we're more and more and more interested in meaning. That's our biggest interest, really. As opposed to form.

Gilbert: Even the colours used are always symbolic.

George: We were more involved with form in earlier times, to a certain extent. Now the form is less dominant.

Gilbert: Everybody just mentions how powerful our shows are. Visually. They are frightened. It's true. All over.

George: It's important that they feel affected, that it means something to them. Not just that they *liked* the colours or liked the show... That's why we're so interested in this film [*The World of Gilbert & George*, see page 98]. Because that is an amazing form. More mad, more bombastic, fantastic...

Gilbert: Overpowering... We like to affect people with our art. Recently we manage to get through much more. Especially to the young people.

George: The galleries always remark that.

Gilbert: Our form is a more direct language to people. They can understand it. We always wanted to do that. Have a simple language that everybody can understand.

George: A piece like *Speaking Youth* [1981] doesn't depend on a knowledge of Cubism or Vorticism or anything else. It doesn't require any specialised knowledge.

Gilbert: Nothing.

George: We wouldn't like that... You always have wankers. But you can always convert them. We do. Professional people in the art world are only interested in the public reaction anyway. Never in their own. They don't have a reaction of their own.

Gilbert: They never know.

George: Museum curators only know what the show means to them after the opening of the show when the people start coming. When you get fifty-thousand road-sweepers coming in who are crazy about it, then they're keen alright. Amazing good toffy-nosed theories immediately. They can see that, independent of them, the show works. Without their permission.

Gilbert: We have always been based on that. We never need any art person.

George: A lot of art absolutely needs specialised professional people to say that it's good in order that it can exist, because nobody else would know.

You have talked in the past about the growing tendency for you not to be invited to art world do's.

Gilbert: We never go… We dislike that stuff. It has nothing to do with art.

George: It's not we who are badly behaved anyway. It's just that they don't understand alcohol, that's all. They think alcohol's for standing around and behaving as though it's water. Alcohol is for getting drunk. That's what it's for. It's silly if you just stand there all evening, all elegant. You might as well not be drinking.

People are frightened of you?

Gilbert: We do have a wall around ourselves. We have to protect ourselves.

George: Even we have stuff within ourselves that does disturb people, I would say. Very much.

Gilbert: Oh yes.

George: From seeing us, or hearing a snippet of conversation or something. Many times when we're in restaurants or in public places, very anonymously dressed, very plainly dressed, we always realise that people are talking about us, or that there's some nonsense going on about us.

Gilbert: Always. We always disturb people. It doesn't matter where we go.

George: What we represent is disturbing to a *lot* of people. [Giggles from Gilbert.] They're not used to that. We are not grey anonymous liberal softies.

Gilbert: A lot of people don't like us because we are very clear in what we accept and don't accept. Our views are very strict.
George: On the whole, people like easy-going people, don't they? That's more acceptable.

Why do you think some people in England are calling you fascists?
George: It's a life-force. It's a life-force we accept very much.
Gilbert: You could say that Christian *goodness* is fascistic. What people used to believe was *good* – religion – you could say that is fascistic. Many people would say so.
George: I mean, we're only here because of the World War II turmoil of fascism anyway. Life doesn't exist without it... Without the good works of the people that the extreme left call fascist there wouldn't even be a civilisation. These anti-fascists never built anything. The Anti-Nazi League never created anything. It is to do with destroying the other stuff; the conventional people that the Anti-Nazi League marchers like to call fascists. It is not a living force in itself. 'Down-with, down-with.' Renta-mobs. It's a negative, anti thing that's all.
Gilbert: For the Anti-Nazi League all of the people who run the world are 'fascist'.
George: 'Western power'. It is often said by young people that fascism led to the concentration camps. In fact, they came from the National Socialists/Nazis. That's what the left never want to hear. Extermination camps had nothing to do with Fascism.
Gilbert: They had to *do* with the left, in fact. Because Nazis in Germany belonged to the National Socialist Party.
George: The most famous extermination camp was in fact Socialist. Not right-wing... That's why it's called right. Because it's the right side. [Laughter.] That's where it gets its name from.

Perhaps we should talk about your pictures Four Knights, Bunhill
    Knight, Whitecross Knight, *and so on...*
Gilbert: We like the idea to lift up completely normal people.
George: Higher spirits. Timeless. That is what man really is, and always will be like that... It's very old-fashioned to oppose that in a way. The power that is in young people like that is fantastic. Amazing. We like to honour that in our work.

The papers have inevitably implied that you are pro-National Front.
George: We're not against people saying that. We wouldn't go out of our way to decry the National Front. It's just a quite insignificant political party.

124

*But they are advocating violence against your Asian neighbours
here.*

George: Pakistanis lead fuller lives than anybody else. My God,
some are even going to public schools. *Expensive* public schools.
They're the richest people in the whole of the street here. They
drive off in cars to the beautiful suburbs. Absolutely. They can earn
super-money.

Gilbert: Some are the most brutal people that we ever met.

George: 'Is it to my advantage?' they ask themselves every single
second. They're not like us, thinking these kind, Christian, historical
things. Courteous and polite...

Gilbert: More timeless. More to do with the spirit...

George: We're not based anyway just on the moment. We're based
on everything so far, *plus* the moment. We don't think just exactly in
this... day.

Do you still think of what you do as sculpture?

George: We're not so interested in definitions any more.

When did that start to disappear?

George: I suppose in the mid-Seventies probably, '74 – '75. People got
too interested in that. 'What is sculpture?' They don't even see what's
in the picture any more. They don't even see what's there.

Gilbert: Even the public are mystified if we say: 'These photo-pieces
are sculpture.' We don't like that. We hate all these academics in art,
and aesthetics and so on...

George: We gave a lot of people freedom to make art with meaning,
because that was away completely in the early Seventies. You could
only concentrate on form. The meaning had to be removed totally –
Minimal, Conceptual...

Gilbert: That's why we had a very difficult time.

George: We emerged at a time when 'meaning' was virtually a dirty
word. The picture or the sculpture had to be totally devoid of meaning.
We were consciously fighting back against that. We had to. To establish
our freedom to do that.

I notice that you now own a television.

George: We restrict ourselves to half an hour in the evenings.
Coronation Street we watch. That is our favourite. *Songs of Praise.*

[The doorbell rings. It is Danny, the drunk from the film.]

Gilbert: 'But I'm a happy drunk. I'm an honest drunk. And I'll be drunk

the day I die.' That's what he said. 'I am the madman who nobody loves
– but I'm quite intelligent.'
George: 'Happiness – now tell me if I'm right; you're quite bright –
happiness is misery, isn't it?' Amazing stuff, yes? Completely serious.
    Why do you like people like him – you clearly do.
George: It's not a question of 'liking'. We can tailor it all in to our
message.
Gilbert: I think there is much bigger philosophy in people like that.
There is more life in them. They are *outside*. Outside the system. We
like all the people that are outside the system, we realised.
George: All these physically inferior, mentally-retarded splendid
people – all perfectly alright. No problem at all. Then we've got this one
educated one, with a woolly hairstyle, yes? And he said: 'My life so far?
Quite interesting. Met a lot of interesting people, been to a lot of
interesting places, but in general I don't describe my life so far to a
camera.' Amazing. And the others did it so splendidly.
Gilbert: We are outside the system, like the drunks. And the ones who
are *not*, they are bad artists.
George: Certainly… We're not anti-establishment or anything like that.
    Have you always been incapable of having what what you call
    'normal' relationships?
Gilbert: I never want that. I never had that before, even… I don't want
to be normal with normal relationships. I have absolutely no interest in
people in that way.
George: The gulf between people is very important. They would be
telling us everything. We have to keep completely free brains.
Independent. One-way, completely. We like to look at them under our
microscope and say what we want to say. Wicked scientists, if you like,
hmmm?
Gilbert: We are not interested in other people's views. We never have.
Not for one second, in fact. Nobody… For many years they thought we
had to do with *nothing*.
George: They thought our art had no connection with anything. They
didn't know what it meant or what it was about or anything. Now they
all fight amongst each other with more and more elaborate theories.
Gilbert: We hate that generation [of Lawrence Gowing]. *Hate* it. They
never did *any*-thing.
George: So patronising. Nationalised their whole life. They're civil

servants, all sitting on committees together. Comfortable lives.

Gilbert: First, they are foreign wankers. Every one of that generation. Totally.

George: They all talk about Monet or Manet or these lock-jaw names. Disgusting. Art from wine-growing countries. It's true. That's all they support.

Gilbert: That was the biggest mistake of English artists. And even the pop generation had a lot to do with that, looking towards America.

George: New York – it's an English city anyway. It's part of England's heritage. But these other people, they go over and they are just overwhelmed by it in a completely idiotic way.

Gilbert: And they are overwhelmed without knowing. Without knowing. It's incredible. Amazing big disease.

George: 'It's a very nice place.' The Americans think that's the most offensive thing you can say about it. They hate it. They ask you if you've seen the latest Terry-Thomas film. It's just a charming, old-fashioned English place.

> *But what about the [New York] club you used to like to visit called The Toilet? And the fist-fucking magazines that you can get there but that you can't get here?*

George: We had an interest in that side of life and so found things to help us follow our interests. Everything is part of our art anyway. We exclude *nothing*. Just at that time we were more centred on that.

Gilbert: We still drink. Every time we go out we are completely smashed. We get drunk when we drink. Immediately. But we don't drink – whatyoucallit – to have a nice time. Wine with luncheon or something... That is why the old generation we dislike very much. That is why we don't ever want to meet them. We are much more famous in other countries than in England. In America we are very, very famous, in New York. They are the biggest buyers of our art. Young people we love. But the old queens in museums...

George: If no one can understand it except them and their friends, then they think it's superior. And better, therefore.

Gilbert: We would like to do plays.

George: We'd do good ones. Very good ones, I'm sure.

[A man appears on the upper ledge of a house opposite.]

George: He's dicing with life. D'you see? It's very dangerous. He might fall off before we finish our tea... People are very embarrassing. Some

people are proud. Some people are proud and shy. We're the proud and shy ones... We normally reserve our social life for when we have to go to an opening of some sort. A social obligation to go to an opening. We save it all up and channel all our bad behaviour into that one evening, and contain it, yes? Get drunk, mess the trousers, and go home.
Gilbert: It's exactly that.

> *The influence of your work is becoming increasingly obvious in commercial art, album covers and so on.*

George: The metallised heads. That was unbelievable for that time. I mean, we did the pieces [*Singing Sculpture*] in the pop world, with The Who and people... Pop festivals, the Lyceum, the Marquee... It's not so obvious in England, the effect we had on popular culture. But on the Continent people are very aware of that.
Gilbert: Every artist tries to put together different subjects; they never know how to do it. And we know exactly, because square-by-square we can do it.
George: It's the standard largest-size cut of photographic paper. But we found we can use that combination to do an endless piece. A 150-part piece, or a two-part piece. Endless combination. Much more graphic and direct and powerful.
Gilbert: And the transport is absolutely nothing. Nobody has such a big show, so many pieces. Our drawing pieces even used to be done like that. In sheets.
George: Everything else is like that anyway. A house is just built up out of bricks. One's life is just built up of days and minutes and stuff.

> *Was it Wittgenstein who...*

George: Don't mention foreigners in this house! [Laughter.]
Gilbert: It is amazing the disease of English people to mention foreigners all the time. It makes me mad. It is so destructive to the English.
George: To destroy Britain. That is the only intention.
Gilbert: In art, just every writing is only to do with mentioning foreign names. Every single piece of writing. Just *incredible*. Even in Victorian times they had so many artists who were so brilliant. That era hasn't been rediscovered yet. But it was just so rich. That has been completely forgotten because of stupid... The Bloomsbury Group. They were the first foreign wankers.
George: *Since Cézanne*. Bell's most famous book. It is the most

poisonous title. You should go to prison for that in a good country.
Absolutely.
Gilbert: That was our biggest success. To become completely
independent of every other artist.
George: Even Lesley Waddington refers to all his English artists as 'the
English Picabia' or the English-something-else. Every time. Terrible.
Gilbert: That we feel is the biggest disease here. We could smash him in
his face for saying that. We would, if he would say that of us. *Absolutely*.
George: Artists on the whole are very shy to say something. We answer
as straight as we can. They're all protecting the reputation of their
intellect, they feel. That's the idea. People think they are very intelligent artists, and they must not destroy that. If somebody thinks we're
idiotic, they can think we're idiotic, certainly. What we will not tolerate
is people saying that they don't accept our work. We don't tolerate that
at all. We don't allow people to say that to us. Absolutely not. Most
people know that they shouldn't say that to us.
Gilbert: We cut them off totally.
George: It's completely uninteresting that somebody doesn't accept our
work. It's a completely stupid idea anyway.
Gilbert: They have stupid heads.
George: I can't think of the last time somebody said that. I'm very good
at replying. I just say, 'well you're an old pig, aren't you?' That's a good
reply. It scares the knickers off them immediately.
Gilbert: They don't *know* what they think. That's the amazing thing.
They don't know. They're pretending. Thay have opinions from other
people.
George: They're protecting themselves, usually. They're afraid that
they'll appear a stupid person if they say that they do accept your work.
Gilbert: Especially here in England, they never want to have a view,
straight out. If you are friends with, like, people at the Tate, that's
finished. You have to be outside attacking them, in a way. Every second.
George: We're very discriminated against there. From beginning to
end. To this day. What was it they said? We were taking the mickey out
of English manners. Incredible, hmmm? Such a lower-class idiotic
thing to say... They like to like it, and they don't like to like us in that
way. Our art is not for the liking classes to like. We don't do it for that.
It's not the reason. Our pieces aren't even likeable in that way.
Gilbert: Boy-Scout art.

George: Druid art... It's quite wrong that they don't have a very, very good representation of our work [at the Tate].
Gilbert: *Nationalised idiots!* They are just that. Just trying to make a living out of it.
George: Cosy lives they want. No trouble.
Gilbert: They always water it down. From the first day that we did art here they try to water us down... They're ashamed of life. I come from a very artistic family. They accept all art.

Have you ever seriously considered having a different base from which to work?

George: We've never thought of living somewhere else, no. It's the most realistic place to live, isn't it, really? It's the best place to see the world from. Whatever happens in London is the same as the world is. Whereas whatever happens in Zurich is just to do with Zurich. London *is* the world in that way. Every rotten corner, every person in the street is a world statement. 'Alright boys!' they say to us. Amazing nice. A country house in Bulawayo would be alright. Really. [Giggles and laughter.] That would be exciting, I must say. Certainly. That would be quite inspiring. In the Sudan or somewhere. I thought you knew we were Africa crazy. Down-town Johannesburg would be lovely. We're more interested in the white man's African culture in a way. Africa's the garden of England. England's allotment. Unfortunately we have no time to travel. We only go where we have exhibitions, really.
Gilbert: I would like to go to Khartoum as a visitor. Stay in a nice hotel. Comfortable. I don't like uncomfortable places.
George: Amazing dreary... But we've become *more worldly-wise,* you could say.
Gilbert: And patriotism. I think that was one of the best things. We managed to crystallise that. We managed to kill off a lot of clichés, for us, in art. For instance, that always everything in art has to be related to some other art.
George: Even artists on television have to say they're influenced by some foreigner. Shows they're good if they say that. Monet: some stupid old French tart having a picnic on a bit of rotten grass beside some foreign dirty river. And they say that is better than Bacon? That is *amazing.* Shocking, really. Some disgusting French bread sticking out of some horrible basket... They don't even know an English name, half of them.

Gilbert: Landseer. It was so heavy with meaning. Very artistic. But at the moment they just laugh at him.

George: Now if they think about Landseer, they just think he's some nonsense old bourgeois capitalist nineteenth-century imperialist rubbish.

Gilbert: We want to be completely outside with – whatyoucall – hooligans and tramps. We don't want to be put inside. Not at all. I always felt that they are not radical enough here.

George: They're nice artists, people like that. That's exactly what they are. Limited down to doing the right stuff.

Gilbert: We know so well that we have nothing to lose. It was very good, because we had so many enemies in the seventies that it made us very, very strong. We could see much more clearly in our heads what we wanted to do because of that.

George: [Smirking.] We have to be on the top of the bus, with the skinheads.

London's Living Sculpture: Interview with Robert Becker 1982

First published in *Interview*, vol. 13, no. 8, 1982, pp. 63–67.

You two met in art school?
Gilbert: We were in the same class. Then we started to show pieces together as students – objects.
How long is art school?
George: I think Gilbert went to school for eleven or twelve years, and I went for seven years. I don't really know what you learn in art school. We hate art school. I don't think it has anything to do with art. Art is completely abstract, intellectual, and you cannot learn it.
There aren't certain givens – the history of art?
George: Who wants to know the history of art?
Gilbert: We don't need to know the history of art to do art.
George: Even though I'm sure we are more familiar with the history of art than anyone else we know.
Gilbert: We never go to museums.
But you did go to art school.
George: We couldn't help it. We were dragged along.
Can you tell me how you spend an average day?
Gilbert: We are working.
George: The film explains our day pretty well. Did you see the film?
Yes, I did, and I enjoyed it very much.
George: Among other things it explains how we spend our days.
Gilbert: Our life is intellectual life. We don't like art – art we don't like.
George: We're into refinement of life more and more.
Gilbert: We think art *is* life. That is what we are trying to do.
That sounds like Oscar Wilde.
George: We're great fans of Oscar Wilde. He was brilliant.
He suggested that life is an art – living life is an art.
George: I'm sure it's true.
Gilbert: We never believed that you could learn art. We don't believe that. Good art is completely vital for life.
I enjoyed your movie, but there were things I didn't grasp entirely.
George: We like to be very clear when we speak in a form, whether it's in an exhibition or a film – our main interest is to speak very clearly to the viewer.

Is it very important that everyone understands what you're doing?
George: As much as possible. We are anti-obscure. We hate obscurity in
art. We like direct contact.

*Do you think that certain forms or methods of communication are
more obscure than others?*
George: Yes. The twentieth century, certainly in Western culture, gave
way to the idea that, if you don't understand it, then it must be
interesting or good. We disagree with that entirely. We think that is
decadence – a cultural decadence. That you understand it is good.

Form is very important to your work.
George: Form is very important in that it is the servant of meaning.
We really believe that form is working *for* meaning. Whenever form
becomes boss it is decadent. Somebody was very interested to find out
what the pieces are trying to say. It was somebody who didn't
understand very well, and we became intensely bored – he wasn't
willing to stand in front of the picture as one did in the nineteenth
century, stand in front of the picture and see what happens. He couldn't
do that so he wanted to know from *us* what it meant. So we got very
angry, and, just to stop the questions coming, we said, 'Well, every work
we do means "fuck you". But we can't sell it very well if we just wrote
that, so we find a different way every time of saying that.' The disaster
was that it didn't shut him up. Then he got completely excited and
started looking at the pictures; at that moment, for the very first time.
Certainly every work of ours doesn't mean just that. But if a picture
doesn't say 'fuck you', it's no good anyway. It has to defy the viewer first
of all, then it can go on to say other things, of course. I think that's the
basic premise. The picture is better than the viewer, first. We hate the
idea of superior people going through the galleries, admiring this and
admiring that.
Gilbert: Ignoring it.
George: That's anti-culture, anti-life totally. They must not feel as
though they know something – then it's all wrecked. If someone says,
'How marvellous, beautiful. It's so much this or so much that', it's no
good. You want them to stand in front of the picture and say, 'What the
shitting hell does this mean to me?'

*I appreciate that because so much art now is being painted for
admiration.*
George: Admiration is anti-world.

So you really don't go to see paintings in galleries?
George: Hardly ever.
Gilbert: We never go to museums – maybe ten years ago.
Are you familiar with what is going on?
Gilbert: They're pushing it.
*For instance, the European and American 'expressionist' painting
that is meant for people to admire – no questions asked.*
George: We're anti-pictures for people.
What are pictures for people?
Gilbert: Pictures to put up.
George: Pictures that people want and like – we don't want that. Liking
– people can do that with their curtains and their carpets. We always
say that we produce our work with our thoughts and with our souls and
with our cocks – these are the three basic elements that we work with.
It's various combinations of these three things that go into each one.
Maybe one is made mainly with the cock. Maybe one is made a bit more
with the soul than the cock. Maybe one is more of the brain and more
cock and less soul – but it's those three things that we work with.
*What would you call the recent show at Sonnabend? [New Photo-
Pieces, Sonnabend Gallery, New York, 1980] There's a lot of cock
in that show.*
Gilbert: Not more than usually.
George: To date that's the most perfect blend for us – so far.
*I found it hard to leave the gallery because I couldn't come up with
conclusions – conclusions I'm used to making.*
George: Conclusion is death, anyway. If you're concluding then you're
dying. You don't especially want to die. It's a beautiful day – maybe
later in the day.
Have you shown your work elsewhere in America?
George: No.
Is there a reason for that?
George: No time.
I think your work is essential for people in this country to see.
Gilbert: We would like to show it to more people.
George: We will make a museum show starting in Baltimore.
Were you disciplined as children?
Gilbert: Yes, very.
George: It's a keynote to life.

Gilbert: Even a lot to do with morality. I was brought up Catholic and George a Methodist.

George: A Hottentot Methodist.

Gilbert: And that's the way we still are. We are very interested in morality these days. Good and bad.

George: Christ on the cross is the basis of our lives. It's the basis of our civilisation.

Gilbert: Even if we don't believe it.

Both in form and meaning?

George: Certainly. The form is taken for granted. The form is every house, every building, every hotel, every street, every car. And the meaning runs through from morning to night – 12 noon to 12 midnight.

Do you participate now in organised practice?

George: No, we would never do that.

Gilbert: We do pray. We don't go into church, but we do pray.

So you're faithful.

Gilbert: Yes, I am. I am faithful.

I want to ask you about messages.

Gilbert: We like messages.

Do you have a message?

Gilbert: Not a direct message. We think our art is full of messages.

Do you want to teach me something with your work?

George: Our work is educational.

Do you want to horrify me by showing me things I don't want to see?

George: We don't want or not want to horrify somebody. We don't exclude anything. We're lifelike. Our education is lifelike. We are anti-artifice.

It's documentary?

George: No, we don't like that.

Gilbert: We like to create – to create a message, not to document a message.

Are you aware of an audience when you're working?

Gilbert: Yes. We only do it for an audience. We are only interested in that, and we are very unhappy when they don't respond. We want people to respond.

Is there a specific – everyone is the audience?

Gilbert: Everyone, we like everyone.

George: Down to every Kikuyu warrior.

That's what I was going to ask, do you think the work goes further than Western Civilisation?
George: We try to do that, we always try to do that. We feel we've succeeded.

Are titles important?
George: Yes, extremely important.

If you had a show in Africa, would the titles be in the language of the country they were shown in?
Gilbert: Maybe, yes. We've always made them in English, but in Europe we don't have to change them. They are even much better. I think titles are very important, because you just have to hear the title and the image comes in front of you. And that's good. If not, you'd have to talk about 'that red picture over there'.
George: 'The green one in the corner', whereas if we say, *Life without End* you have an image, and we like that. We had enormous titles in 1977 when we did the Dirty Words pieces.
Gilbert: We always did the titles from the first moment, like *Shit* and *Cunt*. When Anthony d'Offay told us, remember, when we met him for the first time, what did we tell him? That we wanted to do art to be embarrassed. Art that embarrasses ourselves. I think we still do that. We are very embarrassed sometimes at what we are doing, and that's a good feeling. When it hurts, then it's true for us.

Can a difference be made in the world by art?
Gilbert: Yes, unbelievably, you can change everything.
George: It's the greatest living life force. Fine art, especially.
Gilbert: Everyone really benefits out of it, I believe, in a lot of different ways.
George: It's certainly a bigger life force than any political party is.

The key is to get people to sit and look.
Gilbert: I don't think they have to look – I don't think so. Not directly. Indirectly, it's a very strong force. Some people have to look, but not everybody.

What is an indirect medium?
Gilbert: I mean, everybody is affected very soon...

I see what you mean. So one person saw it and –
Gilbert: It's affecting them in all kinds of different ways. You can say the punk movement came from art. So you had the movement, then the songs, then the way of dressing, then the way of speaking.

What about the title 'Art for All'?
George: It's always been our slogan. We've been talking about it all the time. It's our general theme.
Gilbert: It was arranged innocently, but it's completely true and we always wanted it.
George: It became more true as time went on.
The art isn't just visual, is it?
George: Again, visual is form, and form is the servant to meaning. We're anti-art for posh people. We hate that.
Does art for posh people mean collectors who buy art and put it –
George: It's a certain intellect, a certain understanding. We're not anti-collector.
Gilbert: We like to influence people with our work.
George: We like to shout as loud as possible.
Gilbert: We are mostly interested in young people – we always have been. If they like it, we like it.
Have you always financially supported your work yourselves?
Gilbert: We've always supported ourselves with our work.
George: Private enterprise.
Is Art for All an enterprise?
George: Art for All is an entirely private enterprise.
Do you go to the same tailor?
George: Good heavens, of course. In the next house. We never shop for clothes. We hate buying clothes. We're completely bored by that. We hate it and we just do it when we have to.
Gilbert: We are quite unhappy people. I think we are very desperate, very desperate. We don't believe in an art world. We are not encircled by artists – by nobody in fact. We are completely alone. We see art people very, very seldom.
Is this by choice?
Gilbert: I don't know if it started out by choice, but it turned out that way.
I would think you'd have followers or friends who'd come by.
Gilbert: No, we don't have any friends.
George: We have no one. Nobody. We've certainly never met anybody who's more unhappy than ourselves.
Can you tell me something about where you live, your home?
Gilbert: It's a beautiful house, an eighteenth-century house, all wood-

panelled. We are big collectors of furniture, high gothic furniture and vases.

George: Especially vases; they're exquisite. We have many designs for vases.

Will you do them?

Gilbert: Oh, yes. We started designing vases in 1980.

I've noticed in some of the photographs I've seen of you that you were surrounded by beautiful furniture.

Gilbert: We got interested in nineteenth-century stuff, especially in a man called Pugin, who invented the new gothic in England and all over the world. He was so crazy and so mad. He wanted to destroy St Paul's and St Peter's in Rome. He hated everything.

George: He was like ourselves. He was anti-pagan. And homosexual, like ourselves.

How about ambiguity?

George: We're not interested in being ambiguous. It's like saying enigmatic. We've always thought that we try to make our work clearer and clearer. The more we do that, the more we hear people say 'enigmatic' at the same time. There must be some kind of contradiction involved. It's certainly not on our part – it's not our fault.

How many hours a day do you work on your art?

George: Just recently, preparing the exhibition, we were working twenty-one hours a day. We timed ourselves.

Did you have to rehearse the Living Sculpture pieces?

Gilbert: No, never. Nothing rehearsed – it's just arranged as a system and then done.

George: Lifted from our life.

Gilbert: We've never rehearsed anything.

Was the work just as much for you as it was for your audience?

Gilbert: Yes, very much. You really feel that you are in the world alone. It's a very incredible feeling. You really feel a person.

What do you say to yourself when you're sitting down for eight hours in the same position?

Gilbert: It's wonderful. A wonderful feeling.

Painful?

Gilbert: Pain is nice.

Don't you itch?

Gilbert: No. You can think. It's very fantastic.

It's important that an artist feel pain?
Gilbert: Yes, I do think so. I mean artists do feel pain everywhere.
What kind of pain is it?
Gilbert: They have to carry life with them.
George: Ordinary pain is very important.
Gilbert: If an artist is not unhappy, I never believe he is a good artist.
What is it, separation?
Gilbert: Sure. In the end we want to think about life, and that's why we are artists. I think that life in England is more painful. To be an artist is more painful. It may not be true, but it feels like that.
But you enjoy pain.
Gilbert: I don't know if I enjoy it, but we have to go through it.
George: We accept the realism of pain. We like that it is actual. We feel more of this world. To be soothed by a city, like being in New York, we feel is completely artificial, and we don't want it. We find it very nice, very wonderful, very kind – as visitors. We feel that it is artificial.
Gilbert: We like to be here.
George: We want to be punched on the nose, completely, by every single person who passes us in the street. Everyone you meet, you want to say, 'What the fuck are you looking at?' Then you know that you're alive. The rest is artificial.
Joy is artificial?
George: As far as we've found out, it seems impractical and without meaning. Maybe there is something in it, but we haven't seen it so far.
Gilbert: I think we've created our best works when we were very deeply unhappy.
You look happy.
Gilbert: I mean, everybody's happy. I'm smiling every second.
George: Even Jesus on the cross is smiling more or less.
How about reading?
Gilbert: I hate reading. I just can't concentrate. I don't like to be educated.
George: There are writers and there are readers, we belong in the writers' group. We wouldn't invite anyone into the studio to help us. We have a job. We keep that very clear. We do not participate in others' art.
Gilbert: We do the art, they do the looking.
Have you ever wanted to be something other than an artist?
Gilbert: George wanted to be Oscar Wilde.

George: My first ambition in life was to be Terry-Thomas, and my second was to be an artist.

Who is Terry-Thomas?

George: He was an amazing, marvellous English actor-comedian. He always had a long cigarette holder, and he had a big gap between his teeth. He joked about upper-class life. We bumped into him by chance years and years later in Australia.

How about you, Gilbert, did you have another ambition?

Gilbert: No. I always wanted to be an artist. I started when I was very small with figures. I was nine years old.

George: We're tart artists.

Does the art come first?

George: It depends on the time of day. We're either tart artists or artist tarts.

Morning Coffee with Gilbert & George:
Interview 1985

First published in *Square Peg*, London, 1985, pp. 20–22.

George: Help yourself to milk and sugar if you want.
> *A friend of mine sees you as 'the Morecambe and Wise of the art world'. Do you think this is justifiable?*

George: No, not at all. We wouldn't see that.
> *Is there no element of humour in your work at all? Are you absolutely serious?*

George: We're not conscious of creating humour in any way. In fact, in any case, one of us is not dead.

Gilbert: I think we are changing the idea of art.
> *Which is very serious...*

Gilbert: If not, we would not dedicate twenty-four hours a day to do it.
> *One of the things I've noticed is that you stopped smiling or laughing in your work after about '69–'71. There were two young men who did laugh.*

Gilbert: Yes laugh. We don't do that because it's too serious.
> *Did you find the Seventies very depressing?*

George: I think we began to come to terms with more the idea of the whole person and the whole civilisation, rather than looking at particular aspects. We began to realise that it was important for us to respect the misery and death and violence and aggression and other forms as well. You ask most people what they like. They say, well this; and you say, why do you do that? And in the end they just do everything in order to go for a pint of beer on Saturdays. It's all it boils down to.
> *You are very much a product of the Sixties. The* Bend It *sketch, for example, in your 1981 film is very Sixties. Are you nostalgic for that period?*

Gilbert & George: No.

George: We feel that we belong to this century, the twentieth century. In the Sixties everyone was wearing blankets in fact. Absolutely. They literally were.

Gilbert: Even the art of that period we don't like. Too formalist. It was all full of Art for Art's sake and we don't like that.
> *Was* Bend It *an arbitrary choice?*

George: A very casual choice. It could be almost any pop record.
Gilbert: It's the only one we remembered at the time.
George: We never had a gramophone in our life, never. We never
bought a gramophone record.
Gilbert: But we used to go dancing a lot.
George: The only place we heard music was in clubs.

*There are suggestions of homosexual overtones in your work,
as well as issues of race.*

George: As there are in life, the whole. We have to respect every aspect
of life. Whereas we say in our speech, 'We are fascinated by the richness
and fabric of our world'. In fact our main interest, our only interest and
our only inspiration – the only thing that inspires us is the thing that we
really live for, and that's the idea that, apart from us, the world is
covered with all these people we see. People. That's the only thing that
will ever reduce us to tears. The realisation of that. We're not interested
in formal aspects of picture making, we think that's decadent. Blue in
the corner and a green line down there. We like the idea of bringing a
respect to the individual in the world. Then civilisation can go forward.

British patriotism?

Gilbert: We did want to become artists here, that's quite true. It's very
difficult for an artist to say I want to be here and become an artist, to be
free to do what I want here.
George: In the world...
Gilbert: Very few artists can do that here. They only accept patriotism,
they only want that. They only want French art; that's patriotism. Or
they want American art.

People don't believe in indigenous culture here.

George: That's for sure. That's what we have to work against day and
night. But we're winning that battle very slowly. We just came back now
from America. We had this enormous show at the Guggenheim
Museum. The museum was filled for the opening – 2,000 people.
They've never seen so many people in a museum.
Gilbert: And all classes of people. That was the most interesting thing.
Everybody was there.

*The only parallel with that attendance record would be for an artist
like Andy Warhol.*

George: Yes, that's perfectly true.

Do you have any affinity with Warhol?

Gilbert: He only likes rich people, fame and stuff and we're not into
that. We are into life.

Do you subscribe to any magazines?

George: Not one, no not that I can think of. I don't think we ever did.
We're not great readers really.

Gilbert: Our books, reviews and not even that. Only the bad ones we read.

Do you take much notice of the bad ones?

George: We're always fascinated when people say, 'Are you interested
in criticism? Do you take any notice?' or 'Don't you bother to read it?'
And it's very simple, everyone is affected by that. If I leaned across the
table now and said, 'You Nazi cunt', you would be quite affected, right?

Yes, I would be.

George: Everybody would. Nobody wants that. Everyone's very affected
by it. We have been called everything under the sun. Especially by
people here.

Gilbert: We don't defend ourselves any more.

George: I remember the first thing people said when we started, having
left college: 'Oh it'll never last. Two people as one artist.' And we
thought, 'Oh, my god, when will people ever stop saying that? And what
on earth could they say instead?' Sure enough they found something.
'Alcoholics.' My god, whatever next? It was such a strong label for a
while and they couldn't imagine we would ever change. We thought this
is going to be with us for life. Then we became 'Dandies', 'Edwardian',
'Victorian', 'Fops'. And then we became 'right-wing little Englanders'.
There's no limit to the nonsense. The fact is, whatever they come up
with, they want to be negative.

Gilbert: That's what we believe more, that people either want to be pro
or against.

George: The detail of the accusation is nothing. Like, we could describe
you as this nice chap with a white shirt, or this awful chap with a
horrible white shirt. The detail of the shirt is unimportant, it's whether
we want to be for or against.

Would you like some Ginger cake?

Thank you.

George: Good, have some.

I think we're better able to deal with hostility of that kind than we
ever were before. We're more practised.

Some people would see you as a product of the 1950s working-class

George: But even that, that's a negative/positive thing because if they
want to they could see us as upper-class twits in suits. Prince Charles
always wears a suit. Depends how you want to look at it. We're from
lower-class backgrounds, certainly. I think another reason why we've
been accused of being right-wing or something, is again because we're
not formalistic decadent artists. We don't think it's to do with shape,
colour, texture and that kind of art – which is there in the gallery or
museum to congratulate the viewer on being a sophisticated art lover.
Doesn't do more than that. If you show it to a person on the street and
say, 'What's that?' They will say, 'It's art.' And that's because it's what it
says to them, just three letters. So anything that says something more
than that...
Gilbert: ...is threatening.
George: ...opens up an aspect of the person's life, they think there must
be something wrong. Because art's not supposed to do that. We believe
it's there as a cultural force in life, for change and betterment and
advancement of civilisation.
Gilbert: I'm sure eighty per cent have to be enemies. If you want to do
something new, you must have enemies.
George: You have to realise how many artists there are in England who
have never been accused of these things.

You are avant-garde artists...
Gilbert: Yes.
George: We consider ourselves to be radical, subversive, twentieth-
century artists, world artists.
Gilbert: Among all the young artists that are around now, especially in
New York, they are all following our ideas.

You're not seen so much as fascists in other countries.
Gilbert: The English writers have been spreading it all over, even in
America.
George: Since the mid-Seventies British people have travelled abroad
to besmirch our name.
Gilbert: Even in catalogues! English writers in catalogues.
George: Often when we have shows abroad and we're sent bundles of
reviews, we find one amazingly horrible, destructive review by so and
so. We think, who the hell is this person? We don't remember being

interviewed by him. So we telephone our gallery and say, 'Who's this chap?' 'Oh, it's so and so and he lives in West Hampstead.' From here! Not from Italy or America. Running over, panicky little idiot – to fuck up their own culture.

We wouldn't say that we're not fascists. That's not our interest. One of the most interesting things which we always say to writers is that the most difficult thing it seems (especially with art criticism nowadays) is for the writer to say what it is. They always try to say what it's like and the most interesting thing is actually what it is. If you have a flower from the garden the most fascinating thing about it is actually what that flower is.

Gilbert: Ordinary people see exactly what is in our art.

George: For years the structure of society in Western culture has been based on a cultural hierarchy, so that the profession is completely separated from the public in order to maintain position and salaries in fact. Have to keep the public in their place and keep them mystified. That's why the public is supported almost exclusively in this century; since the collapse of Christian culture they have been completely committed to obscure art. Because as long as there are thousands of people out there who don't know what the hell it is, they can be very grand – and in two weeks' time they can give you a little lecture and tell you what you're looking at. If the public come in and can be spoken to by the work, they're out of a job almost.

We're closing the gap between the public and the profession. We have countless personal anecdotes to support that.

What were you doing at St Martin's School of Art?

George: Learning to be artists. Painting, drawing, sculpture, pottery, graphics, design, history of art, psychology, everything. Just learning, really. We don't believe in artists in college, we believe you're learning in college and the first day you leave, then you're an artist or you're not.

Or you clean windows?

George: We even did that. But we did it at night so we could be artists during the day.

Your 1981 film The World of Gilbert & George *has had controversial success...*

George: It's been shown all over the world at festivals.

Gilbert: They wouldn't show it in a main cinema.

George: When we were showing the film at the ICA [London], when it was first out, it was on in a tiny little cinema and there were people trying to get in – they couldn't actually get in to see it and at the same time in the main cinema were two people sitting watching *Guys and Dolls*. Two people sitting there in this great big auditorium and they wouldn't put our film on because it was 'obscure and artistic'. In fact, the reverse was true. This is again the difference between the public and the profession. The public knew they wanted to see our film. The profession thought they had to show some popular American Thirties muck. But the ICA was opposed on political grounds.

Gilbert: They were very unhappy.

George: We even heard that they would like to kill us!

Gilbert: At the Guggenheim show, not one British official was there.

George: There was a big gala dinner and we were approached by the secretary of the President and she said she'd like to know who was here from Britain to do the speeches. We said, 'There is no one.' She said, 'There must be somebody from the Tate.' We said, 'No.' 'Somebody from the Arts Council or the British Council?' 'No!' Not one, and not one attended the whole tour.

An American won the Turner Prize!

George: That's right, English, but he's lived there for nearly thirty years. It was the nearest thing to a foreigner they could choose. There was nobody more foreign amongst the four. We got a lot of popular support from that decision, in fact. So many students ringing us in the middle of the night in tears. 'Why? Boo hoo…'

Gilbert: In one way it's good for us because we have to defend ourselves.

George: We have no experience of being supported in our own territory.

Gilbert: The reason why the Director of the Tate didn't like us was because of our sexual preferences.

George: He said, 'I don't care much for their sexual preferences'.

Absurd.

George: More than that, because if that is the case he has to judge, he is the pinnacle of modern art in Britain, he is the highest paid by tax-payers' money. That's the leading national collection of contemporary art, he is the Director, there's no better job, he's at the height of that pro-fession. And if that's his view, then he has to go first of all into his library and go through his books very carefully, and chuck out the queer books. Then he has to go through his records and chuck out the wrong records.

And who's the most popular figure for doing that in history? Who had studio inspections of artists for that? Hitler, in fact!

Gilbert: They would have the same in Russia.

George: In Cuba they have it. Extreme right and extreme left cultures have it.

You still have family ties?

George: Very slight.

Gilbert: We do not involve the family in what we are doing. Then we are much freer. And that's what we want. To be free. That's why we don't even want a lot of friends.

George: We like to be very separate.

Gilbert: We want to have our views and put them in front of people with our shows.

George: If you are submerged in normal life, then your view will be normal. So we have to keep separate from normal life in order to be able to say something that is not known. People come to art for something that they don't understand, that's not in their life already.

So you have taken on the role of 'the outsider'...

Gilbert: Oh yes, very much so. We always did. In fact we wanted to be involved, but they never accepted us, and now we never want to go near.

George: We see it more and more in terms of a cultural service, really. Public service for culture. As a giver ... that's why we get furious when people say, 'You must be very happy being given a show at the Guggenheim', and we say, 'Nonsense, we were not given a show, the public have been given a show of our work.'

We've never had a British curated exhibition or a British published catalogue. Even the Whitechapel show which we had was a show invented in Holland. The catalogue was written by an American and printed in Holland.

Are you going to continue doing more photo-pieces?

George: Oh yes, that's our main form. The new works are quite different from our previous works, in terms of content and form.

And colour language? Each colour has a significance...

George: Yes. But not a single significance. Depending on the piece, general atmosphere.

Gilbert: They become so powerful, without knowing, you are completely involved in the pieces.

Some of your models are influenced by your style.

Gilbert: They are doing art like that, 'the Grey Organisation', they are very interesting people.

George: The new works are called *New Moral Works*, the overall title of the show. Because, for us, the art is the friendship between ourselves and the viewer. That's what we call art. And that's why we say the viewers come to the exhibition not with their knowledge of Western culture, or what they know about Cubism and Expressionism, they come with their lives...

Rather like medieval art...

George: Yes, in a sense that they were using formal aspects to speak to people. That's what we say we're doing. The titles are a key part of the pieces, They are like a key – it's the nearest word – to aim the person in the direction of where we want them. Because we say that inside every person there are only three forces: the brain or the head, the soul which we think is separate, and the sex. And one's always working between those three elements, and we're speaking to those three elements.

What will be the logical conclusion of your work?

George: The only conclusion is a whole life. One day there will be a last work that we will make and that will be the whole. That will be our contribution.

What Our Art Means

Statement by the artists first published in 1986 in *Gilbert & George: The Complete Pictures 1971–1985*, catalogue for the retrospective exhibition shown at the following venues: CAPC Musée d'Art Contemporain de Bordeaux; Kunsthalle, Basel; Palais des Beaux Arts, Brussels; Palacio de Velazquez, Parque del Retiro, Madrid; Städtische Galerie im Lenbachhaus, Munich; Hayward Gallery, London.

ART FOR ALL

We want Our Art to speak across the barriers of knowledge directly to People about their Life and not about their knowledge of art. The twentieth century has been cursed with an art that cannot be understood. The decadent artists stand for themselves and their chosen few, laughing at and dismissing the normal outsider. We say that puzzling, obscure and form-obsessed art is decadent and a cruel denial of the Life of People.

PROGRESS THROUGH FRIENDSHIP

Our Art is the friendship formed between the viewer and our pictures. Each picture speaks of a 'Particular View' which the viewer may consider in the light of his own life. The true function of Art is to bring about new understanding, progress and advancement. Every single person on Earth agrees that there is room for improvement.

LANGUAGE FOR MEANING

We invented and we are constantly developing our own visual language. We want the most accessible form with which to create the most modern speaking visual pictures of our time. The art-material must be subservient to the meaning and purpose of the picture. Our reason for making pictures is to change people and not to congratulate them on being how they are.

THE LIFE-FORCES

True Art comes from three main life-forces. They are:

    THE HEAD
    THE SOUL
and THE SEX

In our life these forces are shaking and moving themselves into ever-changing different arrangements. Each one of our pictures is a frozen representation of one of these 'arrangements'.

THE WHOLE
When a human being gets up in the morning and decides what to do and where to go he is finding his reason or excuse to continue living. We as artists have only that to do. We want to learn to respect and honour 'the whole'. The content of mankind is our subject and our inspiration. We stand each day for good traditions and necessary changes. We want to find and accept all the good and bad in ourselves. Civilisation has always depended for advancement on the 'giving person'. We want to spill our blood, brains and seed in our life-search for new meanings and purpose to give to life.

The Fabric of Their World: from Interviews with Carter Ratcliff 1986

Statements by Gilbert & George from interviews with Carter Ratcliff, many but not all of which were first published in 1986 in Ratcliff's essay 'The Fabric of Their World' in *Gilbert & George: The Complete Pictures 1971–1985* (see note on page 149).

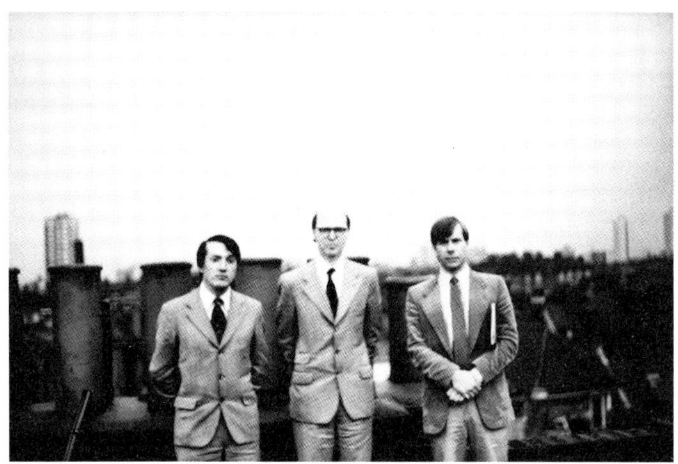

With Carter Ratcliff on the roof of the artists' home in Fournier Street, London, Summer 1980 (*Photo: Phyllis Derfner*)

George: We think of our art as just pictures, not as photographs. We're using photography, not being photographers. The question of our medium is more for the art profession than for the public. A normal person doesn't think about such things. You see a picture, you want to know what it says.

Gilbert: It is important to us to publish our art in books and catalogues, so as many people as possible are able to see it, but we also want them to see the real pieces. We like it very much when the pictures take over. When they're bigger than the viewer. You go to a musuem to look at a picture, but we like it when the picture looks at you.

George: We think there's a certain absurdity in earlier art when, say, a cow is a minuscule spot of colour. It's not fair, in a way. We want our pictures to be true to life.

Gilbert: We want to dominate the viewer with the forces of art. Because art can change people. We believe that.

*

George: The basis of our inspiration is the fact that there are all these people all over the world alive. It's the best thing about everything. And sometimes art ignores that. It ignores the viewer.
Gilbert: We accept the whole world. We accept all the problems. First we try to sort out our morality, then we put it in front of people. They may reject it, but that is advancement, in a way. Of course, just having different views is so difficult. If you have a different view, you are going to be hurt. Just trying to be an artist is like that. You can be very unhappy.

*

George: You know, you can always find something that's like a person's art. For some artists, the nearest thing is children's painting. We once saw a display of the art that is nearest to ours. It was in the window of a tramps' hostel, where they have an art teacher every week. There were the most amazing drawings and pictures. In a funny way, that exhibition was the nearest to us we'd ever seen. It really had some connection to our art.

*

George: A lot of people in the art profession and certainly in the media think that's what art is: a photograph of us holding a sheet of photographic paper in some developing fluid. We've been asked for that. 'Can you do something in the studio for us?' Why should that be art? Crazy idea. Completely absurd. Madness. It's a big twentieth-century cliché to do with form and materials.
Gilbert: The making of an art object is not important. Dressing like someone who makes objects is not important. What is important is putting the work in front of people. So we don't want anyone to see how we make our works. The idea that evidence of the hand is good – that's what we dislike. It's all based on order. But we want the order – and our effort – to be invisible.
George: We wouldn't want people to think, 'My goodness, they must have spent a year on that'. The picture should be completely smooth, as if it had been shot out of our brains, on to the paper like magic. In reality, our pieces are extremely handmade, laboured objects. But they look the opposite. And that is how we want them to look. That is why we would never exhibit our working drawings.
Gilbert: And that is why no one is allowed into our studio. We never learned to be photographers. It was simply the best form for expressing

ourselves, the most modern. A lot of people in the professional art world
don't accept photographic images as fine art. Though, after Duchamp,
all sorts of things have been accepted as art, things much farther from
traditional art than photography. Film is also important to us.
George: We are convinced that we're the only ones who have managed
to use photography in a real way, to use it to really make a picture. So
many artists have played around with the idea of photography, but they
were never unashamedly able to use it to really make a picture. They
always had to do a little bit of Rembrandt on the top.
Gilbert: Even nineteenth-century painters took photographs – tableaux.
And Andy Warhol nearly made a picture, but he still used a canvas. He
wanted it to be a painting.
George: Photography is good because it's real. If you think of all the
pictures of Christ, for instance, all the paintings, and then discovered
that, through some strange trick of history, there was in existence a
photograph of Christ, it would be amazing.

*

George: The grids are a natural part of making large photo-pieces. It is
like a week has to be divided into days, for convenience. A house has to
be made of bricks. You can't make a house from one big brick. You
cannot make a skyscraper with one enormous sheet of glass.
Everything is in sections.
Gilbert: You cannot have a sheet of photographic paper big enough to
put it on, all together. Technically it is impossible. And you cannot have
a single big sheet of glass to protect the work, so each panel is framed
and each frame contains a sheet of glass. Like a skyscraper. When we
went to Houston, we saw these big glass skyscrapers. They are all like
that – framed. It is all based on structure.
George: The same as when we are talking. We cannot say what we want
to say to you in one amazing long word. We have to structure it –
vowels, nouns, pronouns. You have to build it up. So we have built an
individual language for our art.

*

George: We believe that art is there for the meaning, and that artists
who make what we call art-art, just to add to this funny, quirky history
of technique and isms, are very wrong. They're missing the whole point
of the function of art. We believe that people should be different having

had contact with our works. If they bring their life – as opposed to their knowledge of isms – it will be thrown into contrast by the works. It's like if you travelled to India, your life is thrown into contrast by another reality, and that advances you in a way. You accept or reject or combine. But you are never the same.

Gilbert: That's progress. We show in galleries and museums, but we are doing our art for everybody, not just for art-world professionals. For the professionals, especially in England, we are two monsters. And we hate talking with artists about art politics.

George: Yes, we especially dislike talk about money. It seems as though certain artists are simply in the art business, trying to get the best out of it for themselves, manoeuvering it. Dreadful.

Gilbert: That's why we used to get so drunk, so we wouldn't have to listen to all that.

*

Gilbert: We would like very much to make an art that has nothing to do with the art world, just with the public.

George: We have already achieved that, in some measure. It's quite obvious to a wide range of viewers that they don't need a knowledge of twentieth-century art history for our pieces. It's difficult having to show in art museums, it's unsatisfactory, but it's the only way. We're sometimes asked if we would like to have our work put up on billboards, but we're against that. The viewer has to know that it is art, that it comes from that platform. Otherwise, it would be like chucking all the books out of the library onto the street.

Gilbert: But just one, lonely piece of ours on view in a museum is very difficult.

George: It's always too much like an example.

Gilbert: One G & G, one this, one that. So we prefer to exhibit our work in big one-man museum shows.

George: Some recent statistics showed that, in Britain, more people go to a museum or to some cultural event than attend church services. It's quite amazing. Extraordinary. And the most popular room at the National Gallery is the modern one. Surprising, though we shouldn't be surprised by it. People are more interested in things that are nearer to their own times.

Gilbert: It's nearer to themselves. Young people now all like art, in some way. They make their own hats – it's all art, we feel.

*

George: At the time of the Nature pieces, we didn't know how to make a picture. We couldn't figure that out.
Gilbert: We were trying to create our world around ourselves. So we brought things together. We were very interested to see the sum of our pictures, because the jungle – 'Nature' – was part of our world. Shrubberies, foliage, we were just walking in this crazy world with all these feelings with which we used to make the works. But we didn't like the idea of the woods alone. We liked there to be handmade parts.
George: Yes, manmade but without man.

*

George: The Human Bondage pieces show the Christian cross quite often.
Gilbert: And, anyway, the swastika is a version of the cross. The Nazi swastika runs one way, and others run the other way. We have them going both ways. Reversals. We weren't trying to say anything about fascism or the war in particular.
George: You see a swastika and you have this immediate, extremely powerful feeling about what went on all over the world at a certain time.
Gilbert: We were interested in destruction. The destructive element of drinking, for example.
George: People thought we had offered some obvious sort of provocation, whereas our intention was to make our art more relaxing.
Gilbert: Even with the earlier Drinking pieces we liked very much to be free to say that we were drinking, that we don't mind being called drunkards.
George: We like the idea that one could deal with the destructive elements in one's life, in oneself, as human bondage, as something to be accepted. An aspect of life that you needn't avoid at all costs.
Gilbert: But even some people we thought understood our art said these pieces proved we were supporting the Nazis.
George: Yes, young journalists often start their chats with us by saying, 'We've heard a lot about your being right-wing. Fascist. Is it true?' What the hell does one reply to that? It's impossible.
Gilbert: There's no correct political line on our works. We are interested in morality.

George: If someone asks us, 'Are you Tory?' we say that if we wanted to make a work saying we are Tories, we'd have done so. It's very easy to make a work like that. But we didn't do that. It's not a piece we did.
Gilbert: I don't know what we are, politically, because we're not involved with politics. But we have a morality. We are interested in that because we believe that comes through morality – what is good and what is bad. The shifting of good and bad – what one accepts today, and the next day one doesn't accept any more.
George: And we believe our art can form morality, in our time. We're not here to congratulate society for how it is. We want to see change. Improvement and advancement.

*

George: We had already started to sign our names in red. Now we tried to find ways of using the colour red in the pieces.
Gilbert: We were looking for a more aggressive, more powerful image. Red has more strength than black. Black and white is powerful but red on top of it is even more so. It's louder.
George: The violence of the East, the extreme discipline of martial arts in the Orient fascinated us. The name *Cherry Blossom* originated in that fascination.

*

Gilbert: In the early 1970s we did the Living Sculpture pieces. We came into contact with people through the art.
George: And we were no longer totally alone, as we had been during the time of the Nature pieces. Alone in our work, but we saw people then. We drank. We were nearer to the violence of life than we are now or after we began to work on the house.
Gilbert: We had all the fighting pubs. Sometimes the police were called.
George: We always managed to get out of being arrested. Though we did get beaten up. And, in fact, we did end up in jail for the night. Twice. People seemed to find our stance a bit aggressive.
Gilbert: Freedom. We were after that.
George: The violence shows in *Cherry Blossom* and *Bloody Life*. Then our work became more sterile.
Gilbert: It's what we wanted then.
George: There's still a little drinking. A glass in the hand or a bottle standing by on the floor. And different shots from angles, through the

windows. A tree through a manmade window, for instance. Just a little 'Nature'. Combining those feelings about manmade things and natural things.
Gilbert: Just a little shift from one window view to the other. Very depressing and simplistic. When it goes from *Bad Thoughts* to *Dusty Corners*, it gets worse in a way.
George: We were very desperate at this time. In *Dusty Corners*, there is only the fabric of the building and ourselves. No other elements at all.
Gilbert: And that is how we felt.
George: Yes, our works are always true, literally. Just lifted from where we were when we made them.
Gilbert: We never tried to invent anything.

*

George: We came to a point where we could actually say this is all getting more and more mental – more a matter of thinking and of madness, both of which are involved with the head. We got used to the idea of both meanings of the word being attached to our work, so that we were no longer embarrassed or tempted to lose faith.
Gilbert: There was no end, no way out. You just see us looking down or looking up, facing right or left.
George: Always with a perfect system, at least at first. In one piece you might see Gilbert going out of the picture and, in the next panel, me coming into the picture. Facing forward, then facing backward. It's always with us, with nature, and the city, and in this group we're always going around in the pattern without an end.
Gilbert: Other people had appeared in some of the other groups, but now we had become more conscious that the human person is an object like any other object, so why not include it? And a flower, that's not a person, or a house – you can always find truth in that.
George: It has character.
Gilbert: It has character. We had used objects for their character again and again in the beginning and not even realised that we were doing that. Later we became more aware. And found that that is what we wanted.
George: We also became conscious that we had arranged some of the red panels in *Mental* [1976] to form a cross. As red panels alternate with black and white ones. And there is an alternation of night-scenes and day-scenes.

Gilbert: Always opposites. And I think that, as two people, we are light and dark and good and bad.

*

George: People don't want something obscure, we find. They want something bold, something which speaks directly to them. People want something so immediate they can just say, 'That's fucking good'. We don't see our work as narrative. It's not a word we would use to describe our work. The only narrative element in our work is really the whole life narrative. Which means that when we are dead, we would have told one, complete narrative. When we're dead we cannot add to it. That will be the Gilbert & George story. But there is no individual narrative element within any one work.
Gilbert: This is more to create feelings – with people – to express new life.
George: We have inside ourselves a lot of thoughts, feelings, desires, dreams, hopes, fears – many things inside. And we, as artists, have a great, burning ambitious need to tell these things and to put these things out of ourselves. So we want to speak to people using our visual language. We developed and are still developing our own visual language. Because we can only say it in our own way. It is only when the pictures are up, working for us, that we are in some way active – when we have a relationship with the viewer.
Gilbert: We create feelings – of fear, of good. It's not a narrative story on 'good'. It's just based on the word 'good', and you start to build up a lot of feelings, for yourself and the viewer.
George: Between us and the viewer. There are always the two things, making a single art experience. Whether or not people feel 'good' as we do, they form a relationship with us as the creators, on that subject. They know what we're saying to them. They know it's a Gilbert & George. They have all their feelings inside themselves, and together with us – it's like a visual sermon or lecture.

*

Gilbert: By putting the word along the top, then something vertical down both sides, it looked like a door. A door of hell.
George: We found much of the graffiti in doorways. In every Western city, you just find it immediately, the moment you look. We became interested to know what makes a person do that.

158

*

George: The human figures for *Red Morning: Bhuna* [1977] were taken very shyly and very frightenedly from the first-floor window at Fournier Street. We continued that technique for the Dirty Words. After a time, we ventured out of the house with a camera, but only with a long lens, so we could take people's pictures at bus stops and things. One or two we asked.

*

George: Until now, we had always kept each image to a single panel. Then we discovered that it wasn't necessary. Before we had thought of a four-panel piece as a four-part piece – four images, sixteen in a sixteen-panel piece, and so on. But 'Bent', for instance, is one word, a single image, running across four panels. Or a single word broken down into four parts. We decided we could do exactly as we pleased.

*

Gilbert: People have an idea of what art looks like, and when they come to our shows they don't know if it is art. But they like it, they are moved by it and it speaks to them directly.
George: They are spoken to, but not through the history of art. We want our works to be mainly content, and the form should just support the content. The form shouldn't dominate the work. We don't want people to come to a museum or a gallery and admire the beautiful art.
Gilbert: Our work has to look new, a new language that can speak to people. We think the most important thing is what we're trying to say. That's more important than art, than the word 'art'.
George: We don't want our works to say 'art' immediately. We want them to become art.
Gilbert: We want them to say 'life'.

*

George: We were always interested to put our feelings in our photo-pieces. I'm sure we shared those feelings with the people we brought into the works. Of course we saw them more as stereotypes – tramps, people in the stock exchange. We thought of the figures in *Leather Workers* [1980], for example, as representative persons. Six different individuals became *Patriots* [1980].

159

Gilbert: Because of the Pakistani in *Patriots*, people said we were
racist. It was even worse with *Paki* [1978]. Here there is only us and
one Pakistani standing between.
George: The criticism was that we were condescending. And there
were objections to the name of the piece. But you can use 'Paki' as
derogatory or as complimentary. It's an abbreviation, like you see in
headlines: 'Seven Brits Die in Plane Crash'. 'Brit' could be a derogatory
if you want. It depends on how you use it.
Gilbert: Critics and reporters thought very much that we were looking
down. But that is their interpretation. We show people like us but living
in a different way.
George: Yet the feelings are shared. We were conscious that we wanted
to confront this other madness, the people we saw in the city.
Gilbert: Life's desperate. We are near to madness every day. And to
happiness. Fear. Many of the pieces from this time are afraid of life, I
think. In 1980 and '81 we made a series of Modern Fears – *Night Fear,
Day Fear, Night Monster, Living with Fear*.
George: We felt the style of the Western world, the fabric of its life, was
very threatened. That's why you have all this crumbling.

*

Gilbert: When a tribal person makes a sculpture, he doesn't think he's
doing art. He wants to make a sculpture for a god. That's what we like.
And we are very near that. That's why some say we don't make art.
George: We don't like the idea that to be an intellectual is to be an
atheist, that every twentieth-century artist, every twentieth-century
writer has, by definition, to be a non-church-goer. We don't want to
divide society into naive people who believe in god and sophisticated
ones who don't.
Gilbert: We think every single person is religious, to a certain degree.
That's what we are, as well. We try to sort out what that means.
Sometimes people are shocked by pictures of shit and so on, but we
don't want to make them run from the gallery. We don't like that. We
want to push forward in our art, so we must keep the viewer there.
That's very important.
Gilbert: We're not religious in a church-going way. We are religious in
the way an athiest is an athiest. I was brought up as a Catholic, but I
don't want to say now that I'm fighting for the morality of the Catholic

Church. Everyone prays. So we are trying to make an art that is beyond art, that expresses that religious feeling.

George: We want our art to be more and more direct, a wider range of feelings.

Gilbert: We feel our art is advertising thought. The Catholic Church used paintings to advertise the ideas of the Church. The Church told painters what to do.

*

George: The cultural force is enormous – more or less unspoken, but an enormous power. The politics are in the headlines, but underneath all that there is the cultural force holding things together.

Gilbert: Morality – what is good and what is bad. And it changes every day. The shifting of good and bad – what one accepts today, and the next day one doesn't accept any more.

George: That we're able to sit here without crazy armies coming through the window is, in fact, something that people have culturally insisted on having a government arrange for them. It wouldn't be like that if people didn't insist. And in some places they don't.

Gilbert: But nowadays people accept being robbed, in some funny way. But it didn't used to be like that. Maybe in ten years it won't be accepted. It's a balance. We want our freedom. We don't like being told to do what we don't believe.

George: Society seems fragile, yet we're moving now shortly into the third thousand years of Christian laws. It's quite amazing. Every bank, every school, every university, every street, every aeroplane – all based on that one thing.

Gilbert: Nobody believes in religion anymore, yet they all accept it. In the background, everone accepts it.

George: The organisation – the law, all police forces, all military in the West – are all based on Christ. Entirely. But often people don't see the Christian power. That's the best thing about Christ – we have all these amazing streets and whatever we want, more or less, we can have. We can arrange it. That's the great thing about the whole example that Christ gave. Christianity shouldn't be seen as abstract.

Gilbert: We stick our necks out for these ideas. We had the idea that we didn't want to be artists making objects, we just wanted to be people. But this wasn't understood. Even just dressing up in suits horrified the English artists.

George: Not the general public. For them, it was no problem at all.
Not at all. We wanted to be respectable in that way.

*

George: Over the years, we've become more convinced that culture
is a functioning force and a bigger power than all normal politics.
Gilbert: And we became more and more convinced that we were
correct. Because people began to attack us, and so we had to sort
ourselves out, to see what we really want to do and why.
George: We were attacked especially for being right-wing.
Gilbert: We became interested in a kind of art that has nothing to do
with art.
George: We were called right-wing by the element of the left that
attacked us which believes that art can be used by them for political
ends. They need vague art. They need an obscure art that permits them
to say what it is. If the art says what it is itself, as ours does, that defeats
them. They're frightened if the art says something.
Gilbert: People make believe that our art is political, not just it is right
or left, but that in trying to do something new, we are political – having
views of morality and things like that. They don't know where we are.
We don't know where we are. They seem to know what one should do.
George: We're certainly very suspicious of the cliché that good equals
left and art equals good.
Gilbert: We became more interested in Art for All. When we started,
fifteen years ago, the phrase was just naive. But we believe more and
more that's exactly what we want to do, make art for every single
person. Not art for art.
George: Walter Crane had a very particular, socialist brand of Art
for All.
Gilbert: They were all socialists, Crane, Ashbee. They were fascist-
socialists, in a way.
George: They had all the best intentions in the world, but the only thing
they didn't actually think about was the people. They left that out a bit.
They knew what should be done to them. It didn't occur to them that the
people should be part of the whole thing.
Gilbert: We believe very much that people are part of our art.
Everybody should be part of it.
George: We say more and more that our art is the friendship between

the viewer and the picture. We like to allow for the viewer in the
picture. Not that we do this thing that comes from inside us and 'Fuck
you, we don't know what it means but take it or leave it'. We believe that
if the art is working properly the person should come to the art with his
life, just come and stand in front of the picture with his or her life. If
you come with just a knowledge of twentieth-century art history, you're
blocked. You're completely blocked.
Gilbert: First, one needs a form the viewer understands. So we try to
sort out a form for ourselves that everybody can understand. And then
what you put in the picture should be feelings that everyone can
understand, that are part of life. So you don't have to be an art-educated
person to understand.

*

George: You remember as a child, when you're taken to a museum once
a year, you don't want to see the dreary, horrible room with the pictures
of the wigs and ships. Fine art. You want to see the stuffed animals,
trains, model boats. Real things. We want our works to be real, lifelike,
true to life. We are interested in the truth. So if someone was to say,
'Don't you think your exhibition was very depressing?' we would say, 'It
is not more so than life.' Is our art ironical? Not more than life. We are
of life, a part of it. We're changing life for many people who come to our
exhibitions. So our images must have that reality. They are real things.

*

Gilbert: I don't think we have changed our ideas. You can see them
in the earliest of our works. The form changed, the way we present our
ideas.
George: We've elaborated on them. But our intention has remained
the same.
Gilbert: We believe in tradition.
George: That's how the world is kept together – the daily activity.
Change together with maintaining. Certain things have to be
maintained. Some things have to be changed. People quarrel the whole
time because they don't agree which should be changed and which
should be left. We just all know that there's room for improvement.
We, for instance, believe in the form of the picture. So we keep that.
Gilbert: On the other hand, we don't feel we must maintain the
traditional role of the artist. We don't think of ourselves doing some

sort of art, like painting, living up to the image of the artist.
George: We certainly don't accept the twentieth-century tradition of the artist as the freaky person.
Gilbert: No, that's why we like the nineteenth-century idea of what an artist was. He was more intellectual then.
George: It was the picture that was important then. He didn't have paint on his trousers – instead a fantastic frock coat.
Gilbert: His ideas were more important than the actual surface of the painting. We think the artist is a priest, a philosopher, of life.

Missionary Positions: from an Interview with Sarah Kent 1987

Statements first published in *Time Out*, London, 8–15 July 1987.

THE MISSION

George: We don't believe in art – we don't want to have anything to do with it. We want to change life. We don't want to reflect society, we want to form it. We want people to go into the gallery and come out different – thinking, dreaming, hoping, fearing, behaving differently.

Gilbert: The museum is the best platform – everyone is welcome. Art is there to stimulate thought – the speaking artist preaching, stimulating the idea of life. Our work is like someone making graffiti – an advertising campaign of pure thought, just as the church used painters to campaign for religion. Except that we are more free – the language that we use is ours completely.

George: We're speaking louder, it's a louder invitation – don't you think there are enough museums and galleries in the world with bland works of art that people glide past? We've had incredible responses from people of all ages, races and classes. Most artists make work for posh people involved with the art profession – pictures which would mean nothing if you took them outside that elitist group. The cleaning lady doesn't like them. Where we exhibit they always remark, 'It's very strange, the cleaning staff never look at the shows, but with your work, they're crazy about it.' We're amongst the few artists who give dignity to the viewer – we allow the viewer's life in front of the picture. There are no franker, more explicit artists than ourselves – we're never ambiguous.

SUFFERING

Gilbert: We are putting up our views and our unhappiness for them to see – we are depressed and unhappy people.

George: We never met anyone more miserable than ourselves, anywhere. It's better, more serious. Everyone is chasing pleasure – there's never been a greater accessibility of pleasure in the whole history of mankind. Never did so many people have so much fun as now.

Gilbert: I think every good artist is unhappy, that's the driving force.

George: We're anti-pleasure seeking, completely. All the happy people

are dead without having done a thing – happiness is to take, to
contribute is to give. The history of civilisation's advancement is
written in misery, blood, personal sacrifice and controversy, even Jesus
Christ was controversial. That was the Christian message on which
Western civilisation is based. Every school, every university, art
gallery, museum, policeman, hospital is based on the one inspiration –
of misery.

RELIGION
Gilbert: We accept and would like to honour Christian power – we're
happily in debt to the Christian tradition. We do not say we're
sophisticated atheists, let the peasants go to church – which is what all
people of intelligence said this century. They had a classist attitude
towards religion. We don't even know where we stand exactly, we're
trying to work it out – our religious pieces are pro- and anti-religion.
George: When we first did our Jesus pieces in 1980 some of our biggest
admirers thought we were cuckoo. Now everybody talks about
religiosity, morality or politics in art. We are interested in the power of
the individual and the freedom of the artist. In the past they were either
serving the church of the toffs – they either did Christian pictures or
pictures of the toff's house, his family or their animals. There was very
little in the way of serving people. We are at last free and we have a
sense of service, of purpose – we want to give in exchange for the gift
of life. We don't do it to please ourselves – we're just these miserable
chaps trying very hard to give. No joke.
Gilbert: We work as many hours as we can, day and night, until we're
exhausted.

RACISM
Gilbert: We are the only honest artists. We want to be free to speak, to
have a view of the world through art. We are not campaigning for any
parties, but we are political. Secret socialists – that's how we described
ourselves. We are the only artists that are able to accept black people
and white people in our work completely on the same level. For fifty
years you haven't been able to put a black person in an artwork.
George: We have enormous support from people of all backgrounds and
walks of life because of that. In Milwaukee a young black person came
up to us and said, 'I know all about art, and I know all about artists and

it's always looking down its nose at me, but you guys are different –
you speak with the heart.'

HOMOSEXUALITY
George: A white boy – he couldn't have been more than thirteen or
fourteen – his eyes filled with tears, said, 'I would like to tell you how
comfortable I feel standing in front of *Naked Love* [1982].' It meant
something to his life. We would say that the acceptance of sexuality is
important. Sex is sex – I don't want to decide what a person does with
their hands and their sexual organs. We are freedom fighters in that
way. The narrow-mindedness of educated people on those subjects is
appalling.
Gilbert: We use the male because the image is not so used up. A woman
is immediately seen as sex symbol. We are the first artists to tip the
balance.
George: The image of woman has been used largely to terrorise men –
have you never thought of that? It's very simple, people order more
drinks in a topless bar. We are opposed to the bigotry of people who say
that the people in our pieces are 'nasty boys' or yobbos. They're being
classist. We say they are people. If you pick some flowers for the table,
you won't choose a bunch of rotten droopy ones, you'll pick the
teenagers. They represent life, before they've been wrecked by the
system. They are there like extensions of ourselves.
Gilbert: We believe they are our roots.

ISOLATION
George: We never decide how to do a piece. How we are is how the
work is – we trust that entirely. So if in the early work we looked lost,
sad, naive and old-fashioned that's because we were – we are – lower-
class, uneducated country people.
Gilbert: We want to have our ideas, put them up and that's it. We don't
want to discuss it, we would never agree anyway.
George: The discussion is between the viewer and the picture. We want
our effect to be cultural not social, otherwise we'd have to go to every
damn silly dinner party. This is a working tea, after all – we're not
personal friends.

Art for Art's Sake: from an Interview with Jim Shelley 1987

Statements first published in *Melody Maker*, London, 25 July 1987, p. 32.

ART
We don't think about art. We don't believe in Art. We have nothing to do with it.

Art is pure thought. Each bottle, each shirt, label, cigarette all stemmed from Art. Art does affect people's lives. We would like to make art more popular, more democratic. All other artists are involved in self and chasing pleasure and being superior. We are not here to reflect or illustrate life. We want to form it, change it. We have already subverted the profession. When did you last see a contemporary exhibition at the Hayward? Twelve years ago. It's incredible. We should like it to be a scandal. It's the chance of a lifetime. It'll be ten years before we go back and how many people will be dead by then? The Hayward is like *The World of G & G*.

We now have a growing band of extreme intellectuals supporting us, matched by amazing hostility by the profession. Some people would like to see us dead. Dead. We never think 'That doesn't work'. We never think about a picture in advance. How we are at the time, that's how the picture will be – how we hope, dream, how we love, hate.

IDEAS
We're not based on ideas. We never have them.

Our reason for making pictures is to change people not to congratulate them on being how they are. We want people to go out of our exhibitions thinking differently, hoping, loving, hating, fearing differently. We don't go out into the street and scream what we want people to hear. We do a picture and if a person says, 'It's rotten. You shouldn't have done it or been allowed to exhibit it,' we say WHO CARES! It's too late. The subversion is taking place. The world is already a different place because of us. We never want to be revolutionary in a simple way. We like tradition. We like to try and change it slightly. We are not like the other intellectuals of this century who say if you are educated and superior naturally you are an atheist, that only the peasant classes go to church. We believe in Christian power. We are interested in pure philosophy. We want to provoke thought, make people accept life, we want to stimulate life. We want to spend our lives preaching our philosophy (says Gilbert). In service (says George). We are completely without self. We will continue until we are dead.

OPTIMISM
We like to say it's all fantastic.

We never feel bored. We wouldn't want to be involved with that destructive thought. We don't like the artistic, educated idea that there's something wrong with things. When we were children you could either have a brown jumper or a green jumper. Now there are 50,000 jumpers. The skies are black with aeroplanes. I never went outside my home town until I was twenty-one!

Travel, literature, music, television, film. It's a revolution. Fantastic world. Fantastic life. But we don't enjoy life, no. We already gave our life away for our art. We're the dead rabbit on the plate. We want to spill our blood, our brains and our seed for our art.

MISERY
You cannot be serious and happy.

We are depressed and unhappy people. Every good artist is unhappy. We're not interested in enjoyment. It's distracting. The history of civilisation is written in blood, misery and sacrifice. We never think about living in another way. We have no opinions.

FRIENDS AND FAMILY
We have no friends. We are opposed to that idea.

We have no social commitments. Gilbert's father died last year. George met his for only two hours in his whole life. If you have friends you have to compromise. Families interfere. We want total freedom. The family *is* the greatest unit on earth, yes. Highly positive.

CONTROVERSY
Even Jesus Christ was controversial.

We are trying to fight for a certain freedom where everybody can do whatever he wants. We always tell people they should go out there and do it. Just do it. We are the only artists able to put a black person on completely the same level as a white person in an artwork. London is

the most democratic city in the world. Everybody can now do whatever
they want. Everybody can have a job if they want. Look at the vacancies
in the papers. Every foreign person is completely jealous of the spirit of
London. We liked punk rock. Human Bondage was pre-punk. We used
the swastikas as a symbol of human bondage. There's nothing
homosexual about our pictures. All men have cocks. *Cock* [1980] is a
48-inch by 59-inch photo of an erect penis. We *are* interested in sex. We
don't do eunuch art. There are no great eunuch artists. We don't want to
decide what a person does with their hands or sexual organs. We are
freedom fighters. 'Super Liberals'. 'Secret Socialists'. More
importantly, we're normal.

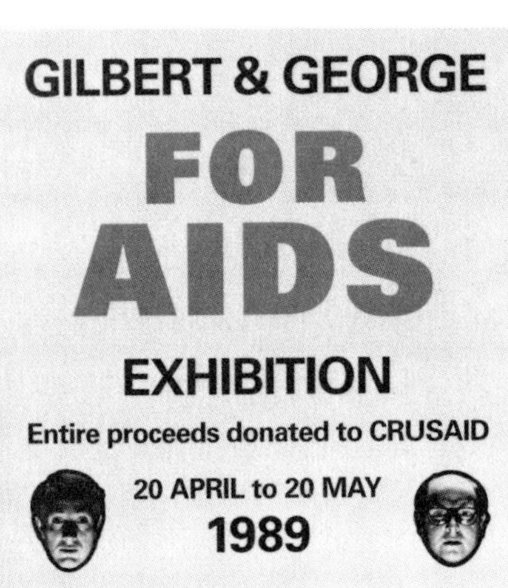

THE FOR AIDS EXHIBITION

Early in 1988 we had a strong feeling that we should be doing something more to help people with AIDS.

Being artists decided us to make an exhibition of our Pictures and donate the entire proceeds to CRUSAID. Anthony d'Offay immediately welcomed the idea and promised to donate the gallery's share as well.

In making these Pictures the forms and meanings in them brought us to a new understanding of the importance of the freedoms of life. In these pictures we provide an opportunity to think and feel a new openness and compassion towards the human person.

London
1989

Cover and introduction to the exhibition catalogue *For AIDS*, 1989   171

We Always Say It is What We 'Say' that is Important: Interview with Andrew Wilson 1990

Interview first published in *Art Monthly*, April 1990, pp. 6–13. This interview was originally commissioned for 3,000 words by Peter Fuller for the April issue of the magazine *Modern Painters*. The version printed here is slightly longer than that originally commissioned. *Modern Painters'* decision not to run it was reputedly prompted by a desire not to confirm the prejudices of their readership and because the interview's length might unbalance the contents of that issue.

You are having an exhibition in Moscow opening on 27 April. What form will this exhibition take?

George: It will be pictures from about the last seven years. It won't be a retrospective over the whole of our career.

Gilbert: It's much simpler, they will understand our vision much simpler if we limit the selection.

George: In Russia, where they know nothing of our work, they need an actual expression of our living selves. They don't want to see an academic show. It would be too confusing for them.

And how did the exhibition come about?

George: It is an old dream of ours. Part of our Art for All theory is our work can speak to people of different cultures, so we always liked the idea of showing in a Communist country.

Gilbert: Three or four years ago we approached the British Council, they told us that they would only be able to do a group show. Then we tried to approach the Russians through Italy – Fiat, because they have a lot of factories in Russia. And then we told Paul Conran about our dream and he told us that if you want to do a show in Russia you have to speak to James Birch, and that is how it happened.

Has there been any sort of censorship exercised in the choice of images?

George: In every country, wherever you show, there is always some form of censorship, and we always like to do that in advance. We like to pre-empt any difficulties, we always like to take it up to the line but not over. We don't want our work to be banned. You strike a balance.

Gilbert: Our show in Basel was different, because the museum director wanted to shock the audience.

George: In fact he made a special room of the sexual pictures.

With Francis Bacon's exhibition in Moscow there was some

*censorship of his more pornographic paintings. Are you worried
at all by this precedent?*
George: No, we have already made that sort of adjustment in the
selection, and the authorities there are perfectly happy. It is not the
interesting thing about art to get people running from the museum in
horror; that would be very unproductive.

*This exhibition is going to be happening at an historically
important time with the fall of Communism. How do you feel about
that?*
George: We are very excited about that, to be part of that movement, it
has always been of interest to us.

And you visited Russia last year?
George: Just to see the space and meet the people – they were very very
appreciative of our work, I must say that.

*What do you think Gorbachev will think of your work? Will he see
the exhibition?*
Gilbert: We don't believe he should have to have a view about it, only
the person who goes to the exhibition can have a view on it. It's like
here, we don't want politicians, we don't believe they have to have a
view of our work.

George: We believe that culture comes first, and politicians follow that.
It has always been the case in history. Whenever the artists arrange a
certain culture amongst the people, they think, 'I want to do this or that
because of the paintings I have seen, or the books that my grandmother
read', they then vote for a particular type of government. So the
politicians are following the culture.

Gilbert: The recent revolution in East Germany was started by artistic
people.

George: The 'New Forum' was a group of people with paintings in the
room and poets.

Do you think the same way about Margaret Thatcher then?
George: Here it is different because you have the vote, you have
freedom in the West. East they do not have the vote. Here it is easy,
because the people can vote for what they culturally expect of the
government. There are parties representing every single opinion in
Britain. There is a Communist Party here you can vote for. People have
to vote for what they want.

Gilbert: But you can only change the view and the vision of the human

person through culture, through different books, through art, pushing
forward the frontier of knowledge, making it a much freer society.
Tolerance, I think tolerance is the most important thing. If you have
tolerance then everybody can have different ideas, and different ideas
are very important. A more complicated richer life.

George: That is why the best role the government plays is like you have
here in the West, where they just arrange opportunity. They don't say,
'This is a good artist or a bad artist', they arrange a system whereby in
the last ten years the number of galleries in London quadrupled and
where the number of artists living by their work is ten times more than
it was under Labour. More and more.

*So, you don't think it is important to worry about what Margaret
Thatcher's taste in art is, or even if she has a philistinic attitude
towards art?*

Gilbert: That has nothing to do with it, we don't worry what politicians
think, that would be giving them too much power.

*But don't they control to a large extent the purse-strings of arts
funding?*

Gilbert: Not ours. Arts funding, that is very difficult, because we don't
believe completely in arts funding ourselves. We believe it is much
better that you make your art, you try to sell it, whoever wants it can
buy it. But once the State tells you what kind of art you want, and
support it in buying it – then we don't like it.

George: That was Mrs Thatcher's greatest achievement in the arts
really, wasn't it, privatisation of the artists? Because before this
government, the artists were nationalised. As well as doing their
paintings you had to work at the Slade for thirty years and for that you
were given a funny award and a pension that was enough to drink
yourself to death but not enough to rescue your career as an artist. And
so they all died unhappy. They had a small memorial show at the back
of the Tate, and that was it. Now they are privatised – it is much better.

Gilbert: Anyway, that is what we believe, very much. You have to be
free. It's not important what each member of the government thinks
about art, as long as they arrange a freedom that you can do whatever
you want. If they would start to knock on our door and telling us what to
do, then I would change my mind!

*But take another position. Say Margaret Thatcher's attitude to
homosexuality and, say, the censorship implicit in Clause 28.*

George: We are not interested to lecture the Prime Minister on her views on heterosexuality or homosexuality, and anyway we have never heard Margaret Thatcher's views on sexuality. And we don't believe that she is the architect of Clause 28, which was in actual fact from the extreme small bookshop that pushed the case so violently that it was bound to receive the sort of response it did. I mean if you go on the street now from this house with a photograph of two men fucking, and say 'You do agree to this, don't you?' to every single person, I would think that is a rather stupid way of doing it, no? That leaflet that caused the trouble could never be published with public money in any country in the world.

Gilbert: We never want to confront – subversive we like to be – never confront, because if you ask too many questions...

George: All the people who have brought about Clause 28 have just made sexuality divisive, which is a very bad thing. We believe that everyone is a sexual person, that is all. After all, you don't need to know the sex of a piece of meat you are eating for dinner, do you? It is just meat. Or flowers, if you send a beautiful bunch of flowers, you don't check which one is spunking off with the next one.

Do you worry about the oppressive attitude towards homosexuality in Russia?

George: Yes, we heard a good joke about that, but I think the attitude is more oppressive towards sexuality, I am sure that is the case.

Gilbert: What was the joke about homosexuality in Russia?

George: Oh yes, this is not actually our joke. One of the organisers was at the Marlborough Gallery talking to Bacon's organiser there and she said, 'When choosing pictures don't you have to be rather careful? Is homosexuality legal in Russia?' And he said, 'Yes, of course. In prison!' What an amazing reply!

How much do you think that your work is appreciated in this country, and do the art critics understand your work?

George: Yes, we have an enormous following here, not less than any other country and probably more. But a wider range of people, from all classes and walks of life. In a lot of countries only a particular class go to galleries.

Gilbert: But critics don't want to look because they are racist.

Racist in what way?

George: In that they will only attend to art that is from wine-growing countries. The educated bigot in Britain just likes foreign art. Art equals foreign to them. That attitude came about through people like Roger Fry.

You have also expressed your dislike of what you term left-wing liberal critics.

Gilbert: Yes, and sometimes we call them 'Black Shirt Marxists', because that is what they are. They want to dictate taste, and we don't believe in that.

Critics like John Berger also seem to hold similar beliefs to you regarding the death of aesthetic meaning, the use of photography or the redundancy of the artistic gesture.

George: I wouldn't know what their beliefs are.

Gilbert: We have never read John Berger but we heard that he was interested in the force and capacity of the photograph as a means for mass communication. We believe the camera is the best modern brush today – because the artist wants to speak to the world. That is what he has to do, so that is the best form.

You have all these Christopher Dresser pots and so forth around this room and in the rest of your house; do you see Victorian values as corresponding to your own values in any way?

George: Well, we never think of it in those terms really. What we like is that they were Modernists, they were completely new, fresh – when they were alive – totally modern. We could also be interested in art from all sorts of periods or even from before that period. There are always artists who are interested, as we are, in the meaning and the force of culture in all periods. At any stage in history, there is always somebody pushing the barriers of civilisation in the Western world forward, and we like to contribute to that. We don't believe it is time to stand still, there is still room for improvement.

Gilbert: What we like is a complicated art, that is the kind of art we like to do. We don't believe in having only one view – it is many views we believe very much in. We never believe that the artist has to be good, and doesn't accept bad. We believe in the whole circle with everything in it – the flower and the shit. You can also fit our art into different frames. You could say it looks Japanese, if you want to; it looks medieval, if you want to; it looks like high tech, if you want to; or like computer art. So it fits in on every level. What we are interested in is speaking, having a vision.

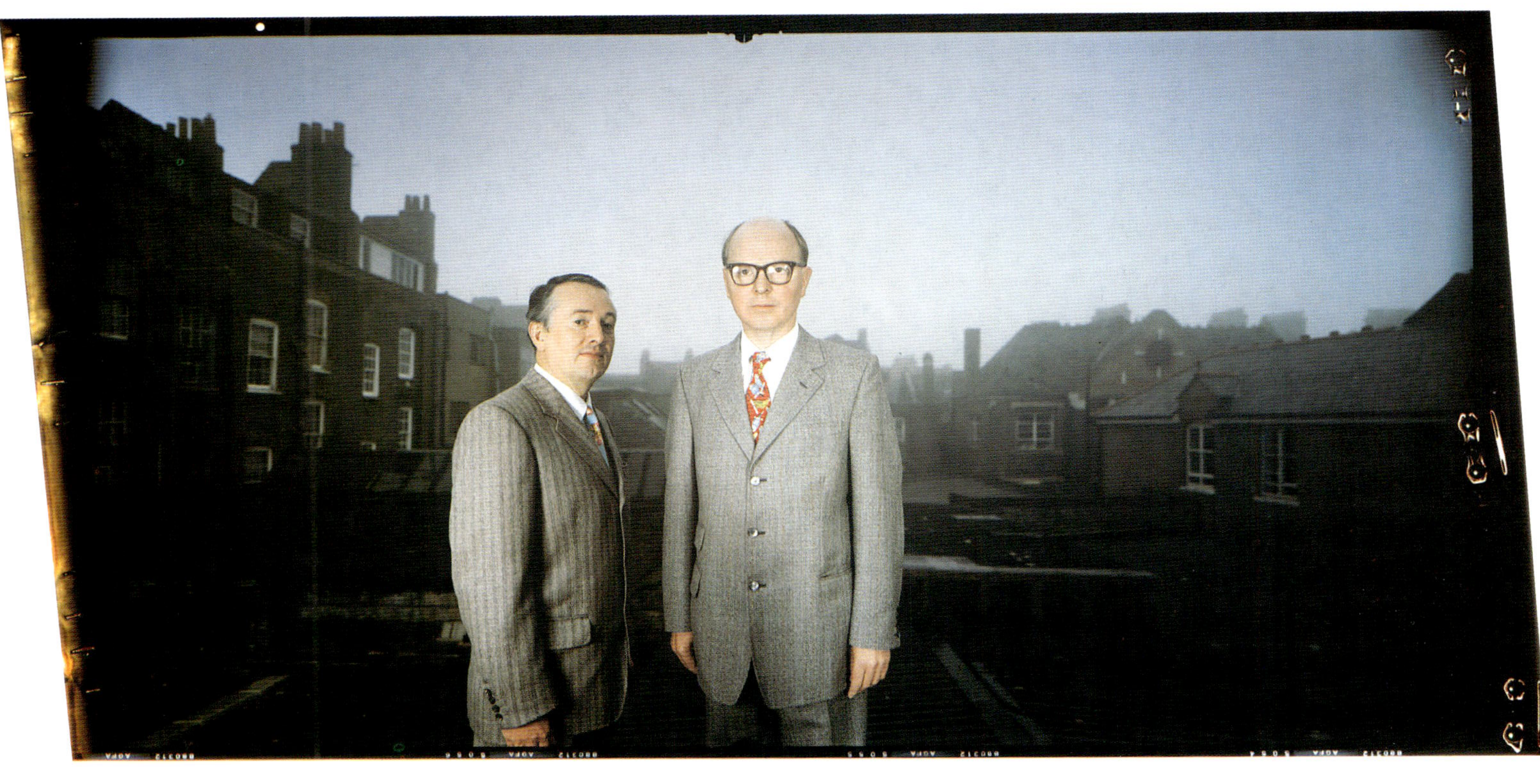

42 Portrait by Alastair Thain, Fournier Street, 1989

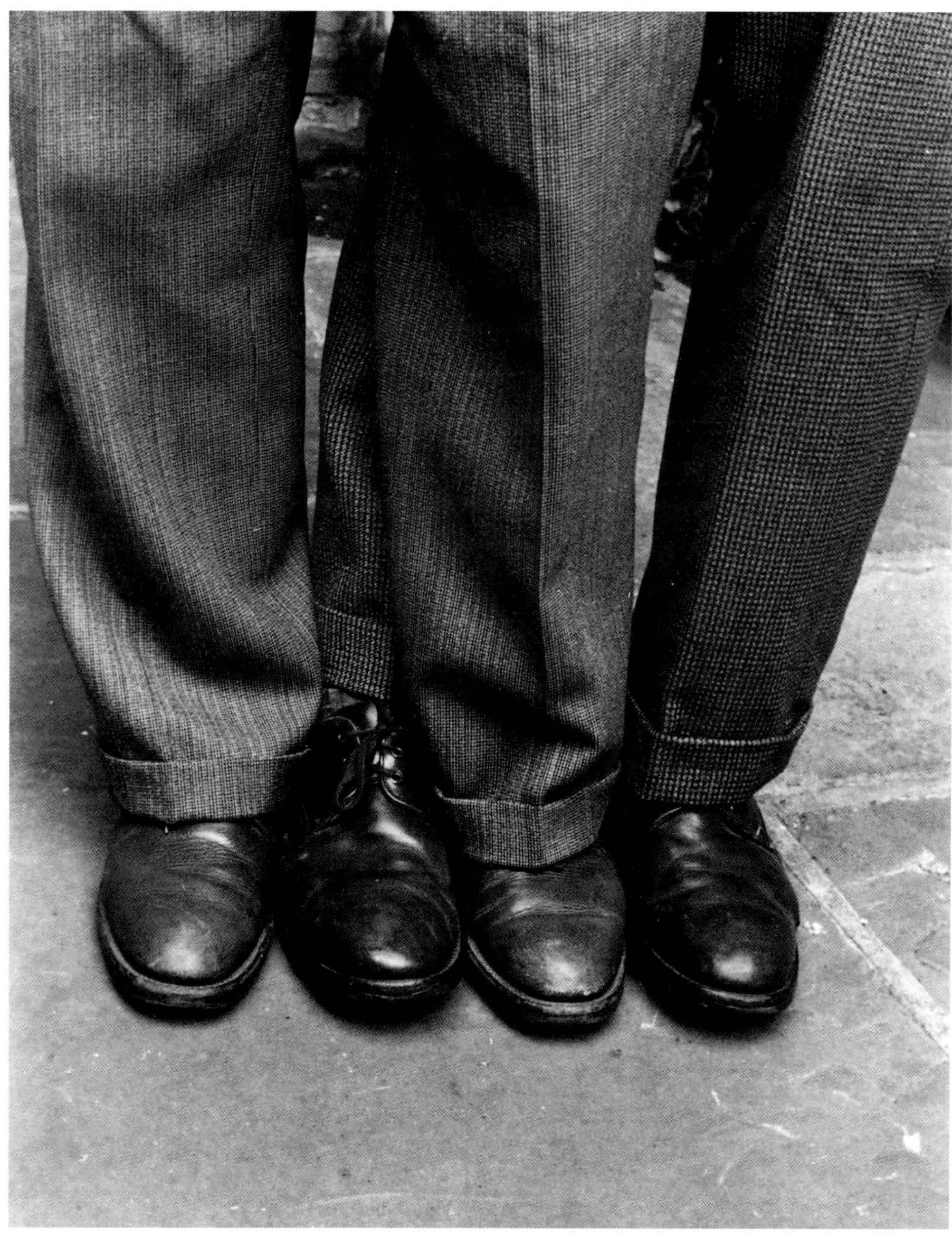

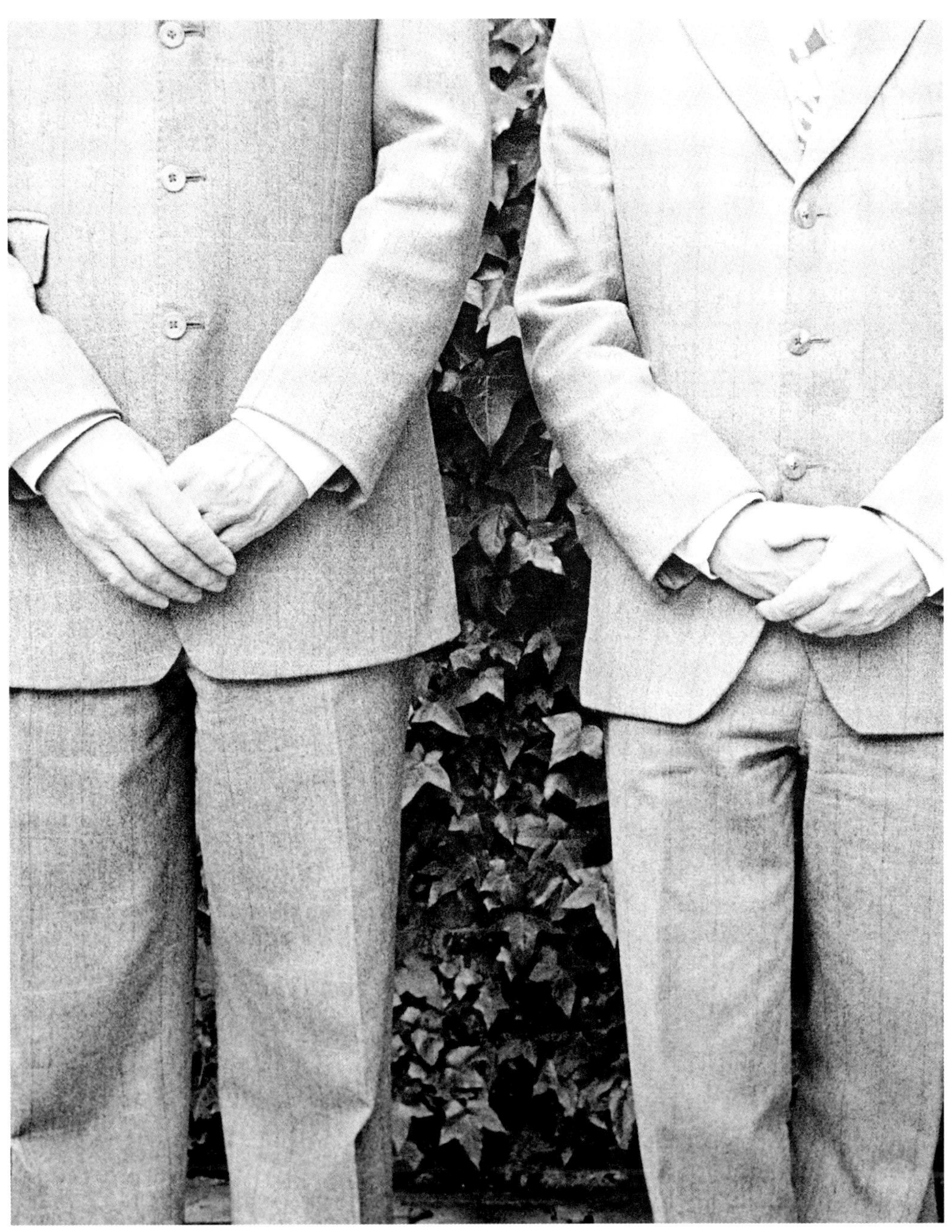

43 Portraits by Rankin Waddell, Fournier Street, 1989

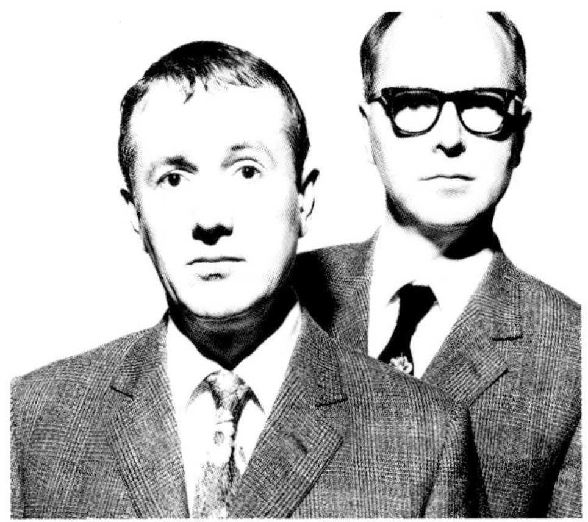

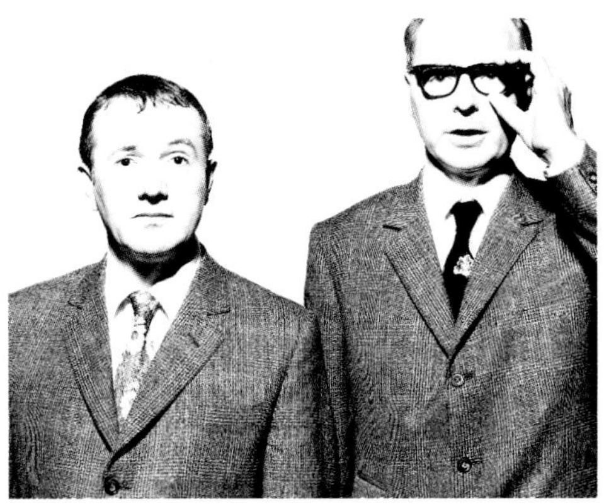

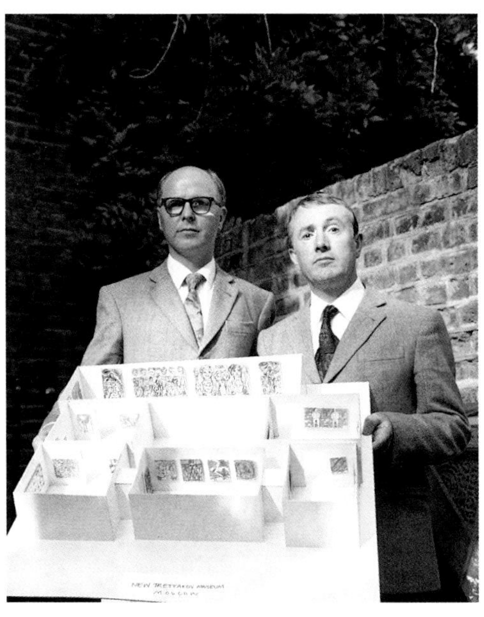

45 Portraits by Daniel Farson, Fournier Street, 1990. *Above*: with scale model for the artists' exhibition at the New Tretyakov Gallery, Moscow; *opposite*: in the artists' home

44 Portraits by Jerome Schlomoff, 29 June 1990

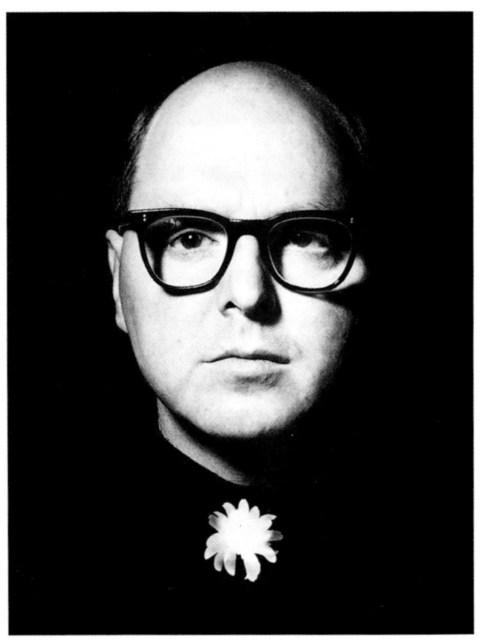

46 Portraits by Chris Garnham, London, 1990

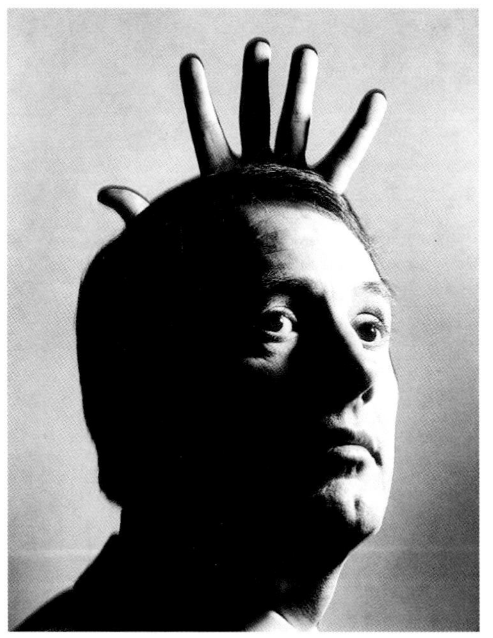

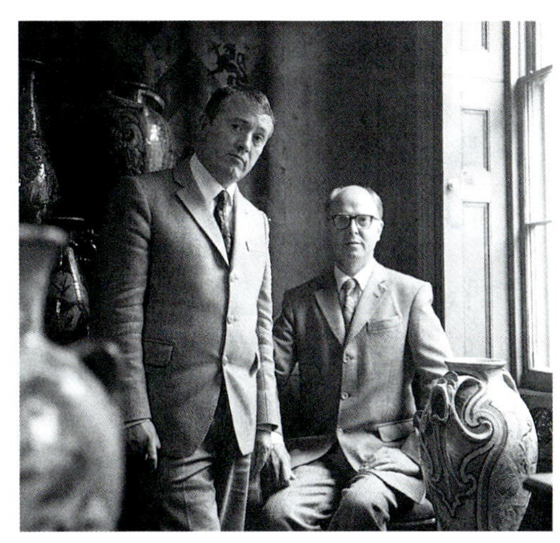

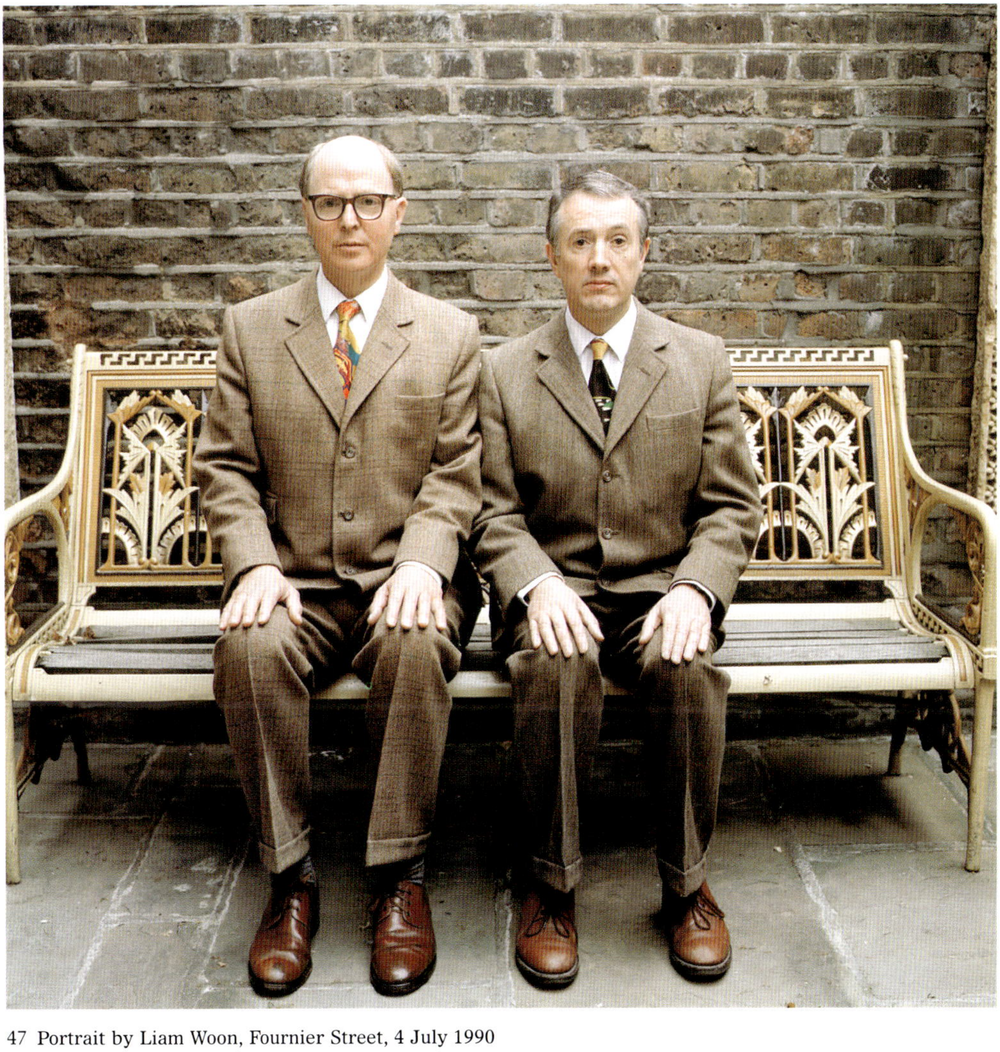

47 Portrait by Liam Woon, Fournier Street, 4 July 1990

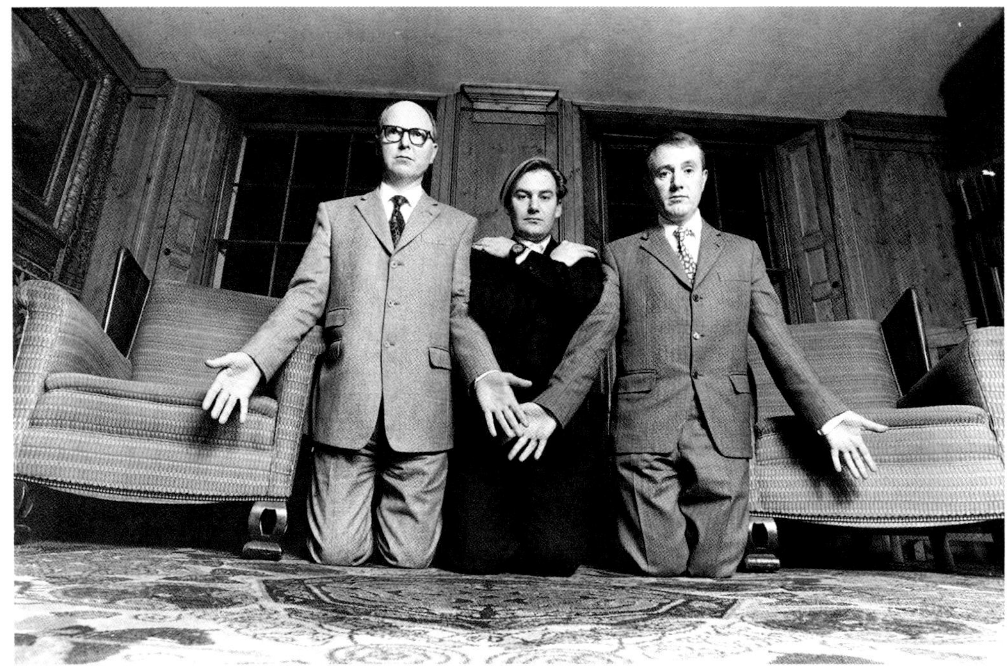

48 Portrait by Simon Townsley for *The Sunday Times* with James Birch, originator of the artists' Russia and China exhibitions, Fournier Street, 1989

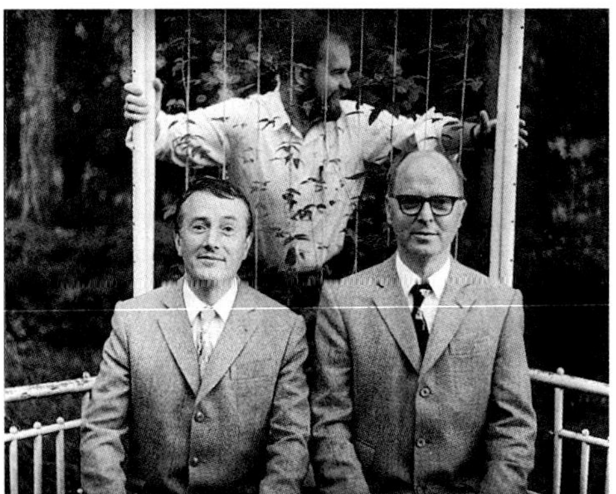

49 With Sergei Klokhov, James Birch's Russian counterpart, Moscow, 1989 (*Photo: V. Zamkov*)

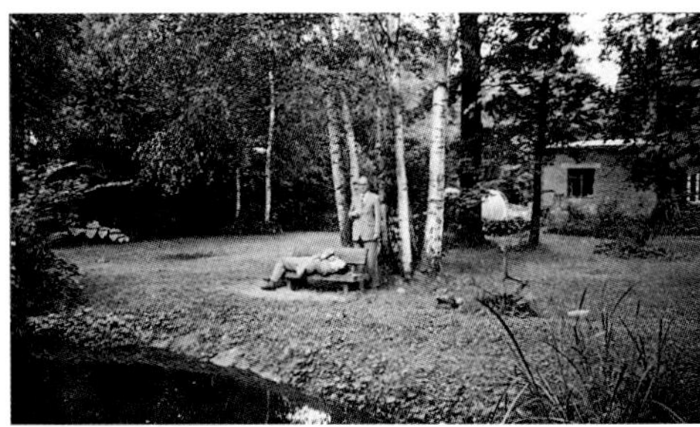

50 At Nikita Sunnikov's dascha in Vernukova, near Moscow, 1989 (*Photo: James Birch*)

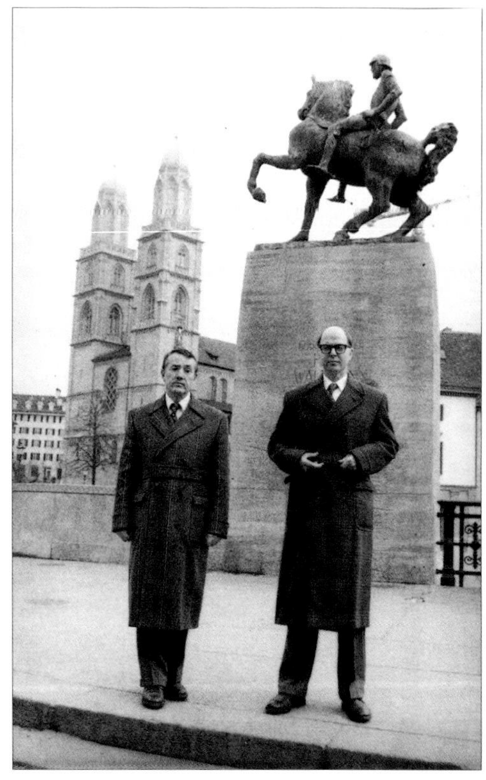

51 In Poland for the artists' exhibition *The Cosmological Pictures* at the Palac Sztuki, Krakow, 1991 (*Photo: Táña Hojcovà*)

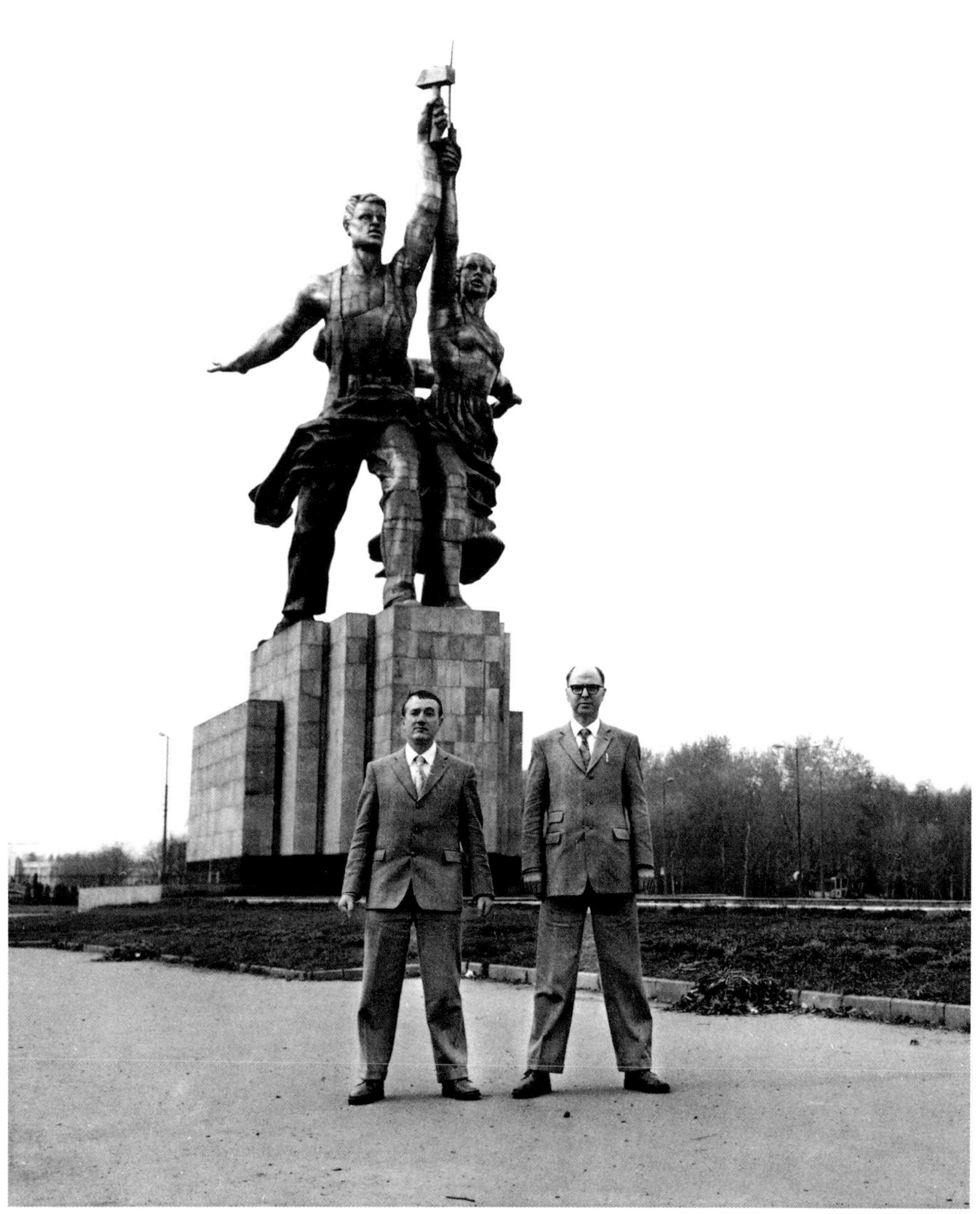

52 Portrait by Daniel Farson in front of Vera Mouchina's 1922 sculpture of Soviet workers, Moscow, 1989

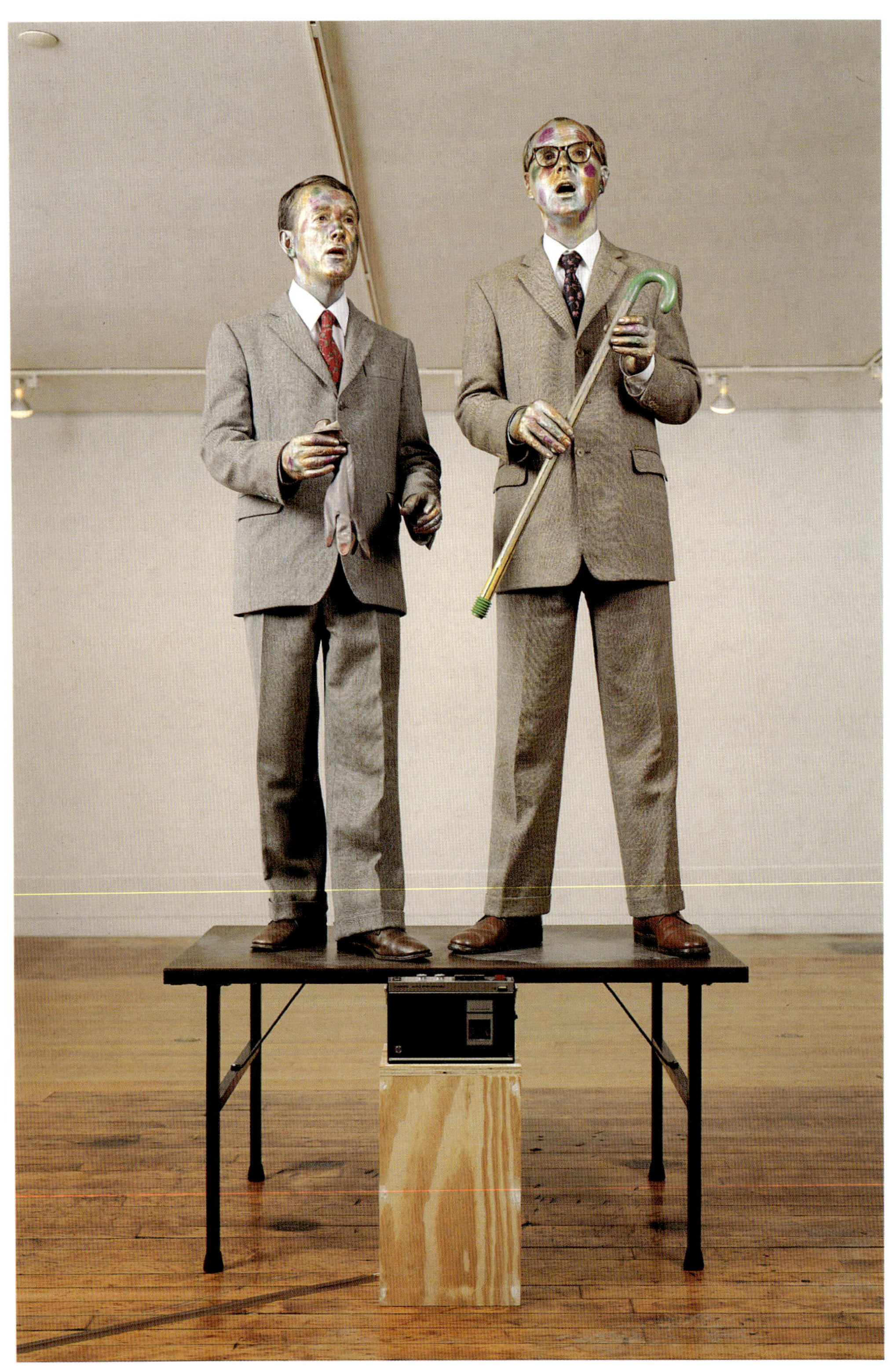

53 *Singing Sculpture*, Sonnabend Gallery, New York, 1991 (*Photo: Jon & Anne Abbott*)

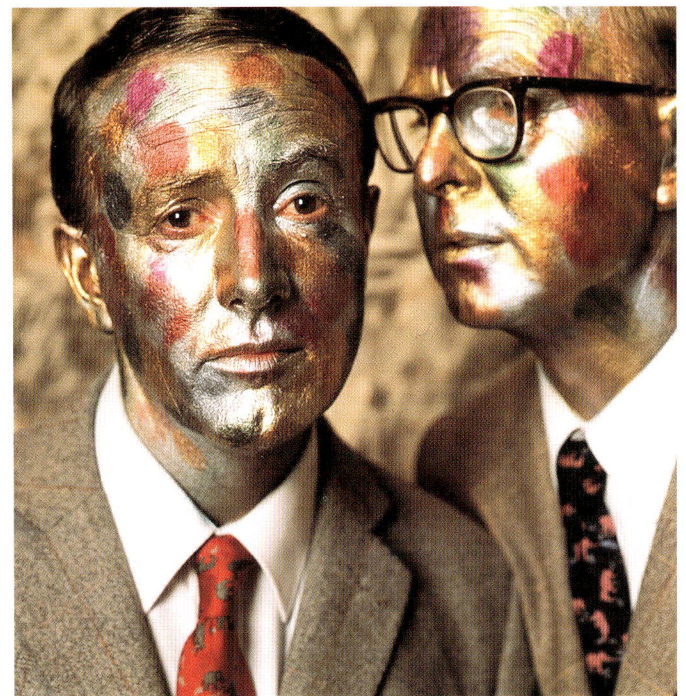

54 Portrait by Abe Frajndlich at the time of the *Singing Sculpture*,
New York, 1991

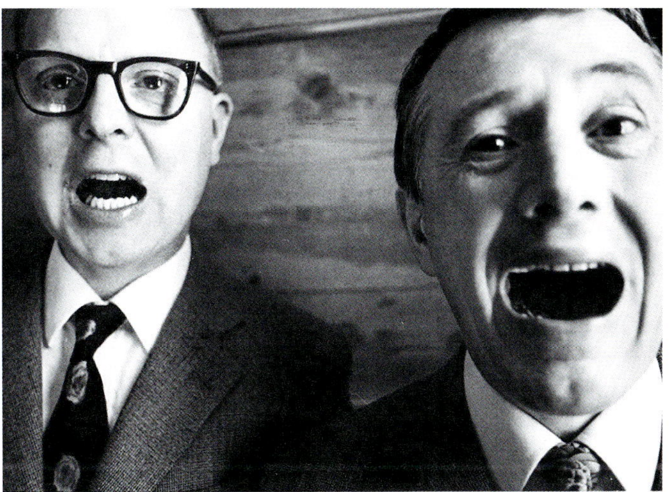

55 Portrait by Caz Gorham, Fournier Street, 1990

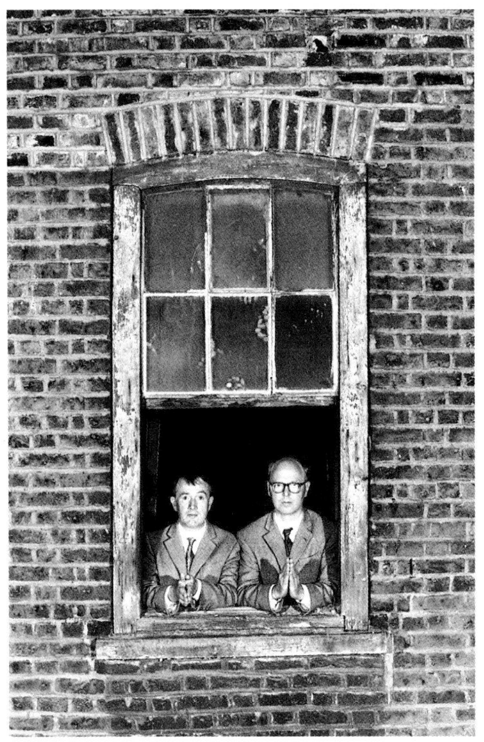

56 Portrait by Herbie Knott, Fournier Street,
August 1991

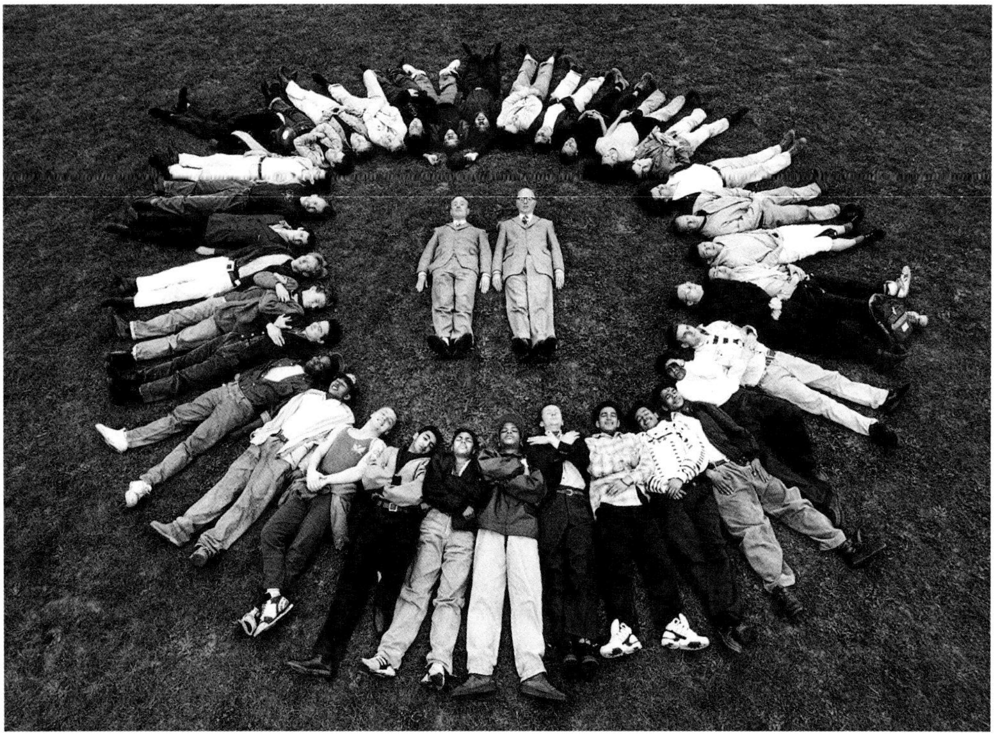

57 Portrait by Herbie Knott with youngsters who appear in the artists' pictures, Roman Road, London,
May 1991

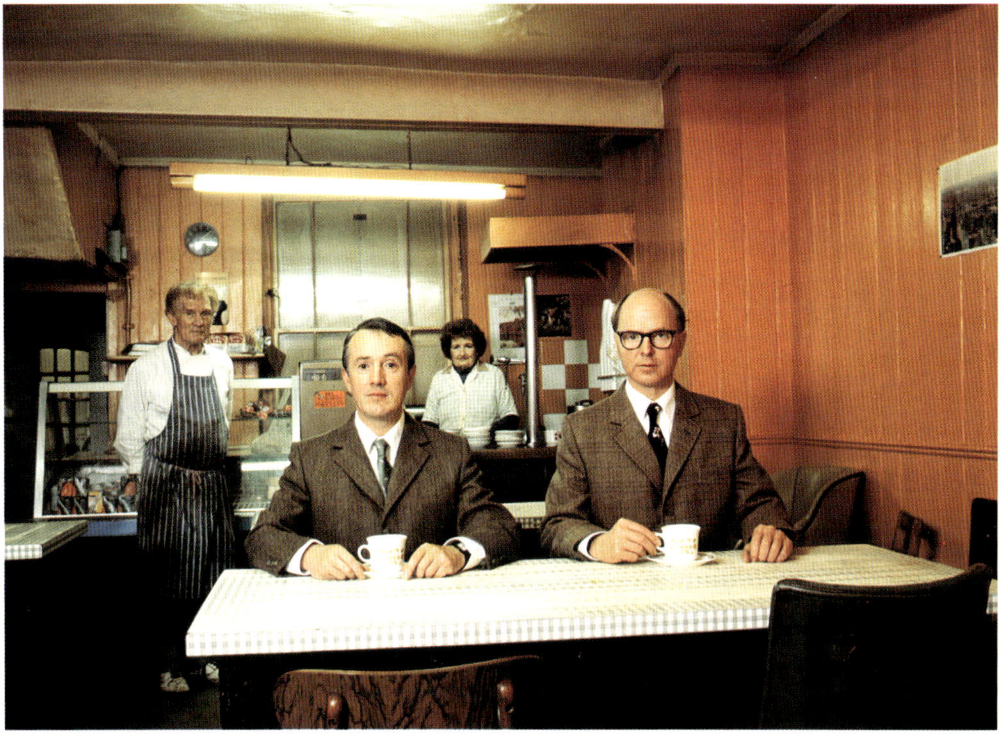

58 Portrait by Vincent Knapp with Clyde and Phyllis at the Market Cafe, Fournier Street, December 1991

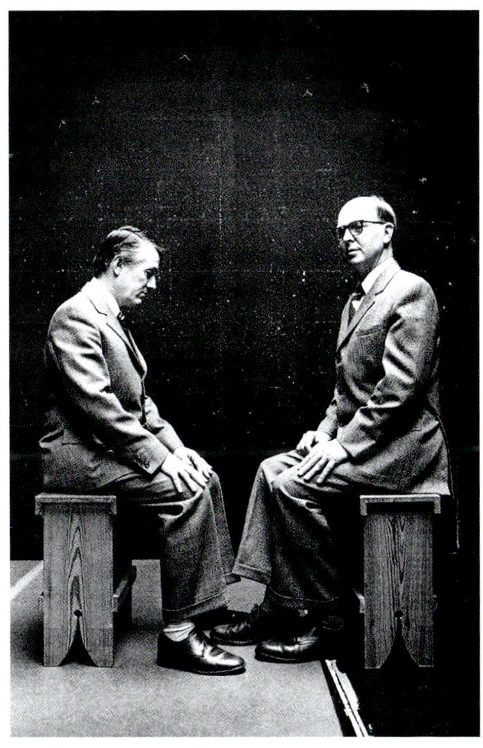

59 Portrait by Robert Goldstein in the artists'
studio, Fournier Street, March 1991

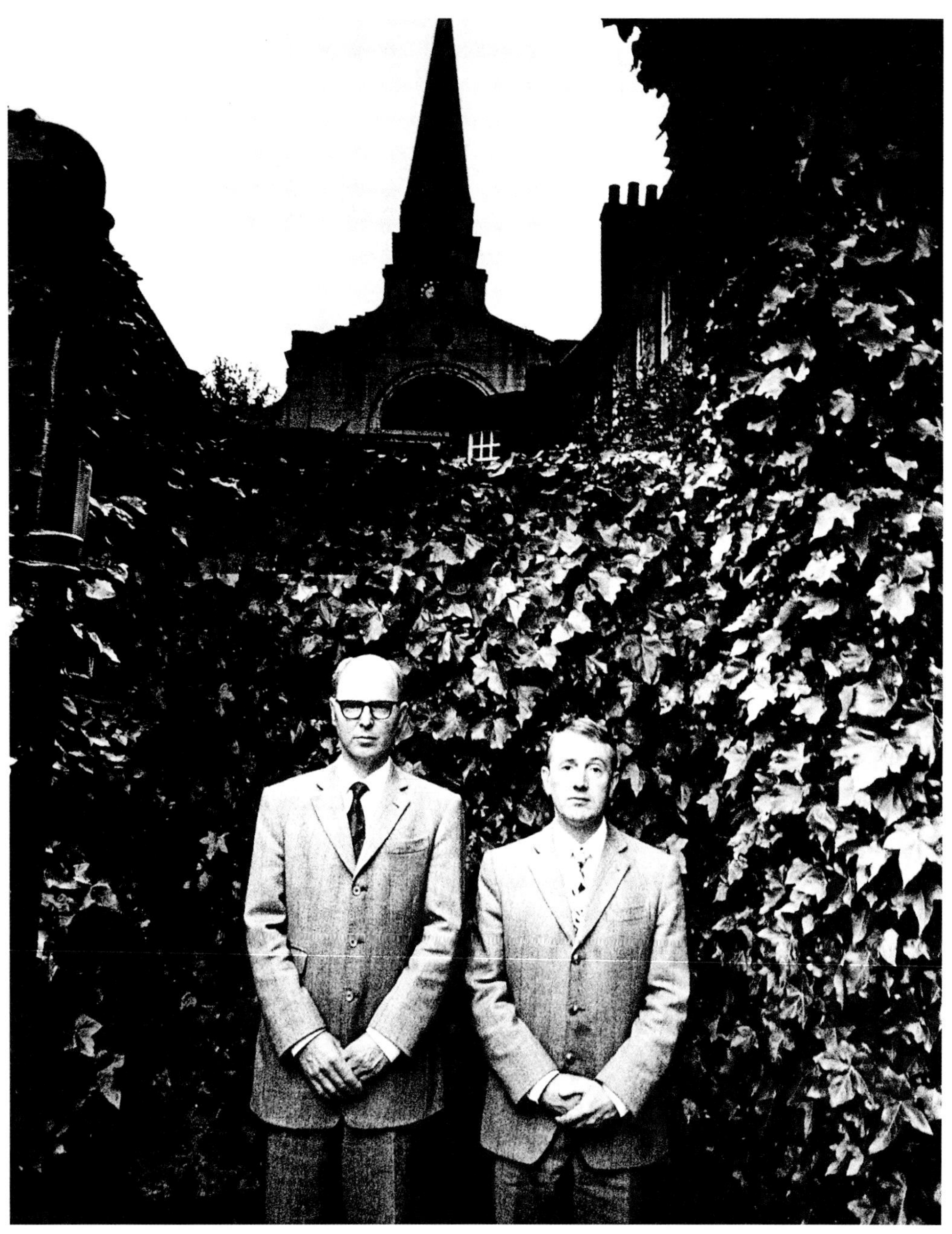

60 Portrait by Pat Pope, Fournier Street, July 1991

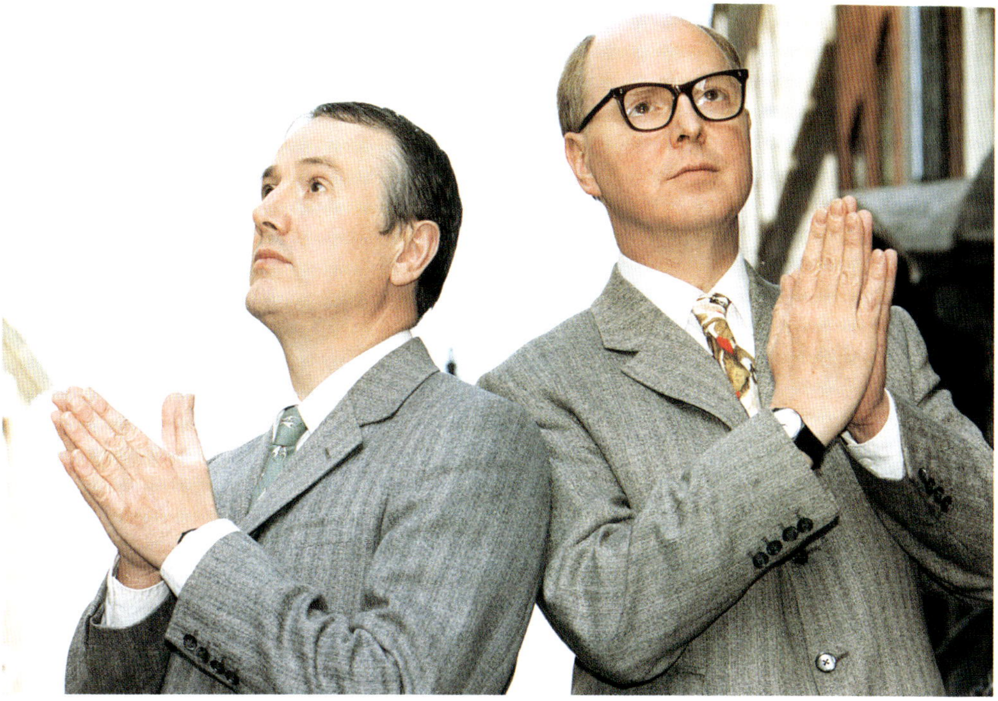

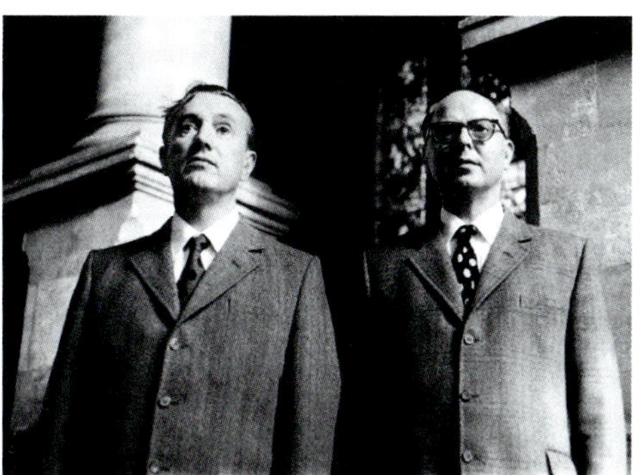

61 Portrait by G. Copus for *The London Evening Standard*, Fournier Street, 1992

62 Portrait by Michael Clement in Christchurch Spitalfields, Commercial Street, London, 1992

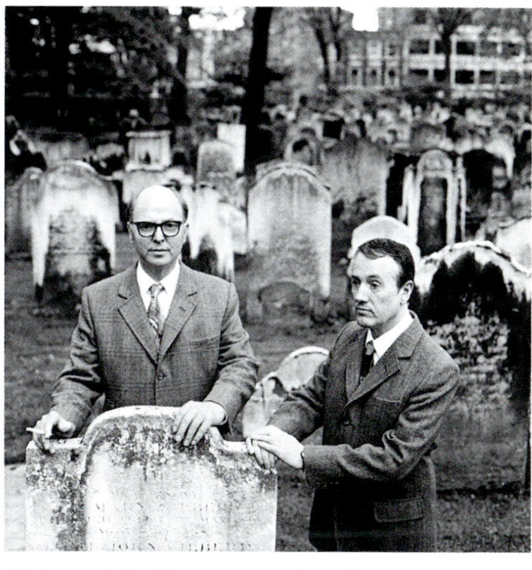

63 Portrait by Liam Woon in Bunhill Fields cemetery, London, 1992

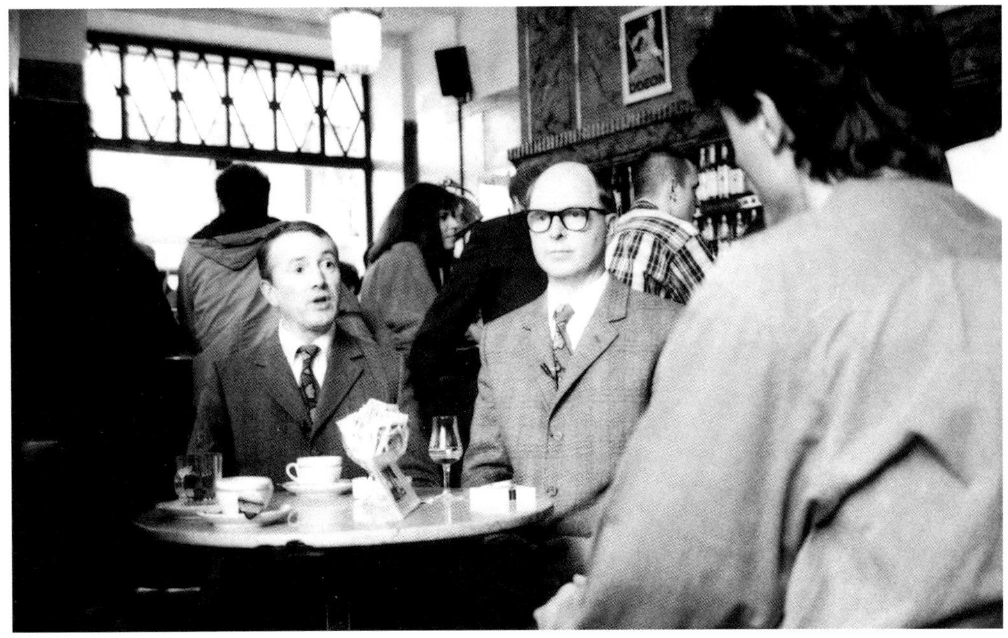

64 At Café Odéon in Zurich, Switzerland, at the time of the artists' exhibition *The Cosmological Pictures* at the Kunsthalle Zürich, 1992

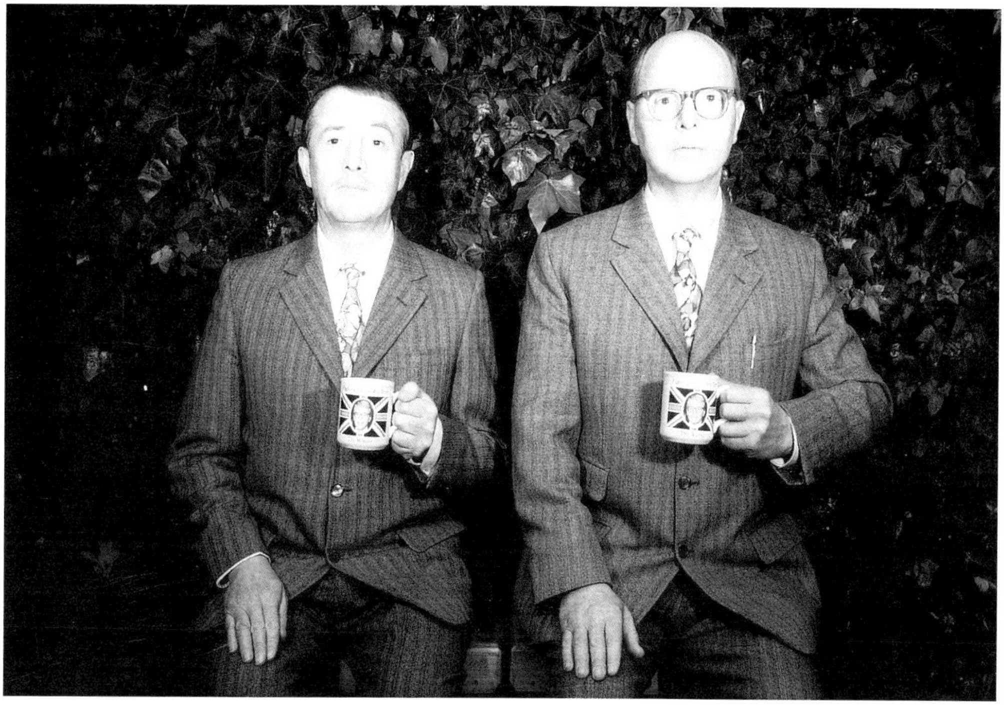

65 Portrait by Michael Lange, Fournier Street, August 1993

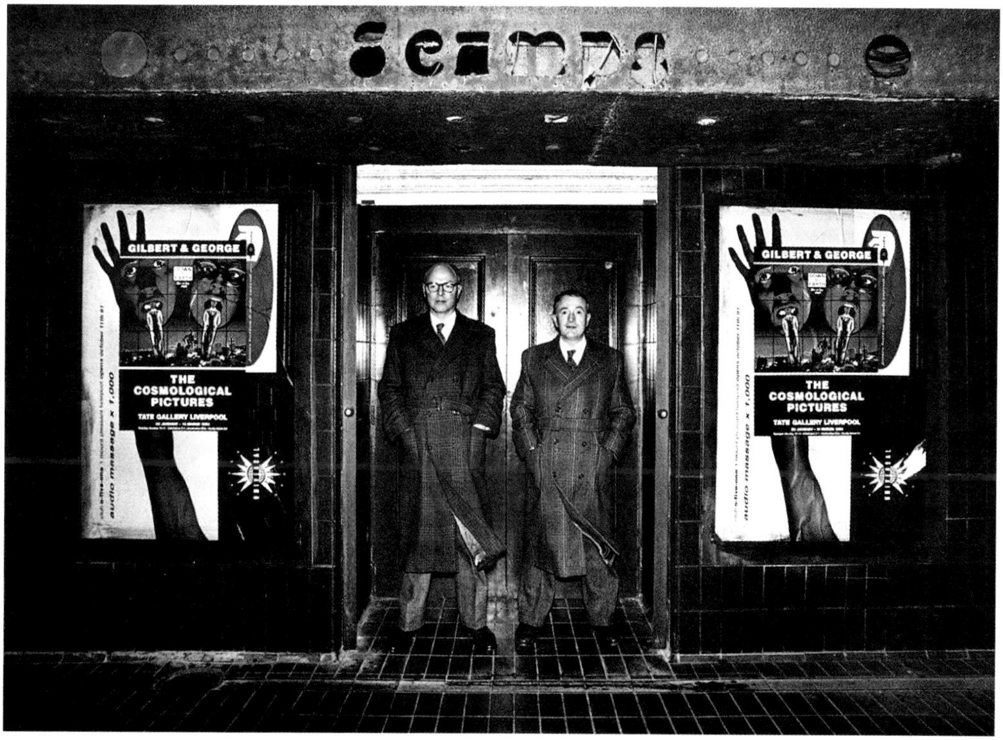

66 Portrait by Herbie Knott in Liverpool at the time of the artists' exhibition *The Cosmological Pictures* at the Tate Gallery Liverpool, January 1993

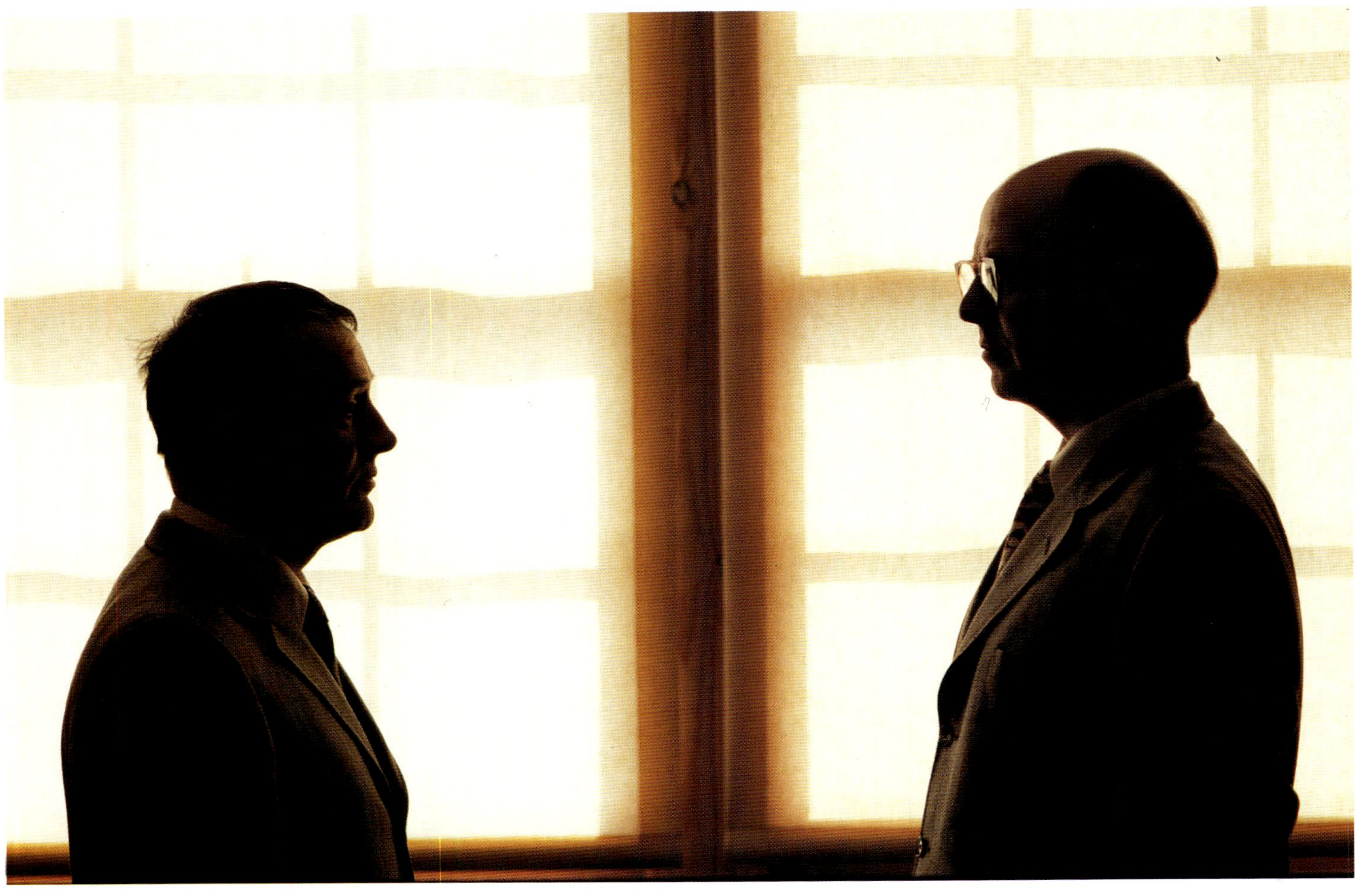

67 Portrait by Michael Lange, Fournier Street, August 1993

George: We were against the elitism of those forms. We realised that
with all the discussion around sculpture at that time, they were
building up a language that was outside life and which the minute you
got on to the Charing Cross Road would not mean a damn thing. It was
only within that club. It was too elitist. We say that the picture is there
in the museum or the gallery for people to view in the light of their own
life, agreement or disagreement is not the crucial thing. If they say, I
don't think those artists should have made that picture, and it shouldn't
be put on the wall, it doesn't matter, you see, it is too late, they have
seen it, and we've got 'em. Bad luck, right? That picture's gone into
their heads, it is too late.

Gilbert: But we know that there is so little that speaks to viewers, even
if they visit the National Gallery they don't understand what it means:
these Renaissance artists, or this king going up and down this
mountain.

George: Fifty dead Jesuses. Why does every Western city have to have
another fifty dead Jesuses? Quite crazy. The form of the painting should
serve the meaning. The form can be as elaborate as necessary in order
to serve the meaning, it should never be the issue. With our pictures
nobody ever says, we like the nice bit of red in the corner or the nice
line going down the middle.

Gilbert: Art is a re-examining of life. That's what it is. Every day we are
all the same – we still have the same bloody stupid face, but we are still
worried every day, so we re-examine ourselves, you know?

George: Oh, we just studied, we used to go to different lectures and
experiment, it was a time of experimentation. We are probably the most
trained artists in London, I'm sure. We both went to art schools for
many many years – twelve years – studied painting, sculpture, drawing,
history of art and architecture, psychology. Everything.

Gilbert: I think that our biggest invention was on the day that we said,
'We are the art and the artist', I think that was the best. We are still
doing that, we have never changed from that. We believe that all good
artists have to do that. Every artist – even Constable – it is his vision
that is important, not the landscape.

George: You still are looking at a 'Constable'. You don't say what a
lovely field, you say it is a fantastic Constable. It is him speaking to you.
It is the living artist. It is the life of that dear, dead man coming out, not
the elm tree.
Gilbert: We only believe in the vision; that is why if we could just chuck
it on the wall, we'd prefer that. But the vision is important, because that
is what changes the world.
George: We always say it is what we 'say' that is important, you see.

But does art have a role to play in Society?

George: The very reality that we sit here now is a cultural reality.
Everyone wants to say nowadays that it is a political reality that we live
in, we don't believe that. We think that we are what we are culturally.
Without culture you would just have some crazy army crashing through
this window at this very moment with machine guns. In countries where
they don't have art, you don't have freedom. You have to have shelves
and shelves of books. Culture has enormous power. If you just say the
name 'Charles Dickens' to anyone in the street, even if they have never
read a book in their whole life, something of the dear man's life will
come into their heads and live again. That is the force of culture which
must be very important, otherwise they would not lock up poets. In
extreme right-wing countries and extreme left-wing countries they lock
up all the artists and writers. The left here would love to lock us up.

So are you apolitical?

Gilbert: We always say we are boring Conservatives.
George: Normal. Normal.
Gilbert: That is what we like to be: normal.
George: Average. Lower-class, uneducated Tories!

Do you have political beliefs beyond that?

George: We are always perfectly amazed that in every other walk of life
– except the art world – it is perfectly normal to be either Labour or
Conservative, or even something else. Taxi drivers, when they start
raving about politics, can be Labour or Tory, some are one and some
are the other, it's not such a big problem. 'What gets up my nose is this',
he says, it is just a discussion. Whereas in the art world it seems you
have to be anti-Tory because it is a big, mad, violent-to-the-death fight,
which is crazy. It is a free country, you can be either, so what is the
problem? It is fairly normal to be a Tory, if it wasn't they wouldn't have
been in power for so long. It is not so unusual. We always say if artists

are supposed to be so original, so creative, how come they have all got
the same damn political party? That can't be so original, they should at
least have a variety of opinion. American artists all love Communism.
Gilbert: We dislike millionaires who want to be Communists, it is
obviously so hypocritical. But in general party policies are becoming
less important – like in Europe – because it's only going to be a kind of
middle party.
George: Well, like the Conservatives are, in fact.

> *Your early works, made with charcoal and oil paint with images
> which are largely concerned with a reaction to Nature seem to nod
> towards a traditional concern of the artist.*

George: Yes, but those large pieces were all based on photography,
without which they could not have existed. We then developed that
language: how to actually make a big one. A lot of people come out of
art school, look in a museum, see what it is, and say, 'Oh, so I will do
something like that'. They start with a box of colours, a box of oil paints.
We didn't do that, we started with ourselves. It took us four years to find
red, whereas the artist has all the colours there immediately, first thing.
We had to go out and buy red. We didn't have all the colours there that
the artist normally has. It took us another three years to find yellow.

> *Should artists intervene in or reflect society?*

George: We have no interest in reflecting or showing society – we are
only interested to be forming it. What we believe tomorrow is what the
artists are today. Already we see the world as very very different from
when we started, and we have been a part of that, I am sure. Good
writers don't reflect society, they form their tomorrows. D. H.
Lawrence didn't reflect the morality of his time, did he? He formed the
morality of the next generation – don't you think? Everyone fucked
differently after that book, they actually started shagging differently.
There were plenty of writers then who just reflected the status quo –
but you don't remember their names, do you?

> *Yet, how do you react to Prince Charles's intervention in the daily
> life of Society, and his concern for forming a new understanding for
> architectural standards?*

George: We are very supportive of the monarchy, we should say that
first of all, more than any other artist we know. But we don't believe
that a person from such a privileged background as Prince Charles is
able to have a clear, modern view. He has not had the opportunity to see

a wide spectrum of life really. He can only walk along the streets surrounded by men with guns in their waistcoats. He cannot 'see' life, and you have to see life, and you have to see life very clearly in order to know where to go next.

Gilbert: And it is very simple: would he understand or like our art or not? He wouldn't. He would be against it because he would say that our images would have to be painted and he is wrong here as he is with architecture. I think that high-tech architecture will never stop, you cannot stop it, it's fantastic, I like it very much. We prefer Prince Albert's views on modern art and architecture.

George: He [Prince Charles] is a fantastic future king who has been badly advised really. I think that is the case.

> *It seems to me that your work is founded on, among others things, a concern for the values of the surface. What to you is the nature of reality, and in what way is it your subject matter?*

George: Our subject matter is the world. It is the Pain. Pain. Just to hear the world turning is Pain, isn't it? Totally, every day, every second.

Gilbert: Our inspiration is all those people alive today on the planet, the desert, the jungle, the cities. We are interested in the human person, the complexity of life.

> *But as far as reality in art is concerned, would you agree with what Wyndham Lewis wrote in* Tarr *that art is life with all the humbug of living taken out? Is art life or a purified version of life?*

Gilbert: For us, art is searching for life, a re-examination of life for the new generation. It is artificial, because we don't know what life is all about, so you have to put up a new idea.

> *Do you agree with Wolf Jahn's interpretation of your work in terms of an ascension analagous to the Life of Christ?*

George: That we like very much. We always saw all of life like that.

> *You don't feel that that is blasphemous at all?*

George: As Christians, not, absolutely not – we are the most Christian artists we know.

Gilbert: I don't believe in blasphemy because that is against freedom.

George: Most people who worry about blasphemy are not Christians in any sense. Jesus Christ came on Earth to be a sinner like all of us. I think that is the basis of the Christian inspiration, wouldn't you say?

> *Critics like Peter Fuller have said that your work is a blasphemous obscenity.*

George: But he is not a Christian by his own admission. I mean, Jesus Christ didn't reflect the life of his time, he formed the tomorrows.

Do you go to church?

George: We are not churchgoers or religious in the formal sense, no.

Gilbert: But that is too limited, saying that it is blasphemy, what does it mean today?

What about drawing a parallel with the Salman Rushdie affair?

Gilbert: But even that, the Muslims will have to give in, in the end, they cannot kill people for religious intolerance.

George: Blasphemy equals religious intolerance.

Were you involved in the publication by Thames and Hudson of Wolf Jahn's book on you, in a financial sense?

George: Yes, absolutely. Of course. All our books are helped in some way.

Gilbert: Every art magazine has to be funded, even by advertising, that is sponsorship.

George: We are always amazed that art critics sometimes write in newspapers against commerical sponsorship, and on the same page as a whisky advertisement! It is very hypocritical, no newspaper that carries an art column can be published without sponsorship – it costs £3.70... without the ads. Sponsorship of art books is very important, because then we can invest in the minds and the lives of the future. Go and look in the bookshops: it is ninety-nine per cent Van Gogh. Do you want that? When I was sixteen, and first became interested in modern art, I couldn't find a book on modern art... didn't exist. And that was wrong. With tennis, which is sponsored, that is different. Oh yes. Every art critic is sponsored.

Gilbert: Publishers, they don't believe they can sell books on modern English artists. So why shouldn't the gallery help in creating a book, if they make money out of it, why not?

Judith Collins of the Tate Gallery has cited you and Andy Warhol as great spiritual artists of today. Would you like to see your work as stained-glass windows?

George: 'Stained-glass windows' is the interpretation of over-educated people. There are vast sections of Society that weren't taken to country churches by toffee-nosed parents who just see it as computer art, just as space-invader art. That reaction depends on your social background; it is to do with class.

George: There is one big difference between Warhol and ourselves
which I think is an important one, and that is his interest in very
famous material. He likes very famous film stars and famous
politicians, rich superstars, rich film stars. We are not involved in that,
we are interested in the human person, regardless of class or
background or anything. All the people in our pictures are humanoid –
they are devoid of class. They could come from any background: they
could be South American or English or Russian or Dutch or Australian.
They don't have to be famous, mad or drugged before they can go into
our work, which they have to be to get into Warhol's. We respect all
artists because they are all working for a particular purpose and aim,
and obviously you have to respect and admire that. But, on the other
hand we are working for something different. One cannot just look at
fine art here.
Gilbert: I like Dickens.

Your read Dickens?
Gilbert: I saw the films like *The Old Curiosity Shop*. I was very
impressed. I like the complexity of life, the structure and the morality
and all that. And it speaks...
George: ...across the history, doesn't it, and across the classes. They
seem to stand the test of time very well.

But have you read Dickens?
George: We are not involved in reading books, we are not from that
class really.
Gilbert: We like and prefer the raw world in front of us, let's stay naked
in front of the world and trying to sort it out.

But you have books in your bookshelves over there, are they...?
George: Not so much for reading, they are mostly visual. Lives of the
artists, things like that.
Gilbert: We became interested in reading about the miserable lives of
the artists in the eighteenth century, nineteenth century – they're all
the same, we found out. Miserable, unhappy.

Are you miserable?
Gilbert: Deeply miserable, yes.
George: We are more miserable than anyone else we know. We think it
is very important to be miserable, we don't believe that anyone made

any progress through being cheerful. Civilisation is not 'advanced' by people lying on the beach with a gin and tonic. Everything is subservient to the art, in fact, and everything has to fit in around it. We try to clear out our life and empty it. We give all our feelings and thoughts and fears and dreads and hopes, straight into our pictures – you cannot be more open than that. There is hardly a subject of life that isn't universal that we haven't discussed in our work.

Gilbert: We don't have any other private life: we eat, go to sleep, think about art. When we have an exhibition we get drunk, that's it. That's very simple.

George: Come home, do some more.

You only get drunk when you have an exhibition?

George: Generally speaking.

Gilbert: Generally speaking, yes!

Do you see this rejection of a private life in terms of a sacrifice that you are making?

George: If you go blindfold into a library, take a book off the shelf and it is about somebody who did something, whether it is in the field of medicine or military or politics or poetry, it has always been done with enormous personal sacrifice, it has always been like that in the history of civilisation. Totally. Nobody has a jolly life for giving. A jolly life for taking, yes, but not a jolly life for giving. Everybody gets beaten up, even if you invent penicillin, you just get smacked in, the first day. They didn't say, 'Wonderful, fantastic, brilliant' – they said, 'Get out, banished from the city.'

Why do you think it is necessary that you should do your art together, would you ever make works as individuals?

George: We never considered that, and that has been one of our greatest strengths in fact, being two. And it is very good because it makes the artist more normal because the whole of the world is more or less divided into twos – it is the most common unit, two people. So it makes it a very democratic form, in a way, more normal.

Gilbert: We always believe that every artist has to ask another person. He asks, 'Do I like this, or not?'; he asks himself like another person.

George: 'Do I do a bit more red here or not?' And back comes this horrible silence. Whereas if there are two, it is very useful.

It is a long time since you made a presentation as Living Sculptures – do you feel you might do it again?

Gilbert: We feel we never stopped, because I think the very big photo-
pieces are exactly that even if we are not there ourselves.
George: The form is incidental, the meaning in the end is the important
thing. We see it as a big continuation, we just changed forms.
Gilbert: I mean we like films. We would like to do another film.
	And do you watch a lot of television?
Gilbert: No, less and less. There is so little on that is interesting. It's all
the same, mediocre.
George: We just relax sometimes in front of the set.
	And the cinema as well?
George: We never go to the cinema, to the theatre, or concerts – never.
	What led you to agree to this interview for Modern Painters?
Gilbert: We agree to every interview.
George: It wasn't a big decision really, we like to be democratic. Why
should we refuse someone? We are not such toffee-nosed artists, we are
not snobbish, we even will do an interview for *Modern Painters*!

The Correspondent Questionnaire 1990

Compiled by Rosanna Greenstreet and first published in the *Sunday Correspondent*, London, 23 September 1990, p. 46.

What is your idea of perfect happiness?
Being miserable.

What is your greatest fear?
Being happy.

With which historical figure do you most identify?
Charles Darwin.

Which living person do you most admire?
Jesus Christ, HM Queen Elizabeth II and PM Margaret Thatcher.

Which living person do you most despise?
Brian Sewell and Waldemar Januszczak.

What is the trait you most deplore in yourself?
Level-headedness.

What is the trait you most deplore in others?
Negativism.

What is your greatest extravagance?
Treating younger people.

What objects do you always carry with you?
Contraceptives.

What makes you most depressed?
Educated bigotry.

What do you most dislike about your appearance?
The signs of ageing.

What is your favourite word?
Masterpiece.

Who are your favourite writers?
Charles Dickens, Samuel Beckett and David Robilliard.

What are you reading at the moment?
The Ariosophists of Austria and Germany 1890–1935 by Nicholas Goodrick-Clarke.

Who are your favourite painters?
William Blake, J. M. W. Turner and Francis Bacon.

Who are your favourite musicians?
Elgar, Britten and The Beatles.

What is your favourite building?
The Houses of Parliament.
What is your favourite journey?
From Heathrow to home.
What or who is the greatest love of your life?
Each other.
What would your motto be?
'Art for All', as it always was.
What do you consider the most overrated virtue?
Egalitarianism.
On what occasions do you lie?
In reply to 'How are you?'
Which words or phrases do you overuse?
Dick.
What is your greatest regret?
Not having discovered bad behaviour earlier in life.
When and where were you happiest?
Sober in our studio.
What single thing would improve the quality of your life?
A cure for all the dear people who are suffering from the Aids virus.
Which talent would you most like to have?
Dunno.
How would you like to die?
Famous, with our boots on.
How would you like to be remembered?
As the artists we are.
What keeps you awake at night?
Sexual fantasies.
What is your present state of mind?
Very disturbed.

G & G Daytripping: 1992

Transcript of Gilbert & George's statements in the short film *G & G Daytripping*, produced and directed in 1992 by Ian McDonald for Anglia Television.

Who?
Gilbert & George: We are Gilbert & George.
Where?
George: We are down from London for the day, attempting to imagine that we are soothing our nerves.
Gilbert: We always take the train to Thorpe Bay and walk through Southend to Leigh-on-Sea, because we like very much the smell of the sea.
What?
George: We as living artists believe in a democratic art, an art which is able to speak to people of different races, of different age groups, of different social and educational backgrounds. We want to create a human art, which is fair to all people.
Gilbert: We believe very much in a moral art. We like to create the morality of tomorrow. A work that is more complex and more tolerant.
Why?
George: We as living artists believe in the advancement of culture in the service of the individual. We want to make pictures that provide the opportunity for change in the viewer. We want to serve the people.
Gilbert: We believe very much that the artist has to ask questions. Why we are here? What we should do here? What we should improve? That's the only way to change the world.
How?
George: When we make our pictures, we go to our studio completely blank, completely zonked, without ideas and without plans because that would be wrong. We want our pictures to discuss all the thoughts and feelings that are simply inside of ourselves, and therefore inside the lives of the viewer, whether they are in the city, or in the jungle, or in the desert. They are the basic concerns of all human persons.
Gilbert: We would like to open up our hearts to everybody. We like to expose ourselves in front of the viewer, with all our hopes, our fears, our disappointments, to try to create a feeling that the viewer can understand ourselves.
Gilbert: We had a really wonderful day.
George: We are very pleased, very happy, very disturbed.

Gilbert & George: Interview with Andrew Wilson

First published in *Journal of Contemporary Art*, vol. 6, no. 2, Winter 1993.

Why did you decide that you wanted to show your work in China?
George: We simply believe that it is very good for people to have access
to what is going on in art, just as they have access to what is going on in
any other arena. Our message is global. It can be shown to people from
all races and backgrounds. To most Western people China is this great
magic land with this enormously mysterious history and the idea that
we, as living artists, can go there with our pictures and put them on the
wall, for people of all ages and from different walks of life to come
in and see, is for us an amazing and exciting opportunity. They are not
people who know our pictures or have seen them before, so it is a
completely fresh and experimental idea.

With your exhibitions, to what extent do you want to break down
barriers?
Gilbert: We are all one. We are part of everything – East and West – it is
all part of life. We should be able to understand and mix up the cultures.
I think that is very important.
George: The barriers between people and nations and societies can
only be broken down with culture.

And do you have any idea what the reaction of the Chinese
audience might be?
George: Multi-layered human. The debate in China is not so different
from the huge debate which is going on in Europe now, which is the
question, 'What is an individual?'

Your pictures often indicate a subject matter without defining it.
How important is this degree of openness?
Gilbert: In some way we do know that art is everything and also that it
is nothing. So it is complete. We are just trying to express ourselves in
the most visually simple way and the viewer has to be able to be woken
up in front of it. It is like a discussion. I think that if you take a group of
people into one of our shows, each person will interpret it in a different
way, if they are allowed to be totally free.

Is that the moral foundation of your work – that it is open for
anybody to get what they can from it?
George: Yes. It is an incredible new idea – art for people. Art for All.
It is increasing the idea of the individual. Making the individual a new

idea, instead of just having groups of people. Art is a choice. It is only opportunity. You cannot impose a picture on someone.

Is that why you have to be responsible and serious in what you do?
Gilbert: Yes. That's why an artist should be provoking thought.
George: And then the person can be different, if they want to be. It is very important that our pictures are not lecturing to the audience. We believe that our pictures are an open opportunity for the viewer to compare their lives with the subject matter and the thoughts and feelings. We are not saying that 'This picture is about this', or 'If you don't understand it, bad luck'. We always say that we allow for the life of the viewer in a picture. We don't want to be selfish when we make our pictures. We want to love the viewer. The success of the artist is in the viewer, and in their life. The viewer has the success, not the artist.

And you call the suits that you wear 'Responsibility Suits'.
George: They are our working clothes. We do believe that we can speak through how we clothe ourselves, as well as through how we do our pictures. It is a very important part of our democratic idea. We can go anywhere, and be in any situation, after all we never wanted to be the freaky artists in that bohemian way. They are very typical, normal suits.

Why did you choose to live in London's East End?
Gilbert: It was the cheapest part of London and also the most romantic part as well. It was so incredible. The first time I went to the East End I felt as if I was in the nineteenth century. All around here it was like something out of Charles Dickens: Dickens's village.
George: Where we live is steeped in history, but it is also very actual and very up-to-date. We really believe this is a typical 'planet Earth place'. It is an ideal example of roughly how the world is. We are both country boys who are up in the city, and we love it. We live in what seems like an ordinary house in an ordinary street. On the other hand, it is quite extraordinary because it is a street that was built by French people who were driven from their country by prejudice.
Gilbert: The East End of London is a melting pot of different cultures. That is why it is so exciting. Everybody in some way is much freer here than in other parts of the country. You have to be more tolerant because there are a lot of different races, different religions, and different people.
George: It is not partisan. It is not narrow-minded in any way. It is like our pictures. It is open. It is gentle to everyone.

Do you find your immediate surroundings inspirational? Is London important to your work?

George: Important that we are here. But not in terms of subject matter or anything like that. There is nothing in our pictures that doesn't exist all over the world, and inside every person. It is local and global at the same time.

Gilbert: We don't feel we need inspiration. We feel we have to look inside ourselves for what we feel and think.

George: Looking into any person's face anywhere in the world is very, very inspiring. We are not looking at the fabric of our world in any way because we don't want to represent the world as how it is. None of our pictures can be found in reality. You can't find or see our pictures in the real world. They are totally artificial.

Gilbert: We are trying to look in, instead of looking out. We are trying to look inside our brain, and I think that is more interesting because that is where the confusion is. 'Outside' is always the same. It is only what we think that changes every second because it is all an artificiality. How we look at the world every day is all artificial, and that comes from the brain. We believe very much that art is about reinventing life. How we walk, how we speak, how we behave, how we look at things. That is art. That is creative. We don't believe in the artist with a brush. Art is about having new ideas. We don't care who or what it actually is, as long as it is reinventing something. In some way we believe in a mad art, a desperate art. We are searching for the truth.

George: A picture is a frozen example of thought and feeling and you can stop life with it. When you are looking at a picture it is a stopping of life, to consider for a moment.

So, should art shock and cross barriers? The avant-garde is often understood in terms of transgression.

Gilbert: 'De-shock', that is what we always said.

George: And not to shock by form but by content, by the meaning. We don't want people running away from our exhibition because they find it freaky or too unusual or not part of their world. We want to seduce the viewer into entering our friendly world, to discuss together with us.

Gilbert: And I do believe that it has to be shocking in the beginning because if it wouldn't be shocking, then it wouldn't be new.

George: Anything that is new in any field in any subject is bound to upset a certain section of society. There are always people who want to

hang on to the present and freeze it, people that just want to hold on to life as it is. We believe in the future, and it will be an amazing future, a very different one. We do not believe that the greatest advancement from now on will be a redefinition of the person. We think that change is very good. We are not the artists to demolish everything. We see what we do as a combined effort: upholding certain things and changing others and that always changes. Next year maybe that does need demolishing.
Gilbert: We are not revolutionary artists. We aim for evolution, always. We like tradition. The line between what is good and bad changes from day to day. It is not fixed. Even to accept the idea of 'bad' in art, as Baudelaire did, is also a new idea. Morality is there for changing. The world is changing all the time and that is what we want. We don't like the idea of a rigid morality. It's all much better to mix it all up and make it a little more chaotic.
George: If you believe in the system that Western civilisation was based on – which is that you give in exchange for the gift of life, that you are here and have this fantastic life and that you do something for that – then we can't believe that we are here as artists to congratulate people on how they are. We cannot give to the people pictures that they want, we have to do the pictures that we believe the world needs, otherwise we are just reassuring and restating what is already there. We believe that the artist has a responsibility. We believe that an artist should have a sense of duty. They're not here to please themselves. We do believe that art should be for something, for people. We believe that all culture creates the future and we want to be part of building the future. We want the world to be a little different because of our pictures. Most artists do not want to do pictures for people because there is a huge personal cost involved in that. They are scared to pay that price. The artists who are leading the life are unhappy.

> *And do you think that the more unhappy you are perhaps the more you will find out?*

Gilbert: No. The more you find out, the more unhappy you become.

> *You are interested in the Aesthetic Movement of the 1890s and the work of Oscar Wilde. Were they 'leading the life'? I would have thought that they were to a certain extent disinterested in life.*

Gilbert: It was very contradictory. They said that nothing else was important except for 'art for art's sake', a beautiful beauty, but they didn't do it. Oscar Wilde was the most miserable person in the world.

In the end, every sentence that he wrote is always searching for the
truth, so truthful. He had to die in the end for his reinvention of life.
It was not for the beauty.

George: We think that they were the first true subversives because they
were saying one thing in order to get away with doing something
entirely different. Wilde is the best example of that. He said everything
was all just pleasure – and one puff of a cigarette, and one lily that lasts
all day – in fact, he was getting away with murder at the same time as
saying that. He created a world which is entirely different. We would
not be here if it hadn't been for Oscar Wilde.

Do you like work?

Gilbert: We don't like work, we only like the result and the effect. We
don't like the 'doing' very much.

George: We're not selfish enough to actually enjoy doing it. The process
for us is unimportant. We like the pictures to look as if they were made
by magic. We wouldn't like people to look at our pictures and say, 'My
goodness, I can see that took ages to make,' and to admire them for that
reason.

Gilbert: The work is totally unimportant except for the end result. It is
only the message that is important. Not the aesthetics of brushes and
painting. Just the power of that image.

Do you feel that as artists you are driven people?

Gilbert: Driven mad, yes. As an artist you always feel unhappy and
dissatisfied because you feel you are never going to be able to reach
what you actually want. You have this goal in front of you and you are
never able to reach it. That's it, we have this amazing urge and we don't
know why: deep down inside us, we want to live. We more and more
believe that everything in the world is art, it is all artistic. It is all art.
There is nothing else. A complexity of life.

George: You could say that culture creates human love, to make a
better world that everybody wants. It doesn't matter where you go in
the globe, everyone will say we need a better life. We have a very high
ideal of art and for ourselves. This is a 'serving idea' in a way and not
that you are locked away in a studio going crazy. We believe that artists
can create enormous effects on people's lives. Art does filter through all
levels of life and have its effect. How we think about each other, how we
love, how we hate, how we dress, how we live, how we travel – all this is
an artistic idea.

Gilbert: We are one of the only artists who actually believe that art means something.

George: Many other artists believe that it is wonderful and fantastic but that it doesn't have anything to do with life. They don't believe that it has any effect on life. Most artists have enormous disregard for the viewer. It is important to have a love of the viewer, not a love of the art. A love of the art is a decadent idea.

Do you think that there is such a thing as Eternal Truth?

George: I would say so. The thrust of human activity is the Eternal Truth.

Gilbert: We are searching for the truth.

George: The Eternal Truth is that the majority of people get up in the morning each day. When you don't have an Eternal Truth organised society collapses and then you have dead people lying in the streets with other people driving past. There are countries like that where you just drive past the dead bodies. They have lost the idea that there is a truth. There is a human God and we are it. We have got to do it, if not we are all lost.

Gilbert: That must be Eternal Truth.

Are you at all religious?

Gilbert: We believe that maybe there is an Eternal Truth. That's the God that we believe in. Yes, we believe in truth.

Are your personal political beliefs anything to do with your art?

Do you have any political beliefs?

Gilbert: No, we don't have political beliefs. We are not involved in politics. We are just Conservatives. We don't want to be the strange artists. Most people in Britain vote Tory so we're like that. Also, we feel that in some way we are Socialists, that's what we are. Even when we say that we are boring Conservatives. I think that the reality is that we are Socialists because we like to do things for people. That's what Socialists means.

George: Once ideology becomes more important than the individual you are lost. It doesn't matter whether it is an extreme Communist country or an extreme right-wing country, both of those regimes will lock up the artist and writer, with the same key. So, it is not just a matter of right or left.

Are your works ever intended to have a politically explicit
message?

Gilbert: No, we never think of politics. We never analyse anything. We are just drifting into this. We have this feeling that we want to express ourselves in a certain way but we never consciously want to do political works ever.

George: It is political enough to be an artist. That is a political enough statement. We are not involved with the details of life. Politicians will only be different in the future if they have looked at work like ours and other people's – that is how we are politically effective. It is a more human idea.

Why did you both renounce the use of your family names to become 'Gilbert & George'?

George: Partly because it is simpler and it is more friendly. We reinvented ourselves at that moment, and we became something different.

Gilbert: We were taking our personal history away. We left the family behind and just became human sculptors with two names, like a brand name – like Van Gogh who signed himself 'Vincent'.

Do you think however that in a sense your past – before you became Gilbert & George – is what formed you into what you are now? Can you identify what made you want to become artists?

George: We were both very very interested in art from an extremely early age. I remember when I was young being very excited by the idea of Van Gogh. I thought that it was amazing just to be an artist in the world.

Your description of yourselves as Living Sculptures implies that as artists you use yourselves as the material for the sculpture – creator and created become one and the same. What does this entail?

George: It is the artist speaking through the picture. It is not an artist making an aesthetic composition but making a letter, a visual letter to the viewer.

Gilbert: We think that was our main idea. I think that is it.

George: We believe that every picture, whatever it has got in it, is still based on that. It is the foundation for everything. In fact, we are inventing our language.

Gilbert: We are only interested in the message and that is art and life for us – 'vision', 'art and life', 'us' – and not the actual structure of the painting.

*In the same way you have spoken of form and content being one –
what this amounts to is that you are abolishing aesthetics.*
George: We have the form there only to support the meaning, never
never for its own sake. It is never red there to be a nice red.
Gilbert: It is there to create moods: of desperation, of happiness, of
unhappiness, whatever. Through combinations of colour you can create
and trap a mood. It is the combinations that are important. The subject
and the combination. That can create an amazing atmosphere.

*You have made your work together for about twenty-five years now.
Why did you decide to work in this way?*
George: We didn't. No decision. We always say it was something that
came over us. We were already doing it in a way before we realised.

Do you think as one artist or two?
Gilbert: Two people make one artist.
George: We think that we are an artist.
Gilbert: Two visions make one vision.
George: A family is made up of people who have different views on
different subjects but there is always a family feeling or a family
direction – as well as the individual – where they share a common
ground in going forward.

Would it be pointless to make your work individually?
Gilbert: I think it would be totally impossible. It would finish us. I mean,
it is totally impossible. I think I would be totally lost. It would be like
cutting the legs off the *Singing Sculpture*.

How do you work together when you are in the studio?
George: When we go to the studio, it is not what we think, it is how we
feel, how we dread, how we hope, how we love, how we hate. We just do
the pictures like that. We trust that. We are not consciously deciding
whether to do a picture with trees or without trees – how tree we are
that day will decide on that. It is like using ourselves as a rubber stamp
and we will see what prints off that day. We cannot fall into making a
marvellous picture by concentrating on doing it. We have to be
completely empty, completely dead, and maybe manage to fall into
some mistake or some new way of seeing that subject.
Gilbert: In a funny way it is like having a big ball of throbbing material
inside you. And you don't want to analyse it.
George: Also we would be doing something that we have already done
because we were familiar with that; and if we're familiar with it we've

said and done it already. We have to fall into a new hole in the road every day, and we don't want to fall into the ones we have fallen into before.

Gilbert: We know little of what we want to take, but mostly it is done subconsciously and we don't want to think too much. That is why we feel it is always like a funny dream in front of us, the untouchable dream, or like a big shout – 'AAAH!' – but never analysing it and never trying to sort out how exactly it should be. In fact, we are making our pictures in some way half-asleep. We want to make them when we are half-conscious, never when we are totally conscious. We are not looking for an end result; drifting, drifting into something.

But this sense of drifting seems to be a contradiction.

Gilbert: I'm sure it is.

You have this very strong sense of purpose, and yet you are drifting.

George: Because we do believe that creativeness is based on inspired thought. Millions of people tried to fly, but some crazy person actually got it together and invented the jet engine.

Your art is born of contradiction...

Gilbert: Not more than life, we do believe that.

Are you visionary artists in any way?

Gilbert: Yes, I would say so. A vision is new thought, a new morality, a new way of seeing the world. A new way of thinking; that is our vision.

George: We knew that we were artists in the egg and that when the last day of art school came the egg would crack open and out would come these fluffy yellow new artists.

Gilbert: The day we said that we are the Living Sculpture, that was it. Art and life became one, and we were the messengers of a new vision. At that moment that we decided we are art and life, every conversation with people became art, and still is. It becomes like some object speaking. Normally sculptures are completely dead. But we are living ones. Speaking ones, complex ones, unhappy ones. That is a fantastic difference. I think that was a big breakthrough for us. That's what the basis of it all is: Art and Life. That is the title of our Art.

The China Statement

Statement read by the artists at press conferences in China on the
occasion of their 1993 exhibitions at the National Art Gallery, Peking,
and The Art Museum, Shanghai.

We, as unhappy artists, are very happy to be able
to hold this exhibition of our pictures in China.

Our art fights for love and courage
and universal celebration of the individual.
Each of our pictures is a visual love-letter
from ourselves to the viewer.

This visit has been a human revelation to us.
We have never before seen so many
good-looking people and Beijing is now
our favourite city.

Boot, Blood Heads, Tears, Seen, Eight, Attacked: from an Interview with Keith Pointing 1995

First published in Great Britain in 1996 by Brockhampton Press, a member of the Hodder-Headline Group, London, in the poster book *Gilbert & George*.

George: The form has to be the servant of the meaning. We don't like the idea of a person coming in front of a work of art and saying, 'I love the drawing technique', or 'I love the brush strokes'. They have to get a direct feeling in front of that picture connected with their lives, they are not admiring the craft.

Gilbert: We do believe we have managed to find for ourselves a form that is very direct and a form that we can totally change day in day out and that we are able to use everything that is in the world. Other sculptors who let's say use plaster, are not able, but we can use any object, air, noses, eyes, landscapes, inside the body, outside the body. Everything is part of our material. We felt that the form of painting is becoming so old-fashioned, that it doesn't speak of today. Except in caricatures.

George: We realise that even in the ordinary person in the street sense, ninety-nine per cent of artworks being produced today, or last week or last year if you asked your mother when was it done, she'd say, 'I don't know dear, 1930, 1940.' She wouldn't know that it lives and breathes this time particularly. We think that is one test of Art; it should live and breathe its time. Our work really started in 1971. It was using the negative image. We didn't want to be like a photographer or like a newspaper photographer with one image, because that belonged to photography history. We wanted to make an artwork in a gallery or museum representing a work of art not a photograph, and the only way we could find in the first place was to make a group of photographs which looked like an object together on a wall. Then very, very slowly this came together into shapes. Sometimes into an oval, sometimes into a strip, circle, decorative shape, then we used a rectangle, like any classical picture, then we lost the gaps in between the sections; towards a single picture away from the idea of a group of separate images. In 1977 because we did The Dirty Words we realised we could do images which crossed sections of the picture. So, slowly they became a single picture. Then, when we invented a way of making a mask it gave us a new freedom again. In 1980–82 we started using colour photographic dye, initially each sheet, one sheet all yellow or all red within one panel two colours.

Gilbert: We had a black line in between and a black base so that we could change it.

George: Later on we used a gum so we could colour an eye, so it was an ongoing slowly developing language.

Gilbert: We think a picture is based on a lot of different ideas and that's why we started out with not one photograph but lots of different ideas put together in a group but we didn't know how to put them together. A modern painting is a picture which is full of meanings at different levels, but we didn't know how to do it and it took us a long time to work out how.

George: It is all of those levels of meaning that we're out for; that's our interest, to find different ways of approaching a person's life. When we had the show in the South London Art Gallery [Naked Shit Pictures, 1995] somebody said to us, 'What is going on in there?' as thirty to forty people were looking in the gallery. It is impossible to quantify that. A very complicated thing happens when someone looks at a picture.

Gilbert: And they are based on the inner feelings that are in every human being. The idea of fear, the idea of death, the idea of sex. Sex as subject in art is in some ways forbidden. The corner porn shop has in some ways more freedom because the artist has to justify it morally.

George: David Sylvester [the art critic] said, 'All the artists have struggled to do "naked", but they've only succeeded in doing "nudes". But you've succeeded in doing "naked",' and we hadn't actually thought of that. Every person who goes through the British Museum, the National Gallery, the ethnographic collection, won't bat an eyelid when they walk past etchings or marble statues, but when they see our naked pictures it's different.

Gilbert: We even try to erase racism from our work. We have all kinds, black people, Japanese people and white people and mix them all up. The reason we only have one sex in our pictures is that we [Gilbert & George] are the living statues.

George: It would be an amazing idea if we were to dress up in frocks as it would be to put women in our pictures. We are the sculptures.

Gilbert: After a time we put people in instead of us to represent ideas of ours. Also we realised we are doing something for the first time. Artists

for the last 300 years have mostly used women. The beauty of the nude
was a female nude.
George: That's the cliché. We are providing something for which the
majority of women are involved. Some of our biggest post is from
feminist women.
Gilbert: Art critics say that it is full of homosexual people, which is
totally untrue. How do you recognise if somebody is? We never wanted
beauty for beauty's sake, we wanted humanity. We couldn't have
children, can you imagine the outcry? And old people we did try with
outsiders...
George: Now we're doing that! Slowly.
Gilbert: Ha ha! Yes, we are becoming that, it's very interesting!
George: We never wanted to use a person who represented a class, a
social class. We wanted to represent humanity not its social position.
When you look at our pictures you never have an idea who they are, or
their social position.
Gilbert: Just the loneliness. The loneliness of being alive.
George: We never go to the studio to make a 'humorous' picture, so we
don't understand why some people giggle in front of our pictures.
Gilbert: Perhaps they free themselves by laughing. We are pessimists
in ourselves but are optimists on behalf of the viewer. We wanted to
make truthful pictures, to encircle you.
George: We don't even think they are large, because the world is of that
size. Streets are very big, cars and buses are very big.
Gilbert: It also depends how or where they are viewed. We do know
someone who had one of these in their flat and it completely changed
their life.
George: Small easel paintings were made for the connoisseur. You look
into them, cows, houses are actually tiny.
Gilbert: But what we are dealing with is what is inside everyone. Some
sexuality, some fear, loneliness, happiness. We always say the viewer is
always trying to find themselves. They are not interested in art. They
are trying to find a way of feeling happier within themselves. We really
believe that. They are all searching for themselves.
George: Just as when you read a novel, you look for a character with
whom you can identify.

*

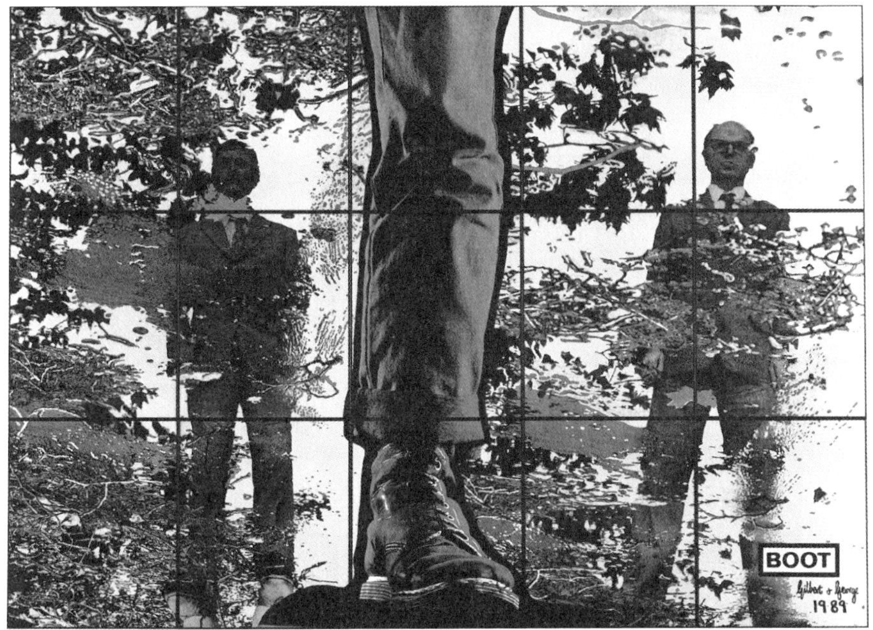

Boot, 1989, 226 × 317 cm

BOOT

Gilbert: It's bleeding in the sky and we are reflected in it and are being stamped on.

George: It's not actually us, it's us reflected.

Gilbert: What is interesting for us is that we were accused in 1980 of using boots in our pieces. Not that we actually did.

George: Boot boys. East End bovver boys.

Gilbert: And we turn out ten years later to find every girl is going around in these boots. It's a most fashionable idea to have. We always say they accuse you of something, then they turn into it.

George: It's exactly that. The two main subjects of the educated left are boots and skinheads. Now boys and girls of the educated left have shaven heads and wear boots.

Gilbert: And we had such a big problem not that we actually used it, there was one big picture *Patriots* [1980] where there was a lineup of skinheads. But they only pick that picture to demolish us.

George: They call it a racist picture. But they refuse to see. We used to telephone them and say, 'Have you got the catalogue there? What do you see?' [catalogue page shows people from the Indian subcontinent,

201

flowers and an outsider] 'Well, it's just a row of skinheads', they'd say. And you say, 'No, no, tell me what you see left to right. What's the first thing you see, what's the second?' And they say, 'Oh well I suppose you're right.'

Gilbert: And now it's turned upside down.

George: So peace and anti-aggression forces such as an Anti-Nazi League march, they've adopted the dress of the enemy. This is a very important piece.

Gilbert: All our pictures are very simple. Nature, human and manmade. When you take images, we use fifty, sixty, seventy models and we take pictures of the head, the body, the ears, the arms, the legs, shoes. In the end we think that's a good idea to make an image and we use that boot to make a composition.

George: In our composition we always need these elements. This is one negative this is another and we combine them.

Gilbert: We always say we have a bank of images. We used to pay a model and thereafter by word of mouth, people approach us.

George: People stop us on the street and say, 'Are you the artists? I'd love to be in your pictures.' We get many letters always enclosing their photograph.

Gilbert: We've taken so many photographs but we use so few.

George: When we first started taking pictures of people we just took photographs on the street in 1980. Then we wanted to take them in the studio but the idea of asking a male person to model was a dangerous thing. But since then half the men want to be male models!

Gilbert: At that time it was anti-masculine, queer. But then that changed... all those magazines.

George: *GQ*, and so on.

Gilbert: When we make these kind of pictures [*Boot*], we trust our inner feelings like here sometimes and we feel totally beaten up.

George: But not consciously. We trust our intuition, which is what the viewer tends to use more with our pictures than with others. It is easier to get a lady in the South London Art Gallery to tell you something about what she feels. Whatever is in their head is in their head.

Gilbert: They are not consciously constructed. That's what we like.

George: We always say that nobody wrote a great novel unless they knew how to do it. Once you know how to do it you teach it or study it or something. We always divide the artists into those who could do this sort of picture or that sort of picture. Some artists could only paint that sort of picture. There is no other possibility. You can never imagine Van Gogh doing anything other than those pictures.

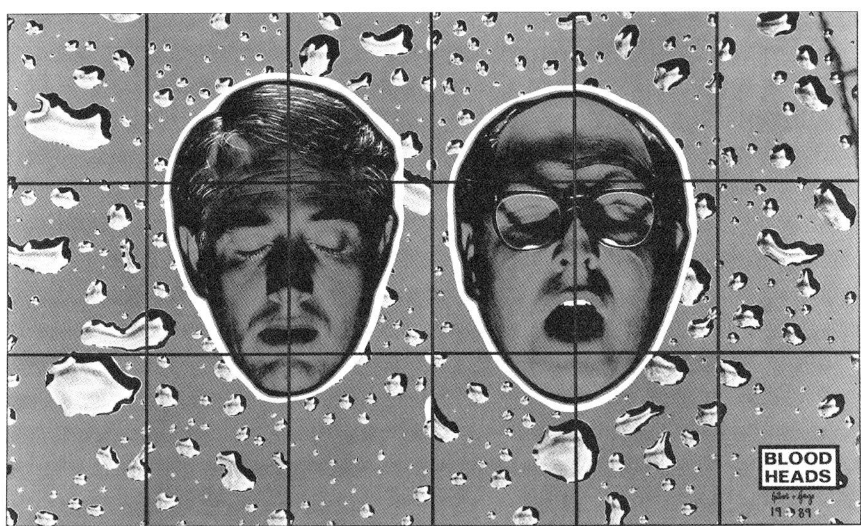

Blood Heads, 1989, 226×381 cm

BLOOD HEADS

Gilbert: In 1987, because a lot of our friends had died through Aids, we started to realise how blood is life. There is nothing else except blood.
George: We did many pictures – *Blood Eye, Blood Nose* – and this is one of the few where we show the blood is us, and this is moisture rather than water. We also find it fantastic that every drop of moisture is a cosmology of the world. Even if you can't see it, reflected in each one of these is Fournier Street, and every single one is different.
Gilbert: Every drop is the whole world. Everyone became terrified of the whole idea of blood. But it's funny because in some way blood is life.
George: We are all on the edge of disaster.
Gilbert: The lighting is a most important thing.
George: Side lighting.
Gilbert: We invented that. Photography is only lighting. We make drawings out of light. When we light it we can give some parts a different intensity.
George: When we develop it we can change it, take some parts out.

203

Gilbert: In some ways we are like very old-fashioned artists. We create artificial light to create an artificial picture. We are also limited by these frames and in the end the frames are useful to help compose the picture.
George: We are not totally free to put anything anywhere, which is good.

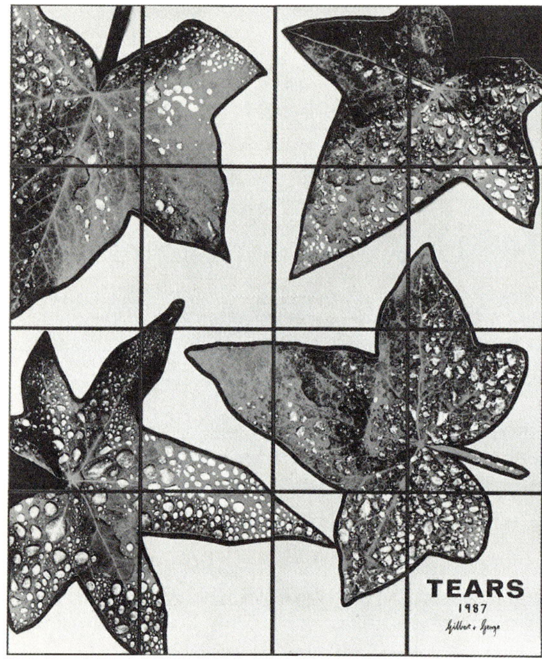

Tears, 1987, 241 × 201 cm

TEARS
Gilbert: We had some ordinary leaves and we tried to humanise them.
George: They are crying in a slightly different way. There are these two black holes which we like to think is like us. The rest is a void, an empty sky. There is a sadness which is quite odd if you consider the subject matter. We felt the world needed a picture of that subject.
Gilbert: We did other ones.
George: But this is the saddest one.
Gilbert: We tell you that, but a picture has to speak for itself. Once we give that title they have to be able to think.
George: Absolutely. Does the viewer agree with the picture or disagree, or more likely a combination of the two.

204

Gilbert: It depends what sort of people you are dealing with, what kind of life they are having. Some would laugh at it. They see it in a different way.

George: Some people will view a catalogue or show and say, 'That's me, that's me.'

Gilbert: It's very funny, when this book [*Gilbert & George: The Complete Pictures 1971–1985*] came out it was just the beginning of this big Aids disaster and so a lot of museum directors, artists and those interested in art liked our work for the first time.

George: From that disease it went into every aspect of life.

Gilbert: Young artists nowadays are only dealing in sex and fear and death. Mostly.

George: It is 300 years since every aspect of society is involved in a sexually transmitted disease. In the nineteenth century it was syphilis, we had the two world wars but medicine was more advanced. Then suddenly every world leader had to form an opinion about Aids. Reagan had to say one way or another, every film star had to come out, every newspaper on the planet, television had to form its ideas about sex and sexuality. Unbelievable. It affected everything.

Gilbert: All the designers, the dancers who died. The actors, the artists.

George: The hospital workers, galleries, ballet, the auction houses, art historians. Unbelievable. Suddenly life and death and sexuality took on a vast range of meaning for everybody. People said to us, 'Is this an Aids picture or not?'

Gilbert: They never did that.

George: But you cannot go to the studio and take Aids out of your brain. It's impossible to ask. It's the Third World War.

Gilbert: But there is enough information in this picture to spark the idea of tears, of life.

George: There are two black holes which you don't find in a long, long time.

Gilbert: It's just the idea of tears falling down. We don't do symbolism. We don't have colours for special meanings.

George: That's why we don't show the whole face. Just the feeling part. It is reflective.

Gilbert: We never try to say exactly what we think. It is not like a minimal piece of art in that you have a cube and a square, etc. Here are hundreds of chaotic ideas.

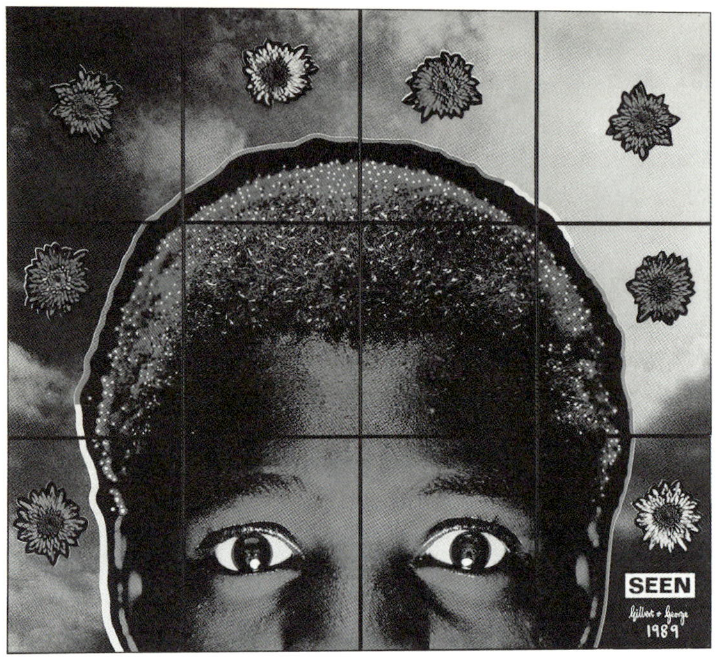

Seen, 1989, 226 × 254 cm

SEEN

Gilbert: All our pictures are based on the complexity of life. That's why we became very anti the idea of totally abstract art because it's too simplistic. We are only interested in chaos and complexity.

There is never a straight answer. And I think that is very important.
George: This is also the result of one of those pictures which is very preposterous on one level. But nobody says, 'Why does he have green hair and a red face?'

It is preposterous but because it's inner, you can accept anything inside imagination. We used a crazy colour combination reversal.
Gilbert: It was created in a period when we started using used clashing colours. It was very anti-aesthetic.
George: They used to call it garish. Colour for fifteen or twenty years of our careers is still a very class concept. A professor's wife wore a sludge-green sweater, a prostitute a yellow handbag. They really thought it had something to do with class. Yet the same professor's wife will happily go to Kew Gardens and gaze into flowerbeds. All these colours exist in nature; fish, birds.

206

Gilbert: We still find colour is not accepted in art. It's grey, black or white.
George: It's changing, though.

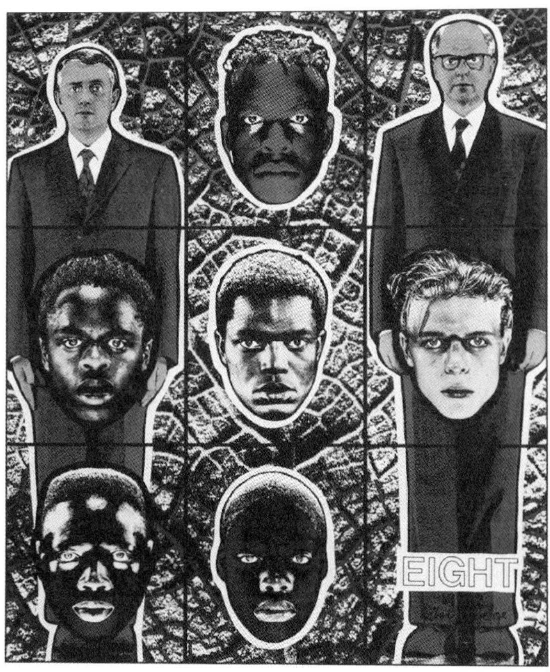

Eight, 1989, 253 × 213 cm

EIGHT

Gilbert: We have put ourselves in, we are one of the eight, everyone is a human being. The background shows a skin of a leaf and so we are all part of the same material.
George: You see, when the skin is red, the eyes are green. The colours were based on a traffic light. We are always trying to sort out the elements which are most important: Sex, Money, Race and Religion. And we realise there is nothing apart from that. So all around us are these four things. Just as we had: Death, Hope, Life, Fear.
Gilbert: We liked the idea of having black human beings, because they have incredible, visual, powerful heads which makes totally powerful art.
George: Totally normal.

Gilbert: Totally normal.
George: It is very difficult to find examples of non-Europeans in the national history of art, except in say Regency slavery paintings. But in contemporary art it hardly exists.
Gilbert: Not even in America.
George: In this great international world we are in.

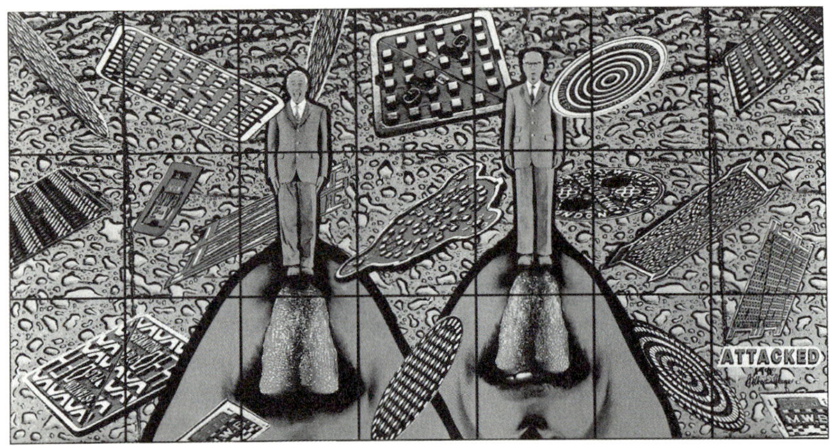

Attacked, 1989, 253 × 497 cm

ATTACKED
Gilbert: In some ways sticking your tongue out is the rudest thing you can do.
George: And the most defiant. From Maoris to children, in China it's an extremely rude thing to do, apparently.
Gilbert: These are manhole covers but in some ways they look like space invaders coming in at you.
George: Or stealth fighter bombers. The yellow moisture we normally use as meaning piss. That's how we normally see it.
Gilbert: We are being attacked and that's it.
George: We always say that it's the eye and the tongue.
Gilbert: Everybody seems to feel the same under this picture, although they wouldn't tell you that, because everybody is hiding something.
George: Some aspect of their life is under attack.

From Wasteland to Utopia – the Visions of Gilbert & George: Interview with Simon Dwyer 1995

First published in 1995 by Creation Books, London, in *Rapid Eye 3*.

QUEER

You don't get called 'gay artists' any more.
Gilbert: We try very much not to go down that road.
George: We never thought of ourselves as that. We don't think of that as an issue. Sex, yes, sexual yes.

But it's not relevant to be necessarily gay or hetero.
George: No.

Then what do you think of the gay subculture? I think it divisive now. When you go 'out', you also go 'in' to a micro world of fashion, clubs, literature…
George: We're not so keen on the divisions. We realise that in the Seventies they had to make a big stand, which was a good thing, but now it's become a very habit-ridden idea. We don't accept the idea that every middle-class couple accepts the two chaps who live at the end of the road and wear jeans and leather jackets as being 'gay'. It seems such a bore.

But I would have thought that it's better than not being accepted.
George: But you see before they would have accepted them just as the two chaps who live at the end of the road. They wouldn't be thought of as 'gay' or 'queer'.

So you're not politicised about it.
George: Not at all.
Gilbert: We're interested in mixing it all up. In making it normal.

Not a division. Making it a normal aspect of life so that people don't have to be defined by their sexuality.
George: We think nobody knows what 'queer' and 'straight' really are. We don't even understand what man and woman are.
Gilbert: We believe much of it is cliché. With cliché people don't have to think and you can make them do anything.

So it's easier socially to manage them.
George: Yes.

Your art and writing encourages change, particularly in young people – who you call 'modern people'.

George: That's the main...we know much younger friends...post-
G & G people you can call them...they just don't think of sexuality in
divisions.
Gilbert: And you can talk about anything.
George: They don't think 'gay', 'straight' or 'queer'. They don't ask if
the friend coming over to dinner is queer or not, it's not an issue.
Gilbert: And that's very good.
George: It's not 'this is the straight one, this is the queer one'. You don't
know. Until the law changed in 1967 most homosexual men were
married with children – lots of people.

> *You only use young men and boys in your photos. Many say that*
> *they are homoerotic...*

George: Only if you accept that every Page 3 girl is lesbo-erotic. No one
ever says that.
George: All men have cocks and we *are* interested in sex. We don't do
eunuch art. There are no great eunuch artists. We don't want to decide
what a person does with their hands or sexual organs. More
importantly, we're normal.

> *How do you get your models?*

George: Word of mouth, locally. We pay a certain amount.
Gilbert: They tell their friends.

> *Do they know the implications?*

George: We show them the catalogues. They love them.

> *I don't suppose previously they've had any attention.*

George: They love posing. They feel that during the session they are
something after all. They all mention it when we ask them. We like to
use models who have prominent eyes – we can't use people with deeply
set eyes – and this gets around, so one day we open the door and there
are a group of local Pakistani kids asking if they can be models, and all
of them are forcing their eyes wide open to make their eyes look bigger.

FEMINAZIS

> *One PC criticism of you is that you don't include women in*
> *your work.*

Gilbert: We are not politically correct.
George: Perhaps *too* politically correct. Actually we don't get much
criticism from feminists, except the feminazis in America who hate gay
men. Modern feminists should agree with us that we are not exploiting

women. It became interesting because all over the world people started asking us about women. They never ask Anthony Caro about women. But we know nothing about women. Most other artists have used women's images for centuries, the art world is run by men.

So, you're aren't objectifying women in any way...

George: Also, men are the sex that women are most interested in. The moment you exclude something in art it becomes important to people. We didn't even think about it.

Gilbert: They decided for us.

George: But it became a very important issue since then. Before that it was all women, women, women in the media.

Gilbert: Now man is becoming a sexual being again.

George: For the first time in centuries. When we were young students at St Martin's there was no male image available except the Sandeman Sherry man and the Moss Bros man – the English gentleman. Young men in *chippie* trousers, black men, workmen were just not published in the Sixties.

Gilbert: And we had to fight very hard because, as you said, they thought that every male image in our pictures must be homoerotic. We always deny that. We say they are men.

George: Persons, in fact.

I think men have had a rough time in the media and so on over the last twenty years. Practically all magazines are edited by and aimed at women, if a guy gets his penis cut off by his wife it's thought of as a joke, whereas if he cut out her cunt he'd be lynched. In every TV advert or sitcom the man is the stupid one, and the butt of all the jokes.

George: We're very opposed to that prejudice. We see it so much on TV, when the wife takes the chip and puts it under his nose... because the other way around is forbidden. The man in the sitcom is a wretched creature. But this view will not last. The feminists can never win an argument now because it is people like us who are doing a better job for a new truth, opening doors, to find new ways of living... and I'm sure we had a lot to do with that.

Gilbert & George: We invented and are constantly developing our own visual language. We want the most accessible modern form with which to create the most modern-speaking visual pictures of our time. The art material must be subservient to the meaning and purpose of the picture.

Our reason for making pictures is to change people and not congratulate them for being how they are.

Gilbert: It became important to us to show naked pictures in museums, put dirty words in museums... In America they wanted to take them down, even in New York.

Have you had problems with censorship?

Gilbert: Oh, yes.

George: Our film *The World of Gilbert & George* is basically banned from television. It's been offered every year for fourteen years to BBC2, Channel 4. They show arty films but they won't show us. One producer, said he'd rather drop dead than have Gilbert & George's film on his show. Nowadays *The South Bank Show* features jazz musicians and alternative comedians as art.

And the paintings?

George: We always try to do it in a delicate way. We think we know the line you can go up to in any city and we take it to that line and get away with it. We don't like the idea of confrontation. We don't think it's productive to go up to someone and say, 'You do agree with this don't you? And if you don't you're a stupid cunt.' It's much better to be subversive, to get away with it. Once people see *Shitted* [1983] that's it. They might say we shouldn't exhibit it but it's too late because they're already commenting on the picture.

Gibert: All these art critics love to accuse us of using dirty words and they love to write them all down, the 'Buggered' and 'Fuck Off'.

George: 'These disgusting artists did these pictures...!'

Gilbert: All the time.

George: And that's very funny as these words will be printed in a newspaper that can't publish those words otherwise. Infiltration. To be against, they have to be won over partly, to become a part of it.

Then they should at least think – though they probably don't – why they are opposed to it.

Gilbert: It's very interesting because we have a young Polish friend who is trying to write a book on us and he went through the press of the show. It was a huge success, so it took the critics' power away. So instead they talked about 'The fulfilment of Goebbels' dream'...

ART
I think people feel uneasy responding to your pictures because they are direct.

George: People are not used to that in art. That's the trouble.

Gilbert: There's nothing that speaks in art at the moment. Abstract canvases don't speak. Nothing speaks.

George: They only exist... I remember when I first came to London when I was twenty, I went to the Tate. There was one of those groups being lectured looking at one of those ballet pictures by Degas, and this posh man asked them to say what they were looking at, and the poor things said 'a ballet dancer'. And then he put on a very superior smile and said, 'No, what you are actually looking at is the shapes between the legs.' Jesus Christ! Complete nonsense. It's unbelievable... complete shit.

The art world talks out of its arse. The interpretations get more ridiculous as people try to justify themselves.

George: It's very interesting that the same class of person that is pro-humanist is totally anti-people when it comes to fine art. They're the most patronising decadent bores. Totally hypocritical in fact.

The problem is that you have chosen a medium that is dominated by rich people and academics.

Gilbert: The problem is that art is based on rich people... what you are allowed to do is dependent on the money of these rich people. If we do things that are so extreme they don't want to buy them we'd have no money to do our books. It's difficult.

George: I think we've got around that more and more. A lot of people who love looking at our pictures have their own reasons, whereas what we call decadent art is only good if it's supported by those professionals, who don't know themselves what it's about. There's a bucket of water in the corner of a gallery, you don't know if it's good or not but if you know the leading museums in the world say it's good you accept it. Whereas we think people accept our pictures – person-to-person pictures.

I often find your pictures disturbing.

George: I'm sure they are.

Why do you think I find that?

Gilbert: Because we always like to get involved in taboo subjects. First we decided we are the art and the speakers – that's how we started the Living Sculptures. We are speaking through images, through postcards, drawings. The subject... we thought we should just continue to have a man, instead of just us we should have other men in our pictures. That became the big subject.

Do you see your pictures as being able to be read in a narrative way?
Gilbert: Yes, if people want to. It's not so simple. We don't make a story out of our pictures.
George: We know from the variety of responses.
Gilbert: I would agree that some pictures are more narrative, some less, they are all based on deep inner emotions, feelings.

You want those emotions and pictures to reach as many people
as you can.
George: Yes, as ART. That's very important. We don't believe in the art going out to a wider public if it's not known as art. They firstly have to know it's art.

This is why we like them to know they are going to a gallery to see art that is very emotional and speaks directly to the viewer. Doesn't matter who he is, he has been spoken to.

Is it important that the viewer understands your original motives
for doing it?
Gilbert: If it's so true it becomes true for the viewer. They see themselves, they are searching for themselves. The viewer is not going in to see G & G, he is going to see that art does relate to him.
George: We always say that if we can take our catalogue on to the street and show the first person and they are interested in some way that's OK because with every other catalogue they don't know what the fuck it is. They have just been told it's an art exhibition.

We spoke earlier of the people who run art, but I think the artists
themselves are so pretentious...
Gilbert: Totally pretentious.
George: Most people don't say that.
Gilbert: They are going down that road again totally.

And it's elitist.
George: We like very much the platform of art. The formality of it... the idea of a rectangular picture. But we always fight for a more generous art world.

We hate the inner circle based on the artist. They do such weird stuff that nobody understands.
Gilbert: And they're accepted by the inner circle and that's it. And they all LOVE each other.

214

Gilbert: The fewer people who understand it the more they feel superior. It's all based on fear, fear of looking stupid. That's why we prefer publications. That's how young people contact us, through catalogues, not through exhibitions… too difficult. Once in a lifetime they let you into the Hayward Gallery and they don't want you after that.

SHIT FAITH

George: We have a fan in H Block in Belfast who writes to us. He's seen our catalogues. He writes to us regularly. It's quite exciting.

The troubles in Ireland are the epitome of stupidity, and religion doesn't help it.

George: *Shit Faith* [1982]. We just had a letter yesterday from a German student.

Gilbert: Studying philosophy. He found a post card on the floor, which illustrates the point, the picture of four bums with shit coming out of them forming a cross, and he said it changed his life completely.

What does Shit Faith *offer?*

George: Amazing freedoms if you haven't come across that before.

Your only political act seems to have been in criticising religion in your pictures.

Gilbert: We are anti-religion. Eat and shit. If you are able to say that in Europe that shows amazing freedom. In Munich they made us take it down.

George: We do think the church should be taken to the European Court.

Gilbert: For lying.

George: You could get them under the Trade Descriptions Act. We've had to go to funerals recently and the vicar said this person is not dead, he's already in heaven. He should be summoned immediately.

Gilbert: And the Pope.

George: You have to think of the number of people dying due to his discouraging the use of condoms – with Aids being probably the world's most common killer soon. In South America every day people get HIV because they're Catholic.

Gilbert: This German was saying how difficult it is in Germany now with all this back-to-basics morality.

George: Neo-Nazis.

This new morality is worrying, particularly in America. It's informed by Aids.

Gilbert: Yes, an excuse.

George: Must have been the long dream of the bigot. Fulfilment of all their hopes. They are all there. You have these intelligent people, they are all bigots inside. Can you imagine *The Times*, which has been regarded for the last twenty years as a platform for liberal ideas, may actually dispute any connection between HIV and Aids. Incredibly irresponsible.

We did the Aids show as we've had quite a lot friends die. It changed the way some critics looked at our work. They had never looked before. They started to see for the first time, It's taken a long time.

George: We didn't plan to work together, people just pointed out that we were. It just came over us.

Was the Living Sculpture period a statement that all life is art?

George: Partly, yes. And partly because we didn't have anything else. We left college, had no money. Every student who was a goody-goody went for a studio or teaching job. We knew we could never have that. We were already discriminated against. We realised that all we did have was ourselves so we thought that must be the art. It worked like magic.

Gilbert: We hated formalism very much.

George: Lines and squares and circles.

You went for a walk in Hyde Park and filmed it, coinciding with the NASA moonwalk that day.

SINGING SCULPTURE

George: It was a democratic idea. We thought that we could be art and artists without the profession.

Why use yourselves so much in your art?

Gilbert: That's how we started.

George: It's our best invention. When people see us on the street it's a different experience than seeing, say, Howard Hodgkin or any other artist.

Gilbert: We are the art.

George: Politicians and sportsmen are like that.

Gilbert: Even when you talk about Oscar Wilde, I only know the name and that he went to prison. He was a living sculpture.

Your imagery now is very much associated with the powerful image of fascism. Even your post cards are called Sculptures, which implies that they are monumental, significant...

George: We think there are things lurking in people that come out when they look at our paintings, not if they look at an abstract painting. If they have feelings about race they will probably start saying them in front of our pictures. If they have problems with fascism it will bring it out. That is what art is for. Isn't it funny that all that class of people who attacked us for having skinheads in our work *became* skinheads? If you walk into a private view of a new artist it's like going to a National Front meeting. Girls and boys who look like skinheads.

Gilbert: Queer and posh.

George: The anti-Nazi movement look like skinheads or Auschwitz victims – just what they are opposed to. All the girls have thin faces, are skinny and wear black clothes.

Gilbert: They are totally censorious.

George: Anti-fun. In fact, a disproportionate number of black people come up to us in the street and compliment us on our work.

Gilbert: One black businessman told us he liked our pictures because he saw himself... that it was not an issue ... and that he was sick of seeing these anti-apartheid posters with someone being strangled over a collage of a black person.

> *In newspapers black people are always portrayed in one or two ways, as a criminal or as a victim of famine or violence. They will show close-ups of black people dying, but never show that in Northern Ireland.*

George: I think there's a free prejudice to do that.

Gilbert: As in the Western films. The cowboys can shoot them down by the thousands. When John Wayne gets shot you get a big conversation as he takes thirty minutes to die.

George: It's a cliché. Calling someone a fascist. In every sitcom if the dad doesn't let the daughter go out to a party she says he's a fascist. In fact, fascism came out of socialism and conservative politics. Very boring. We don't mind being called fascists. There's nothing we haven't been called anyway. One critic accused us of being homophobic. I didn't know what it meant.

Gilbert: It's very silly.

FACISM
Is this area very Bangladeshi?
George: It is now.
How long have you lived here?
George: Twenty-seven years. It was entirely Jewish when we moved here.
Gilbert: We like the Indians very much.
George: We have one Indian family who we are very friendly with. They come here for drinks, the kids sit on my knee... Our adopted family.
You're in a financial position to live anywhere. Do you find this area resonant? Could you produce work in LA?
George: Not for one moment. We always say that if a spaceship landed and people got out and said we've got five minutes to film planet Earth and want something typical, we'd say go to Aldgate [around the corner]. You wouldn't tell them to go to Zurich as typical planet Earth. Not even New York. We think central London – not south like Kensington – central and east London is very actual and up to date. Expressions in the eyes of the people are very modern.
Gilbert: We believe it is one the nicest cities in the world.
George: Very ill-understood.
Gilbert: Total freedom in some way. It's a kind of anarchy that's accepted.
George: No European city has it.
Gilbert: None have the total freedom. Like when you walk down Commercial Street nobody cares whatever you do, however you dress.
George: There's such variety of architecture. Nicholas Hawksmoor's church, a Turkish market around the corner. Then you have Broadgate, very modern, and Bethnal Green and Brick Lane. We can feel London, even when we are away.
Do you find London masculine or feminine?
George: Not masculine. Masculine would be Berlin probably.
Gilbert: Queer maybe. In a modern way.
Do you consider yourselves to be modern people?
Gilbert: Yes.
So you're happy now?
George: We're fighting for the future, we want the world to be a little bit more like our pictures. That the world would become more complex, that every person could get out of their bedsit and in a moment be

feeling a new idea or a new person. We always think that when you read
a novel of the eighteenth century we realise how much the idea of the
person has changed since then, and we know that it could change
incredibly again. It could be a different type of person that develops.
Only if life became more elaborate, and more gentle. More tolerances –
that, I hope, everone can find. As artists we want to respect and honour
'the whole'. The content of all mankind is our subject and our inspiration.
We stand each day for good traditions and necessary changes. We want
to find and accept all the good and bad in ourselves. Civilisation has
always depended on advancement of 'the giving person'. We want to
spill our blood, brains and see in our life-search for new meanings and
purpose to give life.

Do you want to be loved?
George: Oh yes! Have to be… there is nothing else. People come up to
us in wine bars and say something fantastically complimentary. We
love the viewers. All the artists of this century have become
distinguished through their love of our culture or art or something.
We think that's a lot of nonsense. Most artists this century also had a
critical position. We feel that we are different. We are not against
anybody or anything. All the artists think that the general public is
stupid. We don't believe that. Every single person is a fantastic person.
Gilbert: Sometimes we have a problem because whatever you say here
in Britain, they always run everything down.
George: The media, not the public. Even the everyday news.

There is an enormous smugness and cynicism about everything.
George: They even destroyed comedy and humour, again they adopted
this cynical outlook. It's not humorous. People attacking vicars or the
middle class or the government. We think that if you have a table and a
bottle and an ashtray you can be very creative and make something
hilarious without being against anybody. The critical comedy is going to
make a lot of people unhappy. A lot of people are very hurt. I get quite a
wretched feeling when on comedy they do this patting on the head of
the bald man… I get so hurt. I try to say it doesn't matter. And I think
every chubby lady thinks that way… everbody. Like the superior artists
with the bucket and people not understanding, it's the same thing.
Gilbert: The problem here in England is that… well if you say English
Food they say, 'Bad'.
George: English holiday resorts… dirty. English class system…

Gilbert & George: 'Bad!'
George: English economy...
Gilbert & George: 'Bad!'
George: English Prime Minister...
Gilbert & George: 'Bad!'
Gilbert: English artists...
Gilbert & George: 'Bad!'
George: English cricket – lost.
Gilbert: English film – bad.
George: It's just the biggest nonsense. A disease. A hunger for
negativity.

*

George: We were very offended when people ask if we use dog shit in
our work. It's all ours!

The Ten Commandments
for Gilbert & George

First published in 1995 by Editions Janninck, Paris, in a signed edition of 299 copies.

I.

THOU SHALT FIGHT CONFORMISM

II.

THOU SHALT BE THE MESSENGER OF FREEDOMS

III.

THOU SHALT MAKE USE OF SEX

IV.

THOU SHALT REINVENT LIFE

V.

THOU SHALT GRAB THE SOUL

VI.

THOU SHALT GIVE THY LOVE

VII.

THOU SHALT CREATE ARTIFICIAL ART

VIII.

THOU SHALT HAVE A SENSE OF PURPOSE

IX.

THOU SHALT NOT KNOW EXACTLY WHAT THOU DOST,
BUT THOU SHALT DO IT

X.

THOU SHALT GIVE SOMETHING BACK

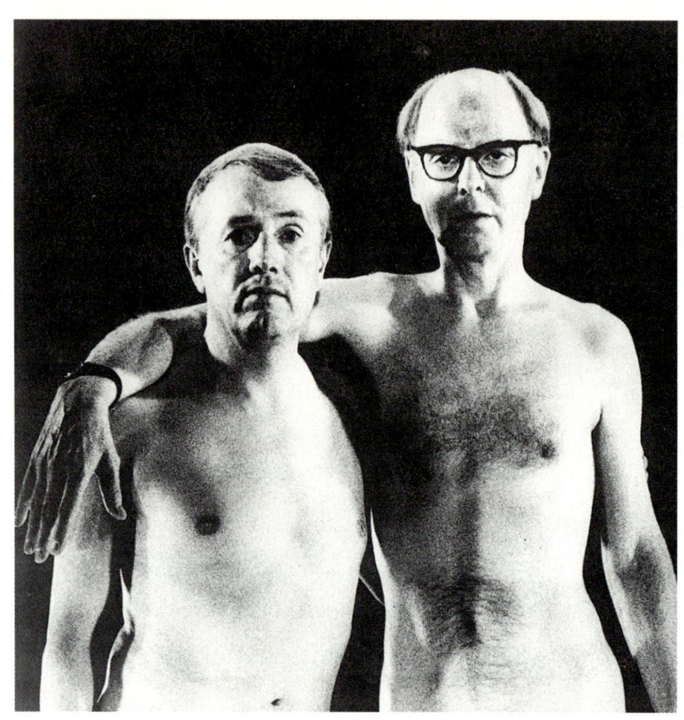

I.
THOU SHALT FIGHT CONFORMISM

Relationships between people and the world are fraught with enormous misunderstandings and frustrations. Barriers can only be broken down by culture. In our pictures, this is probably our greatest concern, now more than ever before.

Frustration comes because people have a dogmatic belief, and have been told to believe. They think that there is some real core inside them that tells them how to be. They are Britishers, and they are EEC persons, they are male, they are female, and have a sure feeling of their roots, their destiny. In our opinion this is not true, it is totally artificial, and we could change it altogether. Maybe we do not know what a man is, maybe we do not know what a woman is, it has changed so much in the past. Everyone is crying out. Every woman is completely mad at being a woman, every man is completely unhappy about being a man. When we go to a restaurant in the evening, we always hear horrible conversations from the next table, connected with boyfriends and girlfriends and marriage and money.

It seems that people are going through the most terrifying life. We believe that this is because they have not understood, as we did not understand, that there might be a new way of seeing ourselves. This is going to be one of the biggest discussions of our lifetime. In our small way, with our pictures, we could contribute to this debate. People's idea of love, people's idea of marriage, people's idea of society, will have to change – as it always has changed.

For centuries religion used to dictate how to behave morally. Somehow, that has now disappeared. The idea is that culture has taken over that role, how to behave, how to speak, what is love, what is family...

Art was first in the hands of the church, later in the hands of the aristocracy. Then the Aesthetic Movement liberated art from meaning. It was said that art had nothing to do with content any more, just with the beauty of lines, forms and colours. The aesthete Oscar Wilde propounded such theories, but – strangely enough – his voluntary sacrifice was one of content, and not form. He suffered and died for human meaning.

We do believe in structures, in systems, but their roots should be based on the idea of freedom, not of restriction. For us, forms should always serve meaning.

II.

THOU SHALT BE THE MESSENGER OF FREEDOMS

Our greatest ambition is to advance the freedom of the individual. Despite our increasing privileges and opportunities, all of us are still very restricted.

We can remember what a different world we were living in twenty-five years ago. Culture has effected great changes since then. If you do not want to work, you do not have to work. If you do not want to believe in God, you do not have to. If you do not want to be homosexual or heterosexual, you do not have to be. You can do whatever you want. But behind the scenes there is still a lot of unhappiness and oppression, from religions and political habits of mind. People are scared of life, and we are just as scared as everybody else.

Freedom by itself does not mean much. It can only advance at the

same pace as the personal sense of responsibility. It is only if we all feel
an equal responsibility for each other that we can make a real advance.
There has to be a greater love, a new idea of love. In our pictures we
try to provide some delicate new way of seeing an aspect of life, what
a person is or is not. The message transfers itself to the viewer, and he
or she then has some information. The picture provides information
which leads to understanding, understanding leads to tolerance, and
tolerance leads to love; love is the mother of invention. And invention is
the key to everything, because it forms our tomorrows. Without
invention we die.

People need attention, everyone needs attention. That is the
greatest cry. It surrounds the world every day. And all the artists in this
century seem to give their attention to art, and we think that is an
enormous misunderstanding. We want to give our attention to life.
Christian thought urged us all to join together in praise of the Lord –
Far round the world, thy children hear thy song, from East and West
their voices sweetly blend, praising the Lord... That ideal failed
because everybody was encouraged to be identical, there was no
individuality. We do not want that. We want everybody to be free to
have their own ideas but at the same time tolerant towards each other.

III.

THOU SHALT MAKE USE OF SEX

Art must create a shock if it wants to be new. But at the same time, we
believe in 'de-shocking'. To the person who comes to us and says: 'That
picture called *Shitty* should never have been created, certainly never
exhibited, and I don't want to see it,' we answer: ' Too late! You've said
something about the picture we did, it's actually made, it's in the
world.' He is 'de-shocked'. And one person who comes and says, 'I love
the picture called *Shitty* – he is 'de-shocked' as well.

In fact we are provoking thought. We want to make 'de-shocks'
normal, the idea of sexuality must be normal. Everybody says: 'Oh! A
penis on our wall! Disgusting!' We answer: 'Why?' If we can accept,
together with the viewer, pictures of ourselves like *Bum Holes* – then
we shall all be different.

We all have wicked roots. The whole Western civilisation is
founded on that idea. Whether with atheists, with Protestants or with

Catholics, at the foundations of Western society one feels the inspiration of Christ. 'We are sinners all.' Our new sense of the individual sexual person is born out of this.

We believe that artists who love art to the exclusion of all else produce decadent art. The greatest inspiration we have is closing our eyes once a day and trying to imagine all the people alive on the planet, wherever they are killing each other, having sex, making revolution, going through the desert or jungle or cities. This is our greatest sadness and inspiration.

IV.

THOU SHALT REINVENT LIFE

A long time ago we made a big distinction. Art about life, and not art about art: that was our biggest personal discovery. Art means discovering, reinventing life, not just a new shape or a new form. All is based on human beings, reinventing a way of living.

We are all cultural entities. What you are today depends on what novels your grandmother and your great-grandmother read or did not read, what music they were or were not listening to.

The day we realised we were living sculptures, that was it. We gave ourselves to the viewer, instead of keeping ourselves as artists separated from the people. The moment we were on that table, singing, then, we were making a life gift.

We managed to become at the same time the object and the artist: a speaking, living object. Normally the artist creates an object which is always dead; we became the living force. It was a commitment.

Real art does not show or reflect life, but it can form our futures – a new world.

V.

THOU SHALT GRAB THE SOUL

We are trying to grab the viewer by his or her emotions. We want to get inside the person. We want to succeed, we want to be right, so we are trying to enter the viewer's inner soul, to make him remember that picture for ever. Life is already a little bit different because our pictures exist.

VI.
THOU SHALT GIVE THY LOVE

We are totally obsessed. We want to love the viewer. We want him or her to see our pictures as visual love letters. And we want a love letter back, probably. Mostly we get one, but sometimes we don't.

In an organised society, if we are burgled, we have to telephone to the police. If something is wrong with a leg, we have to go to hospital. After all these things have been looked after, there is still a sort aching hole inside every person which can only be addressed through a novel, or music, or poetry, or pictures – through a cultural force, through love.

We like to do things for people. Are we socialist? We accept the complexity of thoughts and ideas. Our pictures are based on showing our souls, ourselves. Viewers are able to look and search for themselves. Every human being is searching. He only reads a book because he is trying to find out what he is, by comparison with this particular piece of writing. How does he compare himself with the artist? All is comparison. You need a viewer. We believe that a work of art is finished only when it is in front of the viewer. If not, it is a dead, a meaningless piece of work. In front of the viewer, it starts talking.

VII.
THOU SHALT CREATE ARTIFICIAL ART

Art is artificial, because it is inventive. There are no definite rules. We have artificially arranged new ones, and we can break these down and build again.

We think very slowly. When creating a new picture, we know that we must be concentrated, and very empty. We can stumble into it, we can fall over it. We can make a picture on a very simple subject, but we will make something very truthful.

Everyday reality is invisible. When you have a frozen moment of life, as in our pictures, then it is supposed to mean something. You can pass ten thousand people, crossing London Bridge in the morning, but if there is one who comes to you, takes you by the arm and says: 'I want to say something to you', then you remember.

226

VIII.
THOU SHALT HAVE A SENSE OF PURPOSE

If you have to go to the doctor, because there is something wrong with you, you would like the latest advanced technology. You do not want a doctor who says: 'I'm going to cut around, I don't really know what I'm doing, let's just see what happens.' You would like somebody very professional, very precise. In the same way, we think the artist should have a sense of purpose, should know what he is doing. Not like the traditional twentieth-century artist who says: 'I don't know what I'm doing, I just do it. If you like it, good, if not, fuck you!' That is an old-fashioned idea.

When we step into the studio, we have to be crazed and empty-headed. We want to take away all our consciousness, leaving only how we love, how we hate, how we fear. We can't go to the studio and think: 'Well, should we do a picture of a tree or a monkey, a yellow one...?' It does not work. To feel this state of love, this desire to reach people, we have to be completely empty. And then how we actually are is how the picture will be. We have always found that this is the only truthful way.

We are convinced that our art is psychological. But we would not describe ourselves as doctors of the subconscious. By being living sculptures we became the preachers of life.

IX.
THOU SHALT NOT KNOW EXACTLY WHAT THOU DOST,
BUT THOU SHALT DO IT

When making pictures, we have to be completely convinced that we are wrong. There is no example in the history of mankind of someone writing a book or composing a piece of music because he already knew how to do it. If you believe you are wrong in the first place, at least you have the chance to discover something.

We can never really pinpoint what we want to think. This year we seem to have been developing the idea 'What is a man?' or 'What are two men?'. We are probably trying to humiliate ourselves, as in The Naked Shit Pictures.

Once the picture is finished, we are liberated, it becomes an amazing force, a psychological power. Are we destroying ourselves? We are in search of the truth. It is never rigid. Clouds of ideas are in front of us. There is nothing in the world which is not inside a human being. Everything is inside every single person. We are experimenting alone. And, by making pictures, we can feel our way along with the viewer. It is a journey we are making together with him or her.

In The Hague, somebody came up to us and said: 'This is an amazing exhibition, I've never seen anything so depressing and so miserable in my life. I was absolutely fascinated to see all these subjects being addressed.' Then we shook hands and drifted off. Within two seconds another person came up and said: 'I'd like to congratulate you on this exhibition. It's such a celebration of life, I feel so rejuvenated and so hopeful having seen all these pictures.' Same pictures. The reaction depends on the life of the viewer.

X.
THOU SHALT GIVE SOMETHING BACK

We identify with anyone who has given his life, abiding by the traditional idea that we are not here to please ourselves or to make ourselves happy. In exchange for the gift of life we have to give something back.

We would not say that we are anything other than what people say we are. Let us experiment together with the viewer. We do not know whether it is all for the best, but who does? We are all lost.

We are all here by mistake, don't you think?

We're Just Lonely, Miserable, Terrified People: Interview with Dave Stewart 1995

First published in *GQ* magazine, September 1995.

I was in Cologne recently and I saw an invitation to your new show and I just fell about in hysterics. I thought it was hilariously funny.
George: So you saw *Flying Shit* in other words. [He opens a bottle of champagne.]
Gilbert: It was quite an amusing show. You must have only seen excerpts; the reality of the whole show was much, much more powerful.
I remember the last time we met you were saying that the first piece of art that you ever do – as a baby even – is …
George: … to form the shit. In fact, it's the only sculpture that exists naturally in the world; it's modelled in that way. [He lights a cigarette, a Piccadilly, and chain smokes throughout the rest of the evening.] It's people's first adventure in form, and it's one that everybody in the world understands, whether they are rich or poor, come from a desert or a city, or are three years old or seventy. It's a great unifying theme.
Gilbert: It's the first clay that you have. Children naturally make sculptures out of shit…
But then they get told not to.
Gilbert: The first picture that we ever did, in 1969, had 'shit' in it.
George: Yes, that was with our two names: George the Cunt and Gilbert the Shit.
Gilbert: We don't believe that there is anything wrong in doing pieces to do with shit because shit is part of us. Or to do with nakedness – especially of men. It's strange: a naked lady is wonderful; two naked ladies, very interesting; but two men naked …
George: One man naked is a male study; more than one, well… that's quite serious – two men naked are more naked than one.
Gilbert: Collectors only want to buy middle-class art; they love meaningless, empty-of-feeling art. The moment art says something, they are terrified. That's what happened with our Dirty Words show in '77, which had pictures with titles like *Bent, Shit, Cunt, Fucked Up* and *Communism*.
George: Even our biggest fans thought that we'd gone nuts, that we were excessive or idiotic or something.

I've had a lot of trouble with the Shag *picture I bought from you
that hangs in my church.* [Stewart owns a deconsecrated church in
north London which he has converted into a recording studio.] *It
gets rented out to all sorts of people, a gospel choir sometimes, and
people walk in there and say, 'You can't have that picture in here!'*
George: How ridiculous! People are always shagging in churches –
I remember my days in the choir. [All laugh.]
*From the very first time I saw your pictures I completely loved
them, and I've loved everything ever since. It got to the point where
Annie [Lennox] and I, when we had the band Eurythmics, almost
copied everything from you.*
George: How did you do that?
Oh, we searched out suits...
George: Very flattering.
*And at first we didn't actually perform. We copied you to the point
where, instead of playing live, we would go and sit on the stage and
the record would play and we'd just sit there.*
George: Amazing. I'm sure it was very effective.
*Anyway, to go back to your work, I've read a lot of the books that
you've brought out and...*
Gilbert: Did you see *The Ten Commandments* that we did years ago?
That's quite amusing.
Yes, I do remember seeing that. Have you got a copy?
George: Yes, I think so. [He goes to find it, and returns.] Well, these are the
Ten Commandments – for us, not for other people: Thou shalt fight
conformism. Thou shalt be the messenger of freedoms. Thou shalt
make use of sex. Thou shalt reinvent life. Thou shalt grab the soul.
Thou shalt give thy love. Thou shalt create artificial art. Thou shalt
have a sense of purpose. And our favourite one... Thou shalt not know
exactly what thou dost, but thou shalt do it. Finally, Thou shalt give
something back. That's it.
You could have written that, though, in 1971.
Gilbert: Oh yes, we've never changed – ever.
*You know I have a feeling, looking back, that it's almost as if you
took a pill or something in the Sixties and since then it's just got
stronger and stronger. Following your work is like going through
a trip, a journey.*
George: Well, we always hated what they call the development of an

artist, which is normally the development of a style, of his ability. We would like not to have that.

Gilbert: When we make a work of art, we always want to feel like we are in a black bag, completely empty, completely black, so that you don't see anything.

George: Zonked!

Gilbert: Zonked! We don't ever want to look back, or look at anything; we just want to look inside ourselves, at our feelings, no? And then we just punch those feelings out of this black bag, and whatever it is, that's it – that's our art.

George: We never go to the studio with any ideas because that would be wrong. We realised very early on – from what we know of pictures and novels and music and medical advance, or anything – that nobody created something that they regard as important because they knew how to do it. The people who know how to do it are probably very good at teaching it or something, but it's the people who don't know, who manage to trip up, fall over, smack their head, swab off all the blood, and then realise.

Yes, knowledge can get in the way.

George: Leave it blank, leave it blank. And try to push through...

Gilbert: Push through! One repeats oneself all the time. In fact, we don't want to make different pictures; we want to find the truth of ourselves.

George: [Opening a second bottle of champagne.] It's all one big picture anyway, because one day there will be a last picture that we make and then that will be one whole story together. The strange thing is that when you say 'artist' to a person they think of dead people anyway because most of the artists that we all know are dead. So even if you talk about living artists they imagine that you're going to be dead quite soon because they prefer them dead anyway.

Gilbert: If you aren't dead they don't know what to think.

And they want you to die anyway so you can become a Legend.

George: Yes, dead is good. [All laugh.]

What do you think of people who claim your work is a kind of voodoo, a black magic?

Gilbert: We used to have a local vicar – he's retired now – who we had a big battle with. We had this show with Anthony d'Offay in 1984 and we had this first piece we called *Shitted* – a very good piece, no? – but my

God, they did a short programme about us on television...
George: ...and they interviewed the vicar without us knowing, and he
said some amazingly wicked things about us. He said, 'I think they're
sick, sad and serious.' [Much laughter.] It sort of reminded us of the enemy
because S-S-S sounds like the SS!

*But it's so interesting the way you live your life and the way you are
exactly what you say you are, that you are this sculpture or you are
the art. It opens up a whole new world. I mean, you have not only
reinvented art, you've reinvented your own lives.*

Gilbert: Only if we are able to win over the viewer are we happy; if not,
it doesn't mean a thing.
George: The twentieth century has been filled with artists who think the
viewers are stupid and will never understand. It's not true. We believe
that when we make our pictures we have the viewer in mind. Everybody has their fears, their hopes, their loves, their dreads – they can
look at a picture and make up their own minds about art.
Gilbert: Yes, it's very interesting because if you take normal people to
let's say the Tate and they're confronted with modern art, they will say
they don't understand it and that they are terrified, and they walk out.
Or maybe they pretend to understand it. But when they see our
pictures, maybe they hate them, can't stand them, but in that moment
they understand it. And that's perfect because then you are touching
them, which is what we want to do. We want to grab their souls.

*Yes, as you say, people are terrified of art, especially of naked,
shitty pictures.*

George: We believe that if the artist, in whichever field it is, provides
information, informs about something, then at that moment you have
some understanding. And when you have understanding you become
tolerant because you understand more. And when people are tolerant,
they begin to love. And if you love something enough you actually do
something about it. You declare it. So it's a sort of a change.

Have you ever thought of making a recording?

Gilbert: Well, we used to have this amazing drunken tramp in the street
outside our house. He was very nice to us when he was normal, but
sometimes he would start shouting the most violent stuff, like he was
going to kill us. It was fantastic. We always wanted to make recordings
of him.

Do you have a CD player?

Gilbert: No. We don't have a record player. We've never listened to a
record in our entire lives. We don't even have a radio. It's not that we
are against music; we just made a big decision a long time ago not to be
involved. What we are interested in is freedom, and sexual freedom is
still a big battle.

What do you think of John Major?

George: He's the most decent, darlingest man to do the job there is.

Gilbert: I don't see what he's doing so wrong. I'm not a Tory, but of
course Tony Blair is becoming a Tory after all. George had this idea
that there's only one person that's able to beat Tony Blair at the general
election.

Who?

George: Bugs Bunny! [All laugh.]

I take it you're not supporters of the modern Labour Party then?

George: [Opening a third bottle of champagne.] There is no modern Labour
Party – it's just a Tory Labour Party.

Gilbert: Art is based on capitalism; if it isn't, you're finished as an
artist. We cannot have a Labour Party – freedom in the end is capitalist,
no? Socialism is not freedom, socialism is based on making everybody
the same and equal; you're not *allowed* to be a free person. Maybe
socialism is good for society, but as an artist you have to be a capitalist.

George: We're old enough to remember art under socialism – there
were two West End galleries that sold so-called international art and
that was it. Everybody who left art school had to go and teach for
twenty years and then they retired and started to paint and then
realised they'd cocked up their whole life and used to drink themselves
to death. So never be an artist under socialism.

Gilbert: Even if the capitalist system is not the best system, it's the only
way to create free art. In Russia, they had state artists and they were
dreadful. All these young English artists now are very clear people,
very articulate, very driven – because they don't have anything, they
have to be extremely artistic. But the Labour Party would give them all
a job or something, and they would be finished. They would become
teachers not artists. There's a very famous academy in Düsseldorf
which wanted us to become professors.

George: They wanted to be the first to make two people one professor.
I said, 'Does that mean we get half the money?' and they said, 'No, no,
no – we'll pay you both.'

What was your reaction to the idea?
George: We told them certainly not, under any circumstances, would
we do that. Why should we go and teach German students how to be
good artists? We'd be traitors, wouldn't we? Absolutely.
Would you teach art to English students?
George: We wouldn't even do that. For years and years and years they
would never have wanted us or let us anyway. They wouldn't trust us
with the students would they? And quite right. Entirely right.
Gilbert: We don't believe in teaching art.
George: Whenever students ask our advice we say, 'Fuck the teachers;
that's your only chance.' Because all teachers of art have one fear in
life, one big fear, which they never spell out, and that is that one of their
students will go on to become an artist. They dread that.
Because it will make them feel even more like a failure?
Gilbert: Yes. We have the best art schools in the world here, and at art
school they tell you oh, you are a fantastic person, but the moment you
leave art school you are the biggest shit in the world. And that's what
we fight.
Gilbert: Shall we go to the restaurant?
George: Do you like Korean food?
Anything.
George: Do you like raw fish? Raw meat? Raw wine?

[They go off to a small Korean restaurant in Islington which, as it happens, serves the
most exquisite and unusual delicacies – dishes such as boiled bracken and giant mint
leaves. Bottles of beer and four bottles of red wine are also consumed.]

You clearly like eating out.
George: We have no choice because we don't have a kitchen – never
have done.
All those rooms and no kitchen – why not?
George: We wouldn't like to shop for food, we wouldn't like to think of
what to cook, we wouldn't like to cook it, and we wouldn't like to wash
up, and we wouldn't like to dispose of the remnants, and we wouldn't
like to store food for the next meal.
What if you feel hungry and it's the middle of the night?
George: Bad luck. Eat something else.
Gilbert: It's very good discipline. There is no drink and there is no food.
We only have a drink when somebody's coming round, and then we go
out and buy it.

George: We have a fridge in which we keep the paper for our pictures because it has to be kept at a certain temperature, and we keep the champagne in that. So we keep the paper, we sell the pictures, and then we buy some champagne.

You have a favourite local cafe, don't you?

George: Yes. The Market Cafe, in our street. A brother and sister have owned and run it for forty years – Clyde's the cook, Phyllis is the waitress. And they're the most angelic, Christian, honest, decent people you've ever met. Totally honourable in every single way.

Do you eat there every day?

George: Every day for breakfast and lunch for twenty-seven years. We first went there when we were students, but it was very difficult because at that time it was mostly the Spitalfields market porters who ate there and they were very aggressively lower-class. They were very exclusive and very elitist and they didn't like us coming into the cafe. But we liked the food and Phyllis liked us, and she thought they were wrong. And then very slowly they accepted us, they stopped teasing us and doing wolf whistles and things.

Gilbert: But the food is so fantastic.

George: It's the best English food in the world.

Gilbert: The council health inspectors tried to close it down twice, but we did it up and got it opened up again. We worked on the cafe for one and a half months.

George: Every friend we dragged in.

They must have been really pleased.

George: Oh yes, they couldn't get over it.

Gilbert: That's why every time we go there they don't want to charge us.

George: I always give Phyllis a £10 note for lunch and she always hands back £8 change. For whatever we have, whether we go alone or with friends.

Gilbert: The thing about the Korean restaurant we are in now is that recently one of the waiters became so friendly towards us, and we became such big friends. But he was so naughty, don't you think George?

George: Naughty but innocent.

Gilbert: He was twenty-six or something and had the most incredible face. He looked like a Buddha.

George: Probably the most beautiful we've ever seen – or ever likely to.

Gilbert: But he's a moralist – it was nothing to do with sex. Just to do with friendship. Total friendship. Wonderful.

Gilbert: One time we ate so much that I said to him, 'Please don't bring any more food – I feel pregnant.' And he said, 'I want your baby.' [All laugh.] One time we took him out and he came back to our house so we offered him champagne and he drank so much he was totally drunk. And then he started to ask us the most personal questions – absolutely shocking.

George: Questions like, 'So, is sex better with a man or a woman?' And, 'How many times do you do it a week?' One night he ran out of our favourite wine, so I said, 'We're going to have to think of some sort of punishment for you.' And then he looked at me and said, 'I like anything.'

Gilbert: The amazing thing is that he's the biggest queen on earth, what with his walk and everything – it's incredible. And what does he say all the time, George? That he's not gay?

George: Extraordinary! Wonderful chap! When he returned to Korea, we said we'll come and see you one day. And he took us so seriously that we had to do it. So we went to Korea.

Gilbert: George used to know this Mauritian boy...

George: Steady now, Gilbert. Steady now.

Gilbert: He was lovely and he introduced us to Mauritian food.

George: Well, we sponsored Raj through one year of college here and he said that when he went back to Mauritius he would name his beach-hut restaurant after us. He was a real tart.

Do you ever go to shows or exhibitions?

Gilbert: We never look at art.

George: We don't see anything.

Gilbert: And we don't want to – because the moment you start looking there is no end to it. You become a viewer and we are not viewers, we are the makers.

George: We look at the raw material of life. We prefer to come out of the front door, it's been raining, there's a puddle there, and there's a bit of vomit from a Chinese takeaway, there's a pigeon eating it, there's a cigarette end, and that's all there is. And then you know what it is.

[One of the dishes arrives.]

I've never seen anything like this in my life, what is it?

George: It's cuttlefish.

It has the texture of a tongue.

George: Oh, we like that – we're always tonguing. As long as there's tonguing, there's hope. [All laugh; George is becoming increasingly drunk.] So Dave, are you a Christian or non-Christian chap?

Well, my stepfather, who was my biggest influence, was a Zen Buddhist. He was absolutely hilarious – he never ever used money, ever, he found everything in skips, he got up at five in the morning, found his newspapers, found croissants outside bread shops...

George: But do you think we're all God's creatures?

No, I don't.

George: So whose children are we?

Gilbert: That's the vicar in George.

George: No, no, no – not true. It's the artist, artist, artist.

Gilbert: OK.

George: OK. Or not. It's right or not. The *artist... I'm* not the vicar...

I'd agree that we're all God's bad children. Do you believe in God, George?

George: No. But what we do believe in, more than anyone we've met, is the heritage of Christian belief, and we honour that. We accept that probably 300 yards down the road there is a church.

Gilbert: We don't believe that there is a God out there, like the way Renaissance painters did, but we do believe in Christianity. Christianity is just a moral code – lead your life in a good way.

Do you feel that you're not validating your existence unless you're doing something?

George: We only believe in responsibility. But, you know, we never did anything.

That's a great headline for this piece. Maybe we should just have that headline, the photo, and blank pages.

George: It's true – we're just lonely, miserable, terrified people every single day. We get very disturbed sometimes.

What, as a pair or individually?

Gilbert: No, no, no – we just get frustrated.

Like a feeling of angst?

George: Oh no, there's nothing *German* about us.

Well, you don't like taking holidays, do you?

George: We don't like pleasure.

I find that hard to believe.

George: Really, we don't. We only went on holiday twice in our whole
life: we went to Korea and to Portugal.

How was Portugal?

Gilbert: It was so bloody dead. Because we didn't feel threatened by
anything. They are the most peaceful people we ever met. They watch
the sea and they have the most melancholic souls in the world. We also
went to India – although that wasn't completely a holiday; we were
trying to find out spaces to show.

[Towards the end of the evening, Gilbert & George become decidedly worse for wear –
their minds wander over a bewildering array of subjects and at one point George sings
a song he learned at Sunday School. They remain, however, extremely generous and
polite.]

You know in Thailand the women, to get their babies to sleep,
masturbate them, suck their penises and...

George: Well, the standard book for nannies in England, up until
1927 or something, advised that if you want to put a boy to sleep, suck
him off.

How come you're reading standard nanny books?

George: Well, I check on these things. And we learned recently that the
police manual says that if a policeman wants to make his dog loyal to
him, he must masturbate him.

Gilbert: And if one of their police dogs attacks you, we know how to
stop him.

George: Yes, just ram a stick up his bum – then the jaw opens.

And how do you get round to the bum?

Gilbert: Behave like a gentleman!

The Singing Sculpture: Interview
with Wolf Jahn 1995

Previously unpublished extract from a forthcoming book-length interview.

You met at St Martin's in 1967.
Gilbert: Yes. First we made objects of our own and showed them together, then we did one object together – one mask, a head. I would put in whatever I wanted, and then George put in whatever he wanted, and so on, and then it was finished.
George: You could say that was a collaboration. We've never collaborated in that way since.
Did it take a long time for you to become friends?
George: No, we were friends immediately. We used to go for dinner, explore the East End, Hampstead, everywhere, every afternoon.
Gilbert: It's very simple. George was the only one who accepted my pidgin English.
And then you did the Living Sculpture?
Gilbert: In a way, that happened by mistake. Because at the end of the year we posed with our objects, holding our sculptures –
George: – and then we did the same without the sculptures.
Gilbert: We realised we didn't need the objects any more. It was just us.
George: And in our little studio in Wilkes Street in Spitalfields we played that old record *Underneath the Arches*. We did some moving to it, and we thought it would be a very good sculpture to present. And that in a way was the first real G & G piece. Because it wasn't a collaboration. We were on the table as a sculpture, a two-man sculpture.
Gilbert: First it was like a lot of other stuff we did, like walking, or like *Reading from a Stick*. Then it became a revelation for us. The time and endurance made it a new way of art for us, and made us into art. When we started doing it for eight hours or two weeks on end, we realised that the *Singing Sculpture* was our first solid idea. Before that, we could have gone anywhere – we could have been pop stars or anything else.
George: We soon discovered that wherever we did the *Singing Sculpture* it worked every time. People were always glued to that sculpture. The older people, the children sitting on the floor – all the bloody time, always a success – and that was a fantastic feeling. And we

discovered that people could get any meaning out of that piece. There
was one small boy who wanted to travel with it for ever, and wind up
the gramophone for us; there was one lady who cried because it had
something to do with the memory of her father. I think that's the seed
of what we have in our pictures today. It's open to different responses.
Gilbert: And it even started to speak to us. Unhappy, lonely, alone.
George: Just finding that you can do an artwork for people in a simple
way. People feel better for it. It wasn't like a normal artwork around
that time, which some people liked and some didn't. Everybody took
photographs. It's like famous paintings: you have millions of postcards
of them. We felt like that. There were photographs in all the newpapers.
It became a famous piece.
Gilbert: It caught people's imaginations totally – and we were the art.
We realised that we could speak, that we were able to create messages.
We became the speaking art object. I think nobody ever did that before.
George: Not in that way.
Gilbert: It became a living, walking sculpture that spoke to everybody.
We believe the turning point was in November 1969, when we posed on
the stairs at the Stedelijk Museum in Amsterdam.
George: It was semi-official. An artist friend, Ger van Elk, knew Wim
van Beeren, who was a curator there. We weren't invited exactly; it was
sort of tolerated, and it turned into a sensation. It went on for five hours.
And there are so many people who remember it from those days. It's
still the most popular postcard. Some people spoke to us; a lot of people
took photographs; some Germans threatened us with a knife. Some of
our old tutors – Anthony Caro – saw it. It was a sensation.
Gilbert: We believe that we were born on the stairs of the Stedelijk
Museum.
George: If we had been more like some of the other students at St
Martin's, we would probably have got involved in pop music. They
actually wanted us to do these Living Sculptures in the pop world. One
or two people said, 'Couldn't you do a record, or let us hear a tape?' So if
we had been a little more like the hippie, guitar-playing people we
knew, we'd probably have gone in that direction. But we had no interest
in pop music in that way.
Gilbert: George told a story at the Lyceum once.
    What kind of story?
George: The story of my childhood. I read the story out to Gilbert and

discarded the sheets. They fluttered into the audience. We also did the Living Sculpture in Hyde Park during a pop concert. They asked us all sorts of personal questions at that concert. They assumed we were some sort of funny modern gurus.

Gilbert: The make-up takes you away from the normal person and makes you special. That's it. It makes you a god in some way – a sculpture, in fact. It wouldn't have worked without make-up.

George: And we had these very distinctive, ordinary suits. At the pop concert, that stood out a mile. Everybody was wearing kaftans and muslin dresses – nobody had a normal suit like we had. Not one. The other important feeling we had was that we wanted to do something nice. We didn't want to do this grubby, fake-serious stuff. We wanted to do something that was attractive and emotional.

Gilbert: I remember we were very against the Arts Lab, where they did Happenings, because Happenings were disgusting. They were just rolling around with toilet paper, wires, beds falling down, rubber.

George: Always dirty.

Gilbert: We wanted a clean object in a museum, but a living one.

George: Happy, bright, light, beautiful even. That's why we used to look at Easter cards, things like that.

You kept your first names but dropped your surnames.
Why was that?

Gilbert: At college we were GPGP. But when we left college we became simply Gilbert & George.

George: More catchy.

Did you want to break with your past?

George: We were happy to leave it all behind. We got out of it. It was fantastic. We were even very happy to get away from the world of art at St Martin's.

Gilbert: We hated that. We knew it was nonsense. We still hate it – all those fake sculptures. In one year we managed to move from small objects to nothing.

George: That's why we like the idea of the Postal Sculptures, which we mailed all over the world. There must be millions of villages that don't have museums filled with horrible sculptures. But every village gets letters through the letter box, and everyone understands that.

Gilbert: That was a form we liked, so that we could send very personal messages. We told them how we felt. It had to be from us, handmade.

And those Postal Sculptures were an incredible success.

How long did you go on sending them?

Gilbert: For six years, concurrently with the *Singing Sculpture*.

George: It didn't feel like a lifetime activity. It was something to go through and leave behind. But the Postal Sculptures were the seeds of our pictures.

Once the Singing Sculpture *was defined as form, wasn't it risky for you to continue with it, to keep on doing it without change or evolution?*

George: Everyone said you can never do anything after that, it's so successful, so well-known, you can never do anything better.

Gilbert: When we first did the *Singing Sculpture*, the form was difficult to survive on – financially, even. There was no system for making money out of it.

George: Because we didn't want to make variations on it, we couldn't go back to the places we'd been to before with a new record or a new make-up. It seemed silly. The *Singing Sculpture* is it. The most famous living thing we have done in our whole life, and it survives in film form.

Gilbert: The *Singing Sculpture* was very limited: what you can do with it, say with it, express with it. So in 1972, when we started drinking, we decided to do decadent sculptures – pictures, in fact. But we were still the objects. We realised that we had become the *Singing Sculpture*, and it didn't matter whether we were doing it in a gallery or not. Our existence became the artwork.

East London, Sex, Shit, Death: Interview with Hans-Ulrich Obrist 1995

A shorter version of this interview was first published in the catalogue for the 1997 Gilbert & George exhibition at Magasin 3 Stockholm Konsthall, Sweden.

EAST LONDON

The East End is a place where you would bring people to show Earth.

George: Yes, we would say that around here is one of the most actual places. The look in people's eyes, the variety of expression, is very up-to-date.

Gilbert: Because we studied here and then moved to the East End of London, we made a big decision that to be artists we didn't want to go anywhere else. A lot of artists, to become successful artists, had to move to Berlin or to Paris or to New York because it felt like being here was not the right place to be. But we said we will stick our shoes in the mud and be firm. We wanted to become artists here, and that became very important for us.

George: The East End is as multi-racial as any other place on Earth. We always say that our pictures are not involved in London, and not involved in our immediate surroundings. When others say, 'But you use the Church from the end of your street', we say, 'That's the church inside of you, inside the viewer'. You can live in Sydney or Johannesburg or New York and you will find very similar Christian symbols.

The East End is also Jack the Ripper.

George: Even Jack the Ripper exists everywhere.

Gilbert: Everywhere, even in Switzerland, in Hanover.

You once told me that this church at the end of your street, Christchurch Spitalfields, is built on strange foundations.

George: It was a brilliant idea. Hawksmoor first built the foundations and then, by finding an excuse to sack the builders, he secretly had seven horrors built into the foundations and cemented over: one strangled prostitute, one baby cut into three pieces – magical horrors. When it was all covered up, he rehired the builders and the church rose on top of that evil. He said that to *defeat* evil you have to *do* evil, which in medical terms is of course perfectly reasonable. It is the vaccination theory, isn't it? They have to give you a little bit of the illness to make you immune to it.

What about Fournier Street, the street where you live?
George: It changes always.
Gilbert: The Huguenots had to leave France, so they moved to the East End of London. All of the streets around here are French streets.
George: Constant change. The Huguenots had to leave here too because English law was against them.
Gilbert: They are weavers, silk weavers. They became rich so they had to leave this part of London for tax reasons.
George: Complicated reasons. Then this area was inhabited by German people. There were still two German churches in the district. Then it became Russian, Jewish.
George: It is constantly in flux. Even during our time, it has changed so many times. The Jewish people left and Maltese people came, and then people from Somali land came, then the Bangladesh people arrived, and now it's more mixed.
Gilbert: Eccentric people arrived.
George: It became very queer for a while. Even now I am sure it is changing in some strange way that we don't really see. Now it's becoming more hippie and macrobiotic, more artistic in a way. There are galleries here for the first time. There are probably four or five galleries within two minutes' walk.

Spitalfields Market has changed a lot.
George: We like that change.
Gilbert: In some way it is a very extreme district. It is on the edge all the time.
George: Yiddish was very commonly spoken here when we first came.
Gilbert: Now it is a mixture always moving from Cockney to Jewish to Indian. But it is all quite extreme, the mixture of cultures, and that is very exciting.
George: The man at the string shop used to add up the bill to himself. He spoke while adding it up in Yiddish and had to translate it for himself into pounds, shillings and pence. Then he had to translate it from the decimal. Extraordinary.

I often observe in the streets of the East End these crashes, shocks of differences. It is not about different communities becoming homogeneous. It is about crashes of differences, in a Victor Segalen kind of way.

Gilbert: What is exciting is that in some way they all know us. George always says hello to all of England. We are totally protected.

Like last night with the taxi driver; you didn't even have to tell him the address. He said, 'Fournier Street?'

George: They are life-long friends.

Gilbert: We already know many middle-aged, or say forty-year-old Asians who speak to us who we can remember from when they were very glamorous teenagers. That's interesting.

The coexistence of elements from the past and the present is also apparent in your house, such as your collection of Christopher Dresser vases.

George: That's what Christopher Dresser said was modern for him. Modern was the steam-ship travel, so he could encompass the world easily for the first time. It didn't take months to travel to Japan or to San Francisco. The depth of history was just becoming available. They were digging up the pyramids. They were digging up Mayan temples. For the first time you could have a total grasp of history and of the world. Dresser thought that together past and present was very modern.

Gilbert: We believe very much that we are trying to accept the modern and the old at the same time. We don't want to say that only what is modern is right.

George: All history together with today is what is modern, not just the now modern.

Gilbert: The complication of it, we believe, is so good.

SEX

George: The biggest issue of our time has been, and will continue to be, what is a man and what is a woman. This is the main issue under discussion. We have always believed that, and it always became more and more true. We never thought we would live to see an *Evening Standard* headline saying, 'It's Official: Marriage is Defunct', and this was a headline giving some new statistics on divorce and marriage tendencies.

Gilbert: We always used to say that the heterosexuals can sort themselves out only when they accept, when they are able to understand, the homosexuals.

George: At the moment the so-called 'straight' community is more intent on copying the gay community. That's the tendency at the moment.

Gilbert: Gay culture has dominated straight culture recently, don't you think? Everything that is new or even amusing in pop music comes from that. It is at the forefront of sorting out amazing difficulties.

Your work has had an enormous impact on advertisements, where, for example, in the last couple of years there are more men than women.

George: Enormous changes. That is post us, really. Post G & G. We always fought against the divisions of sexuality. We were always encouraged by the art profession to believe in the idea of gay or straight and we don't believe in that. We just believe that every person is a sexual person. There literally is no such thing as a heterosexual or a homosexual. We think it is completely an invention. Now we think it is not such a useful definition anyway.

Gilbert: But it will change, very, very slowly. Only on the day when there is no problem, when you can be whatever you want to be and nobody has to write a big article about it, then that's it, then you can stop.

George: It is happening more and more anyway. How many times have you told somebody something that was said to you at a party that was very interesting without having to say the sex of that person.

It is also about identity I think. The notion of identity is fluid and saying that there is a heterosexual identity and a homosexual identity means fixing and limiting identities. Sade said that everything is in permanent transformation so there is no such thing as a fixed identity. It's all fluid.

Gilbert: That's it.

George: Totally. We are happily capable of being so much more complicated than anyone says and therefore one has to leave these divisions aside to allow us to be as elaborate as we can be.

*

George: Even when people say 'gay' they don't realise that gay is a modern term and was stolen from female prostitutes in London who were known as 'gay ladies' for 120 years. Even the word 'homosexual' is just a Hungarian invention from 1865. It didn't exist before. All the early writings on sexuality classify what we now would call homosexual activity only in terms of excess, so that a person who was having a drink was having a drink and if you got drunk it was excessive. If you are having sex with a woman you are having sex. If you fuck about with a man you are just being excessive. It wasn't different, it was just doing a lot.

It's the same thing with 'obscenity'. One tends to think of obscenity as negative. But if one goes to the roots of the word, 'obscenity' means 'beyond the scene'. When people are small-minded, what is beyond their small-mindedness is 'obscene'.

George: When I was reading the history of pornography by Montgomery Hyde it said that there have been seventeen international conferences since 1971 to try to decide on a term and a definition of 'obscenity' so that the postal services of the world can have some common legal legislation and not one of those conferences has ever resulted in a signed paper. They can't decide on what is 'obscene'.

Gilbert: They cannot agree. But it is quite clear in America what is 'obscene'.

George: 'Obscene' in America means images or text which appeal to the prurient and show nakedness and excrement.

Gilbert: It's incredible. That is exactly what we do.

George: So we are doing very anti-American pictures at the moment!

SHIT

You once said, 'Beauty is our art'. It has always been a big theme. Beauty has also been a taboo in art.

Gilbert: We did it many times and many times we wanted to make beautiful pictures.

George: As a force.

Gilbert: As a force.

George: Not as an end. In Eastern poetry there are poems about something very beautiful and very simple. Four-line poems which describe a few pieces of grass, and then there is a stone next to it, and then a little rain hits the stone. So it is describing something beautiful but at the same time you get an amazing feeling from it. The force of beauty brings some new understanding.

Gilbert: Because for a long time beauty meant kitsch. Even that we tackled many, many times, the idea of beauty.

I think your work would not threaten people so much if it were not beautiful.

George: I think if all of the Naked Shit Pictures were done without using our negative form, if they were done with charcoal and some

brown paint, and done a little rough, not so polished as ours are, I think
they would have no...

Gilbert: ...impact...

George: No service to people whatsoever. None. They would provide
nothing to help one single person.

Gilbert: They would have no power.

George: If they were collaged, with a little bit of polythene. Even if they
had some real shit and lavatory paper stuck to the pictures, they would
mean nothing. They wouldn't have the connection to the inside of the
person.

Gilbert: We think that through the form we use, through the negative
that becomes so hard and so polished, the pictures become so powerful
and so aggressive in some funny way. We always say that our flowers
are totally aggressive.

George: Recently people said that we even made shit beautiful in some
way, that we gave a way of looking at it.

Gilbert: The first time they can actually look at it. I think that's
incredible.

George: To the people who say, 'Surely you've manipulated these
shits to make them look like penises, I don't believe they are actually
shits,' we say, 'Have you looked at yours? Because if you look at them
every day, come next Thursday you probably will have one like that.'
If you never look at the shit, you cannot say that it shouldn't look
like that.

Gilbert: The morality that we are allowed to eat but not allowed to look
at our shit is morally wrong. If not, it is perfect.

> *It was in your first work, in the* Shit and Cunt Magazine Sculpture
> [1970], *that shit first appeared.*

George: That's entirely true.

> *It's a big theme. Roland Barthes once said, 'Photographic shit
> doesn't stink'.*

George: That's true. But I think people think ours does. I'm sure of that.
We recently had an article where it said, 'The artists and their pictures
stink'. It's also very interesting that people are alarmed, as probably we
are as well, by the combination of naked and shit. It's interesting that
that should be alarming, because the fact of life is that you have to be at
least partly naked in order to shit. You cannot shit with your clothes on.
So it's very natural, the combination of those two subjects.

Gilbert: It is based on degrading ourselves. Then critics cannot attack you in the same way! I always believe that.

George: We are as serious in exploring the feelings and thoughts around shit at least as much as local government have to be. Local government constantly have to monitor drainage systems. Whenever you build a new housing estate you have to build a sewage plant. So local government, central government, have to be involved. The medical profession has to be totally involved with shit. They have to take samples from people: 'Could I have a stool sample, Sir?' they say. Then they have to analyse it. Restaurants by law have to provide lavatories. Public parks by law have to provide lavatories. The manufacturers of lavatory paper are very seriously involved in the subject of shit and have to be, quite naturally. There is a whole mass of attention given to it and we are giving it artists' attention.

I recently saw an Aztec exhibition with beautiful ancient earrings in the form of shit. At that time, unlike now, shit was not taboo.

George: How marvellous. What a commercial item that would be today. They would sell like hot cakes. We think it is important to say about taboos that a lot of people think we are very free, mad, crazy fuckers who want to impose our free way of life on them. This is not at all the case. We are filled with taboos. We are terrified of shit. It is an adventure together with the public, together with the viewer.

Gilbert: Even in the pieces where we have the trousers half down, it is not the nakedness that is taboo, it is having the trousers half down.

George: It is very interesting that those pictures are always described as the trousers half way down, whereas one could equally say that they are half way up. They are always seen as taking the trousers off, not putting them on. One could say that they are very coy because we are in the act of putting the trousers on.

It is in between.

George: Yes, absolutely.

Gilbert: We manage to take away the sexuality of the works in some way so that they become for the first time like you are able to look at the nakedness of humanity...

George: ...in a way that you can't with a pin-up magazine, for instance, or with a glamorous young person in a movie.

Gilbert: That's totally different.

George: It was very interesting that David Sylvester, having seen these pictures, said something which we hadn't realised entirely. He said that all of the Modern artists tried to do pictures and only succeeded in doing nudes, which they were very unhappy about, but that we have done naked.

Gilbert: Because the pin-up magazine is not naked, it is a sexual stimulant. It is different.

George: We believe that if you look at pin-up magazines you are looking at those models, you are looking at that material. We believe that people looking at our pictures where we are naked are looking at their own nakedness as well. It's not just us. They realise their own nakedness under their clothes at that moment. In that way the pictures are as much about the viewer as about us, really.

*

George: There is a famous quote from the bible where it says – and one has to be careful with these texts as they have been interfered with by scholars time and time again – 'Beware of the men who sit on the wall and eat their own dung and drink their own piss'. Those words appear in the bible twice. In Barbara Thiery's book, *Jesus the Man*, she says that in one of the Bible's original texts it says that Jesus was taken from the cross and laid temporarily in a urinal. This is so interesting because our picture *Urinal* [1991] shows a urinal set in a church. But all of the classical texts, Greek and Roman, have been interfered with, haven't they? Things left out, things introduced...

You used a lot of Christian iconography in the past, such as your Jesus pieces at the beginning of the 1980s. But it was always for the individual that you used it, wasn't it?

Gilbert: Faith. We are always playing true and against, trying to say is it good or is it bad. Like *Black Jesus* [1980]: we made it black.

George: People say, 'Oh, it's not clear whether it's for or against. Is a Christian person supposed to be flattered or offended?' And we say that that is only two of the many possibilities this picture can bring about. We always say that we are not fighting for freedom, we are fighting for freedoms.

Gilbert: We are brought up by this. Religion, faith, is still with us, in the back of our minds. We are fighting for and against all the time, every single day. In every corner of the world we are confronted with a church. Even the laws of all these countries are religious, based on religion.

250

George: Shit and faith put together, like in *Shit Faith* [1982] or in the big shit cross in the Naked Shit Pictures, should be great unifying themes. All people, wherever they live, have some involvement with shit. All people have some faith or attitude towards faith. Wherever you live, whatever your age, whatever your education, those two things are common elements.

So it's about fusion?

George: Those two things would have something to say to anybody, anywhere.

Gilbert: But the combination is dangerous.

George: It is exciting. Do churches have lavatories?

There is an interesting church in Vienna, in a psychiatric hospital in Steinhopf, built by Otto Wagner. He made the floor slanted so that water could directly pour off the excrement.

George: Amazing. Do you think this church has lavatories? Every church must have a lavatory presumably.

Gilbert: Normally they don't.

Maybe a private one for the vicar.

George: Oh yes. An elitist lavatory. Surely Christians say this is the house of God, so if it is a house it must have a lavatory.

DEATH

When you use Christian iconography it is also often to do with death.

George: That is the basis of the Christian faith. The example of Christ dying on the cross is still with us totally, isn't it, that one example. It is lived out endlessly by people as well.

Gilbert: We liked it for the idea of the suffering man and that is why we became quite interested in the idea of Jesus, as a suffering person. Beaten up for saving the world. That is what we like.

George: From our reading we realise that in every field, wherever someone advanced a cause, whether it was in medicine or art or, every field, there was always enormous suffering involved. Who didn't get beaten up in history for doing something? It's just an endless heritage for that. Van Gogh was discriminated against, Rembrandt they tried to put in prison, Oscar Wilde ended up a disaster. The list must be endless. The man who invented anaesthetics was completely discriminated against. Darwin was beaten up in texts all over the world.

Gilbert: And you will be very soon.

George: It's your turn soon.

You also have this notion of de-shocking with regard to these
pictures.

Gilbert: Always, always.

George: I think this is more the case now.

Gilbert: But it is very funny that we have been saying 'de-shocking' for
ten or fifteen years, and even in this article yesterday, they think we
only want to shock.

George: We don't think our pictures are shocking in the moral sense of
shocking. We think television coverage of the Rwandan killings, daily
on the news, whether it is in the press or on the television, you see
death and sport, death and sport, death and sport and we think that's
very, very alarming, that diet.

Gilbert: When you see these big tanks moving down the street, that's
more morally wrong because you know that they can blow your head
off. You can hurt other people, and we don't do that. I think that is very
interesting. We are not damaging people like war does.

Your pictures are profoundly human.

George: We even believe that the news has this insistence on death and
sport and it is a very wicked thing really. There should be legislation
imposed with guidelines that news presenters should have a more
humanistic range of what is news. There are many things that will
happen next week apart from death and sport.

Death in itself is a very dull event, but thinking about death is
interesting.

Gilbert: The fear of death, that's it...

...which has to do with energy, the thinking and fear...

George: You only have one go at death. With most things you have a
variety of occasions. Death we have just one chance.

Gilbert: Every second it is nearer to us, we are nearer to death.

Since the Renaissance, in Western culture one rarely sees a dead
body in the street, in the public sphere. It is banished outside.

George: From the Western world, yes. The embalmer, the person who
lays out the body in the coffin, has to put a cork into the anus to stop the
body doing anymore shitting. So even that's a connection. Even Van
Gogh when he shot himself, he shot himself on a dung hill, interestingly.
I wonder why that?

Interview by Martin Gayford 1996

First published in 1996 by Edizioni Charta, Milan, in the catalogue for the retrospective exhibition *Gilbert & George* at the Galleria d'Arte Moderna, Bologna.

Could you each tell me something about your background?
George: First of all we both come from fairly similar poor, country backgrounds, I would say.
Gilbert: I'm from the Dolomites, Italy. We speak a different language – Ladino. I went to art school when I was fourteen years old. I always wanted to be an artist. My first figures were sculptures when I was seven, eight years old.
Can you remember what made you want to be an artist?
Gilbert: I liked art, I liked figures, I wanted to make figures. The only artist that was really important was Michelangelo, he was big enough as an image. And even my uncle was painting a little, so the family was a little artistic. I was always looking.
What did your family do?
Gilbert: My father was a shoemaker, we lived in a small village, that was about it.
Were your parents pleased that you decided to be an artist?
Gilbert: My father was never very interested, but my mother yes, because she always wanted us to do exactly what we wanted. She was the big force behind us. But they never understood exactly what an artist is, which was good, they never actually looked into it very closely. So they didn't see the big disaster that could occur.
George: Similar in a way. I was already going to evening classes before I left school, which happened when I was fifteen. Then I continued with evening classes. I was working in the local town, in a shop. Then the teacher at the college said, you should become an art student and go on to art school. At that time, in that part of Britain, it wouldn't have occurred to me to think of it.
You lived in the West Country?
George: Yes, in Totnes, a small town in Devon. Because the classes were at Dartington [a well-known progressive school], the teachers were quite progressive, and all the students were private, so they wanted to experiment with me in a way. So I went to college there, full-time for two years. They gave me a grant, which was an experimental idea.

Can you remember what prompted you to want to become an artist?
George: Probably seeing Van Gogh, and reading about him, I think.
That freedom of somebody being completely crazy, without having to
answer to anybody, and producing pictures and becoming very famous
– a free spirit.
Gilbert: George has very good pictures that he did when he was
fourteen, fifteen years old.
George: My mother wasn't so keen on the idea of my becoming an
artist. That was just because people were very backward there at that
time. It wasn't a fear of modern art. I don't think either of our families
was aware of the possible disaster of living as an artist. I think my
mother only said, 'You shouldn't do that darling, you wear glasses.'
You were brought up by your mother?
George: Yes, just the mother.
Gilbert: So I went to Munich then, to the Academy. I was the youngest
student there. I was seventeen and a half. I stayed there for six years.
So you did life classes and all that sort of thing?
George: Oh, yes, every type of training.
Gilbert: I did it all, and I was very good.
Do you think all that has been of any use to you?
Gilbert: No. I don't believe it has been after that.
George: I think it's very good to find out what you don't want to do by
practising it all.
Gilbert: George did fantastic paintings at Dartington. When a
newspaper did a big interview with us once, we went out and bought a
copy, and we looked at it and said, 'My God, there's a Morandi on the
cover'. But it wasn't a Morandi, it was one of George's paintings.
George: When I was at Dartington, students would go on from there to
become teachers of some kind. There were only ten or twelve students
altogether, mainly girls, and they all went on to Corsham [a West
Country art school which was associated with modernism and
abstraction] to do the teacher's course there. So I applied with all the
girls and I was the only one who was turned down. I was horrified, and
my teacher at Dartington was amazed that the best student was
rejected after years of these twitty girls all being accepted. So he
contacted them, and they said, 'This person might be an artist, but he
is unlikely to make a teacher'. So that was very good, a very good
moment.

Lucky escape.
George: They were right.
So you both ended up at St Martin's School of Art in London.
Gilbert: George was already there in 1966. I arrived in 1967.
George: The college was extremely famous, that was why Gilbert came.
Gilbert: It was so famous all over Germany because of the younger
generation sculptors.
*Caro [Sir Anthony Caro, exponent of welded-metal abstraction]
and his circle?*
Gilbert: Caro and Philip King and Tucker and all that stuff. When
you're young you have this vision that you have to go where everything
is actually happening. You cannot stay in a village, you have to be part
of it if you want to understand it all and do something new.
So you thought St Martin's was the centre?
Gilbert: And it was. Absolutely.
How did you get to St Martin's, George?
George: I ran away from home to London. Then I met an old college
friend who said I should go to Oxford and look after a small boy whose
mother was going to Africa for a year. So I looked after him for a year,
then I went to the art school in Oxford, which was very good because a
lot people had just graduated from St Martin's – from the Caro, King,
Tucker school – and were taking teaching jobs around the Country.
They were teaching in Oxford.

Then I went to London for the day, and I was walking down the
Charing Cross Road to look at the book shops when I met one of these
tutors from Oxford. He said, why don't you come and look at my
college. I said, 'Where's that?' and he said, 'There it is, there'. I didn't
know where St Martin's was.

So we went into the college, up in the lift to the top floor, to this
famous department. I went in and he introduced me to Frank Martin,
head of sculpture. We chatted for five minutes, maybe. Then he said he
was busy. On the way down in the lift, my tutor said, 'That's alright
then, isn't it?' I said I didn't understand. He said, 'He's accepted you on
the course'.
*So you weren't consciously aiming at St Martin's as the centre of
the avant-garde.*
George: No, not at all, but the result was the same. Extraordinary.
You were both on the same sculpture course.

Gilbert: Yes, same room.

Did either of you contemplate, even for five minutes, producing welded metal sculpture in the Caro mode?

George: No. The group we were part of had already decided against that. There were some goodie-goodie students – about four, it was a very small course anyway – who did work in the Caro/King style. They were predicted to have very, very rosie futures in the world of art, to go on to become famous artists. None of them did, of course. Among the others while we were there was Jan Dibbets, Bruce McLean, Richard Long, Hamish Fulton, Barry Flanagan.

Gilbert: The list is enormous.

And you were a group, were you? Socialising and exchanging ideas?

George: Yes, chums, more or less.

Gilbert: I think that what was exciting was that if you didn't want to do anything, you didn't have to do anything. You could just be totally abstract. They didn't make you make forms just for the sake of it. That was a big freedom. That's why we, in some way, changed the idea of art in that school. I think Caro will never forgive us, because after that those objects of his were finished.

Gilbert: A little while after we left college, and had already done some small shows together, we wanted support from our teachers. So we went to see them all, and it was an unbelievable revelation. They did not want to know us.

George: They were very hostile. There are two stories that illustrate that. One was that we asked a friend of ours to write a letter to ask if they would recommend us for some project or exhibition. So she wrote to Frank Martin, and he wrote back and said, 'Dear Madam, under no circumstances have anything to do with these people'. We still have the letter. The other occasion was when we went to see Caro. We went to a pub near his studio and sat and had half a bitter and a cheese roll, and explained where we wanted to take our art. He listened very carefully, quite politely. Then he said, 'I hope very much that you don't succeed, but I rather think you might'.

Encouraging in a way. What form did your work at that time take?

Gilbert: It took so many different forms – nuts, paper...

George: Hardboard, plastic...

Gilbert: Transparent objects, with dust inside. Cast things, like a cast of my head, or my hand.

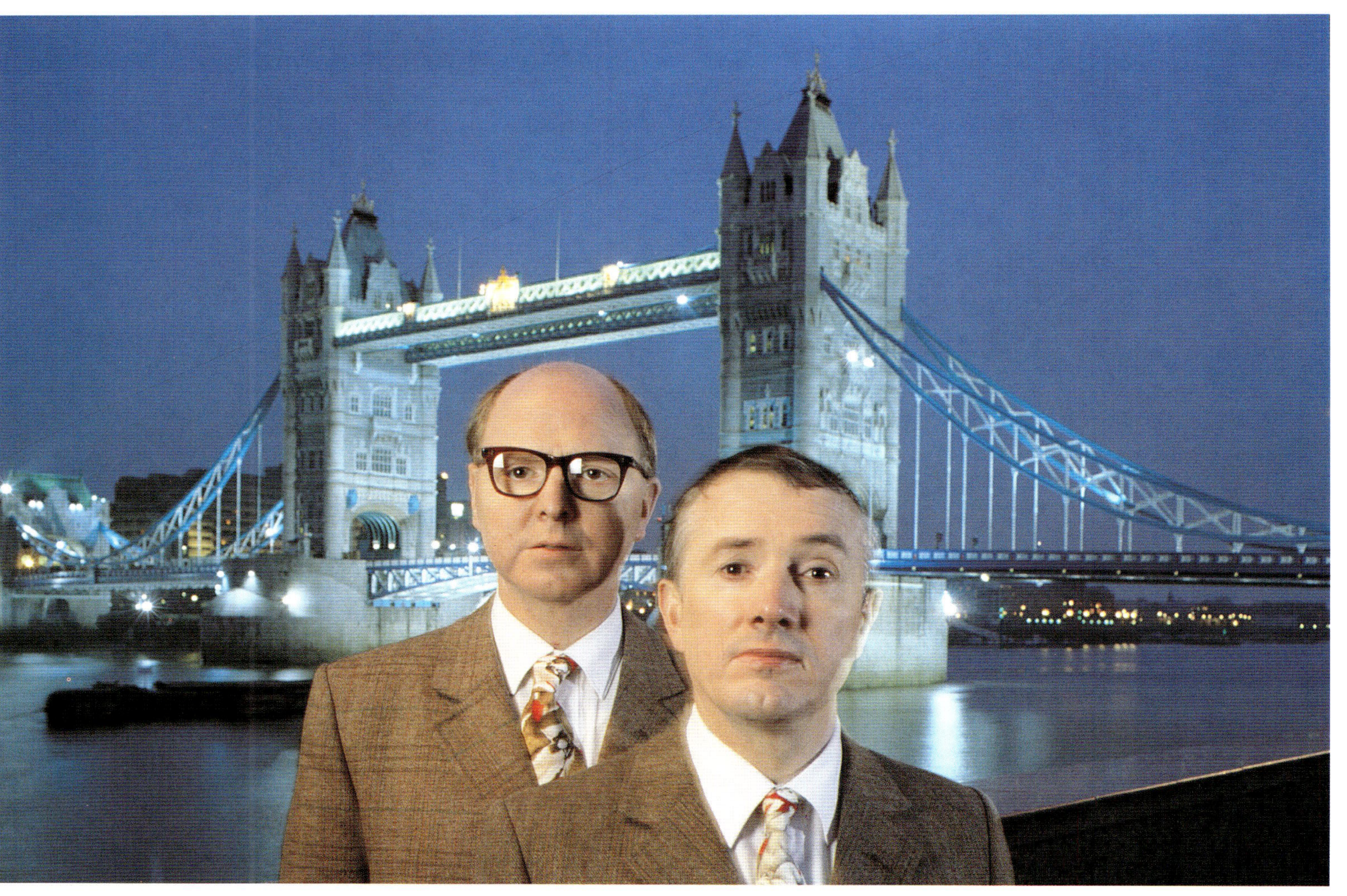

68 Portrait by Michael Lange at Tower Bridge for a German-language travel guide to London, August 1993

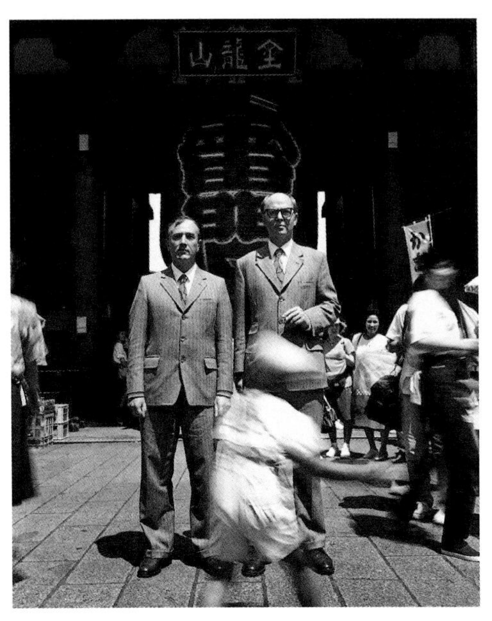
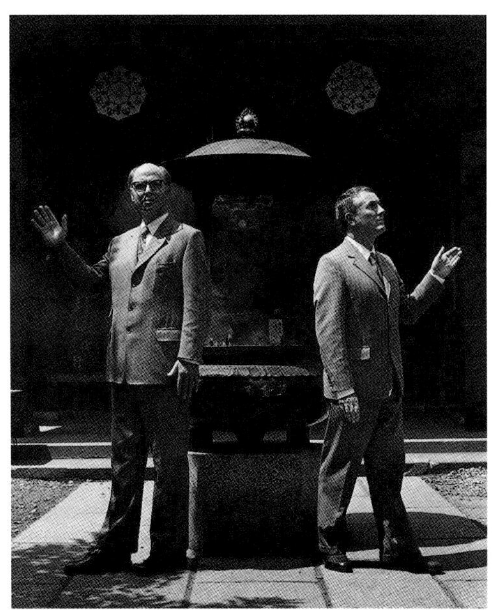
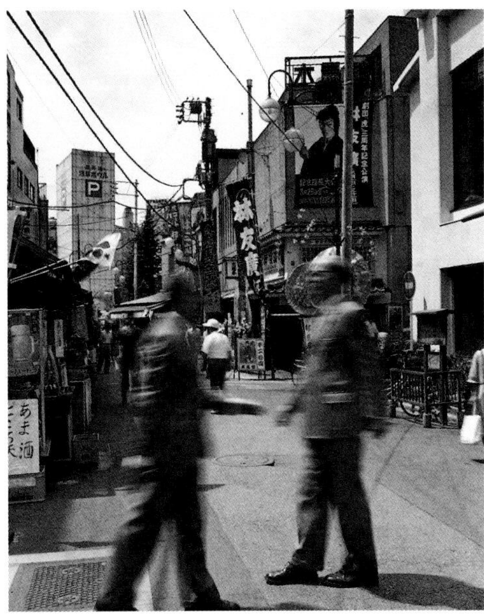

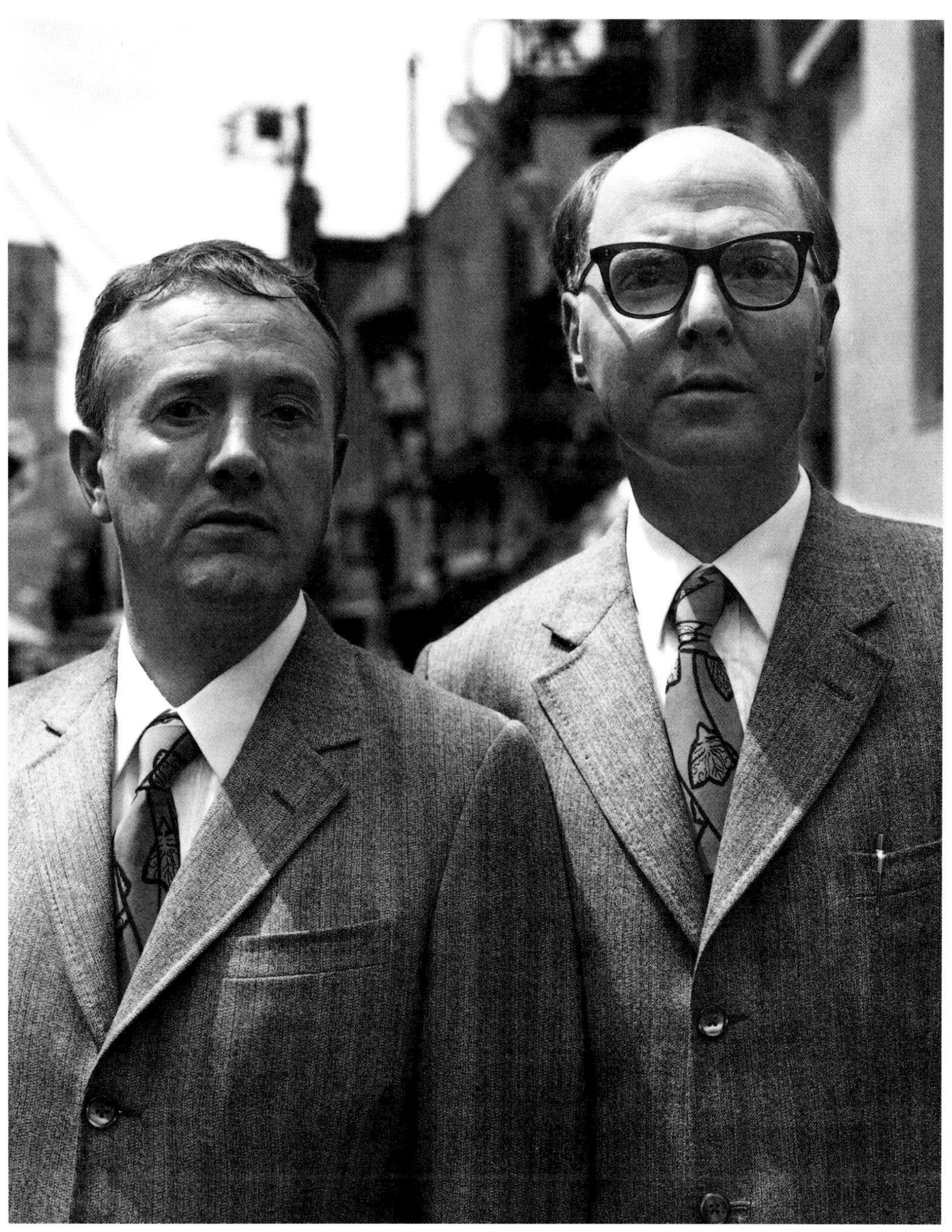

69 Portraits by M. Hasui for the Japanese magazine *Switch*, Tokyo, 1993

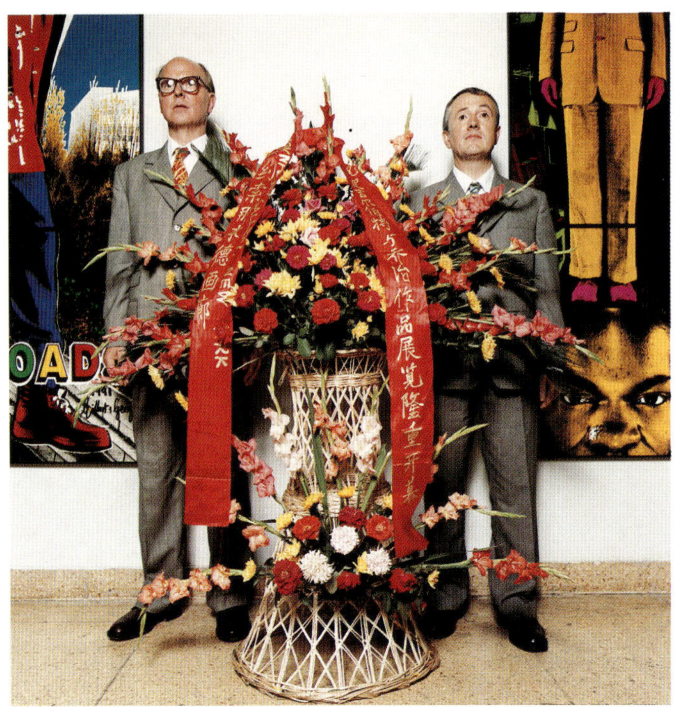

70 Portrait by Dana Lixenberg at the National Art Gallery, Beijing,
during the opening of the artists' *China Exhibition*, 3 September 1993

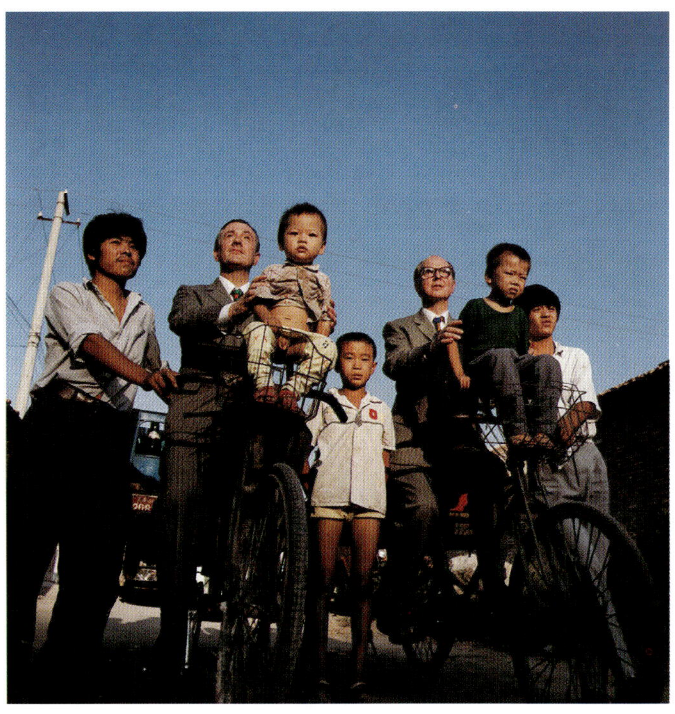

71 Portrait by Dana Lixenberg, Beijing, September 1993

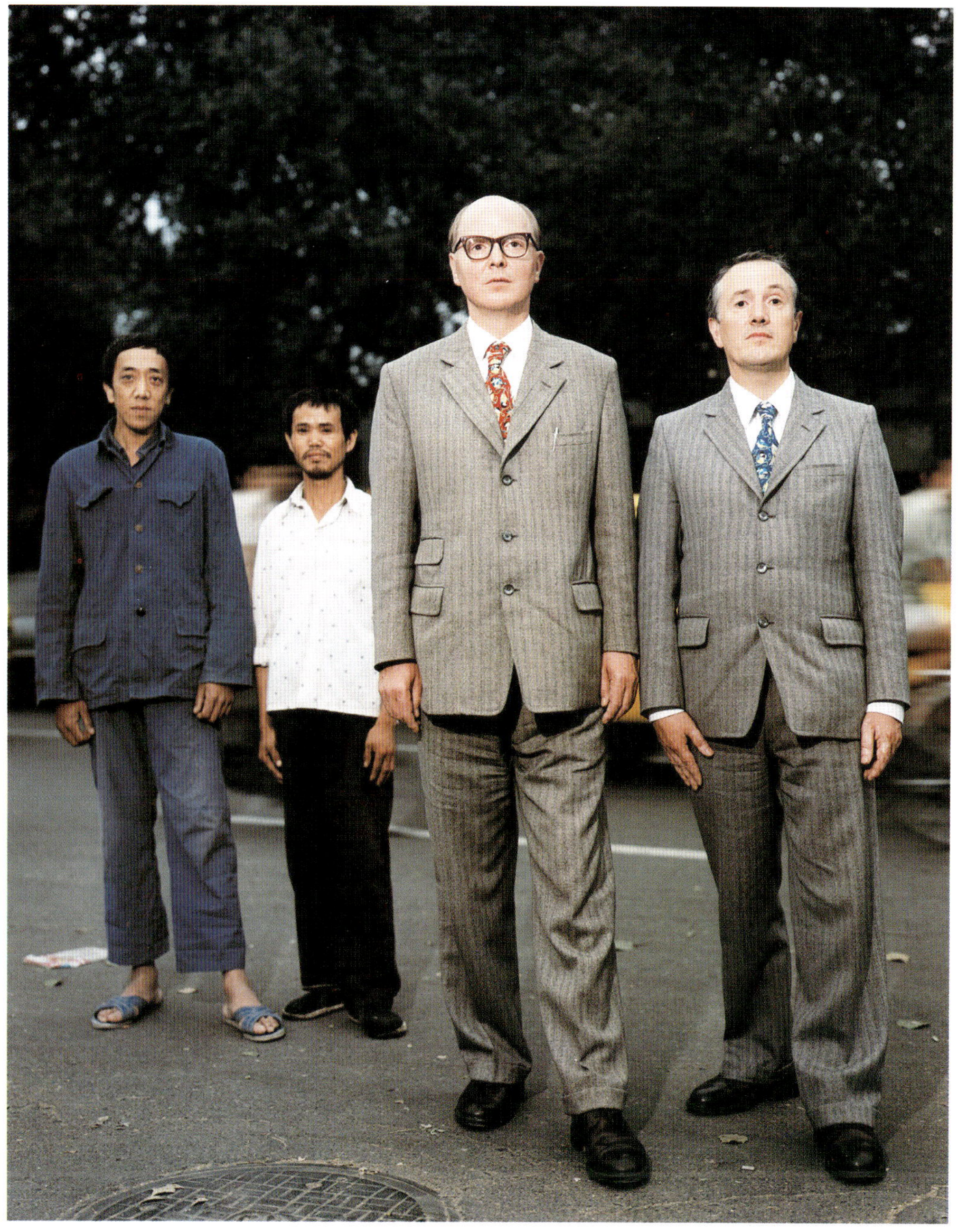

72 Portrait by Dana Lixenberg at the Temple of Heaven, Beijing, at the time of the artists' *China Exhibition* at the National Art Gallery, Beijing, and The Art Museum, Shanghai, September 1993

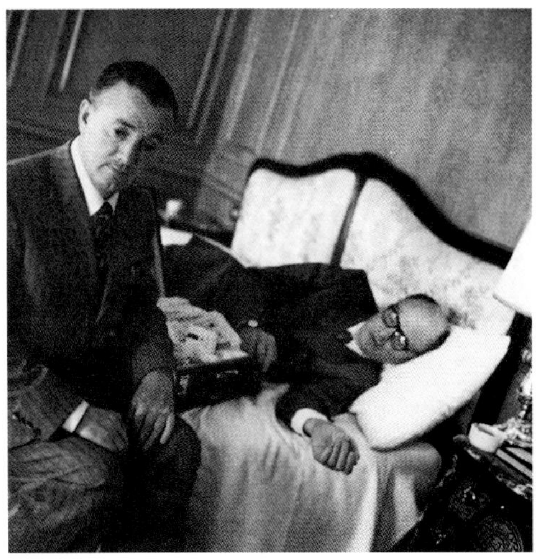

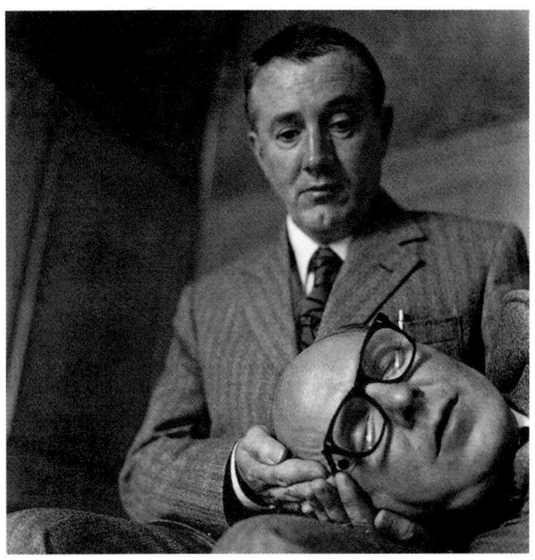

73 Portraits by Andrea Cometta in Suite 402
at the Hotel Splendide Royal, Lugano, Switzerland,
17 June 1994

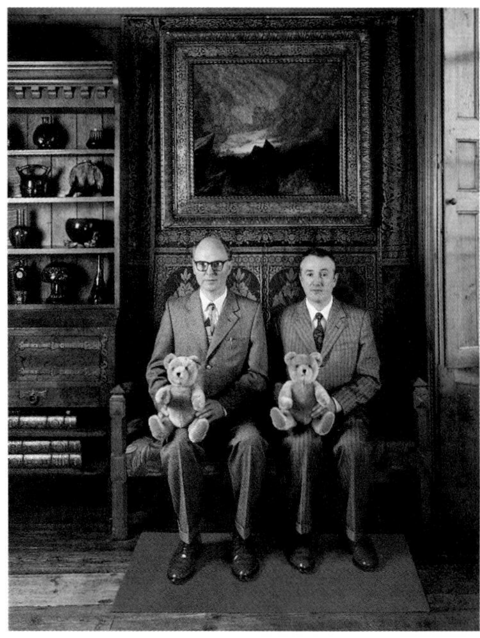

74 Portrait by Simon Beer, Fournier Street, 1994

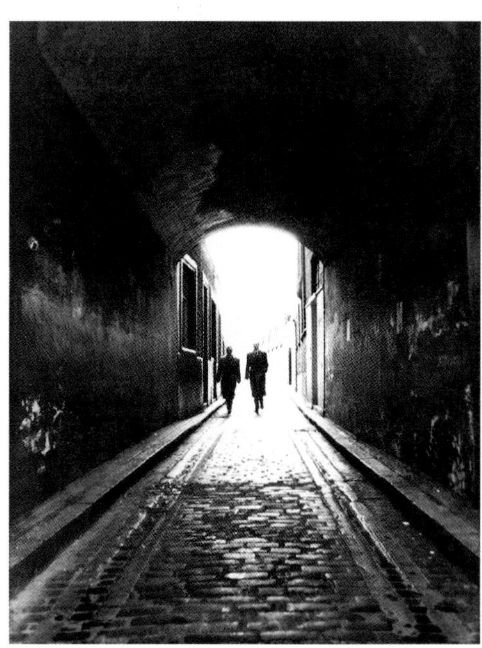

75 Portrait by Giles Moberly, Angel Alley,
Whitechapel, December 1993

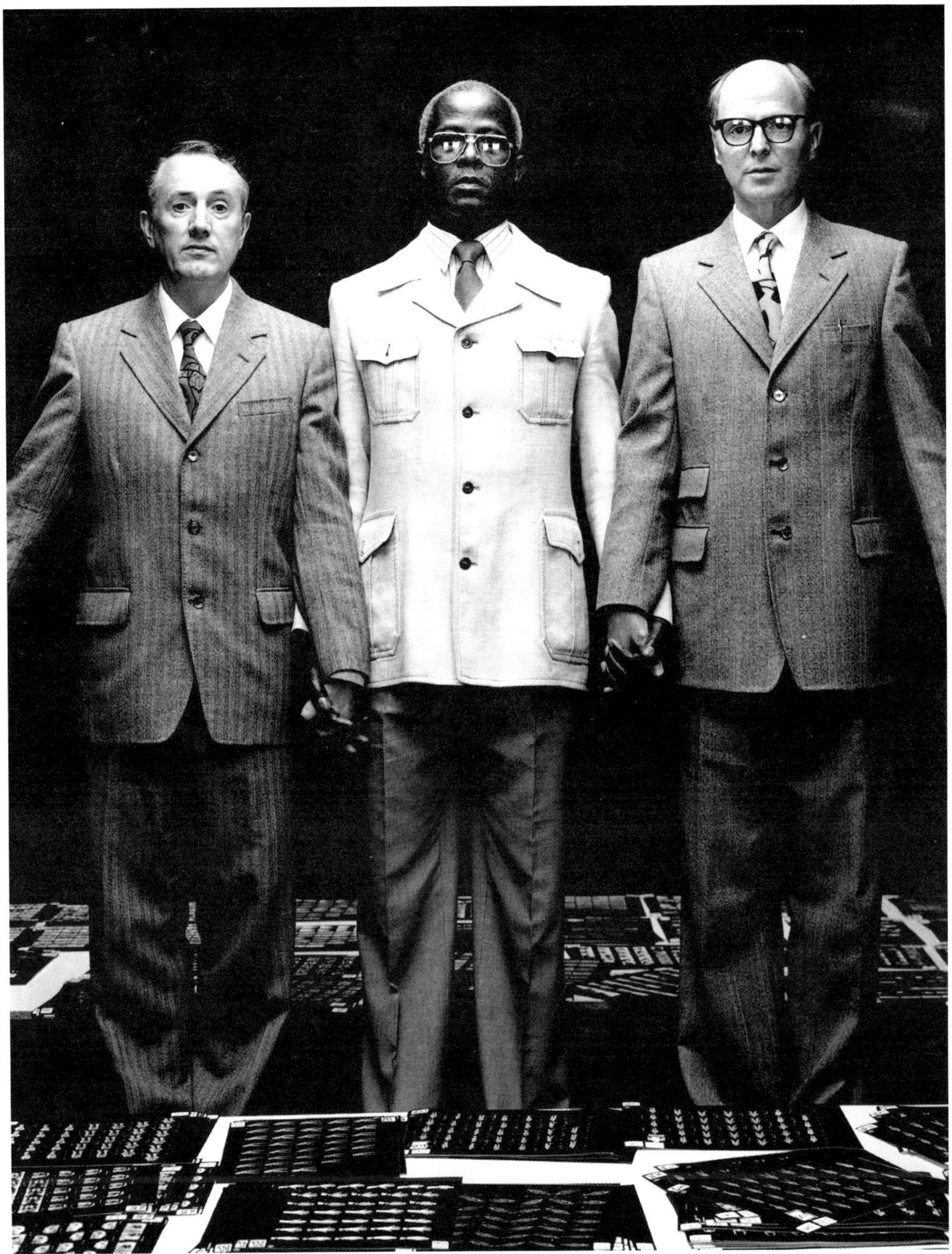

76 Portrait by Jillian Edelstein with Stainton Forrest, the artists' helper and friend, photographed in the artists' studio for the *Telegraph Magazine*'s 'Soulmates' series, 1994

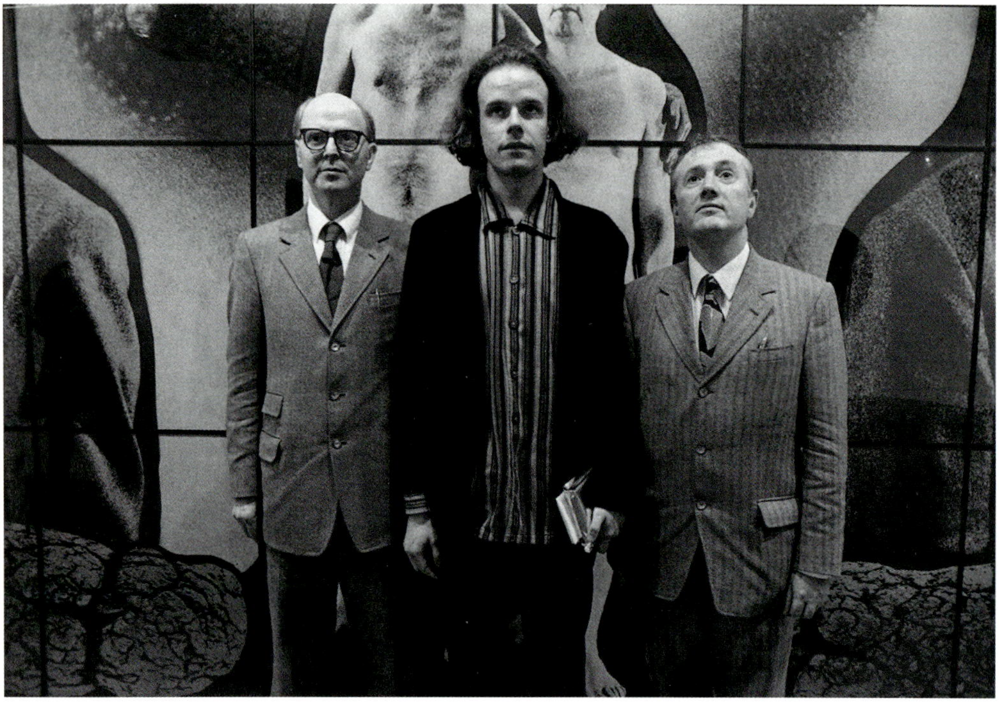

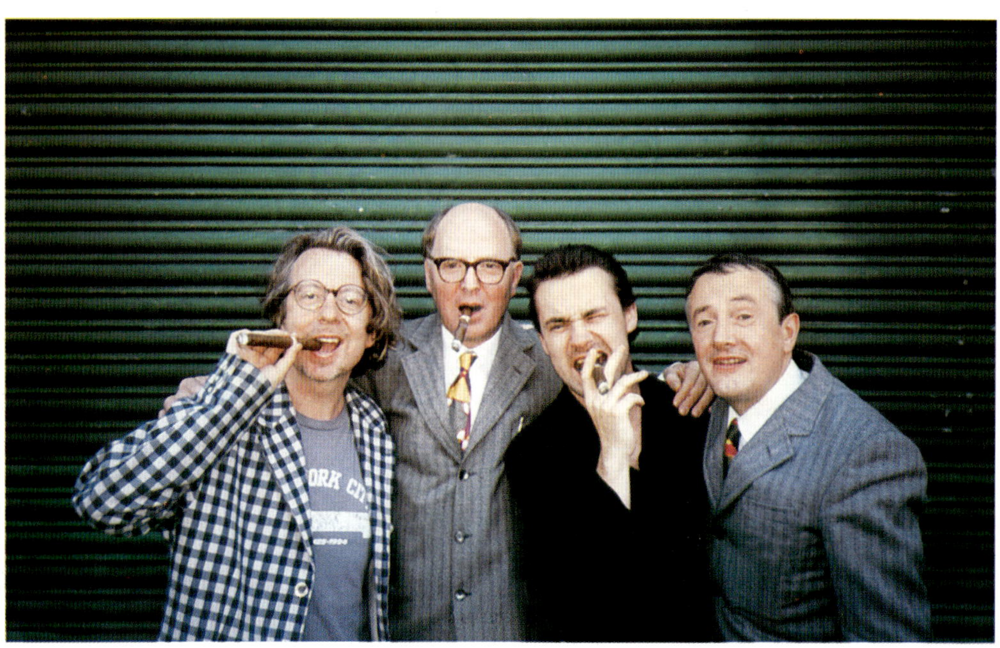

77 With Hans-Ulrich Obrist in front of *Human Shits*, 1994, during the installation of the group exhibition *Take Me I'm Yours*, curated by Obrist for the Serpentine Gallery, London, March 1995 (*Photo: Armin Linke*)

78 With Dave Stewart and Damien Hirst, Spitalfields Market, London, 1995

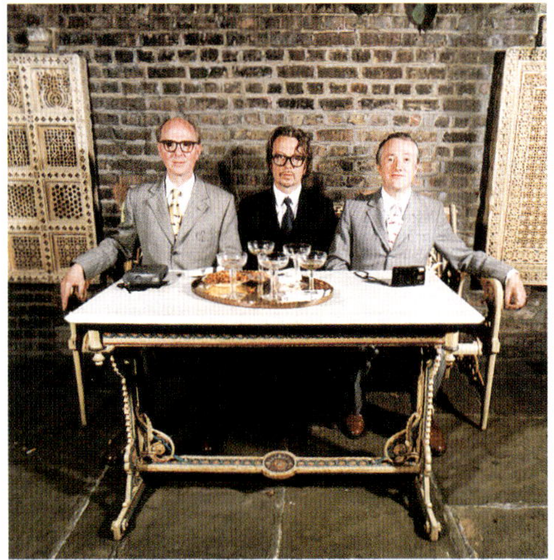

79 Portrait by Dave Stewart (seated with the artists),
Fournier Street, 1995

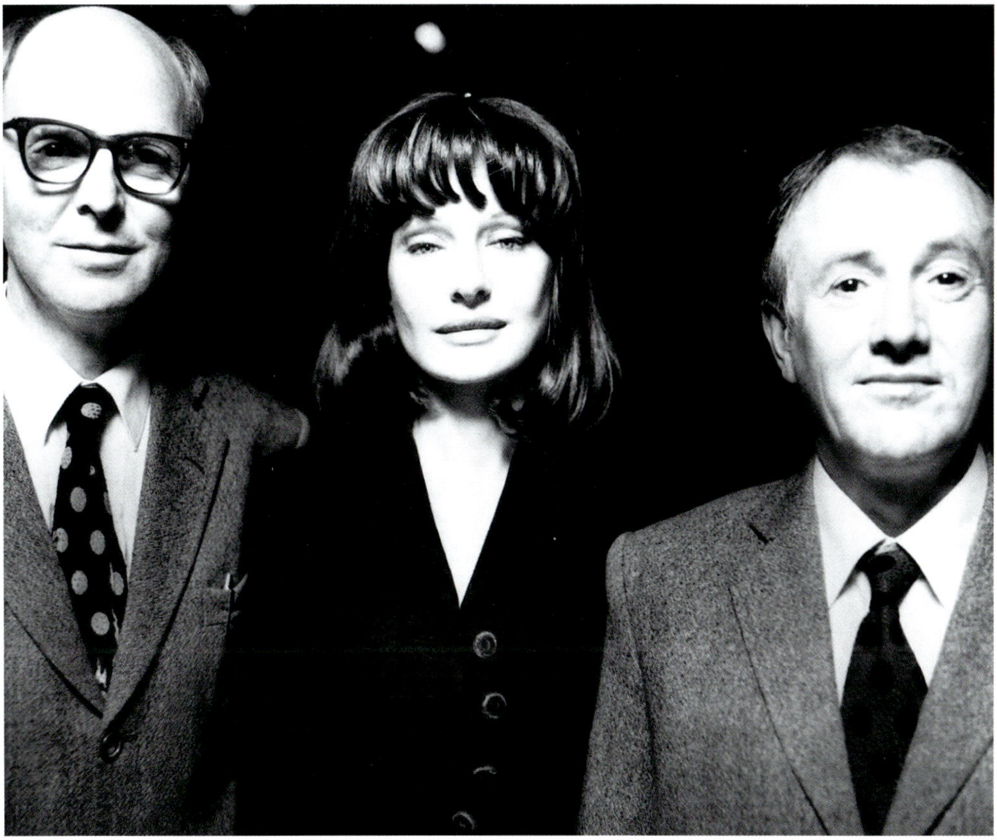

80 Portrait by Justin Westover with Shere Hite during filming of The South Bank Show *The Fundamental
Gilbert & George*, Fournier Street, 13 September 1996

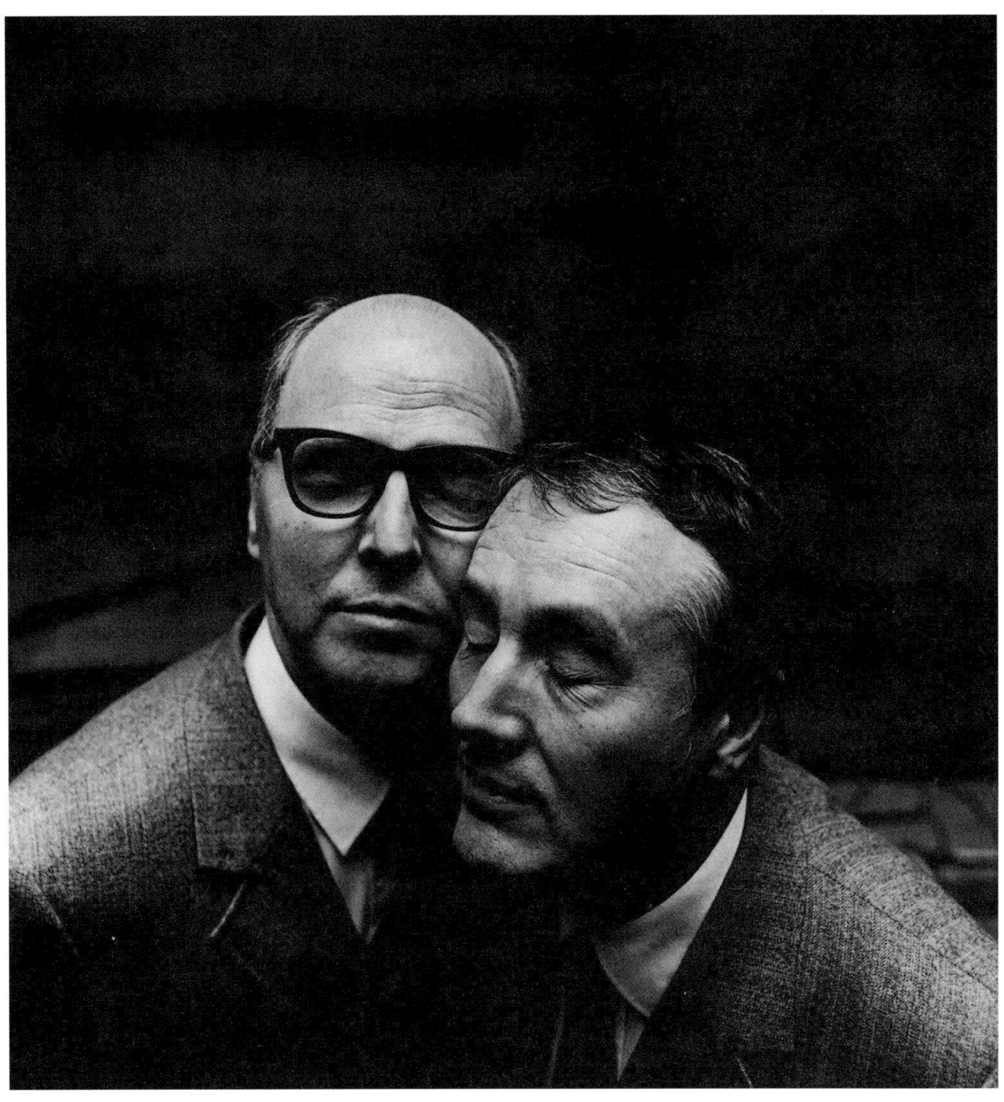

81 Portrait by Kevin Davis commissioned for the catalogue of the exhibition *Minky Manky* at the South London Art Gallery, 1995

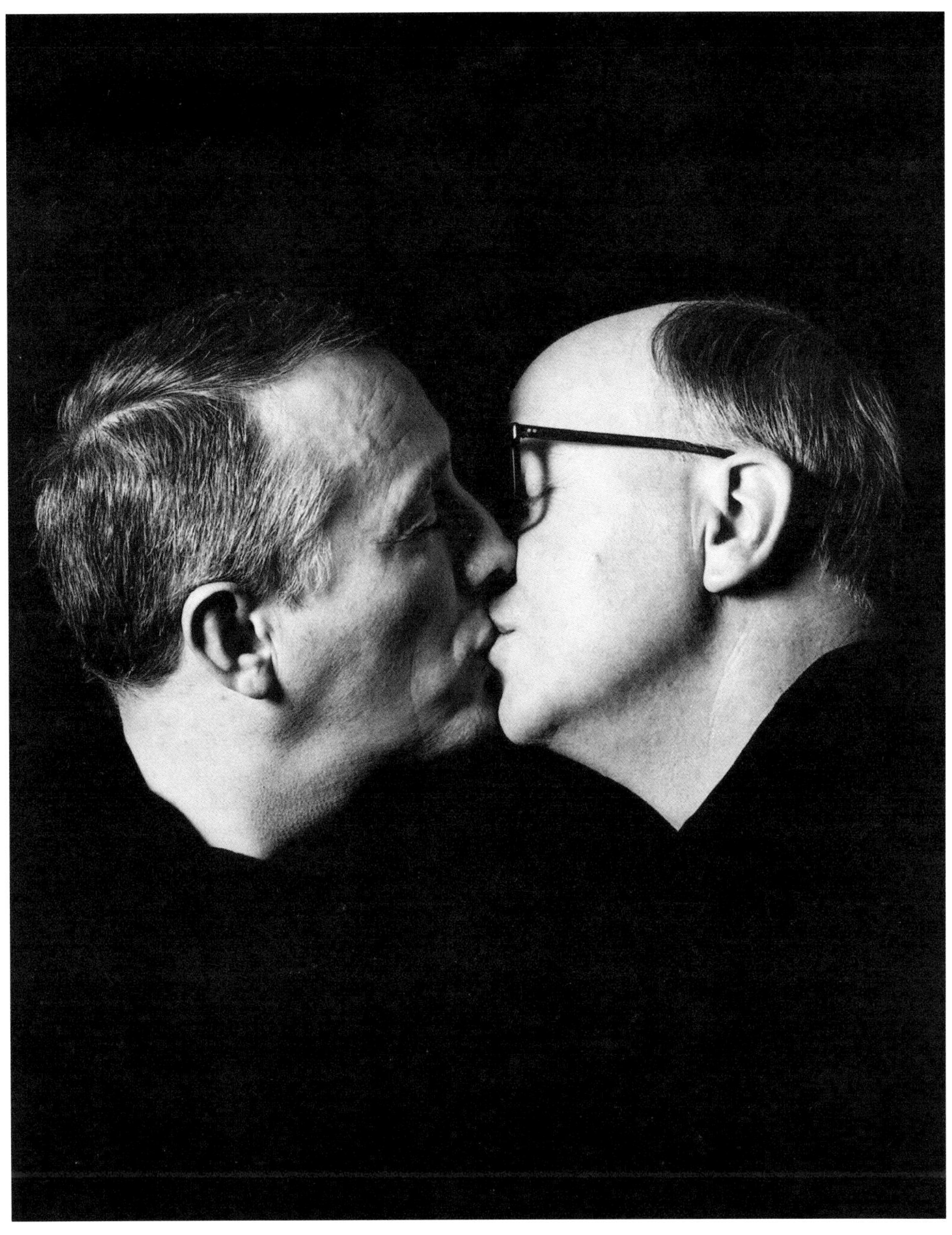

82 Portrait by David Seidner, 1994

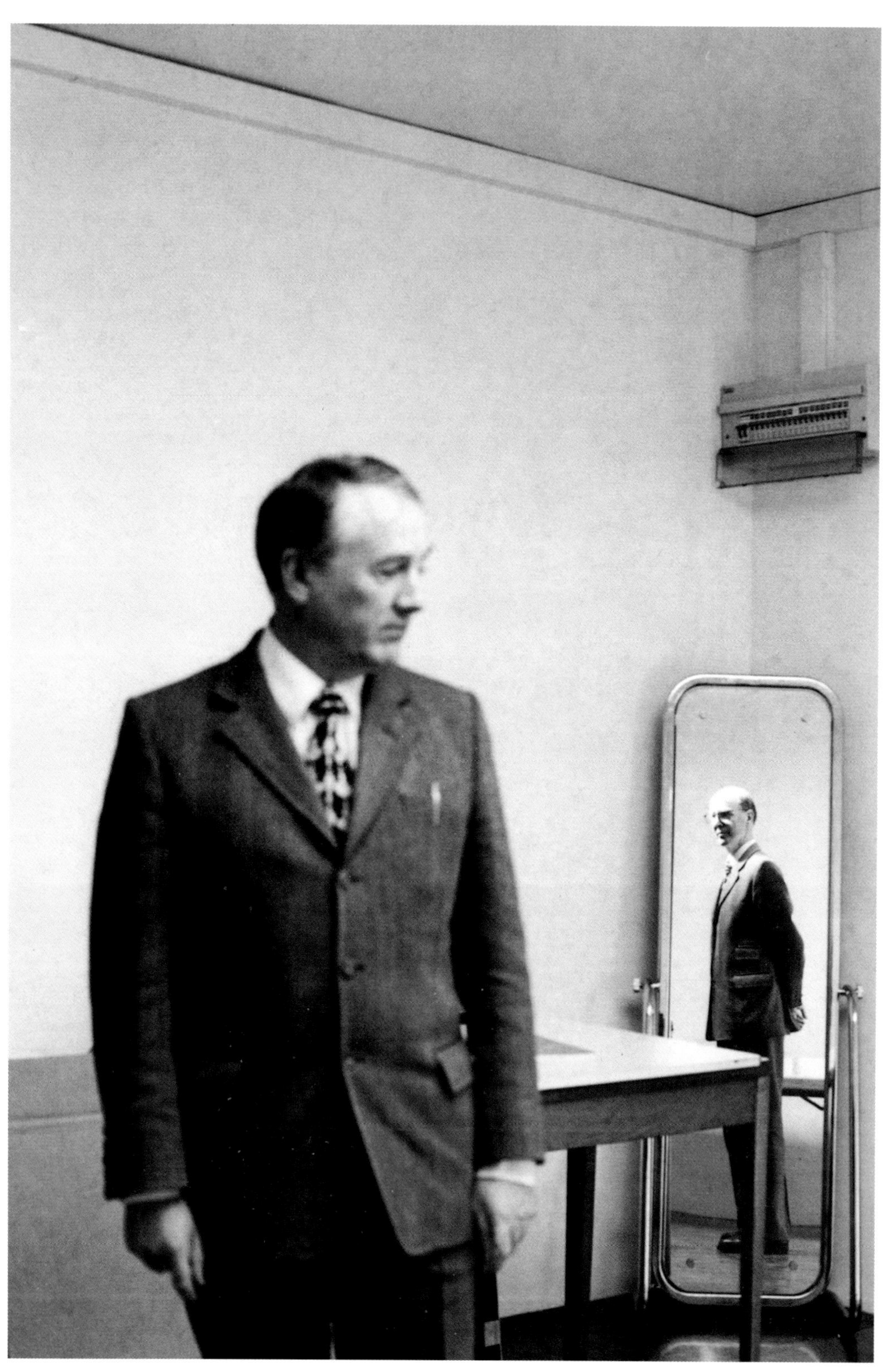

83 Portrait by Wolfgang Tillmans in the artists' studio, Fournier Street, 1997

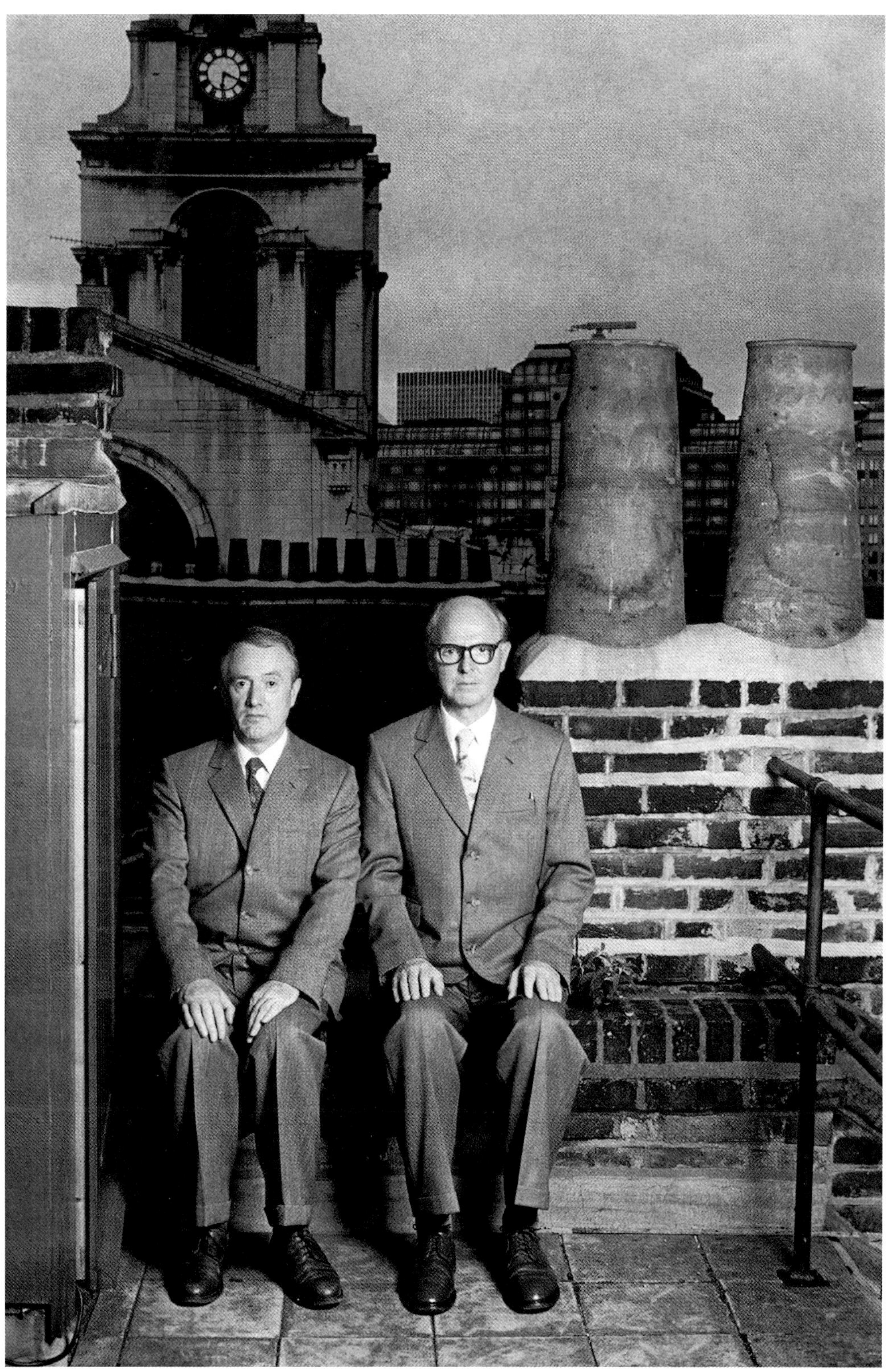

84 Portrait by Herbie Knott photographed for *The Independent* in the same place, at the same time, ten years and one day after Knott's 1986 portrait of the artists (see portrait no. 30), September 1996

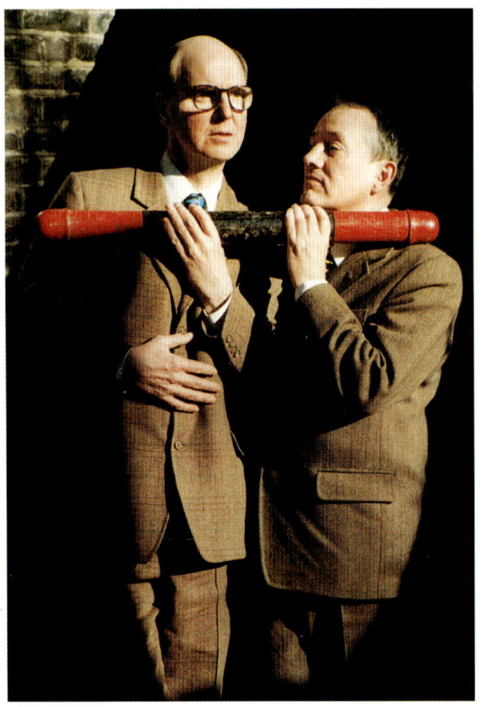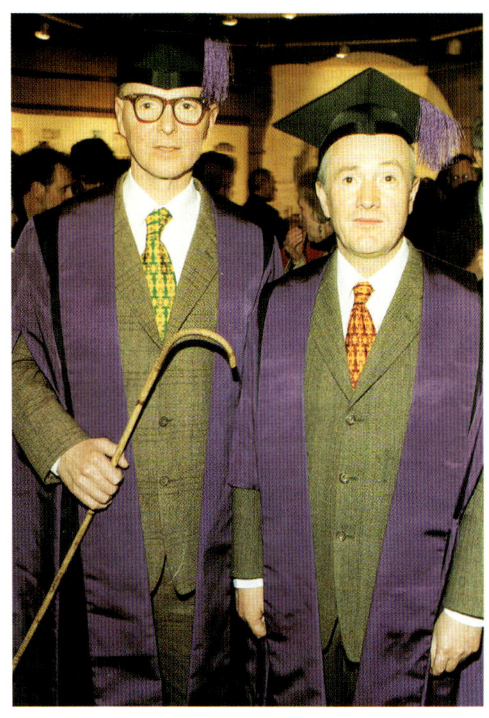

85 Portrait by Dominic Dyson with Indian lingham from the artists' collection, Fournier Street, February 1997

86 At the Cochrane Theatre, Holborn, to receive an Honorary Doctorate from the London Institute, 13 May 1996 (*Photo: Hugo Glendinning*)

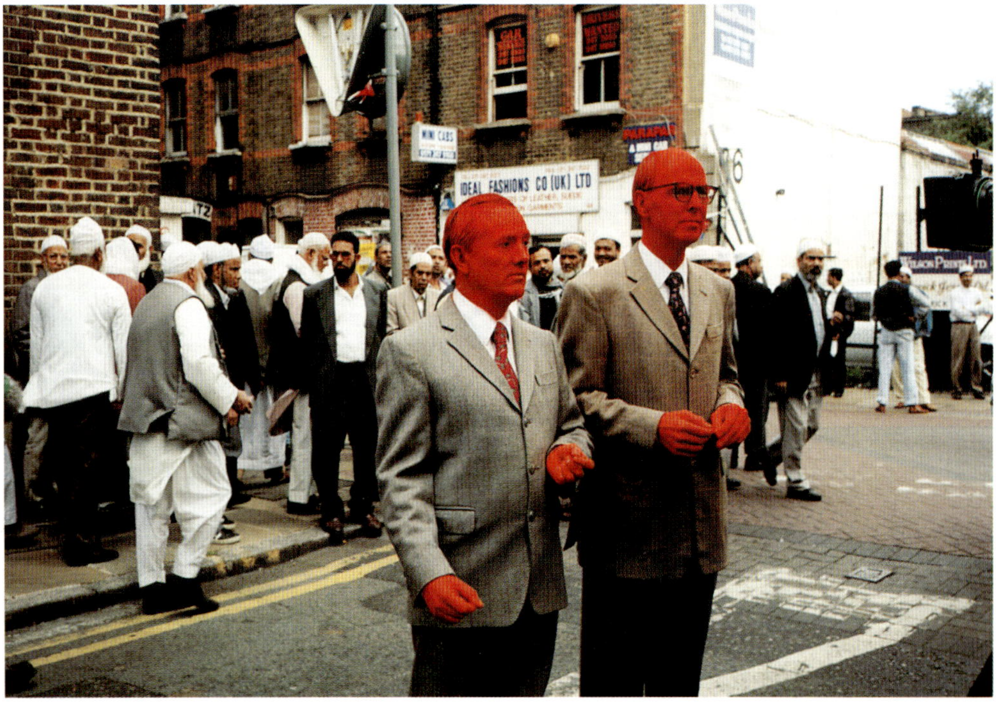

87 As the *Red Sculpture* during filming of *The Fundamental Gilbert & George*, Brick Lane, 13 September 1996 (*Photo: Gerald Fox*)

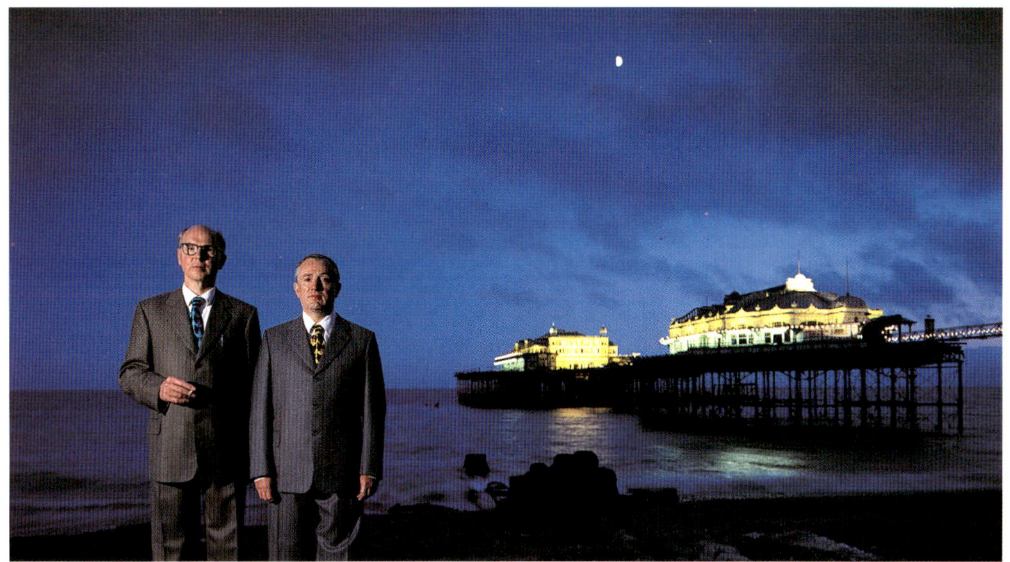

88 Portrait by Herbie Knott, Brighton, 13 July 1997

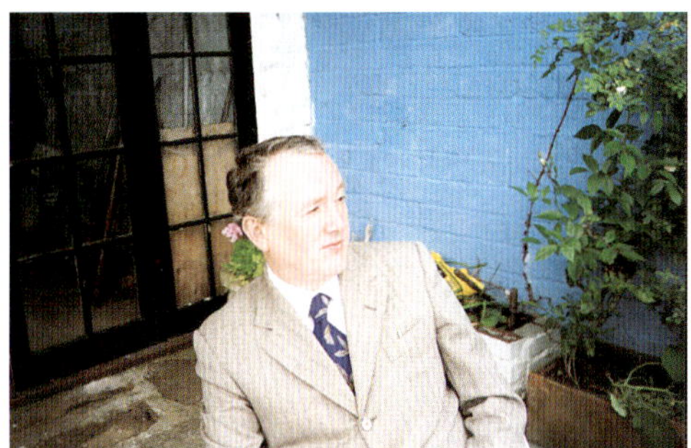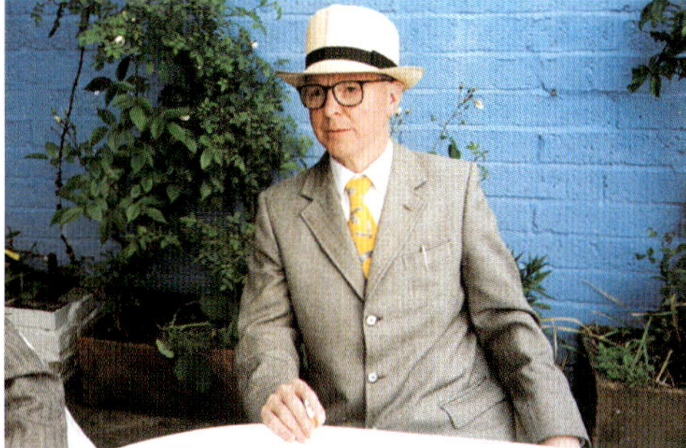

89 At Daniel Farson's home in North Devon, June 1997 (*Photos: Dan Farson*)

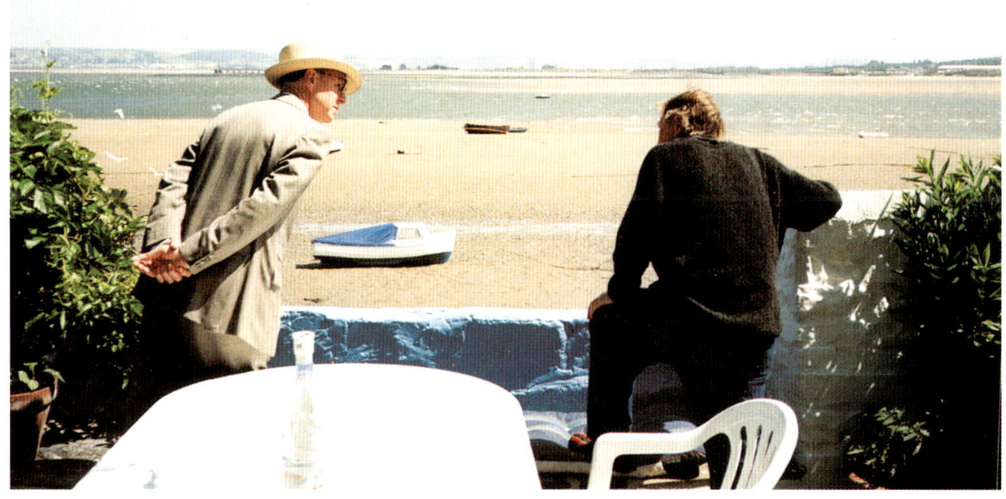

90 George with Daniel Farson, North Devon, June 1997

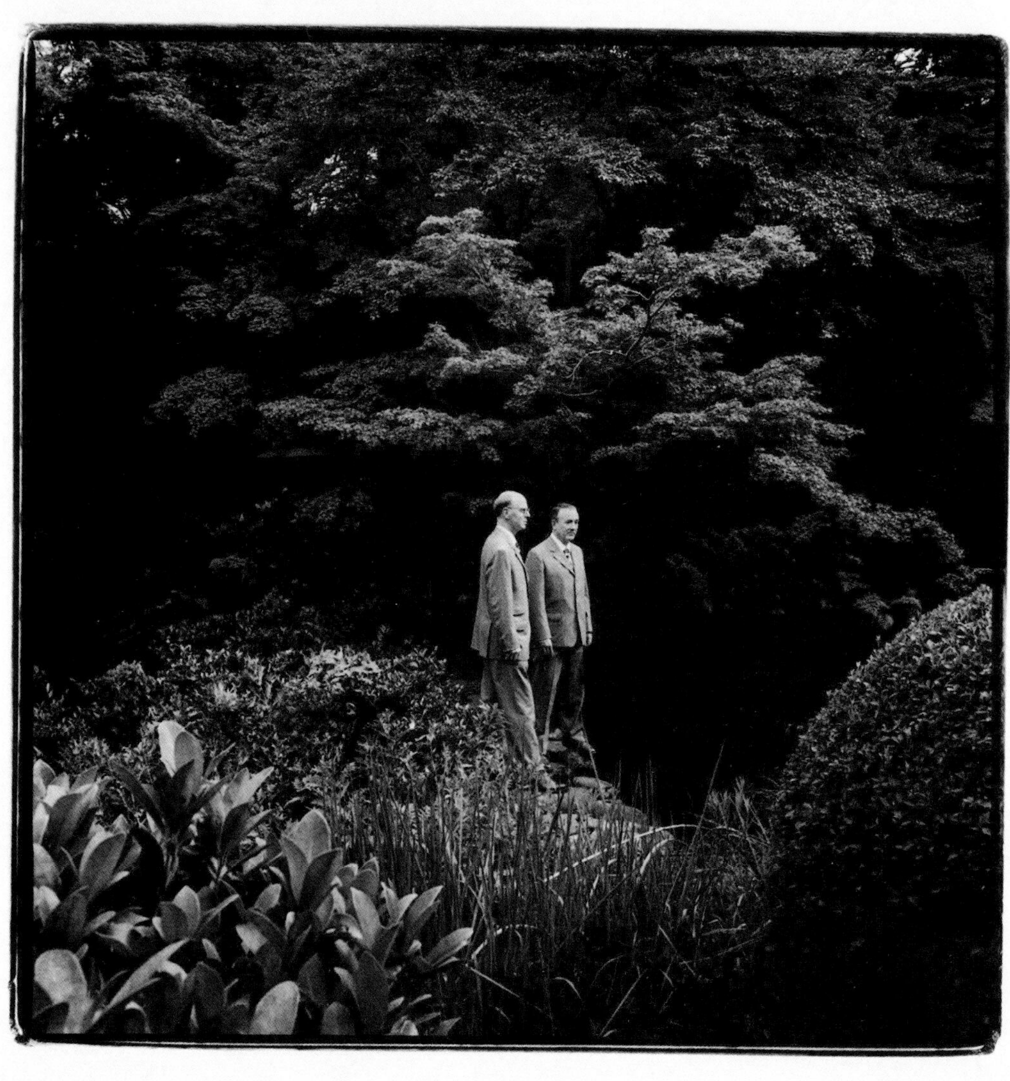

91 Portrait by Shigeo Anzai in Japan at the time of the artists' retrospective exhibition at the Sezon Museum, Tokyo, July 1997

A lot of people are doing that at the moment, too.
Gilbert: Or George put in his cigarettes.
George: The most famous college piece was a box which had Plexiglas, then glass, then chromium-plated bars like a prison, very perfectly executed, then inside when you looked inside all you saw was a stubbed-out cigarette.
Gilbert: One day we were taking images of us holding sculptures, we did sculptures you could hold – like a stick was sculpture.
George: Or a sphere.
Gilbert: Or a small cube you could hold. Then we realised the idea that we ourselves became the sculpture. That was it.
At what point did you decide to fuse into one artistic entity?
George: We didn't.
Gilbert: We did a mask together once, and I put on a colour, then George did.
George: Taking it in turn, supposedly we could be very irresponsible that way. There was no single one artist. So it was a way of getting away from self. But I don't think we were very conscious about why we were doing that then. Although we were already arranging our graduation show, showing sculptures together in a room, so you couldn't tell whose was whose.
Gilbert: What we did was put plaster on the floor to make it all white like snow, then we put the objects in. Then we closed off the door with Plexiglas so you could only look through. And when you looked through you could see all these objects in a snowscape, and you could see this whole landscape of London through the window in front of you as well.
George: The window on the far side framed it up like a picture on the wall. Like our pictures now in a way. Because you couldn't move very far, it was like a still image. But we never sat down and said, 'Let's work together'. We just drifted into it. Some of it happened to us. It wasn't so conscious.
Gilbert: The biggest problem for us was that we actually didn't have any money, but we still wanted to be artists. We couldn't even have a studio, nothing, and we were very anti-formalism. We didn't want to have anything to do with shape, anything to do with art for art's sake.
George: We had already at that time done very primitive exhibitions, like in a local meat-packing factory on the Bethnal Green Road, for the working people there. All the staff were given an invitation when they

came to work at 7.30, then in the staff canteen lounge we put up an exhibition.

Gilbert: Then at Liverpool Street Station we put out leaflets to ordinary people to go and see it.

There was one in a restaurant, wasn't there?

George: In a sandwich bar in Soho, again an Art for All idea. Then we telephoned the Savoy and said we would like to provide a Christmas nativity scene. We would provide a donkey and some sheep and instead of Mary and Joseph we would be the two figures.

Was there a political idealism behind all this?

Gilbert: No.

George: But we knew already as students that there was some enormous nonsense, we felt, when for example on Friday afternoon everyone toured the college with tutors, stood in front of sculptures and discussed them. And we realised that what was being said, and indeed the sculpture itself, couldn't be taken out of the college. The language, that commentary, had no application to the rest of the world.

Gilbert: So we thought we ourselves are becoming more and more the object if we have nothing, and we realised that the best thing was to accept it. That was incredible that moment. Our speech became the art. We used to send out letters for example and they all loved it.

George: We did Postal Sculptures. Magazine Sculptures. Living pieces. Anything that was possible that day. Our contemporaries, not the good ones, but the lousy ones, were always getting jobs and going to the Arts Council to get some money, to save up and have a show. We didn't believe in that. We thought, today we have to do whatever we can do.

That was how the Singing Sculpture *began, was it?*

Gilbert: That started out very slowly, and as something different, without metallised heads. We did it in all the art colleges, only for two minutes, three minutes, just the length of the record. We would get on the table, and that was our new sculpture. But we would make sure everybody would be there. We did amazing publicity in advance, with a tape-recorder, a loop repeating, 'Come to see our new sculpture at three o'clock'.

George: We even played it on the phone to people we felt would be important to be there. Recently David Sylvester said that he had one of those calls in '71. 'It was very sinister,' he said, 'Very sinister'. Because we didn't speak, as they answered we just put the tape recorder to the phone, and it said in unison: 'Our new sculpture, our new sculpture, at 2.30, 2.30.'

So you were spreading the word.
Gilbert: We were very keen to have an audience, we still are. We wanted to say something, and they would respond.
George: We went to every gallery in London, including the ones that no one had ever heard of, we just went through the list. We went to every one with this life box, with these images and objects in it. And we said that we'd like to have an exhibition. They all wanted to see slides of our work before they decided, and we explained that it wasn't like that. That if they said 'Yes' to an exhibition, then we would do something.
Gilbert: Like an installation, something for that situation.
George: But of course, everybody said no.
Gilbert: Except for Robert Fraser. He let us use the gallery for one afternoon to show this piece, the *Shit and Cunt*, that we did.
George: The really big moment came when there was an international exhibition called *When Attitude Becomes Form* – originating from Italy and America. The idea of the show was that it would tour the world, and in every venue a local curator would be appointed and would add to the show from that neighbourhood. London chose Charles Harrison, and we thought, 'That's fine, we're in'. But then we weren't in, we heard. And we were very, very shocked. We thought there are only three or four people in London that he'll add to the show, we're certainly the leading ones. But he didn't include us. So to overcome that we went to the private view as the Living Sculptures with multi-coloured, metallised heads. We just stood in the show, very still. That was amazing. That just smacked the whole show in, really.

Was the metallised head idea a reference to bronze in conventional sculpture?
George: It's to remove the person, so that you can look at a person freely, people can just come up and look. They can't do that otherwise. They'd be embarrassed. And we can stay there like that, we're not shy to do that. We feel like an object.
Gilbert: You have to become different, otherwise it doesn't mean anything.
George: A Living Sculpture was the idea, a sculpture that was living. During that evening presentation a man whom we knew very well by name, but hadn't met – extremely famous, Konrad Fischer from

Düsseldorf – came up to us. He said, 'So you do a show in Düsseldorf, uhh?' That was an amazing moment for us. It was immediately a launch into a new level of contacts and possibilities. He arranged for us to do a show in the Düsseldorf Kunsthalle.

Gilbert: After that it was just total success overnight.

George: We immediately had a Dutch gallery, a Belgian gallery, an Italian gallery, a New York gallery, even a London gallery.

I read a description by the writer and jazz singer George Melly, of how around this time you were doing the Singing Sculpture *in an upstairs room at a gallery. He tried tiptoeing so as to catch you not doing it.*

George: That's what we imagined would happen. We were very determined just to do it the whole day – eight hours. Because we knew someone would try to do that.

Gilbert: It was very important that we came from a tradition of making sculpture. Even St Martin's School of Art was not looking towards Europe. It was looking towards America. In Europe there was a Fluxus movement going on that we didn't like, because we felt that it was based on dirt. It was muck. There were experimental happenings – that were a little more like Fluxus. But we hated that, because we wanted to do just static sculptures.

George: We wanted to be tidy and clean and good, not alienate 90% of the public. Most people who went to a Fluxus thing would by offended by it and walk out.

This is the idea of Art for All again.

George: Yes, children would be fascinated by the *Singing Sculpture*, old ladies would love it because it reminded them of different thoughts and feelings. And it did work.

You're very keen not to exclude people.

Gilbert: Yes, still.

George: That's the idea. The idea of the suits fits in with that, and the ties. We knew that a lot of art and sculpture offends ordinary people, and ours tends not to do that.

Gilbert: It worked totally.

How did the suits come about?

Gilbert: George always had suits, so did I – not maybe when I was working – but otherwise suits.

George: Because we come from the country. In the '50s, on any

important occasion – if you went to church, or someone got married,
if you went on holiday – you had to put on a suit.
Gilbert: George used to have a black suit he always wore at art school.
He was a dandy a little, already in '65. In the beginning when we didn't
have money they were second-hand suits.
George: We had our Burton [British chain of tailoring shops] suits in '72
probably.

Why three buttons?
Gilbert: We like them.
George: It's normal. We always think that if you took a suit from every
decade this century and made an average, you'd probably end up like
this – they're not particularly 1990s, not particularly 1950s.

But why do up all three buttons?
George: That's to be tidy, I think. Tailors always tell you to leave the
bottom one undone, they even tailor it like that now. We have to change
the cut to do up all three buttons. When I was a teenager, the family
always told you to leave the bottom one undone.

I was taught just to do up the middle one.
Gilbert: It's the country style to do them all up.

You mean someone in the old days in Totnes or the Dolomites
would have done up all three?
George: Absolutely. You can see it in old photographs.
Gilbert: But it's become so everybody copies our suits. What's exciting
is that we have all these photographs of artists from 1971, -2, -3, -4 – at
parties, all drunk. And we always looked the same. The others looked
like hippies, with beards, flared jackets. Everybody has suits now – the
young artists, the pop stars.

The charcoal pieces came next, didn't they, which were quite a step
from postal art, and so forth.
George: Not such a big step as it seems in a way, because we did those
charcoal pieces, not as drawings – which is how some people think
of them – but as sculptures. Every one is based on a negative image.
We had a photograph from a negative we'd taken squared up then we
copied it on to cheap paper. We didn't know then how to make an
enormous piece using negatives; and we certainly didn't have the
money to do that then. But we could just buy rolls of paper and boxes
of charcoal. So they are very primitive photo-pieces, in a way.
Gilbert: It was very interesting because, when we started to do all the

Living Sculpture pieces, and sending art as post-cards, and all those things, we felt we also had to leave something behind. But we didn't want to leave messages. That's why we did them like big documents.
George: We even scorched the edges of the first ones to make them look like big, antique scrolls. We felt we wanted to make them look as if they'd always been there, these big documents, as if they were 300 years old.
Gilbert: That's why we stained them brown.

So you moved towards something flat which you put on the wall and look at. Most people who started off making very abstract, conceptual work found some way of producing a lasting object.
Gilbert: You have to, if not it's very difficult. But we didn't want people to think that G & G are very good drawers, that's why we wanted them to seem as if they already existed.
George: That's why we abandoned them. Partly because we were able to financially, but also because people sometimes admired or were interested in the technique of the charcoal work. Therefore they weren't getting what it was actually saying to them. They weren't reading the text at the bottom and getting a feeling, they were just admiring the art, and we hated that.

You are puritanical in that way, aren't you?
George: Is that puritanical?

You know, you like to stick to the message and cut out the frills.
Gilbert: Yes. I think that this was a period of experimentation. We even did films, drawings, paintings, to find out how we could leave some amazing feeling behind – a feeling like you get from a letter, not an art work.

So at that stage you were looking for a form. The feeling you are talking about is the same as the message, is it?
George: We always say that you can't remember every word of the book you've just put down, but you know what every bit of you is different because you've read that book. You know that you'll never be quite the same about that subject.

When you say a message, it's obviously not a message that you could write down on a post card or something, otherwise why bother to do this great big thing and put it on the wall?
George: Sure. Art is also the effect on the household: of having one or two members having gone to see the show.

Do you think that what you're doing is different in principle from Van Gogh or Michelangelo?

Gilbert: No, not those.

George: Both maniacs weren't they?

So at that stage you were looking for a form to make your effect on the world, create this mood, transmit this message.

George: That's why we were very keen to include words as a key.

Gilbert: Yes and we realised that the Living Sculptures were very limited. The message was very limited, because after a day or two we had gone away. And you cannot change every day and do a new one, it's very limited.

George: You can do sad, or happy. Certain range of emotions, but you cannot have a great tree beside us, you can't do three people kneeling together. All the world is there but only in that way.

Gilbert: It's very powerful, but you can't do a new one every day – impossible idea – because it's to do with existence.

So how many different ways did you do Living Sculptures?

George: There was only one *Singing Sculpture* which was miming to the same record all the time.

Underneath the Arches [a powerfully-evocative recording from the '40s by a music hall double act, Flanagan and Allen].

George: We also did just being still, that was when we went to the Stedelijk, in Amsterdam, which was extremely important for us.

Gilbert: Then we did the *Red Sculpture* which was in '75. That was again based on a recording that we did – one hour of recorded messages, and we would act out the words.

George: With matt red flesh. It was very powerful, quite tense. Quite different from the *Singing Sculpture.*

Gilbert: Then we re-did the *Singing Sculpture* again in New York in '91, twenty years later. It was more powerful because in the twenty years art had moved more and more in our direction. Everybody is doing themselves now. There is not one young artist who is not using part of his body or doing autobiographical work.

George: Self-representation, whatever you want to call it. It's already five years since we were asked by a journalist why we were always in the picture. They've stopped asking that, because everybody is doing it. For years and years and years they didn't understand that, now it's normal.

Gilbert: At the same time, we were already doing movies, videos.
George: They were the first videos in the way that people think of
videos now, but they were so primitive at that time that they were
actually made on film, then transferred to video.
Gilbert: It was very successful.

   *Would it be true to say, though, that as with the Living Sculptures,
   these videos had severe limitations?*
Gilbert: They had enormous limitations. Maybe you could become a
film director, that's something different, but as art it has amazing
limitations.
George: You can't leave it on the wall, you can't have a postcard of it,
it can't appear in the catalogue. Not in the way a picture can.
Gilbert: It breaks down all the time, it's very expensive to make.
George: Like a book it is much less democratic than a picture. If you're
discussing a picture on TV you can have it there on the screen. It's that
frozen, forever-there, picture. We think it's an absolutely amazing
form. You can put it on a matchbox.

   So the final answer really was the photo-pieces.
George: Yes, and a picture in the classic rectangular square format.
We moved very slowly towards that, in fact. The first ones were groups
of panels.
Gilbert: At first we didn't know how to make a big picture with
photographic paper, because nobody had done that before, using
photographs like this. So we wanted to make something bigger, that's
why we scattered groups together, with different subjects.
George: Then very slowly those scattered groups came together into
rectangles.

   *The work of the mid to late '70s has a documentary look, because
   it is monochrome with one colour.*
Gilbert: It was grey first, then black and white, then black and white
and red, then black and white and yellow, black and white and green.
Then full colour.

   *I've always felt that there is a sense of place about those early
   works particularly, that they are rooted in this part of London
   where you live.*
George: It's true and not true. We always feel that we never have to go
far. We don't have to travel the world to find subjects, because we're
just looking for the subjects that are inside you. What are your hopes or

fears about the people on the corner, the church, the sky, the policeman,
the wet pavement? So you don't need to go anywhere except just outside
the front door for that.

Gilbert: The first ones were landscape pieces, and they were done in
Regent's Park, Hyde Park or Kew Gardens, those three places. Then
the drinking pieces were done in two pubs, one down the road there.

There's a pastoral side to your work, isn't there?

George: It was more pastoral at first, and that's because we didn't know
how to use the city. For instance, in the charcoal works there are some
buildings and things, but we didn't really know how to use them. I think
that's because we didn't read newspapers. We never thought about
politics or TV or anything, and we believed that whatever these strange
feelings around us were – this confusion of life, and fears – we could
express by the jungle of nature.

Gilbert: But there was always something handmade near to it.

George: A bench or a bit of path.

Gilbert: We didn't like a pure landscape. It had to have a manmade
element in it. Afterwards, I think what happened was very simple,
that's when we started to get drunk.

George: More worldly. The first time we did an object for a gallery was
after we did the *Singing Sculpture* in Düsseldorf. Konrad Fischer said,
'So you do a gallery show', and we bought some paper and did these
huge charcoal works, which we still called sculptures, it says sculpture
in the corner.

Gilbert: And we were living in a small room, so we made them in panels.

George: Then Konrad Fischer asked, 'So how much is this?' We didn't
know because we'd never sold a work of art. So we thought of an extra-
vagant sum of money and said £1,000 – which was absurd.

Gilbert: Appalling.

George: But he sold it in the next few days.

Gilbert: We were amazed.

George: That was enough money to last for two years at that time.
An extraordinary sum of money.

Gilbert: We were drunk every night. We were taking out everybody.
That's why we started to do the Drinking Pieces, and then *Dark
Shadow* came because it became a nightmare. Doomed. All black.
So we did that.

George: At that time we were more socially involved with other artists, and they would all be drinking with us. And the next day they would go to their studios and do a perfect white canvas with a line down the middle. We thought that was completely absurd. What the hell was that? Surely you should be doing something you know about, something people can connect with in some way?

Gilbert: We were very decadent and very destructive, I think, in all those pieces from '73–'74, those Drinking Pieces: *Bloody Life, Dusty Corners, Dead Boards*. They are very easy to read, because we always express what is inside of us – and for that reason everybody is able to identify with them, because they are the same.

George: Even the *Red Morning* pieces which all of our followers would now regard as wonderful, calm, classic pieces from that time, each have a sub-title: *Red Morning – Killing, Red Morning – Hate, Red Morning – Flog, Red Morning – Drowning*. Disastrous titles.

Gilbert: I remember at that time we felt this socialistic cloud moving in '76, '77. We felt that Britain was becoming communist, all red. So we did these *Red Morning* pieces, they were based on that. Then we did the Dirty Words pieces, and we even did swastikas that were very difficult for many people. It was a kind of pre-punk stuff, don't you think? Even Bloody Lives are pre-punk, totally.

Do you think there's a paradox in the fact that you emphasise that you want your work to be as accessible as possible, but you also include elements – the swastikas and dirty words for example – that are bound to alienate people?

George: We always say that we want to be accessible, but not at any price.

So with one hand you're opening the door.

George: And with the other we're squeezing their fingers.

Gilbert: We wanted to do something that was too obvious in England – this graffiti, this amazing destruction of life – and make art out of it, and show it.

That's something that's very evident around here, in the Spitalfields area of East London. Could you say something about why you live here, rather than in West London, for example?

George: We love it. We'd die in West London.

Gilbert: The thing was that when George was a student he was looking for somewhere cheap to live and have his own studio.

George: This was the only chance, it was extremely cheap at that time, the whole district was so run-down, so poor.

Gilbert: It felt like moving into the nineteenth century. And then we loved all the mixtures of people – the Bangladeshis, the Jews, the Maltese, art students, artists and now rich people who are moving in. And we never wanted to have a point of view about the change.

It's also rather dramatic and beautiful. There's one of Hawskmoor's most beautiful churches at one end of the street, an extraordinary baroque monument, slightly sinister.

Gilbert: So it's good, eh? We used to rent the ground floor, and in 1974 we managed to arrange enough money to buy the house, and we never thought of moving, or even buying something different in the same street. That's it.

So on the one hand, you're aiming to be very universal, comprehensible in China, or South America, on the other you're linked to this spot.

George: But we always think that around here is very global, that if a spaceship landed and they said we've got five minutes to report of a typical Earth planet place, where shall we go? We'd say Spitalfields, Commercial Street, corner of Liverpool Street and Bishop's Gate [All within a few minutes' walk of Gilbert & George's house and studio]. The expression on the eyes of people around this district is very up-to-date. In other parts of London it's more typical of the '40s or '50s.

So from the formal point of view, the next stage was colour?

George: That was the most complicated journey for us. Because unlike any other artist, who have a box of colours, we started from a different base. It took us a long time to find black even. Then it took another four years to find red. We didn't start as picture makers, even.

Gilbert: We were sculptors, with a different approach.

George: We looked down on picture-makers. At St Martin's we never once went to the painting department. We regarded that as something very old-fashioned.

So you were working out what colour meant to you.

Gilbert: So we wanted to have colour to express moods – blackness, like *Dark Shadow*, to make it all desperate. Then to have red to make it more violent. Fear. Danger. Love. Then we became more sophisticated, and made some completely yellow ones. Next we thought it would be a very good idea to have, say, four colours, so you could say 'The Red One', 'The Green One', 'The Blue One'. It simplified things, limited choices.

George: We used to delineate. I think the first one we did was *Coloured Faith* [1980], it was a cross four times but each one was a different kind of faith. It's a way of distinguishing. That's why we had four colours first, not every colour in the world. Like traffic lights we had it. *Coloured Feelings* was another. The four feelings.

Colour coding.

Gilbert: It's very funny because now all computers are based on colours, like Windows, for example. You simplify with colours, you don't need words. But in America we weren't allowed to use the word 'Coloured'.

Because there it was used to refer to black people. Americans are very puritanical about words.

Gilbert: When we did the Dirty Words pictures, one was *Queer* – which was totally forbidden.

George: That piece toured America and aroused more hostility among the so-called gay community than anywhere else. Now they're all using the word 'queer'. It was '77 when we did it.

You were going against the grain then of course.

Gilbert: Yes, and in another way we were going against the other artists in '81, '82, '83, because we tried very hard to make *beautiful* pictures. We wanted to make them visually powerful and beautiful.

George: I think beauty was regarded as quite beyond the pale at the time. The word beauty had something to do with lower-class greetings cards. It had no connection with fine art. You said, 'Interesting', or 'It's a good piece'. But nobody said 'Beautiful' about one of these modern sculptures.

Gilbert: They even disliked our use of colour. Because the colour of modern art from the '70s and '80s was grey, black and white, that's roughly it.

Were you becoming less nihilistic?

Gilbert: No, because there were also pictures like *Stream* [1980] which was just a naked boy with piss. But we wanted to make them beautiful at the same time.

The coloured photo-pieces are the ideal formal solution, from your point of view, aren't they?

George: That was also a very complicated journey, like finding the colours. How we actually coloured a picture was something we had to find out. At first we only knew how to colour an individual panel. We only knew how to colour this one red, and this one, and leave these two not coloured. We didn't know how to put a red person here, and have a yellow branch here on the same panel. Then we started to discover with certain colours that we could colour to a black line, and the division between coloured and not coloured would be lost in the middle of the black line.

Gilbert: We would take all our subjects against black, and cut out leaving a black line, in the middle of which we could change colour.

Of course, a lot of people say your pictures look like stained glass, but the reason for the black lines – like leading in a window – is just technical, isn't it?

George: Yes. From using the first colour in '74, to being able to colour freely took – what? – ten years?

Gilbert: Ten years. Until '83–'84.

George: Parallel with those two awkward slow discoveries, there was another one. In all of those early pictures we only knew how to put one negative image per panel. So, for example, this panel would be a view of the Thames, this would be a flower, this would be Gilbert, this would be me. It took us years to figure out that you can have Gilbert there over several panels, as long as you mask everything else off. Then afterwards we can shoot another image, there and another one there, or perhaps put it across Gilbert, as long as we don't shoot Gilbert first. That's something that a painter doesn't have to discover. You can do it with a brush immediately. We had to find it.

Gilbert: What is very interesting is being stuck in certain systems is very good for art. The fact that you don't have total freedom is very good. You are restricted, and that makes you do something different.

George: You are forced to create, forced to find a way. If we'd sat the first day in front of a canvas of any size, with all the colours in the world...

Gilbert: ...We would have been lost. Discipline is very good. And we have another discipline, which is that, technically, we cannot look at them until they are totally finished. And when they are finished they are finished, we can never change them.

George: We cannot see the picture as it progresses, as a painter does. Most pictures you see are thirty or fifty images in one all hidden underneath the paint and muck. Ours are what we felt and thought at that time.

Gilbert: And we never destroyed one.

How long does the process of making a group of works take?
Gilbert: It can take a long time. Sometimes we take a lot of images,
maybe even for a year. Then we design a certain amount that we feel we
are able to produce in three or four months non-stop working. The most
recent ones, the Naked Shit Pictures, took roughly a year, but there
were an enormous quantity – nineteen, and very, very big.
George: It was nearly two years. The previous ones were finished
in 1992.
Gilbert: But we don't want just to make pictures. We could do a lot of
shows if we wanted to, but we have to feel something new. We don't
want to repeat ourselves. We will anyway, every artist does that, it is an
evolution of ideas that is going on. We have to have a feeling that we are
able to accept.

Is your technical evolution complete now?
George: There are many developments that have taken place within
that time.
Gilbert: Technically, there are many things we can arrange. We can
arrange different cameras, micro-cameras...
George: Even in subjects. From 1977 when we took pictures of people
in the street from our first floor window without letting them know,
from that moment until the time when we could actually ask someone
to stand still for us, please, took two years. Then to get them to come
into the studio took four years.

But you are adapting and refining.
Gilbert: Yes. We do accept this language, we don't want to change it.
George: The rectangular picture we think is the most weird form.
Modern art went towards weird, like filling this room with bananas, or
covering the ceiling with umbrellas, or the walls with dead pigeons,
just to be weird. In fact it became completely normal. None of those
exhibitions that I just mentioned would amaze you. In the end the
picture is the weirdest thing.

Because you can put much more in it?
George: Many more levels of thoughts and feelings.
Gilbert: And because in some funny way we are making pictures,
taking a photograph of an image and then compromising a picture out
of it, we can take an image of *anything*. That's incredible. Inside the
body if you want. Anything. But if you are an artist who does

sculptures, it's very laborious and limited. Or even painting, because it doesn't look real. OK, you can do abstract, but that's very limited as well.

George: We feel very lucky that we were able to embrace the negative image. We didn't think we had to transfer the negative image on to an auction house canvas in order to feel that we were artists. All artists used the negative, but they had to make it into a bloody Rembrandt in order to feel that they were artists – all the nineteenth century artists did, Bacon, Sickert.

Gilbert: Hockney, everybody.

Do you think photography has superseded painting?

Gilbert: I think for visual imagery, totally. The artist doesn't produce imagery any more – television, books, it's all through the camera. You cannot paint the news. You can still make interesting aesthetic pleasing pictures or cartoons. There will always be a big school for that. We don't believe painting will stop, but as a powerful form it's finished.

George: We still think that one test is that if you show a normal person a canvas by a contemporary painter, he won't know when it was done. 1930? 1940? He won't say 'Wow! That's obviously done today, that's today living breathing language.' It's not the only test, but it's one test. Art should live and breathe its time. We never think that the Western World around us is already looking a little bit like our work.

So you think you are affecting society, not reflecting it?

George: We never believed that we reflected society. We didn't even want to do that.

Gilbert: We are against the grain in every single way. And going up to an edge that hurts us. I think that's very important. We always got hurt. People think that we couldn't care less. But we were very hurt by a lot of stuff. That's good.

You mean hostile reactions?

Gilbert: The hostility became sometimes so incredible. I think for the last twenty years we've always been some way in trouble. Our art is very confrontational.

You have had amazing press coverage for your latest show, the Naked Shit Pictures, exceeded only by the Princess of Wales.

George: Unbelievable. It's been reported in Japan and Israel, Denmark and America. Beyond our wildest dreams.

You're very pleased with all this response.

George: Thrilled.

*One thing people often say about you is that you're madly
egotistical, all your art's about yourselves and drawing attention
to yourselves.*

George: Which we can answer very easily. If you go to the National
Gallery and see a Constable, you will say: 'That's a wonderful
Constable.' You will never say I like that grass or I like that tree. You
have to know that it's Constable speaking to you. We just took it a stage
further from that.

Gilbert: What is a Rembrandt? He himself. All the inner feelings of the
artist. Or Van Gogh. It's just him, a completely maniac person. You see
his mad vision and that's it. If art is not totally mental, provocative in
every way, it's curtains. The end.

George: I think it's very good we're in the picture reminding the viewer
that it's not a boring art work, an aesthetic experience. It's us saying
something to them. Also you cannot be egotistical as an artist anyway,
because if you walk the streets and ask people to name a politician,
everyone will give you a name. Name a film star, a sports person, same
thing. Name an artist? They'd look blank.

You might be coming close after that last show.

George: It's tiny.

Gilbert: Artists are extremely unfamous.

George: Extremely unfamous.

*Would you admit, as is often said about you, to being great masters
of the art of publicity?*

Gilbert: No.

George: If a person is interested in football he will get four pages in
every single daily newspaper. It's eight years since we showed here in a
public gallery. Football is every day.

You are not uninterested in publicity?

George: We think that there is an enormous hunger out there for art,
and they can never see a Gilbert & George picture. They can buy an
Agatha Christie, they can read about death and sports every day in the
newspaper. We aren't getting publicity, we are bringing pictures to
people. Publicity is not for us, it's for the viewer. Informing the viewer
that there are pictures he can go and see. Isn't that better than learning
that there are another 10,000 bodies going down the river in Rwanda
every day? Art is fantastic for people. We think that if we do a show

once every eight years in a public gallery, as many people as possible
should be informed about it.

We think the art world has to change totally. The Tate is so
complacent and pleased because they have two million visitors a year.
Far more people go to supermarkets. We think all public galleries
should be open from 10 a.m. to 10 p.m. It's totally idiotic closing
museums at six just as the offices close. Never heard of such nonsense.

*You were worried at one point that because the Naked Shit Pictures
were in a little gallery in South London, no one would come.*

Gilbert: We were quite terrified.

George: Yes, and we were worried that the police might be called.

But you'd shown the work before in Germany?

George: Not in the same way.

Gilbert: But before Germany we were nervous. That was why we split
the work up into two groups. One we showed in a private gallery in
Cologne, the bigger pieces went to Wolfsburg and they were part of a
much bigger show. To test them out, that's why we did it. Then we
showed two in the Serpentine in the Summer.

*So you showed them step by step. But you were worried about
getting an aggressive response?*

George: Not from the press. We didn't want it to go wrong. We don't like
counter-productive scandals. It's alright if it's a scandal in a positive
way, but not in a negative way. You know, if the gallery had to be closed
for three weeks while some stupid judge made some decision. We
would hate that. We want to take it up to that line, but not go over it. We
don't want three pictures having to be removed or anything.

Gilbert: We think it's extraordinary that we managed to get away from
this whole idea of gay artists, or gay couple. We hate all that stuff.
Nobody said that. But in the end it became a very big discussion all
over England whether we should say 'shit' or not, whether nakedness
was acceptable or not. Don't you think that's very interesting?

George: The South London Art Gallery was a fantastic exhibition, but
there was a much bigger exhibition going on out in the world. A leading
Danish newspaper had a Naked Shit picture reproduced in colour.

George: People who talk about the nakedness in our pictures could pass
without batting an eyelid at a marble naked, a bronze naked, a
watercolour naked, but when you see ours it's a totally different
experience.

David Sylvester compared the work with Michelangelo and Masaccio.

George: We invited him to see them before the show. We had just laid the photographs out in the studio. He looked at them in complete silence for about ten minutes or more. Then he said, 'These are the greatest old master pictures you have ever done.' We said, 'You've only been here for a quarter of an hour and already you're insulting us'.

He also said two things that we hadn't realised which were very interesting. He said: 'All the artists in this century have tried to do naked but they've only every succeeded in doing nude. But you've done naked.' It's true, that is the difference. No one sees them as nudes, not even naked men, really, naked human beings.

I presume Sylvester wouldn't agree with this, but I think Lucian Freud produces a very powerful impression of nakedness.

Gilbert: We always think they look like sixteenth-, seventeenth-century nudes.

They shock people though.

Gilbert: Shock maybe.

George: There's one in the Ashmolean Museum in Oxford which we saw by chance. It's in a room with old fashioned paintings, and it's just another one. Courbet? Totally the same.

People say that you've produced these new works because you're obliged to find something more shocking all the time to stay ahead of the pack.

George: In fact we did a picture called *Naked* [1980] and a picture called *Masterbator* [*sic*, 1980] fifteen years ago.

Gilbert: That American who did a picture of a crucifix in a bucket of piss, he's a follower of us! I think tomorrow we might do the most beautiful flower piece, if we want to.

George: I don't think we do these things to keep abreast. The truth is that, for us, these works were the most complicated pictures, on an emotional level. All one's feelings about romantic love, psychological, sexual, were completely disturbed by making those pictures. We're still slightly damaged by it. They never think of that. They think we're laughing all the way to the bank or something.

Gilbert: We can't sell them anyway. How can you sell pictures like that? How?

Why do you think you divide people so sharply?

George: We're not sure that we do. Isn't it just media people?

Gilbert: With the general public we're the biggest heroes, we know that, we just have to walk down the road.

George: Nikos Stangos [director with the publisher Thames & Hudson] was saying that it's changing. Traditionally, it was the artist together with the critic against the public. That was how modern art lived, that was the petrol in the engine. He said that with us, it's the artist together with the public, against the critic.

Do you think there's something about your work that irritates a certain sort of person?

Gilbert: I think more and more that the people who are completely irritated by us are the art historians who went to Manchester University or Essex University, where they were only taught Marxism and feminism and all that stuff, no?

George: The *New Statesman* was violently opposed to the show. It's only the lefties who are against us, strangely.

You get attacked from both sides don't you?

Gilbert: Oh yes.

George: Generally speaking, it's the right that's on our side now.

Quite a lot of critics from right-wing newspapers, certainly. But right and left these days are not very distinct.

Gilbert: I think for us, there is a certain left-wing art critic who has an ideology about what good art is, and we don't fit in. We never did. And they very violent.

George: That group of Marxist types, they have a suspicion that somewhere we must be evil. They can't quite figure out what's evil about us.

That's one thing people say about you: 'They're terribly right-wing.'

Gilbert: What does it mean, right-wing? We tantalise them. Once we said we were lower-class uneducated Tories.

George: They can't bear that.

That is of course what middle-class left liberals particularly dislike.

George: They can't stand a Bethnal Green [poor area of East London] Tory. They call us fascists just because we said that Margaret Thatcher was a very good Prime Minister. They call us paedophiles just because we have had young people in some pictures.

Do you still support John Major?

George: John Major is the most fantastic Prime Minister of our
lifetime. I am sure of that. So decent, so honest, so ordinary. Wonderful.
The second lower-class person to be leader of the Conservative Party.

He comes from a strange background.

George: Circus family. Exciting. It's a wonderful name for a Prime
Minister. John Major. Like John Bull. He's thrilling.

I am not a fan.

Gilbert: He didn't do anything wrong. Margaret Thatcher did a lot of
wrong in the end. The collapse of the money was her fault.

George: I think it's very simple, Gilbert, it was very hard to be the first
woman Prime Minister with everybody shouting Nazi queen, Nazi dike.

She has a theatrical, excessive personality, whereas Major...

Gilbert: A dead donkey, hmm?

George: That's the attraction.

Gilbert: There is one thing of which we are very sure and that is that art
has to be based on capitalism, total free capitalism. If not, it's nothing.
If you have art under socialism, it's finished, because they tell you
exactly what to do. Young artists, right or left, all they can do is sell to
Saatchi [Charles Saatchi], who is a Tory, or not?

I suppose he is.

Gilbert: So they are conning themselves.

George: Art flourished under Mrs Thatcher. Under Labour [in the
1970s] we had to go to Düsseldorf or somewhere to sell.

Do you see John Major as a Gilbert & George person?

Gilbert: No, we rather believe that the government isn't very important
any more. It should be run efficiently, and that's it.

George: We were the first people we've met to say that Westminster
should be privatised.

Gilbert: It must be totally free! At the same time there is very little
freedom. We are controlled by the government, more and more. They
take all your money away for tax, or rates, you have to fill in this form
and that.

George: Tax should be 10p in the pound [10%], every pound for
everybody.

You are obviously some way toward the right of the Conservative
Party. That's a right-wing thing to think.

Gilbert: But we are the most subversive left, in one way. Derek Jarman
called himself a left-wing person doing conservative films.

George: And we've suddenly realised that we're the opposite.
Gilbert: We say that we are conservatives, but we're doing art that's so anti-bourgeois.
George: If we got into trouble, we'd have to call on the left to support us.
Gilbert: They would, Ken Livingstone would support us.
George: We are subversives, we believe in that.
Gilbert: It's very simple. I'm not interested in politics. I never voted. But to free ourselves, we said we were low-class Tories. That got us free from everybody. But we are the most socialistic, mad, subversive artist that exist in the world. I think we are nearer to anarchists than anything else, because we are totally self-sufficient. We don't need anybody, we don't go anywhere, we don't take part in art gallery parties, collectors parties. Nothing. We are *alone here doing our pictures.* There's a period when we make them, then there's a period when we promote the show. Then we go back and do some more. They always think that we are trying to manipulate, that we are scheming. Not at all.
George: The other artists are like that. We are reckless.
But are there any taboos you would retain?
Gilbert: Like?
Well, against strangling people who annoy us, for example.
Gilbert: We don't hurt people, we never did. We love people.
Let me put something to you. People sometimes say that Gilbert & George irritate because you present a sort of caricature of a certain sort of Englishman. You're very buttoned-up, apparently, but then you present yourselves doing all these naughty things that Englishmen might like to do.
Gilbert: Or are doing.
George: I think that's true except for the race element. People wear suits in every bloody country in the world.
Gilbert: We are dandies, in some way. We like the idea of Oscar Wilde. He was a gentleman who dressed up, and inside suffered totally.
George: Saying that form was all that mattered, and doing the opposite. We only like the disastrous artists, Van Gogh, Rembrandt, they all got into trouble.
The life, rather than the art.
Gilbert: You mean the vision, we only believe in that. Even when you see a Michelangelo, it's just his vision that's the important thing. Then

you find form is affected by that, then you find your form. but the
important thing is to have a vision. Art for us is inventing the morality
of tomorrow. Nothing to do with canvases, and so on.
George: For us the important thing is that it looks clean, respectable
and not as if someone else could have done it. So even uneducated
people are not enraged. Nobody says a child of five could have done
that. They can see that they are cleverly done. A lot of modern art
alienates those sections of society because of form. If you have three
buckets in the centre of the gallery it's going to alienate 90% of the
people.
   It would alienate me.
George: It would alienate us.
Gilbert: We believe in the artist as a speaker. Even Van Gogh, we
believe that all his paintings are based on some orgasms.
George: Explosions of rage, sex, religion.
Gilbert: A lot of modern art today doesn't speak. It's always based on
Duchamp. It's always the found object. We never did that. Duchamp
was important because he created a lot of freedom, but we want a
moral art in the end. We don't like an art about art, that's very simple.
   *But to communicate it has to look good, that's the paradox of your
   position. What you're left with is the picture.*
George: What you're left with is the effect on the viewer after they
leave the exhibition. We believe that the world will be slightly different
after they leave our exhibition. With the Naked Shit Pictures we came
closer to the viewer than ever before. It's not a stuck-up artist saying:
'Oh all those idiots out there will never understand my work.' Most of
the artists did say that in this century.
Gilbert: Our work is brilliant, technically. A lot of people don't even
know how it's done. You can look at it in details and it's very artistic.
George: We think all that is at the service of meaning.
   *But what you're trying to do, it seems, is to give photomontage the
   punch and authority and presence of painting.*
George: We are the modern painters! That's it. Don't worry about
whether painting is finished and all that. It's alive and well, and in the
Bologna Gallery.
Gilbert: We are the nearest to Francis Bacon. He didn't know how to
paint. He only knew how to make a powerful image. He used any stupid
technique to make it powerful. He was not interested in painting, he

was interested in the result, the ghastly frightening image that ended up on the canvas. That's the big difference, we don't feel other artists are doing that. They are masturbating in their paint. What we like in Francis Bacon is the message.

And what is the message?

Gilbert: The message in Bacon is very simple: humanity, fear, unhappiness.

George: Everything you could find in a person you could find in Francis Bacon.

Gilbert: Like Rembrandt has that. Maybe he was a very good technician, but what I see in there is fear of life.

George: I think we're desperately unhappy people, but in some strange way we're the same as everybody else.

You think everyone is unhappy?

Gilbert: Yes. Life is very difficult. We just struggle to fight each other off day and night to survive.

George: In an organised society, if you get robbed you can go to the police, if you break your leg you can go to the hospital. But after all those things are looked after there is still this great aching void inside all of us.

Gilbert: We always say none of the art critics look at our work, because they have preconditioned ideas about what art should look like. So art has to be a concept, it has to be minimal, it has to be School of London, or performance art, now it has to be post-what-do-you-call-it. Because of that they never look at what is in the picture. They think we are arranging traps for art critics to fall into.

George: They write themselves into traps, not us, then stick their legs into them.

Gilbert: The ones who are very against us, sometimes are very near to us, only the final decision is against.

George: We believe in a new morality. We say it all the time.

What are the components of your new morality?

Gilbert: Complexity, and truth, and freedom of understanding.

George: We all have to become more elaborate, we believe.

Gilbert: You cannot be terrorised for the rest of your lives, just because we say we are conservative. Or if you are left-wing, that is that. There is a complexity of ideas. We have to be more liberal.

George: Or individual. Everyone more themselves. We're probably very primitive compared to how we could be. We're certainly much more elaborate than people were in the eighteenth century, when most people just held somebody's horse all day.

Do you think there's any chance of you're getting religion?
Gilbert: Not for one second! I hate fucking religion.
George: We're religious in the sense of moral fibre, we all come from a Christian culture. And we hate the idea of normal twentieth-century artists saying they're atheists, it's just too snobbish. Obviously the cleaning lady goes to church.
Gilbert: We would take the church to court if we could.
George: We think they should come under the Trades Description Act.
Gilbert: Because they're lying.

You use religious imagery quite a bit.
George: We're for and against.
Gilbert: We love and hate it, that's what it is.

Did you come from religious backgrounds?
Gilbert: I was brought up as an extreme Catholic.
George: And I was extreme Protestant. Methodist. Like Mrs Thatcher.

Do you want to be accepted? It seems you do and you don't.
Gilbert: We want to be accepted in the right way. In the right way.

You're not making it easy. So you can't be surprised if you aren't.
George: We're not.
Gilbert: But every time we start on some new work we think this time they will love us.
George: We always think that. Naive probably.
Gilbert: We want total love anyway. We are after total success, that's what it is. The right way is very limited. Because in the end, they have to change, not us. The middle class out there. We cannot make pictures for them. They have to accept us in the end.

Gilbert & George and Shere Hite: 1996

At the suggestion of Hans-Ulrich Obrist, Shere Hite was invited to London by The South Bank Show to meet Gilbert & George on camera during filming of the documentary *The Fundamental Gilbert & George* (directed by Gerald Fox, series editor Melvyn Bragg). This text is an edited transcript of their previously unpublished conversation, which took place on 13 September 1996.

George: How do you do?
>   *Nice to meet you.*

Gilbert: So you are the friend of Hans-Ulrich.
>   *Yes. That's right. I was glad when he gave me the book of your*
>   *artwork. I've shown it to so many people.*

Gilbert: We read your interview that you did a long time ago in the *Telegraph*, because we always buy the *Telegraph*, and I remember one specific thing.
>   *What was that?*

Gilbert: That men like to be touched up their bum.
>   *When I saw your work I thought it was amazing that nobody had*
>   *ever had the courage to present images such as that before. They're*
>   *very witty of course, and profound at the same time. I'm sure people*
>   *will tend to giggle a lot, but they will also have a deeper meaning.*

George: We were speaking to a policeman once who said that for years his job had been to attend scenes of motor-accidents on the motorways. The first job to do when the policeman arrives is to move the crowds back. He said invariably there's somebody giggling amongst the crowd. Somebody who can't accept the disaster of that awful half-dead body and just responds by giggling.

Gilbert: But giggling is part of liberation, no?

George: As well, yes.

Gilbert: We started to make a big collection of erotic magazines, but all to do with the male because in some way for us it is more interesting. It's more taboo and you can see how it changes, very, very slowly, what...

George: ...what the male figure actually is. A 1950 pin-up book is entirely different from a 1959 one. We also found out that when a person dies the family auctions everything that belonged to him or her except their collection of pin-up magazines. They always destroy that. We think that's very cruel because it was obviously a part of the person's life.

*When I did a book on male sexuality I used questionnaires and
people had to answer them anonymously. They were essay
questions, so people often wrote volumes back about themselves.
Several men wrote me – more than women – that they were leaving
answers to my questions about their intimate sexuality in their will
so that their children could know what their lives had been like in
private, after they were dead. They didn't want to talk about it
while they were alive, but they were willing to leave it that way.*

George: When we started to make the collection of magazines we
advertised so that we had some telephone calls from people living in
the country. They tended to be elderly people, and they wanted to sell
their magazines because they were frightened that they'd die and
they'd be discovered in the house. They couldn't put them in the
dustbin, because it was a small village – the dustmen would know them.
They were thrilled to find that somebody actually wanted them. It was
very sweet. One older country gentleman with a lovely rural accent
said, 'Er, I've got quite a big collection'. And I said, 'Well, can you tell
me roughly what you have?' He said ' have a complete run of *Zipper*
and *Man to Man, Quorum...*', and all these marvellous titles. And I said,
'Can you tell me how much you would like for the collection?' He said,
'I couldn't take any money for them. They've given me a lot of pleasure
over the years.' Isn't that sweet?

Gilbert: Hans-Ulrich was recently in touch with an Oxford professor of
science, and he wanted this professor to be in one of his projects. But he
refused to be in it because we were in it. This professor is a professor of
evolution – *evolution* – but he's not able able to accept the idea of two
men naked, or a bum. He was furious, calling us all the names under
the sun. Can you imagine that?

*I can imagine it, because of course I've had to listen to quite a few
complaints and cries of outrage myself. I'm not surprised either
that men would be more affronted by your work than women.*

George: Amongst the Naked Shit Pictures, the most recent group of
pictures we made, is one called *Bum Holes*, which is a portrait of
ourselves taken from the back. That's the favourite picture of ladies.

Gilbert: And they told us why: because they feel vulnerable, like we
feel vulnerable in that picture.

*It was very courageous that you would make those pictures
because they do look so vulnerable. The ones in which you have
your pants down are also vulnerable moments.*

George: Yes. Much more naked than entirely naked.

Exactly.

Gilbert: We believe the subject of sex in art is one of the most important ones. We believe that in the last, say, forty years very few artists used the message of sex in art. They went away from sexuality in art and started to be involved in the formal aspects of art. We believe sex is the most important thing in art.

Why would you say that?

Gilbert: We believe that the power of living is sex. There is nothing else. We are driven by sex, but we don't like the idea of male sex or heterosexual sex. We only like the idea of sex.

George: We say everyone is a sexual person.

Gilbert: Being.

George: We don't believe in such a thing as male or female or homo or hetero. We don't believe in any of those terms really. We think it's much more elaborate, far more beautiful, much more complicated.

Well when you get a chance to read my book, I say that too.

George: Wonderful, wonderful.

Gilbert: Even the young people, more and more, they believe it.

But, as you say that – and I'm sure that it's true for what you believe in – you don't have any women in your art. Why is that?

Gilbert: Because for the last 300 years, nudity in art meant women.

Females – yes.

George: Every cartoon about modern art was always the female nude, wasn't it? Naked ladies.

Yes, and that's why men would be more threatened by the fact that you're using the male figure in this way, because men are accustomed to thinking of being the artist not the object. The person who looks at something else is not used to being looked at. So women in this society are the object of men's actions...

George: That's why women's magazines throughout history have always shown a woman on the cover. I should think that would be deeply offensive to a woman – or if it doesn't have a woman on the cover, it'll have a cheese flan or something.

There's another view that we think women are more beautiful!

George: [Laughs.] Now we get into trouble.

Of course you're both very beautiful – I didn't mean to say that you were not. Was it a conscious decision to stick with the male figure?

Gilbert: Not really. It was just something that happened to us. It happened because first we used ourselves and then thought it much better to have a young man. All the critics called them names immediately – prostitutes or rentboys – they're not able to accept a man...

No, they're not able to accept it at all. I'm sure they don't consider it art, sometimes. As a matter of principle did you decide to use the male form? Or were you attracted to using it as...

George: No, we weren't conscious of that. We were just conscious of extending ourselves into other figures, and naturally we would have other men. It would be as odd for us to start putting women in our pictures as it would be for us to start dressing as women.

Gilbert: Excluding things is very important, because then the discussion starts. If you have women in art – men *and* women – then it's boring, normal. But if you exclude women, the discussion is enormous. Everybody's up in arms that we have to have women in art, that we have to have women in our pieces. And we say, 'Why?'

If you have a woman in there, then somehow or other it is in a context which they can understand, rather than one which they can't understand. Why would a man want to be come the object for others to view? That's what you're not supposed to be.

Gilbert: But that changes, we think.

How?

George: The convention is slightly broken now. The idea that beauty is female, and that a man can never say to another man, 'You look beautiful this evening'. That's changing.

It's not so much that the taboo is that men are not beautiful. The taboo is about the fact that men are supposed to be those who control the world. Therefore, having more power means being covered, not using your body and so on, don't you think? So therefore people would look at your pictures and think that they're giving up power somehow, because you don't have to do that.

George: Even if the figures are not naked it's the same issue exactly. If you had a group of clothed females in one of our pictures, the issue for the man-viewer would be whether they are attracted to that one, or that one, or not.

And what do you think they think when they look at yours?

Gilbert: They are shocked, terrified.

*What do you think men are afraid of when they look at your
pictures?*
George: The convention has gone...
Gilbert: ...of male nudity.
George: Terrified also because it's *not* dead. If it's something from
central Africa, or something from Florence from the fifteenth century,
it's much easier then. But if it's living art saying that, that's already
something different.

I'm thinking of that famous painting, Le déjeuner sur l'herbe
[Manet, 1863], *where, of course, the women are naked and the men
are dressed. You're doing the reverse of that, in a way.*
George: Strangely it doesn't matter if it's mythological or antique, like
all of those Rubens paintings with huge pot-bellied elderly gentlemen
with grey beards rolling around. No one would bat an eyelid at that
either. That wouldn't threaten anyone, because it's a magic, from the
sky or something.
Gilbert: It's art, religion...
George: ...Moses, or something. If it's actual and truthful then it's much
more complicated to view it.

Exactly. Would you consider some of the things you do erotic?
George: No more than life itself is. We would never go into the studio
thinking, 'Should we do erotic or non-erotic things?'
Gilbert: I think we kept eroticism in some way out of our pictures.

I think so.
Gilbert: I think we did, almost did that.
George: On the other hand, a flower is erotic in a picture in the end.

*The fact that you've also pointed out the human function of the
bowel in your pictures makes one uncomfortable. 'Is it sexual, or is
it physiological? Are they going to the bathroom, or are they having
sex?' We're brought up not to combine in our minds that we're the
same person: we go into the bathroom, we close the door and that's
a completely separate room, and so on...*
George: Yes. We read recently Montgomery Hyde's history of
pornography and I think that to this day American law still states that
one of the definitions of pornography is nakedness and excrement. Could
that be written somewhere? I think so. Yes, it's one of the definitions.

*Well, to stand up for the United States for one second, I notice here
in England that the toilet is always in a separate room from the*

washing-up room, or the bath-tub or shower. In the States it's all in one room. I am often put to wondering if this is a benefit, or exactly why it has to be in a completely separate room. Usually there's very little else in the room.

George: It's part of convention...

Of course you know there is one other famous male nude – Jesus Christ. He's always portrayed as nude, practically. You have one depiction of him here. How do you feel about Jesus on the cross?

George: Jesus on the cross is one of the great suffering S & M images. Every national gallery in the world is filled with dead Jesuses, and it's always seen as positive. No one ever thinks that it's suggesting you do that to people or something. It's always seen as a goody-goody picture.

Gilbert: It's kind of cinematic.

At the same time he does seem more real than classical sculptures or idealised male beauty pictures, even though he's idealised too.

Gilbert: He's so alive. We're not Christians, but more and more people believe in this crazy idea of Jesus...

George: Because Jesus became a man... that he wasn't only a god.

Gilbert: He became human, and probably sexual.

The glorification is that he gave up the world and things for the world, that he wasn't sexual. They say it's wonderful to be a man who isn't sexual – be spiritual, not sexual. Would you ever put women in your pictures?

George: Well, we never thought of that. There are many different answers to that question, of course. We always have to think of different answers.

It would be such a cliché probably, because it's been done so often.

George: Millions and millions and millions of times.

Gilbert: I think we would ruin a simple idea that we have.

I think so too. And it's much more powerful because there are two of you. If there were just one it wouldn't work the same way either.

George: Absolutely.

More powerful as two also because you seem to be giving each other permission to do that. Somehow you're colluding with each other. That must be very irritating to some viewers.

George: Even a double male naked figure is a modern idea and it wasn't even allowed in many magazines for years. As long as there's a single figure it was alright because it was art.

286

*But I think that it's not upsetting to women to see two men together
in your art at all. It's upsetting to men, really.*

Gilbert: Women are much more liberal. Women and children, we
always say, are the freest, without doubt.

George: Children have no problem whatsoever with the Naked Shit
Pictures. They love them, especially the shit.

Gilbert: Women are much freer, always have been. Women have been
our biggest supporters from the first day. When we first showed the
Naked Shit Pictures in London [South London Art Gallery, 1995] we got
a lovely letter from a small boy written by his mother saying that her
son loved the exhibition and loved the shit. He just had one question to
ask about the exhibition: 'Where is Jesus?' An extraordinary question.
Extraordinary.

Gilbert: He wasn't there. Yesterday we went through the Bible to find
pieces about sexuality. There are many. Even to do with homosexuality,
there is one small piece. But there are hundreds of other pieces about
just looking at a naked lady.

George: You were put to death just for seeing your daughter naked. The
one against so-called homosexuality is just part of an enormous list. We
think that the Church should come under secular law. We think it would
be very good if the churches and the vicars had to conform to the law of
the land. They shouldn't have separate rulings.

*This is the big fight of the moment. Some Islamic leaders, and even
the Pope, have asserted that moral law should come before secular
law. There is an enormous debate going on today about that very
issue. If you could have men understand one thing looking at your
pictures, or if you could have women understand something, what
is it you would like them to know?*

Gilbert: Complexity of life.

George: Elaboration.

Gilbert: Elaboration of the individual.

George: That there is nothing in the world that is not also inside each
one of us.

Gilbert: Complexity. Nothing else. More gentle and more complicated.

*The idea has been that you have to be ashamed of your sexuality, or
have to have it as a separate part of your life, that it is not really
something that on a daily basis you can be proud of.*

George: Yes, without doubt. There have been enormous changes during our lifetime, but we see a lot more coming. Before we are dead there will be an enormous change of understanding.

Do you ever envy women being viewed in the nude so often, or do you think that it's a put down of women?

George: If we were women we would be quite cross about that. We would feel quite used. If I were a woman, I would like to buy my weekly magazine with a boy on the cover.

If you were a heterosexual.

George: Yes, because the sex that the majority of women are involved with would be male. So In that way our pictures are quite feminist, you could say. We provide pictures for women.

Well, what you say is based on a heterosexual premis, that...

George: We don't believe in heterosexuality anyway.

In Ancient Greece they had to pass a law telling men to have sex with their wives because they were not reproducing enough.

Gilbert: They were seducing all the young boys instead.

George: It was a different type of sexuality, based on class as well as on age.

Already at that time sexuality seems to have had connotations of something elicit, or something not connected to the higher parts of the world. A strange dichotomy.

George: It varies anyway throughout the world. We all discuss it but we're only discussing one Western system. The age of consent varies enormously throughout the world. Attitudes towards sex vary enormously.

Gilbert: We don't want to make a homosexual art or a heterosexual art. We never wanted to do that. We want to make a sexual art. We think that's very important.

The Fundamental Gilbert & George: 1997

The following previously unpublished statements by Gilbert & George represent a small part of the extensive interviews conducted by Gerald Fox (director) and Sarah Wason (assistant director) for The South Bank Show, *The Fundamental Gilbert & George*, which began filming in 1996 and documented the artists' work on their most recent group of photo-pieces, The Fundamental Pictures. *The Fundamental Gilbert & George* premiered on 8 February 1997 in London at the Tate Gallery and at the National Film Theatre and was first broadcast on Channel 4 in two parts on 9 and 16 February 1997.

MAKING PICTURES

George: We think that we have developed a way of making pictures that needs two people, really. Very difficult for one person to make pictures like this from the physical point of view, even from the emotional point of view.

Gilbert: Emotionally it would be very difficult for one person to go through this kind of image that we do. I think it would be impossible.

George: We don't argue, but even if we did we wouldn't tell. [Laughter.] We believe that the world is one big enormous argument, and we think we at least should try to keep away from that.

Gilbert: If we would start to argue everything would fall apart very fast. Because it is based on accepting the two, the view of two people together. If not, you are finished immediately. It wouldn't work. It wouldn't work.

George: It's that area of common ground that we believe in. We don't believe so much in the individual in that way. We like to think of ourselves as an artist, and that's it.

Gilbert: That's why we always say that we don't ask too many questions. We are pushing ourselves forward without knowing too much. If one has too a strong view that would be impossible.

George: A little blind is very good as well.

Gilbert: Blind. And accepting the certain feeling that is driving us, and that's it. Don't ask so many questions.

George: It would be difficult if we were doing it for ourselves, for instance, because then there would be an enormous personality problem. But we really are doing it for the viewer and that removes immediately the problem of individual sense or sensibility, or the pleasure of doing it or the interest in doing it. We really are creating pictures to go out there, to be in front of people.

Gilbert: We are only interested in the end result. We are not interested in the making. Not for one second.

George: Once we've taken a group of images, like the ones we took for The Fundamental Pictures, we will go on drawing on that bank of images for a long time. Having created these pictures will make us changed people anyway. We will be very different people having created The Fundamental Pictures from how we were before. We will already have a different outlook, a different feeling about everything.

THE VIEWER

George: We think we are very gentle in our approach to the viewer, really. We know how fragile we are, so we can imagine that the viewer is equally fragile... One of the main subjects under discussion [in the Naked Shit Pictures] is the human reality that there is no nakedness without a viewer: we are not naked when we are alone.

Gilbert: For us, being naked in front of the public, we are trying to make ourselves vulnerable in front of the viewer. That is very important because art is based on making ourselves more vulnerable and opening up what is inside us. We never look at what is outside the world; we always look inside the world, and this kind of picture [*Naked Eye*, 1994] in some way is showing the world what we actually are inside. It's all the difficulties, all our problems and all our complexities.

George: That is to reveal purely the eyes of the viewer, because you don't need to have your eyes open to feel naked in front of another person. The other person is looking.

Gilbert: You can concentrate on the inner feelings if you close your eyes.

George: We always say in our pictures that it is through our eyes that we take in the world and from our mouth that we speak out and form or re-form it.

Gilbert: If not, you only have skin, and only through the eyes you are penetrating the other person, or through the mouth you are pene-trating, you are speaking to other person, or even the sex you penetrate the other person. So that is the most important thing, because you only see the world and feel it through those kind of things – not through the skin. Normally the world, the general world, accepts one [man], a boy and a girl naked, but two naked men? It is in some way unacceptable, and I think for us it is much more important.

290

George: So many people said, 'But isn't it a reference to Adam and
Eve?', and we said, 'Surely it's more like Adam and Steve....' [Laughter.]
I mean, anything that the artist takes from himself to put into a book or
into a picture, if it is sincere and if it reaches out to people, will in some
way damage the artist. We believe that the artist has to be prepared for
that. You cannot take something out from inside yourself without
wrecking in some way.
Gilbert: In some way humanity is based on hiding everything. You have
clothes, you have hats, you have – what are they called – gloves. You are
hiding everything. But we in some way open ourselves up and I think
this is very difficult because the vulnerability of human beings is so
difficult. Not maybe in primitive societies, but in our society it's very
difficult. We all hide and hide and hide. We always pretend to be
different than we are.

HUMAN BONDAGE
George: The Human Bondage pictures [1974] were very important to
us for many reasons, first of all from the practical, graphic point of
view. They were on the way to a rectangle, on the way to a normal
picture. They were coming together and enabled us to go deeper into
the darker side of things that we hadn't done before. Using that image,
the fyflot [swastika], is already a very powerful statement. We showed
them first of all in Germany, and in a way we wanted to rob the image
back from the last war, because before it had been a positive image for
thousands and thousands of years, and still is in countries that hardly
knew about the last war. We wanted to claim it back in a way, and of
course they were very involved in drinking which sometimes people
forget. They are called *human* bondage, not *political* bondage.
Gilbert: The sign of a swastika from the recent past meant oppression,
total oppression, and we felt that the drink did that. It took over and
made us 'bondage' to the alcohol.
George: The swastika is a very well-known negative image, but
interestingly a local elderly Jewish friend of ours went to see the
exhibition in 1980 [*The Photo-Pieces 1980–1981*], at the Whitechapel
Art Gallery, and came to see us. He was so excited he said, 'I love your
swastikas because they go the other way around!' So there's another
interesting way of seeing it.
Gilbert: Because if they go this way round [the opposite direction of the

Nazi swastika] it's the sign of good luck. That's it, that's what it is, it used to be, but it doesn't have this kind of symbol anymore.

*

Gilbert: In 1972 we had a little success in the art world, so we started to spend the money, going out, drinking, getting totally drunk, totally drunk, so that's when we started to do what were the drinking pieces.
George: *The Major's Port* [1972].
Gilbert: *The Major's Port, Spilt Drinks* [1973], *Bottoms Up* [1973], all this kind of title and all based on drinking. But it was still happy drinking. Later in 1973 or '74, when we started to do the Human Bondage pieces or the Dark Shadow pieces, in some way a big cloud came over us, like all black. That's why we even did a Dark Shadow [see pages 78–92], a big shadow or nearly depression. For the first hour you feel you are overdoing it, you start to feel inside all this pain and all this loneliness. It may have to do with the drink. That's why we started to do this chained-up piece; to be fucked, chained into these rooms in Fournier Street, alone, on the floor, drunk, and that's why we used to call them Human Bondage. The dark comes in towards us every time. Half our body was always in darkness.
George: We think that the drink was a part of a lot of different things. It wasn't just alcohol because of course people can be drunk with anything. There are all sorts of things people can be drunk with, and it was a general human statement in a way. We do believe that we went deeper and deeper inside ourselves in preparation for being able to go out to the viewer more later on. We felt we had to completely destroy ourselves in some way, to find out the worst things about ourselves, all of the worst feelings. *Bad Thoughts, Human Bondage*, all of these titles tell you that, even *Red Morning: Death, Red Morning: Danger, Red Morning: Beating, Red Morning: Killing* [all 1977]. We wanted to do everything that we could inside of ourselves as persons in order to be able to come out from that which we did later on. In the late seventies we came out entirely differently.
Gilbert: It was in some way even like self-flagellation. We had these blackouts and depressions. At the beginning it was very easy to make art. Then in some way it became more and more difficult and in a moment all that you see in front of you is nil, nil, nothing. That's why we did all this.

DEPRESSION

George: We think that the bleakness of *Dead Boards* [1976] and *Dusty Corners* [1975] is a feeling that exists in everybody in some degree. There is some part of the head, the soul and the sex of every person that can identify wherever they live in the world with those feelings. Very delicate, difficult things to talk about, even more difficult to make pictures about. We remember someone who owned a *Dead Boards* or a *Dusty Corners* picture, inviting us to his [home] years after he bought it. We didn't even know who it was, and he said that his wife had died the previous year and he just wanted us to know that that picture had been an enormous support for him during the period of bereavement. That was a very interesting letter to receive.

Gilbert: But they [the works] do describe exactly the feeling that we had. We did isolate ourselves totally, we were totally alone, and we kept to that.

George: Lots do. Depression.

Gilbert: We have to do that. We never had friends after. Sometimes we really felt exactly like that, totally lonely, unhappy in these empty rooms, and they represent that. What I find rather amusing, when we showed them the first time in New York, 'Dead Broads', they called us. But before we did these pieces, like *Bloody Life* [series of 1975], and we had this piece where we'd push ourselves against the wall and all this blood comes down.

George: They're more physically destructive, whereas *Dead Boards* and *Dusty Corners* are more intellectually bleak, more spiritually bleak.

Gilbert: Totally. We always felt outsiders. There was a period when we were going out drinking, in '72–'73, that we didn't feel so much... We felt we were able to be happy in the evening.

George: Pretending to be happy.

Gilbert: Pretending. But after that we retreated totally into our world.

George: We never wanted to become part of normal thought because then we wouldn't have anything to say. It's no good having the things to say that are already in people's heads. We want to find things inside of ourselves and inside the viewer, delicate other thoughts.

Gilbert: You don't want to argue with people in the evening or having to discuss art if you like it or not. You want to make it exactly how we feel it is right for us, and then they see it only when it is finished. But if you

have a lot of friends you always have to compromise, you have to
compromise your souls. In the moment that you have a friend you have
to compromise, and we never wanted to compromise.

*

Gilbert: During this period I wouldn't say that we were bored. I'm sure
we were depressed and lonely, but not bored.
George: We would never say that we were bored.
Gilbert: No, never bored, because in front of us there's just this big
urge that we want to make the most incredible art. We want to open up
in front of the viewer all these amazing feelings that we feel. That is
what an artist is doing, showing what he is, showing inner feelings.
George: We are too involved with searching for complexity ever to be
bored. We think that it's the most incredibly elaborate and complex
fascinating thing, being here on earth. It is an extraordinary thing we
think... I think we want to be able to understand mental breakdown.
I think that's very important for an artist or a writer to be able to do
that. You have to be able to understand the most miserable person that
is alive out there in order to build up and to be able to become in some
way of help or of use.
Gilbert: But I don't think that's something unusual. It's happening in
every family, in every house, in every writer, in every happy person; if
you look into their hearts they would say the same story. It's nothing
new, only we are open enough to show it to the world. Instead of hiding
everything, we open it all up.
George: Part of the depression in the pictures that we make is based on
our ambition and our intention, how we want to take our art. Art is
based on circumstances that surround us.
Gilbert: But it was not the only period. Later it became much more
dark, much more. But we accept that, we accept that what is
surrounding us is our material. Or if we don't go out of the house we use
the house to make the art. At the moment that we are walking up and
down the street you use the street to make art, and that's what we're
doing, looking, looking on the ground or looking up into the sky or
looking onto the floor boards, that's what we do.

ART

George: The basis of most of our inspiration is to try to work towards a more democratic art, an art that spreads across the classes, across the educational divides, across different countries. It's very important to us. Art was so elitist in this century so far, it has to change.

Gilbert: We believe that art is a message, that is why we started to design booklets, postcards, to design books that are very cheap, very beautiful but very cheap, because we know that out there everybody's interested in art, not only the rich people, not only the artists, every single person. So we always try to arrange catalogues and books that are visually very powerful and very simple. Instant success it has to be.

MAKING FILMS

George: When Philip Haas asked us to make a film [*The World of Gilbert & George*, 1980–81] we realised that most films are based on decisions. You have to make a film like this or a film like that or a film about this or a film about that. And instantly we realised that we didn't want any decisions and the only way to avoid that is to make it entirely inclusive. So our fears are in the film, our hopes are in the film, our dreams are in the film, our hates are in the film, our loves. We put everything that we knew about, everything we felt about, everything we hoped for, we just piled it all in.

Gilbert: They are the same as our pictures, only they start to speak and they start to move. There is nothing different. It lasts longer but it is the same, absolutely the same. We rather like our film. But more and more we still believe that pictures are the best way of speaking. Even when today we read an article about making films, we realise that there are so many moviemakers here, let's say in London, who make films and nobody in the end will see them. To make an artwork is much cheaper and you can put them up in different museums and hundreds of thousands of people will see those pictures and they will see them through catalogues, through books, through television. It's unbelievable, it's the best form. And you are much freer because it's not based on expense and nobody is telling you what you can or can't do. So it's the best form.

THE FUNDAMENTAL PICTURES

George: From the beginning of this year [1996], we've been taking
images towards a huge new group of pictures. We've taken pictures of
shit, of piss, which we showed you, of spit, which you see here – spits
on the street and taken in the studio, and of tears and of sweat and of
ourselves. So we're building up a huge group of images based on all
of our hopes, dreads, thoughts, feelings.

Gilbert: And even the landscape outside... urban landscape. We took
a lot of roses because we think they are exactly the same – everything
is the same. If you look into a drop of blood or a drop of piss, or in the
garden or in the sky, or in a piece of shit – everything is the same. That's
why we became very fascinated by that.

George: Absolutely. We became very interested in the universality of
certain images, of simple broken urban landscapes which everyone in
the world understands, of spit which everyone has thoughts and
feelings about, of shit, of piss, of the human person – or the flower even
that they love.

Gilbert: If you look very closely at the flower, it's the same thing, it's
just rotting away like spit or shit... So we are all the same, even us as
human beings we are just like a piece of matter.

George: It's something we've been working on for a long time, but more
recently we believe that we're going deeper and more desperate and
more emotional. In 1977 we already had pictures called *Piss* and *Cock
VD* and we had a picture called *Coming* [1975] which showed sperm,
and we did many, many works connected with piss, in the early
eighties, *Winter Pissing*, many pictures...

Gilbert: *Friendship Pissing* [1983].

George: *Thirst* [1982].

Gilbert: We always want to take our art to the edge, because we know
that this kind of language which we are using here is near to total taboo.
We want to make it that it's absolutely nothing except normality of life –
that's why if you look into these drops of piss you start to see the most
beautiful flowers. It's just wonderful life.

George: Full of emotions and feelings. We were very interested, even
taking images of spits on the street, that it immediately aroused
enormous hostility from people standing nearby, being completely
aggressive that we were actually focusing on and giving attention to a
piece of phlegm on the pavement. We thought that was very interesting

296

that it could arouse such strong feelings... When we are taking these images we don't have exact plans for pictures but we have a general sense of the area of human interest that will be dealt with in the pictures.

Gilbert: We really feel once we have these images that they are happening by accident – most of the images are happening by accident. We don't have clear views of what we want. But once we have these images they fall into pictures. It's very simple to do. It's like going into a black bag and putting them together. Once we have the material, they are finished, they are done.

George: We always say that all of the pictures we create have been lying dormant inside of ourselves. We just bring them to life in the studio. In the same way we believe that the pictures are also lying dormant, sleeping in the viewer, and we can bring them to life.

Gilbert: So from the beginning to the end we have to concentrate non-stop. It's all towards the end result, because the end picture – that's it. We are not interested in anything else except the end result. Is the end result speaking to the viewer or not? Don't you think, George?

George: That's what we're after, exactly.

*

George: We started to take these images very early this year – just after Christmas [1995] – and we will go on now until probably another month and then we will start to create the pictures. We never know exactly what we're doing when we're taking the images. We have to trust ourselves in some strange way. We have to follow – even if it sometimes feels embarrassing to be doing something, we still have to put that to one side and do it. Because we feel that to do something new it's very difficult, so we are pushing ourselves very, very slowly and we are waiting for accidents to happen and in the end we only use maybe two percent of the images but those are the ones that are really important to us. It is a kind of study because when we first started to do shits it felt very awkward and difficult to do. You know, coming from the lavatory with this shit in your hand and going to the studio, and taking an image of it, getting the lighting right, taking a perfect... and then we realised that it was like a study, and we could go on and make a huge visual – it's probably one of the biggest visual studies of shit ever made. We have thousands and thousands of different ones.

Gilbert: The images have to start to speak of a bigger depth and that's
why we try to find a bigger depth and sometimes it takes a long time.
George: The deeper we go into the subject, we know from experience,
the more levels on which it is received by the viewer, so that you
actually have something incredibly intense in the museum or the
gallery. You will find people responding on different levels. Like with a
shit we had people who were collectors of fossils, we had people from
the medical profession, children have a different approach to the
subject. There's no one way in which a picture can speak or reach a
person and we don't want to do every day something different. We want
to make it more solid, this idea of existence, our existence, our compli-
cations, from pissing to eating and drinking, everything should be
there but it becomes more and more human.

*

George: We think that with the subject matter that we took, which will
be in the new pictures now, we are able to go deeper inside the
humanistic idea and come closer to the viewer on different levels. He
or she will be shitting at some point during that day. They will be going
to the lavatory, they will be conscious of illness, they will be conscious
of blood. Everyone is, everyone sees it in the newspapers, in their life,
in their bedrooms, in their bathrooms, and we can get closer to the
person on a human level by extending the range of contacts.
Gilbert: We did do it before in '75. We did this piece called *Coming* and
we did this piece called *Shitted* and a lot of other pieces. But I think this
time we were able to make them visually very beautiful. Even through
the blood pieces that we did in the For Aids exhibition you realise that
all the fluids that are part of us – if you start to look through them you
see the most beautiful... the most beautiful light is in front of you.
George: In fact it was purely by chance that we discovered this
subject. We were setting out to take images of single drops of liquid
which we could colour red to represent blood, and we wanted to take
perfect forms of drops rather like you'd see on the top of a motor car
when it's been raining. And so we tried to take them very, very close,
either with bellows or rings on our machine, or maybe with a microscope, and we discovered that we could do that – take a perfect image
of a drop [with a microscope]. Then we came back to the studio four
or five hours later and suddenly we looked through and saw these

298

extraordinary flowers and weeds, and trees, and different levels of
wonderful strange grottoes and things.

*

Gilbert: [Looking at images on a contact sheet.] This we discovered recently
when we started to put drops of piss under a microscope, so this is just
one single drop of piss – the whole thing started when we wanted to
take images of a drop of liquid or a drop of piss, because we'd always
used that in our pictures but we wanted to take the images more
exactly. It was an enormous surprise to us to find that not only did we
get the shape of the drop but we get this enormous activity inside which
we didn't even imagine or think about, and then we went on with other
subjects. Every single day and every single hour the slides are
different, so it is a non-stop activity that creates itself, like the most
beautiful wallpapers, and then boff, here is another one.
George: This we also find very beautiful. This is semen, or spunk as we
call it. We thought this was very exciting – that you get a fish shape here,
as fish was the earliest sign in the image for Christ, *ictus* in the Latin.
Gilbert: And so when we realised that, we cut ourselves and put one
small drop of blood in the microscope and realised that it is an amazing
world...
George: Tremendous design.
Gilbert: So we stopped cutting ourselves, we ran to the hospital to ask
them if they could give us two, three small bottles of our blood. We
made the most amazing discovery. It just looked like fourteenth-
century or thirteenth-century windows.
George: We realised that it was very connected with what we've always
been doing. We realised during the last few weeks that everything
we're doing now is connected with what we were always doing. In 1969
we sent out *A Message from the Sculptors* [see pages 9–11], a postal
work, and that had little circular microscopic samples from our life for
the viewer to see. A small sample of hair, of breakfast, of our clothing.
This is quite close to that in a way – we've just gone deeper and deeper
into the forms, and into the meanings. They're all designs and shapes
that we would love to produce but we don't like the idea of drawing
them ourselves. We like the idea of finding them.
Gilbert: So in the moment that we add the colour they are going to
become so incredible, beautiful – and that's what we like – this idea that

they look like the most beautiful nineteenth-century or twentieth-century wallpaper, but it is not. It actually is the structure of urine.
George: It's also exciting that as we went along we found endless possibilities from piss. We found that some days it would form into little machine guns all over the drop. Another day it would look like hockey sticks. Another day it would look like flowers.
Gilbert: Another day, guns and roses.
George: Extraordinary – endless possibilities. We never dreamt of that. We just really wanted to find a drop, a way of making a very good image of a drop. We didn't imagine there would be a content there.
Gilbert: [Looking at images again.] And here we have some other ones that are just as exciting.
George: These are drops of piss that have become crystallised through time. These look more Celtic in some strange way, like Celtic jewellery.
Gilbert: And in the moment that blow them up, on a bigger scale, they are going to look incredible.

*

George: We have no aesthetic criteria at all when we are looking for images. We don't say, 'Oh, this one works and this one doesn't work', as the artist commonly does. Whatever we find in piss we are agreeable with. If we find guns there, we will use the guns. If we find flowers, we will use the flowers. It is best because we are not these traditional artists who need a brush in hand, always. For centuries and centuries, everybody loves what they call the hand of the artist, and we absolutely are totally uninterested in that. We are only interested to have the vision that inside ourselves we push that under a wall and that's it – it has to be done like magic, nobody knows how it is done. Only the image in front of the viewer should speak. What you need to do there is totally unimportant.

*

George: We do believe that when we say 'death, hope, life, fear', or general subjects which we believe everyone on the planet can identify with, or if you say 'money, sex, race, religion', those four words are part of everybody's life wherever they live, and it would also be true to say that shit and piss and blood and sperm and sweat and tears are equally universal.
Gilbert: They are very universal, and we are amazed that nobody actually looked at them. Once you start to look at them very close you

realise that they are just like the most beautiful object that you ever saw, they become like the most beautiful flowers, every one is. They have this morality. Nobody likes them morally, but the moment you look at them you realise that it is just like the most beautiful flower.
George: And of course we are all dependent on these forms. Even if you think of flowers they need the earth, they need rotting creatures and other vegetation, they need heat, they need cold, they need moisture. We're all connected in our forms and forces, really.
Gilbert: We need to eat, we need to spit, we need to piss and we need to shit, so it's more important than anything else. Without these kinds of objects we wouldn't be able to survive to live. Why shouldn't we involve this kind of material in our art? It's the most important part of living.

DEATH
George: There are two main developments in our pictures. One is the development of the language – we developed a visual language. The other is how we change as people. Normally when you look at the work of an artist you see his stylistic development. Whereas with our pictures you see how we feel. We started as very innocent shy timid students coming out of college – you see that in the work. Then you see, as we become part of the world, that we become more disastrous and we become more drunken. It's like the viewer's life, in a way. The viewer can imagine their life as a parallel to our development... There were very deep religious elements in the '80s, with the all blue spiritual backgrounds. The human person representing mankind, even representing us sometimes, representing the viewer.
Gilbert: Yes – the flowers, the thorns and all this – the battling for life with all these young people with sticks.
George: The world city, the urban city.
Gilbert: And then we had the disaster – the falling of death that became involved in all the blood of all our friends. All our friends were dying and so we saw all this end of life in front of us, every single day, and I think that had a big effect on us.
George: One of the greatest effects, really – of all our time. As children we were surrounded by the wreckage of war and everyone believed that nothing horrible like that could ever happen again. Most things you could get immunised against. There were very good medical systems and things. We weren't going to have another war. Then along came this

horrible Aids disaster, and that was like a third world war in a way.
Gilbert: Our art was always based this kind of masochism, that we want
to beat ourselves up and to feel it, and that's why we even did the Naked
Shit Pictures, to show to every viewer what we really are. Combined
with the shit that is totally life. That became very important to us,
especially with the last pictures. With the Naked Shit Pictures we think
we did an amazing job at getting very, very close to all the things that
lie deep inside every viewer.
George: Probably it would be true to say that the Naked Shit Pictures
and other pictures from the last two or three years were the most
difficult pictures we ever made, most difficult for us. They actually
involve ourselves in making pictures with shit, with ourselves naked,
and I'm sure we did damage ourselves in some way.
Gilbert: It's very frightening.
George: They are very healing pictures, but very damaging as well.
Gilbert: Very frightening because there is such a big prejudice against
shit and nakedness and two men. So in the moment that we show that,
a lot of people are up in arms. They cannot take it, but at the same time
it's very opening up, because after all, why not? Why, we *are* that. We
are made of dirt.
George: To take those things from inside ourselves – those thoughts and
feelings – and to put them into the pictures, that is at the very least
exhausting and at worst slightly damaging, I'm sure. Yes, to tear
something very truthful from our whole life so far – all the thoughts and
feelings that we ever had or might have – and get that out into the
pictures to the viewer. It is a very struggling difficult thing.
Gilbert: It was always based a little on hurting ourselves, to make it
more truthful.

*

George: We were always very conscious of being dragged at increasing
speed towards the grave, and we don't even mind that. We would like
very much to come to terms within ourselves with the idea of death. It
would be very good if one could become more comfortable with that
idea.
Gilbert: But I would say that for the last ten years, every... every friend
that we had nearly died.
George: We didn't have very many friends, but now we don't have any,
hardly.

Gilbert: That changes you, your attitude towards life.

George: It's something we never thought of because we fondly imagined that because we had two or three friends who were probably half or two-thirds our age, without being conscious of that, we imagined that they would always be there. Then suddenly they're not. This is quite a horrible thing.

Gilbert: And then you start to see these young people in front of you dying. Shocking, and... We understand the meaninglessness of life. It doesn't matter if you're here or not, huh? But there is this sense inside oneself that one wants to live, this life force that keeps your life, you're going to live, you want to make things, you want to change the world...

George: Till the very end, till the very end.

*

Gilbert: I'm sure that we are not *only* miserable.

George: We never said that we were *only* miserable,

Gilbert: George is a comedian. He's the best in the business. But do you know a happy comedian? They don't exist.

George: From what we've found out so far, the history of advance was written in blood and tears, in every field – in medicine or science, or literature. It was always difficult. It was always based on personal sacrifice.

Gilbert: I'm sure we can enjoy ourselves when we go out and get drunk and have an amusing evening, amusing conversation, but in the end...

George: You can pretend anything.

Gilbert: Yes, you can pretend, but in the end when you come back, that's it – you are confronted with the emptiness.

Gilbert & George

Gilbert
Born Dolomites, Italy, 1943
Studied
Wolkenstein School of Art
Hallein School of Art
Munich Academy of Art

George
Born Devon, England, 1942
Studied
Dartington Adult Education
Centre
Dartington Hall College of Art
Oxford School of Art

Met and studied
St Martin's School of Art,
London, 1967

Postal Sculptures

1969 *The Easter Cards;*
Souvenir Hyde Park Walk;
A Message from the Sculptors;
(dated 1970); *All My Life;*
New Decadent Art (1969–70)
1970 *The Sadness in Our Art*
1971 *The Limericks*
1972 *1st Post Card;*
2nd Post Card
1973 *The Pink Elephants*
1975 *The Red Boxers*

Magazine Sculptures

1969 *The Words of the*
Sculptors, Jam Magazine
(Autumn), pp. 43–47
1970 *Shit and Cunt,* Studio
International (May),
pp. 218–221; *With Us in*
Nature, Kunstmarkt
catalogue, Cologne
1971 *Two Text Pages*
Describing Our Position,
The Sunday Times Magazine
(10 January)
1972 *There Were Two Young*
Men, Studio International
(May), pp. 220–221
1973 *Balls,* Avalanche
(Summer–Fall), pp. 26–33

Works in Edition

1970 *The Words of the*
Sculptors (edition 35);
Walking Viewing Relaxing
(edition 13); *To be with Art is*
All We Ask (edition 9); *Two*
Text Pages Describing Our
Position (edition 19)
1971 *The Ten Speeches*
(edition 10); *The Limericks*
(edition 25)
1972 *Morning Light on Art for*
All (edition 12); *Great*
Expectations (edition 12)
As Used by the Sculptors
(edition 30)
1973 *Reclining Drunk*
(edition 200)
1976 *The Red Sculpture*
Album (edition 100)
1979 *First Blossom*
(edition 50)
1987 *Nineteen Eighty-Seven*
(edition 200)
1988 *Nineteen Eighty-Eight*
(edition 6)
1993 *The Singing Sculpture*
1969–91 (edition 20)

Films by the Artists

1970 *The Nature of Our*
Looking (edition 4)
1972 *Gordon's Makes Us*
Drunk (edition 25)
In the Bush (edition 25)
The Portrait of the Artists as
Young Men (edition 25)
1981 *The World of Gilbert &*
George, produced by Philip
Haas for the Arts Council of
Great Britain (70 minutes)
1984 *Gilbert & George,* South
of Watford, ITV
1986 *Recontre à Londres,*
Vidéo Londres, Michel Burcel,
France; *Gilbert & George,* La
Estación de Perpiñán, TVE,
Spain

Films about the Artists

1975 *The Red Sculpture*
1991 *The Singing Sculpture*
by Gilbert & George, produced
and directed by Philip Haas
for Sonnabend/Methodact
1992 *G & G: Daytripping,*
produced and directed by
Ian McDonald for Anglia
Television
1997 *The Fundamental*
Gilbert & George, produced
and directed by Gerald Fox for
The South Bank Show and ITV
Television

Living Sculpture Presentations

1969 *Our New Sculpture,*
St Martin's School of Art,
London; *Reading from a Stick,*
Geffrye Museum, London; *Our*
New Sculpture, Royal College
of Art, London; *Our New*
Sculpture, Camberwell School
of Art, London; *Underneath*
the Arches, Slade School of
Fine Art, London; *Sculpture in*
the '60s, Royal College of Art,
London (with Bruce McLean);
In the Underworld, St Martin's
School of Art, London (with
Bruce McLean); *Impresarios*
of the Art World, Hanover
Grand Preview Theatre,
London (with Bruce McLean);
Meeting Sculptures, various
locations, London; *The Meal,*
Ripley, Bromley, Kent (with
David Hockney); *Metallised*
Heads, Studio International
Office, London; *Telling a Story,*
Marquee Club, London;
The Singing Sculpture, The
Lyceum, London; *Telling a*
Story, The Lyceum, London;
The Singing Sculpture,
National Jazz & Blues Festival,
Plumpton; *A Living Sculpture,*
at the opening of 'When
Attitude Becomes Form', ICA,

London; *Underneath the Arches*, Cable Street, London; *Posing on the Stairs*, Stedelijk Museum, Amsterdam
1970 *3 Living Pieces*, BBC Studios, Bristol; *Lecture Sculpture*, Museum of Modern Art, Oxford; Leeds Polytechnic, Leeds; *Underneath the Arches*, Kunsthalle, Düsseldorf; Kunstverein, Hanover; Block Gallery Forum Theatre, Berlin; *Posing Piece*, Art & Project, Amsterdam; Konrad Fischer Gallery, Düsseldorf; *Underneath the Arches*, Kunstverein, Recklinghausen; Heiner Friedrich Gallery, Munich; Kunstverein, Nuremberg; Württembergischer Kunstverein, Stuttgart; Museo d'Arte Moderna, Turin; Sonja Henie Niels Onstad Foundation, Oslo; Stadsbiblioteket Lyngby, Copenhagen; Folker Skulima Gallery, Berlin; Gegenverkehr, Aachen; Heiner Friedrich Gallery, Cologne; Kunstverein, Krefeld; Nigel Greenwood Gallery, London
1971 *Underneath the Arches*, Show Room du Garden Stores Louise, Brussels; for BBC Television play 'The Cowshed', London; Sonnabend Gallery, New York
1972 *Underneath the Arches*, Kunstmuseum, Lucerne; L'Attico Gallery, Rome
1973 *Underneath the Arches*, National Gallery of New South Wales, John Kaldor Project, Sydney; National Gallery of Victoria, John Kaldor Project, Melbourne
1975 *Shao Lin Martial Arts*, Film Presentation, Collegiate Theatre, London; *The Red Sculpture*, Art Agency, Tokyo
1976 *The Red Sculpture*,

Sonnabend Gallery, New York; Konrad Fischer Gallery, Düsseldorf; Lucio Amelio Gallery, Naples
1977 *The Red Sculpture*, Sperone Gallery, Rome; Robert Self Gallery, London; Art Fair, Sperone Fischer, Basel; MLT Gallery, Brussels; Museum van Hedendaagse Kunst, Ghent; Stedelijk Museum, Amsterdam
1991 *The Singing Sculpture*, Sonnabend Gallery, New York

Publications

1970 *The Pencil on Paper Descriptive Works* (edition 500), published by Gilbert & George, London; *Art Notes and Thoughts*, published by Gilbert & George, London; *To be with Art is All We Ask* (edition 300), published by Gilbert & George, London; *A Guide to the Singing Sculpture*, published by Gilbert & George, London
1971 *The Paintings*, published by Kunstverein, Düsseldorf; *Side by Side* (edition 600), published by König Bros., Cologne; *A Day in the Life of George & Gilbert* (edition 1,000), published by Gilbert & George, London
1972 *The Grand Old Duke of York*, published by Kunstmuseum, Lucerne
1973 *Catalogue for their Australian Visit*, published by John Kaldor, Sydney
1976 *Dark Shadow* (edition 2,000), published by Nigel Greenwood, London
1977 *Gilbert & George*, published by Taxispalais Gallery, Innsbruck
1980 *Gilbert & George 1968 to 1980*, introduction by Carter Ratcliff, published by Van Abbemuseum,

Eindhoven
1984 *Gilbert & George*, introduction by Brenda Richardson, published by Baltimore Museum of Art
1985 *Death Hope Life Fear*, introduction by Rudi Fuchs, published by Castello di Rivoli, Turin
1986 *The Charcoal on Paper Sculptures 1970–1974*, introduction by Demosthenes Davvetas, published by capcMusée d'art contemporain, Bordeaux; *The Complete Pictures 1971–1985*, introduction by Carter Ratcliff, published by Thames and Hudson, London, Rizzoli International, New York, Schirmer/Mosel, Munich; *The Paintings 1971*, introduction by Wolf Jahn, published by Fruitmarket Gallery, Edinburgh
1989 *For Aids Exhibition*, introduction by Gilbert & George, published by Anthony d'Offay Gallery, London; *The Art of Gilbert & George*, text by Wolf Jahn, published by Thames and Hudson, London
1990 *The Moscow Catalogue*, texts in Russian by Sergei Klokov & Brenda Richardson, published by Gilbert & George and Anthony d'Offay Gallery, London; *Twenty-five Worlds by Gilbert & George*, text by Robert Rosenblum, published by Robert Miller Gallery, New York; *Worlds and Windows*, text by Robert Rosenblum, published by Anthony d'Offay Gallery, London, Robert Miller Gallery, New York; *Eleven Worlds by Gilbert & George and Antique Clocks*, introduction by Remo Guidieri, published by Desire Feurele, Cologne; *Gilbert &

George: Postcard Sculptures and Ephemera 1969–1981, introduction by Carter Ratcliff, published by Hirschl and Adler Modern, New York
1991 *Monarchy as Democracy*, introduction by Wolf Jahn, published by Anthony d'Offay Gallery, London, and Oktogon, Munich; *With Gilbert & George in Moscow*, text by Daniel Farson, published by Bloomsbury Publishers, London; *The Cosmological Pictures*, texts by Rudi Fuchs and Wojciech Markowski, published by Haags Gemeentemuseum, The Hague
1992 *New Democratic Pictures*, texts by Anders Kold, Lars Morrel and Andrew Wilson, published by Aarhus Kunstmuseum, Denmark
1993 *Gilbert & George: The Singing Sculpture*, texts by Carter Ratcliff and Robert Rosenblum, published by Thames and Hudson, London, and Anthony McCall Associates, New York; *Gilbert & George: China Exhibition*, texts by Wojciech Markowski, Norman Rosenthal and Andrew Wilson, published by Gilbert & George China Exhibition Project, London
1994 *Gilbert & George: Recent Works*, published by Robert Miller Gallery, New York; *Gilbert & George*, text by Wolf Jahn, published by Museo d'Arte Moderna della Citta di Lugano; *New Shit Pictures*, text by Wolf Jahn, published by Galerie Rafael Jablonka, Cologne; *Shitty Naked Human World*, text by Gilbert & George, published by Wolfsburg Kunstmuseum *Naked Shit Pictures*, text by Wolf Jahn, published by

South London Art Gallery, London
1996 *Gilbert & George*, text by Danilo Eccher, interview by Martin Gayford, published by Galleria d'Arte Moderna, Bologna and Edizioni Charta, Milan
1997 *Gilbert & George: The Fundamental Pictures*, introduction by Robert Rosenblum, published by Cyber Art Publications UK Ltd, London; *Gilbert & George: Art for All 1971–1996*, texts by Robert Rosenblum, Fumihori Nonomura and Yoshiki Sumikura, published by Sezon Museum of Art, Tokyo

Gallery Exhibitions

1968 *Three Works/Three Works*, Frank's Sandwich Bar, London; *Snow Show*, St Martin's School of Art, London; *Bacon 32*, Allied Services, London; *Christmas Show*, Robert Fraser Gallery, London
1969 *Anniversary*, Frank's Sandwich Bar, London; *Shit and Cunt*, Robert Fraser Gallery, London
1970 *George by Gilbert & Gilbert by George*, Fournier Street, London; *The Pencil on Paper Descriptive Works*, Konrad Fischer Gallery, Düsseldorf; *Art Notes and Thoughts*, Art & Project, Amsterdam; *Frozen into the Nature for You Art*, Françoise Lambert Gallery, Milan; *The Pencil on Paper Descriptive Works*, Folker Skulima Gallery, Berlin; *Frozen into the Nature for You Art*, Heiner Friedrich Gallery, Cologne; *To be with Art is All We Ask*, Nigel Greenwood Gallery, London
1971 *There Were Two Young*

Men, Sperone Gallery, Turin; *The General Jungle*, Sonnabend Gallery, New York; *The Ten Speeches*, Nigel Greenwood Gallery, London; *New Photo-Pieces*, Art & Project, Amsterdam
1972 *New Photo-Pieces*, Konrad Fischer Gallery, Düsseldorf; *Three Sculptures on Video Tape*, Gerry Schum Video Gallery, Düsseldorf; *The Bar*, Anthony d'Offay Gallery, London; *The Evening before the Morning after*, Nigel Greenwood, London; *It Takes a Boy to Understand a Boy's Point of View*, Situation Gallery, London; *A New Sculpture*, Sperone Gallery, Rome
1973 *Any Port in a Storm*, Sonnabend Gallery, Paris; *New Decorative Works*, Sperone Gallery, Turin; *Reclining Drunk*, Nigel Greenwood Gallery, London; *Modern Rubbish*, Sonnabend Gallery, New York
1974 *Drinking Sculptures*, Art & Project/MTL Gallery, Antwerp; *Human Bondage*, Konrad Fischer Gallery, Düsseldorf; *Dark Shadow*, Art & Project, Amsterdam; Nigel Greenwood Gallery, London; *Cherry Blossom*, Sperone Gallery, Rome
1975 *Bloody Life*, Sonnabend Gallery, Paris; Sonnabend Gallery, Geneva; Lucio Amelio Gallery, Naples; *Post Card Sculptures*, Sperone Westwater Fischer, New York; *Bad Thoughts*, Gallery Spillemaekers, Brussels; *Dusty Corners*, Art Agency, Tokyo
1976 *Dead Boards*, Sonnabend Gallery, New York *Mental*, Robert Self Gallery, London; Robert Self Gallery, Newcastle
1977 *Red Morning*, Sperone

Fischer Gallery, Basel; *New Photo-Pieces*, Art & Project, Amsterdam; Konrad Fischer Gallery, Düsseldorf
1978 *New Photo-Pieces*, Dartington Hall Gallery, Dartington Hall; Sonnabend Gallery, New York; Art Agency, Tokyo
1980 *Post Card Sculptures*, Art & Project, Amsterdam; Konrad Fischer Gallery, Düsseldorf; *New Photo-Pieces*, Karen & Jean Bernier Gallery, Athens; Sonnabend Gallery, New York; *Modern Fears*, Anthony d'Offay Gallery, London
1981 *Photo-Pieces 1980–1981*, Chantal Crousel Gallery, Paris
1982 *Crusade*, Anthony d'Offay Gallery, London
1983 *Modern Faith*, Sonnabend Gallery, New York; *Photo-Pieces 1980–1982*, David Bellman Gallery, Toronto; *New Works*, Crousel-Hussenot Gallery, Paris
1984 *The Believing World*, Anthony d'Offay Gallery, London; *Hands Up*, Gallery Schellmann & Klüser, Munich; *Lives*, Gallery Pieroni, Rome
1985 *New Moral Works*, Sonnabend Gallery, New York 1987; *The 1986 Pictures*, Sonnabend Gallery, New York; *New Pictures*, Anthony d'Offay Gallery, London; *Gilbert & George Pictures*, Aldrich Museum of Contemporary Art, Connecticut
1988 *The 1988 Pictures*, Ascan Crone Gallery, Hamburg; Sonnabend Gallery, New York
1989 *The 1988 Pictures*, Christian Stein Gallery, Milan; *For Aids Exhibition*, Anthony d'Offay Gallery, London

1990 *Gilbert & George*, Hirschl and Adler Modern, New York; *Twenty-five Worlds by Gilbert & George*, Robert Miller Gallery, New York; *The Cosmological Pictures*, Sonnabend Gallery, New York; *Worlds & Windows*, Anthony d'Offay Gallery, London; *Eleven Worlds by Gilbert & George and Antique Clocks*, Desire Feurele Gallery, Cologne
1991 *20th Anniversary Exhibition*, Sonnabend Gallery, New York
1992 *New Democratic Pictures*, Anthony d'Offay Gallery, London
1994 *Gilbert & George*, Robert Miller Gallery, New York; *New Shit Pictures*, Galerie Jablonka, Cologne
1995 *Gilbert & George*, Galerie Nikolas Sonne, Berlin; *The Naked Shit Pictures*, South London Art Gallery, London
1997 *The Fundamental Pictures*, Sonnabend Gallery, Lehmann Maupin, New York

Museum Exhibitions

1971 *The Paintings (with Us in the Nature)*, Whitechapel Art Gallery, London; Stedelijk Museum, Amsterdam; Kunstverein, Düsseldorf
1972 *The Paintings (with Us in the Nature)*, Koninklijk Museum voor Schone Kunsten, Antwerp
1973 *The Shrubberies & Singing Sculpture*, National Gallery of New South Wales, John Kaldor Project, Sydney; National Gallery of Victoria, John Kaldor Project, Melbourne
1976 *The General Jungle*, Albright-Knox Art Gallery, Buffalo

1980 *Photo-Pieces 1971–1980*, Stedelijk van Abbemuseum, Eindhoven
1981 *Photo-Pieces 1971–1980*, Kunsthalle, Düsseldorf; Kunsthalle, Bern; Musée National d'Arte Moderne, Centre Georges Pompidou, Paris; Whitechapel Art Gallery, London
1982 *New Photo-Pieces*, Gewad Gallery, Ghent
1984 *Gilbert & George*, Baltimore Museum of Art; Contemporary Arts Museum, Houston; Norton Gallery of Art, West Palm Beach, Florida
1985 *Gilbert & George*, Milwaukee Art Museum; Solomon R. Guggenheim Museum, New York
1986 *Pictures 1982 to 1985*, capcMusée d'Art Contemporain, Bordeaux; *Charcoal on Paper Sculptures 1970 to 1974*, capcMusée d'Art Contemporain, Bordeaux; *The Paintings 1971*, Fruitmarket Gallery, Edinburgh; *Pictures 1982 to 1985*, Kunsthalle, Basel
1987 *Pictures 1982 to 1985*, Palais des Beaux-Arts, Brussels; Palacio Velásquez, Madrid; Lenbachhaus, Munich; Hayward Gallery, London; *Pictures*, Aldrich Museum, Connecticut
1990 *Pictures 1983–1988*, Central House of the Artists, New Tretyakov Gallery Building, Moscow
1991 *The Cosmological Pictures*, Palac Sztuki, Krakow; Palazzo delle Esposizioni, Rome
1992 *The Cosmological Pictures*, Kunsthalle, Zurich; Wiener Sezession, Vienna; Ernst Muzeum, Budapest; Haags Gemeentemuseum,

The Hague; Aarhus
Kunstmuseum, Denmark;
Irish Museum of Modern Art,
Royal Hospital Kilmainham,
Dublin; Fundació Joan Miró,
Barcelona
1993 *The Cosmological
Pictures*, Tate Gallery,
Liverpool; Württem-
bergischer Kunstverein,
Stuttgart; *Gilbert & George:
China Exhibition*, National
Art Gallery, Beijing; The Art
Museum, Shanghai
1994 *Gilbert & George*,
Museo d'Arte Moderna della
Citta di Lugano; *Shitty Naked
Human World*, Kunstmuseum
Wolfsburg
1996 *Gilbert & George*,
Galleria d'Arte Moderna,
Bologna
1997 *Gilbert & George: Art
for All 1971–1996*, Sezon
Museum of Art, Tokyo;
Gilbert & George, Magasin 3
Stockholm Konsthall,
Stockholm; *Gilbert & George*,
ARC Musée d'Art Moderne
de la Ville de Paris, Paris

Index

310

Acknowledgements
For their invaluable help and con-
sultation in the preparation of this
book, Violette Editions would like
to thank Judy Adam, David Bailey,
James Birch, Andrew Brooke,
Gordon Burn, Sophie Castle,
Prudence Cuming, Dominic
Dyson, Daniel Farson, Stainton
Forrest, Gerald Fox, Mark Francis,
Abe Frajndlich, Rudi Fuchs,
Giuseppe Gilardi and Grafiche
Milani, Philip Haas, Shere Hite,
Wolf Jahn, Herbie Knott, Natasha
Krosher, Zoë Manzi, Hans-Ulrich
Obrist, Carter Ratcliff, Brenda
Richardson, Robert Rosenblum,
Alexander Roussos, Anne
Seymour, Nikos Stangos, Dave
Stewart, David Sylvester, Richard
Thomson and The South Bank
Show, Wolfgang Tillmans, Justin
Westover, Peter B. Willberg and
Andrew Wilson.